A VISIT
TO
INDIA, CHINA AND JAPAN
IN THE YEAR 1853

A VISIT

TO

INDIA, CHINA AND JAPAN

IN THE YEAR 1853

BAYARD TAYLOR

GYAN

Published by

GYAN

Gyan Publishing House
5, Ansari Road
Daryaganj, New Delhi-110002
Phone: 011-47034999, 9811692060
E-mail: books@gyanbooks.com

Distribution Network
gyanbooks.com
India, USA, Canada, UK, Australia, France

ISBN : 978-81-212-9655-7 (PB)
First Published, 1855

2nd Impression 2023

Printed at: Gyan Press, Delhi.

A VISIT TO INDIA, CHINA AND JAPAN IN THE YEAR 1853
Author: BAYARD TAYLOR

A VISIT

TO

INDIA, CHINA, AND JAPAN

IN THE YEAR 1853.

By BAYARD TAYLOR.

1881.

Dedicated

TO

CHARLES A. DANA

BY HIS

ASSOCIATE AND FRIEND.

PREFACE.

WITH this volume ends the record of two and a half years of travel, which was commenced in the "Journey to Central Africa," and continued in the "Lands of the Saracen." In bringing his work to a close, the author cannot avoid expressing his acknowledgment of the public interest in those portions of his narrative already published—an interest which has justified him in the preparation of this volume, and encouraged him to hope that he will again be received at the same firesides as a gossip and companion, not as a bore.

Although the entire travels herewith presented embrace India, China, Japan, the Loo-Choo and Bonin Islands, and the long homeward voyage around the Cape of Good Hope, they were all accomplished in the space of a year. Hence, some of my descriptions may bear the marks of haste, and I may, occasionally, have founded a judgment on the first rapid impressions, which a greater familiarity with the subject might not have confirmed. I can only say, in answer to objections of this kind, that I have conscientiously endeavored to be correct and impartial, and that, in preparing this work for the press, I have carefully tested the original impressions recorded on the spot, by the truer images which slowly ripen in the memory, and by the light of subsequent experience.

The portions of the book devoted to India and China are as complete as the length of my stay in those countries allowed me to make them. The account of my visit to Loo-Choo and Japan, however, is less full and detailed than I could have wished. In accordance with special regulations issued by the Secretary of the Navy, I was obliged to give up my journals to the Department, at the close of my connection with the Expedition. It was understood that they would be retained and employed in the compilation of the Narrative of the Expedition, now being prepared by order of Congress. As my accounts of the most interesting events which I witnessed had already been published, and were therefore common property, I made application to Government for the favor of being allowed to copy portions of my journal—especially that part relating to Loo-Choo—which would have enabled me to supply the links between the published accounts: but my request was peremptorily denied. My papers will no doubt be restored to me, after the completion of the Government work: otherwise, like John Ledyard, in a precisely similar case, I shall have the alternative of an unusually tenacious memory.

During my journeys and voyages in those remote parts of the world, I was treated with great kindness and hospitality by the English and American merchants and officials established there, and received assistance in the prosecution of my plans, which I take sincere pleasure in acknowledging. I desire, especially, to return my thanks to Commodore Perry, to whose kindness I was indebted for the most interesting portion of my experiences; to the Hon. Humphrey Marshall, late U. S. Commissioner to China; to Capt. Buchanan, U. S. N.; to Edward Cunningham, Esq., U. S. Vice-Consul at Shanghai; to Henry G. Keene, Esq., of the E. I. Company's Civil Service, and Capt. R. Baird Smith, of the Bengal Engineers; and to the American Missionaries in India and China, from all of whom I received every assistance in their power.

B. T.

NEW YORK, *August*, 1855.

CONTENTS.

CHAPTER X.

CHAPTER XI.

CHAPTER XII.

CHAPTER XIII.

CHAPTER XIV.

CHAPTER XX.

CHAPTER XXI.

CHAPTER XXII.

CHAPTER XXIII.

CHAPTER XXIV.

CHAPTER XXV.

CHAPTER XXX.

CHAPTER XXXI.

CHAPTER XXXII.

CHAPTER XXXIII.

CHAPTER XXXIV.

CHAPTER XL.

CHAPTER XLI.

CHAPTER XLII.

CHAPTER XLIII.

CHAPTER XLIV.

INDIA, CHINA, AND JAPAN.

CHAPTER I.

THE OVERLAND ROUTE TO INDIA.

Leaving Gibraltar—Voyage up the Mediterranean—Landing at Alexandria—Distribution of Passengers—A Cloudy Day in Egypt—A Joyful Meeting—The Desert Vans—We start for Suez—Cockney Fears—The Road and Station-houses—Suez—Transfer to the India Steamers—Our Passengers and Crew—The Mountains of Horeb—Red Sea Weather and Scenery—A Glimpse of Mocha—The Straits of Bab-el-Mandeb—An Extinct Hades—The Fortress of Aden—Arrival—The Somali—Ride to the Old Town—Population of Aden—Temperature—The Fortifications—The Track of the Anglo-Saxon—Departure—Disregard of Life—Araby the Blest—Life on the Achilles—Approach to India—Land!—The Ghauts of Malabar—Arrival at Bombay.

My passage to Bombay had been secured a month before; the ticket was in my pocket; the horses I had ridden from Granada had gone back under charge of José, my merry guide and groom; and finally, on the 27th of November, 1852, the mail steamer from Southampton to Alexandria, two days overdue, was signalled from the top of Gibraltar Rock. There was no tie to bind me to Europe: my travelling trunk was already packed, my bill paid, and the needful stock of Gibraltar cigars laid in. My face was turned eastward once more, but I looked beyond the Orient, to those elder lands of India and Cathay, where the sun of Egypt and of Greece first rose. Long before the outward-bound passengers had finished their rambles in the Alameda, I went out the water gate of the town, and the sunset-gun found me impatiently pacing the deck of the *Haddington*.

Our voyage up the Mediterranean was a dreary one, and without any incident worthy of being recorded. There were a hundred and seventy passengers on board, and the cabins fore and aft were stowed as closely as the steerage of an emigrant ship. The raw, gusty weather we encountered, made our quarters doubly disagreeable, while, owing to the comfortable indifference of the officers, nothing was done to alleviate the annoyance. In fact, it required symptoms of incipient ship-fever, and the strong protest of a few resolute passengers, to procure for us the simple relief of a wind-sail in the cabin. The fare resembled that of the Pacific Mail Steamers, during the first year of their establishment; and the price of passage was in about the same ratio. The Peninsular and Oriental Company, like all great monopolies, is a model of meanness.

We ran along, under the lee of the Spanish Mountains, to Cape de Gatte, then crossed to the Barbary Coast, which we skirted to Cape Bon, catching now and then a rainy glimpse of the distant Atlas, touched at Malta, and after a voyage of eleven days—time enough to have crossed the Atlantic—took a pilot off Alexandria, at daybreak on the 8th of December. I looked upon the crowd of windmills on the Cape of Figs, the light-house on the island of Pharos, and Pompey's Pillar in the distance, with almost the feeling of one returning to his native land. A clear, balmy Egyptian morning welcomed us after the gales of the Mediterranean, and the anchor had not been dropped five minutes before the passengers began to make for the shore. We left our baggage in a heap upon the deck, with the assurance that we should find it again, on arriving at Suez. The Egyptian Transit Company has published very strict regulations, limiting the length, breadth, and depth of trunks and portmanteaus to be conveyed across. I scrupulously arranged my baggage according to these rules, but found, on reaching Alexandria, that nobody else had done so, and that packages of treble the prescribed dimensions were accepted and forwarded without objection. Only two cwt. are allowed free, extra baggage to India being charged at the rate of £60 ($300) per ton. Several of my fellow-passengers paid from £10 to £20 for over-weight.

The day before our arrival, a meeting of the passengers was held, in order to decide by lot their respective places in the omnibus vans from Cairo to Suez. As each van held six persons, and there were enough of us to fill twenty-eight vans, we formed ourselves into as many parties of six each, appointing one of the number to draw. Those parties, for instance, who drew the numbers from one to ten, were sent off in the first steamer from Alexandria, and the first batch of vans from Cairo, and were obliged to wait in Suez for the more fortunate drawers of the last numbers, who thus gained a little time in the former cities. As my party had drawn one of the last vans, we had the whole day in Alexandria, which enabled us to get our letters and papers from home, refresh ourselves with a Turkish bath, and lay in a stock of choice Latakieh for the Indian part of the voyage. The hotels were filled to overflowing, more than a hundred passengers from

India having been waiting six days for our arrival. We barely succeeded in finding seats at Rey's Hotel d'Europe The arched entrance resembled a bazaar; venders of tobacco, whips, tarbooshes, pipes, shawls, &c., thronged on all sides, and the clamor of the donkey-boys was something terrible to the uninitiated. I found a number of acquaintances among the motley multitude, most of whom not only remembered my face, but my name also, hailing me with: "Thanks be to God, O Howadji T—— ! you are welcome back!"

At the appointed hour, we went on board the barge, in the Mahmoudieh Canal, and were towed off by a small steamer. In the sweet, mild air of the evening, we sat on deck, watching the palm-trees by starlight, till it grew chilly and damp with the heavy night-dews. We then went below, and spread ourselves out on some bare tables and benches, until 2 A. M., when we reached Atfeh. Here a better steamer was waiting for us. The transfer was soon made, and in another hour we were breasting the current of the glorious old Nile—the river of rivers. The morning was cold and gray, and we had a dark, rainy, disagreeable day. I had never known such weather in Egypt. In fact, until an hour before sunset, when the clouds broke away, it was neither Egypt nor the Nile. The leaves of the palm-trees were all blown one way, the Fellahs lay in their huts for shelter, scarcely a boat was to be seen on the river, the camels and Bedouins vanished from the horizon of the Libyan Desert, and the dull, brown, opaque flood lost all of the mystery and solemnity of its character.

It was after dark before we reached the Barrage, at the point of the Delta. Our Arab firemen heaved the wood into their furnaces, until the chimney was red-hot, and a great mass of scarlet flame, pouring out of the top, flapped and snapped in the wind like a Moslem banner. On we went, throwing aside the turbid waves, past the glimmering lights of Shoobra and the dim minarets of Boulak, till the ruddy glare of torches on the Transit Wharf announced the end of our voyage. Here, the passengers were obliged to give up their carpet-bags, as no baggage is allowed in the Desert vans. This matter settled, we got into the omnibus, drove up the broad avenue of acacias, and into the great square of Cairo.

I went with my friends to the Hotel d'Europe, and found my old landlord, Monsieur Nolté, as fat and obliging as ever. To my great joy, my faithful dragoman, and companion on the White Nile, Achmet, was in Cairo, and as I was obliged to leave early the next morning for Suez, I sent for him immediately. Nothing could exceed the surprise and joy of the honest Theban. We had abundance of news for each other, and old experiences to talk over, and did not separate until long after midnight. Some of my party, by rising early, rode up to the Citadel by sunrise; but I contented myself with a donkey-ride through the Ezbekiyeh, accompanied by Achmet and the little *shaytan* of a donkey-boy who served me a year before. I would have given more than I am willing to confess, for the sake of staying a month in Egypt. Cairo, in the winter, is one of the most delightful cities in the world; and the brief morning glance I had of it brought back with double force the charms of my past Oriental life.

At 8 o'clock, I bade adieu to Monsieur Nolté, and Achmet and the donkey-boy, and took my place in the allotted van. These vehicles bear a strong resemblance to a baker's cart. They are about six feet by four in size, mounted on a single pair of wheels, and entered by a door in the rear. Each van carries six persons, so you may conceive that there is very little vacant space. The driver sits on a box in front, and an Arab assistant rides on the step behind. There are four horses to each, which are changed about every five miles. The distance to Suez—84 miles—is divided into sixteen stages, and the usual length of the journey is sixteen hours.

Our six vans, forming one "batch," as it is called, receive their respective parties, and we dash out of Cairo by the Suez gate. The morning is exquisitely mild, fair, and balmy, and the palm-groves of the Nile, on our left, never looked more beautiful. Outside of the gate there is an encampment of several hundred tents, which we take to be those of the pilgrims preparing for their journey to Mecca. Some of the party are absorbed in the Tombs of the Caliphs, and others in Abbas Pasha's white Italian palace, when, as we climb a long, sandy rise—the first step of the Desert—an eye that knows in what direction to look, sees the Pyramids looming large and blue, far away over the city. You can look at nothing else, when you have the Pyramids in your landscape, and so we watch them fade, and sink, and recede, till our horses draw up at the first station in the Desert.

Yes, this is the Desert: but the young lady who goes out to be married in India would not have thought it. The Nile Valley is still in sight behind us; but even looking toward the Red Sea, here is a broad macadamized road, filled with camels, and Arabs, and donkeys, to say nothing of our six rapid coaches; two telegraph towers on the sandy hills; and five miles before us, the station where we shall again change horses. It is a barren, desolate country, certainly; but it is not the Desert of one's dreams—not that silent, fiery world of tawny sand and ink-black porphyry mountains in the heart of Nubia, over which I had travelled a year before.

I was amused at seeing many of our passengers, immediately on reaching Alexandria, wind great white shawls around their hats, and hang green veils over their faces. While crossing the Desert, although the temperature was not above 70° at noon, they persisted in doing the same thing, and some of them even protected their eyes with spectacles, although there was no glare that would have made an infant wink. According to their ideas, they were in constant peril of having a sun-stroke, or catching the ophthalmia. My companions in the van were inured to an Indian sun, and so we threw aside all fears, and made merry from one side of the Desert to the other. At the fourth station we stopped an hour to breakfast. Here we found a spacious two-story house, with a large dining-saloon, divans, &c., and an excellent breakfast for thirty persons on the table. There were several neat bedrooms for the accommodation of persons who wish to make the journey more slowly.

The country through which we passed was low and monotonous, and we saw no mountains until we approached the Red Sea. There are three trees on the road—one large and two small ones, but no wells. At the eighth, or half-way station, we had dinner, and were allowed two hours rest. The meals were all gotten up and served by natives, the Transit Administration being a perquisite of the Pasha of Egypt. Considering that every thing has to be brought from Cairo, they were very good indeed. Opposite the Central Station, Abbas

Pasha built a large palace on the summit of a hill, where he often went to spend a few days and breathe the healthy desert air. All the supplies, of course, have to be brought from the Nile—a distance of nearly fifty miles. I approve entirely of the Pasha's taste, and should like nothing better than the use of a suite of apartments in the palace for a few months. The long white front of the building, crowning a naked range of gray hills, has a striking effect when viewed from the Suez road.

The sun set before we left the midway station. We drove on in the dark, without other incident than passing long strings of camels laden with our baggage, and the specie and mails for India. Now and then some of our teams would come to a halt in a streak of deep sand, and this would detain all the others, for the orders are very strict that the vans should keep together. There are no ascents or descents on the road worth notice. A railroad could be constructed with but moderate trouble and expense.*

An hour after midnight we reached Suez, and were at once driven to the Government Hotel, a dreary quadrangular building on the sea-shore. The rooms were all filled, of course, but we obtained a cotton quilt and part of a hard divan in the billiard-room, at the rate of a dollar apiece. All the baggage arrived during the night. Even the specie-laden camels, which left Cairo at the same time as ourselves,

* Recent mails from the East (May, 1855) announce that Said Pasha has determined to extend the Alexandria and Cairo Railroad, now nearly completed, to Suez. If the work is prosecuted with the same vigor as heretofore, the transit from Alexandria to the latter place, three years hence, will occupy but eight or ten hours.

were at Suez early the next morning. The two steamers, the Hindostan and Achilles, lay at the anchorage, three miles off, but there was a smaller steamer in waiting to take us out. Our baggage, tickets, and other preliminaries, engaged all our time, and I saw nothing of Suez except the white quadrangle of the hotel, two ugly minarets, and a great quantity of mud huts. I suspect these are about as much as anybody sees. The American flag was flying from a lofty flag-staff, on account of the presence of the Hon. Humphrey Marshall, U. S. Commissioner to China, who was on board the Hindostan. I took leave of a number of good friends, who were bound to Madras, Calcutta, and China, and went on board the Achilles. The day was excessively hot and sultry, and the Captain of our steamer received a sun-stroke while on shore, from the effects of which he was confined to his berth during the whole voyage.

We weighed anchor about 10 o'clock the same evening, the Hindostan having left an hour before us. Our passengers were between seventy and eighty in number, and as the Achilles rated less than a thousand tons, we were crowded rather too much for comfort, though in all respects we fared better than we did on board the Haddington. The stewards were mostly Hindoos, the sailors the same, the cooks two Portuguese and a Chinaman, and the firemen hideous, monkey-faced negroes from Mozambique. Among the passengers were a Portuguese General, the Governor of Mozambique, a Turkish Bey, Ambassador to Yemen, and a Transylvanian, who for fifteen years was Court Physician to Runject Singh at Lahore, and was then bound for Cashmere and Thibet. Amid such a motley gathering of character and nationalities there was no lack of diversion. For myself, when I drank Bombay water, ate real curry, hailed the waiter as "khitmudgar!" and was addressed by him as "sahib!" I felt that I was already in India.

The morning showed us the shores of Egypt on the one hand, and the red mountains of the Sinaitic Peninsula on the other. The Gulf of Suez is so narrow that you have a distinct view of both shores, alike hopelessly sterile, but enchanting in outline and color. The thousand-fold shadows of those sandstone mountains, tinted with the fairest rose, purple, and violet hues, are pencilled with the delicacy of a miniature painting. The loftier range of Horeb, which rises inland, presents a sharp, serrated outline. I tried to persuade myself that I saw the peak of Sinai, but the ship's officers insisted that it was not visible from the Gulf of Suez. In addition to the absorbing interest of the scene, the shores had a grand continental significance. Here was Africa, there Asia. Like the Bosphorus which parts Europe and Asia, or the straits of Gibraltar, where Africa confronts Europe, this part of the Red Sea possesses a grandeur beyond that which Nature gives it.

In the afternoon we passed Ras Mohammed, at the extremity of the Peninsula where the Gulf of Akaba joins that of Suez. We then lost sight of the Arabian shore, while only the higher peaks of the mountains in the deserts of Egypt and Nubia were visible. On the 13th, we entered the tropics, and each day thenceforth showed a marked increase of temperature. By the noon observation on the following day, we were in Lat. 21° 30′, off the port of Djidda, and not more than a hundred miles, in a straight line, from Mecca—

probably the nearest approach I shall ever make to the Holy City.

After passing St. John's Islands, off the ancient port of Berenice, we lost sight of both shores until the evening of the 16th, when Djebel Tor, or Teir, a lofty volcanic island, appeared on the left. Early the next morning we made Djebel Sogheir, and ran along close to its shores. It is about a thousand feet in height, and resembles a huge mass of cinders. Some palms were growing on the northern slope, but there was no sign of habitation. We had a violent head-wind, or rather gale, similar to those which are frequently met with off the mouth of the Gulf of California. Yet, in spite of this strong current of air, the thermometer stood at 85° on deck and 90° in the cabin. For two or three days we had a temperature of 90° to 95°. This part of the Red Sea is considered to be the hottest portion of the earth's surface. In the summer the air is like that of a furnace, and the bare red mountains glow like heaps of live coals. The steamers at that time almost invariably lose some of their stewards and firemen. Cooking is quite given up, and the panting and sweltering passengers drink claret and water and eat dry biscuits.

In the afternoon we had a glimpse of the town of Mocha about ten miles distant. It is built on low land, but a range of mountains rises in the background. With a telescope, I could plainly distinguish the white citadel, and a long line of low, flat-roofed buildings, looming through the hot vapors of the coast. The famous Mocha coffee does not grow in the vicinity of the town, but is brought from the valleys of the interior. Hodeida, further up the coast, is another port for its exportation, but the foreign trade of both these places has been almost entirely destroyed by the rise of Aden. The cof fee is taken down to the latter port in the native coasters, or by caravans from the interior, and there shipped for Europe and other parts of the world. Much of the so-called Mocha coffee, I am told, is actually grown in Abyssinia.

We now approached the Straits of Bab-el-Mandeb, the "Gate of Tears," which we passed about midnight. The passage for vessels is about three miles wide, and not at all dangerous in clear weather. The Arabian and Abyssinian shores are hilly, but not mountainous. Had not the weather been so hazy, we should have seen the lofty range of the Danakil, on the Abyssinian side. The latitude of the Straits is about 12° 40′, about the same which I had attained the previou winter, on the White Nile.

On the next morning we were in the Indian Ocean. The barren volcanic headlands of Arabia Felix rose on our left, point beyond point, till at last a larger and loftier mass was declared to be the Rock of Aden. The pale-green water through which we were sailing told of reefs and shoals, and the ship made a wide curve to the eastward before entering the bay. The main land of Arăbia presents a level, sandy coast, with few indentations, and the Bay of Aden is formed by two narrow peninsulas which project from it at right angles, their extremities shooting up suddenly into clusters of black, ragged volcanic cones, about 1,500 feet in height. No description can give any idea of the savage sterility of these mountains. They are masses of cinders and scoriæ, glowing as if with still unextinguished fires, and the air around them quivers with the heat radiated from their sides. Their forms exhibit all the violence of the convulsion which created them heaps of burned fragments, cliffs divided by deep fissures, and sharp, inaccessible cones, shooting upward like congealed flames from the rubbish of extinct craters. Some profane tourist speaks of Aden as resembling "Hell with the fires put out"—a forcible simile, but very much to the point.

The town and fortress of Aden occupy the eastern peninsula, which was obtained from the Sultan of Lahadj, in the year 1839, partly by force and partly by treaty. The sum of $250,000 was paid to the Sultan by the East India Company, and the chieftain prudently sold what was already more than half wrested from him. Nevertheless, his son and successor did his best to have the bargain annulled, offering to refund the money. This was of course rejected, and the place was for a number of years exposed to assaults from the Arabs of Lahadj, who were violently opposed to the sale, and to the establishment of a foreign colony on the coast. In spite of all precautions, robbery and murder were constantly perpetrated in the town and camp, until the fortifications on the land-side were completed. At present, there is tolerable security inside of the walls, but no one ventures many miles into the interior, unless attended by a strong armed escort. The harbor of Aden was known to the Romans, and its importance as a point of communication with the Indies seems to have been understood by the Turks, as there are still the remains of fortifications, which were constructed in the time of Solyman the Magnificent. The rock is about six miles in length, by from two to three in breadth, and its highest point is said to be 1,800 feet above the sea.

We ran in, along the western base, until on turning a small headland, we came upon a sheltered roadstead, in which half a dozen English colliers and a number of small Arab craft lay at anchor. Here our own anchor dropped, and the ship was presently surrounded by boats rowed by half-naked blacks, some of whom made themselves entirely so, and commenced diving and splashing in the water, in the hope of getting shillings thrown over for them to fish up. A few long, one-story white houses and some heaps of Newcastle coal were scattered over a level piece of sand, at the head of a cove, and on a slight eminence towards the sea there was a group of cane huts, built in the Robinson Crusoe style. On this eminence there is a sunken battery, barely visible from the water, but said to be strong enough to sink any hostile vessel which may attempt to enter the harbor. A few days before our arrival, a French corvette, which had been cruising in the Indian Ocean, came into Aden with her guns ready shotted and manned, in full expectation of being fired upon, her commander supposing that Louis Napoleon had commenced the invasion of England. I went ashore in a small boat, rowed by four Somali, or natives of the African coast, near Cape Guardafui. They appear to be a low variety of the Arab race, having dark brown skins, deep-set eyes, long, straight noses, and handsome, curling hair. They are less partial to mutton-fat than the tribes on the Red Sea, but their long locks, which are naturally of a glossy blue-black hue, are dyed brown, or dark red, which imparts a goat-like, satyric air to their lank, nimble figures. Their language is a very bad Arabic, which I could with difficulty understand. No sooner had we landed than we were surrounded with the owners of donkeys and horses, anxious to hire them to us for a ride to Aden. The old town lies on the other side of the Peninsula, and is not visible from the landing-place.

I took a horse and rode off at once, followed by the attendant native. The road, which is alternately of sand and macadamized volcanic cinders, follows the curve of the bay towards the northern end of the rock, where there is a strong gate, affording the only land communication with the sandy Arabian plains beyond. The natives are here obliged to give up their arms, owing to which precaution there are now but few crimes committed, in comparison with former years. As I rode along, between the black, scorched hills, and over the blistering sand, amid the almost insupportable glare of white noonday heat, my eyes turned to seek the dazzling blue and violet-green tints of the bay with an exquisite sense of relief. After two or three miles of this travel, the road turned inland, ascending the less abrupt slopes of the hills. I came at length to an artificial pass, about forty feet deep, by twenty wide, cut through the comb of the central ridge. It was closed by a ponderous double gateway, and the wall of circumvallation crossed by an arch. An Indian sepoy stood guard at the gate as I passed through. The road was filled with Arabs from the interior, bringing camel-loads of their produce to market, and with the mongrel natives of the African coast. Among the latter I readily distinguished the natives of Adel, the country lying south of Abyssinia. Major Harris, in his "Highlands of Ethiopia," calls them the "mild-eyed Adaël," and truly the expression of their features is feminine in its mildness and gentleness. They, as well as the natives of Aden, speak Arabic substituting only the Hindoostanee word "*sahib*" (master,) for the "*Howadji*" of Egypt.

Beyond the pass, the town of Aden came into view. It lies in a circular sandy basin, almost enclosed by black mountains of volcanic cinder. The buildings, which are spacious huts of wood, cane or mud, one story in height, are scattered over an extent of three quarters of a mile. The dry bed of a torrent which divides the town, proves that it sometimes rains at Aden, although I was informed that a heavy fall of rain does not occur more than once or twice a year. A new mosque, a small Christian Church, and a tall tower (built, I believe, for an observatory), were the only objects which distinguished themselves amid the mass of huts. There were two or three feeble attempts at cultivating small square yards of ground, and these pigmy specks of green gave life and cheerfulness to a scene which would otherwise have been depressing from its utter desolation. The only water on the peninsula is brackish and disagreeable, and is rarely used in an unmixed state. The Arabs bring a better kind from the opposite headland, for which they are paid at the rate of $1.50 per 100 gallons. The only things the place affords are fish and oysters; all other supplies must be imported. There are a number of shops in the town, kept by Hindoo merchants, and there for the first time I saw the Parsee, or Fire-Worshipper, wearing the high chintz mitre which is peculiar to his sect.

I made the tour of the airy bamboo huts on the beach, where the 78th Regiment was quartered. The soldiers were lounging lazily in the shade, for since the wall of defence has been finished, their duties are very light. Some of the officers had brought their families with them, so that there was a small English community. The temperature of Aden ranges generally from 80° to 90°, with a maximum of 98°, and a minimum of 75°, being more equable than almost any other climate in the world. As there is no miasma from vegetable matter, it is considered healthy. An officer who had been stationed there more than four years, informed me that out of ninety men whom he brought with him, he had only lost two.

I rode through the bazaar in the native part of the town. The principal commodities were coarse cotton stuffs, dates, sugar, spices, and bad tobacco. I dismounted at a small coffee shop, but both the coffee and the narghileh were so intolerably bad that I gave them to the nearest native. A large crowd of Arabs collected around me, and the most intelligent of them asked me the news from Damascus and Stamboul. They said there had recently been war in Yemen, and that Shekh Hossayn was then at the head of the tribes. Leaving the town, I returned to the western side of the peninsula and visited the Turkish Wall, which is the main defence of the place, on the land side. The Rock of Aden resembles that of Gibraltar in being attached to the main land by a narrow strip of sand, but instead of presenting an unbroken line of precipice, as at the latter place, the hills form a crescent, with the concave side toward the north. The points of this crescent are connected by a powerful wall, further protected by a deep moat and sloping glacis, and the heights at each end are crowned with batteries. Immense sums have been expended on these fortifications, which, though far from being completed, now afford perfect security against foes by land.

The value of Aden as a naval station has been much exaggerated. It has been called the "Gibraltar of the East," perhaps with reason, since, like Gibraltar, it can be of no use without a fleet. At present it could scarcely be called impregnable, but were it so, might readily be starved into capitulation, as Gibraltar might be, if England should lose her naval supremacy. Nevertheless, as a necessary station on the Overland Route, its possession is of the utmost importance to England, and it belongs to her *geographically*, as the Fillibusters say. The fortifications are most admirably planned. The skill and genius exhibited in their design impressed me far more than the massive strength of Gibraltar I never felt more forcibly the power of that civilization which follows the Anglo-Saxon race in all its conquests, and takes root in whatever corner of the earth that race sets its foot. Here, on the farthest Arabian shore, facing the most savage and inhospitable regions of Africa, were Law, Order, Security, Freedom of Conscience and of Speech, and all the material advantages which are inseparable from these. Herein consists the true power and grandeur of the race, and the assurance of its final supremacy.

The population of Aden, which was little more than 1,000 at the time it was acquired by England, now amounts to upwards of 20,000. It has almost ruined Mocha and the other Arabian ports on the Red Sea, having usurped the greater part of their commerce. It is a free port, and the native merchants are but too willing to transfer their trade to it, thereby escaping the burdensome and indiscriminate duties exacted by the Turkish Government. The resident merchants in Mocha, Hodeida and Djidda have petitioned the East India Company to establish Customs at Aden, but without effect.

The Achilles took on board three hundred tons of coal, and at half-past nine in the evening fired her signal gun for the passengers to come off. One young lady, however, remained nearly two hours longer, the steamer waiting solely on her account. Less consideration was shown to a luckless native, who had fallen asleep in one of the boats and was not observed until we were under way. He was immediately thrown overboard in spite of his entreaties, and left to take his chance of reaching the shore, which was half a mile distant. There was a collier lying about a hundred yards off, but he would not be able to get on board of her so late at night, and the forcing of him into the sea, under the circumstances showed a most criminal disregard of human life.

On the following day, some mountains about a hundred miles east of Aden were in sight; they were our last view of Araby the Blest. We were from fifteen to twenty miles distant from the shore, and the loveliest tints of violet, lilac and rose-color concealed its sterility. After leaving the Red Sea, the temperature became a few degrees cooler, the thermometer showing 80° at night, and 85° to 87° at noon. The Indian Ocean was calm and peaceful, the violence of the north-east monsoon being over, so that, although it blew in our faces, it only served to freshen our nights and noons. We took our meals under an awning on deck, and some of the passengers preferred sleeping there. Where this open-air life is possible at sea, a long voyage is endurable—otherwise, rather a thousand miles on land, than a hundred on the waters.

Our fare was so much better than that on board the Haddington, that we did not complain much. The coffee and tea, however, gave evidence of astonishing skill, for I never imagined it possible that these beverages could be so badly made. The passengers were often quite unable to distinguish one from the other. On the other hand we had capital bread, the baker being a Chinaman, who kept secret his manner of preparing it. The curry was genuine, and would have compensated for many deficiencies in other respects. On Christmas Day we had a handsome banquet on deck, and turkey was liberally dispensed to all on board. The evening was spent in festivities, the passengers dancing polkas on the quarter-deck, the wild Africans yelling and clapping hands amid-ships, and the sailors performing hornpipes on the forecastle.

The distance from Aden to Bombay is 1,664 miles, and after having been at sea nine days, with a prospect of getting out of coal, we grew at last somewhat impatient. Finally, on the morning of the 27th of December—precisely a month after I embarked at Gibraltar—the cessation of the monsoon, the sultriness of the air, the appearance of the clouds, and the arrival of a dove on board, denoted the proximity of land. I have rarely approached any country with a keener interest. Scarce Vasco de Gama himself, after weathering the Cape of Storms, could have watched for the shores of India with more excited anticipation. That vision of gorgeous Ind, the Empress far away in the empurpled East, throned on the best grandeurs of History and canopied by sublime tradition, was about to be confirmed, or displaced for ever. Near at hand, close behind the blue sea-horizon, lay that which would either heighten the fascination of her name, or make it thenceforth but an empty sound to the ear of Fancy.

Therefore, in spite of the breathless heat, I keep watch from one of the paddle-boxes. At noon there is a cry of "Land!" from the foremast, and in a short time the tops of mountains are faintly discernible on the horizon. These are the Western Ghauts, which extend along the Malabar Coast, from Cape Comorin to Surat. The island of Salsette, north of Bombay, next rises, and ere long we distinguish the light-house, at the entrance of the harbor. A considerable extent of coast, north and south, is visible—the mountains picturesque and beautiful in their forms, and exhibiting, in their drapery of forests, a marked contrast to the desert hills of Arabia, which we have last seen. We are now near enough to distinguish the city, the dwellings of the residents on Malabar Hill, and the groves of cocoa-nut and date trees which cover the island. The sea swarms with fishing-boats, and our native pilot is already on board. We are signalled from the light-house, and being five days behind our time, are no doubt anxiously looked for.

The Bay opens magnificently as we advance. It lies between the islands of Bombay and Salsette and the mainland, and must be fifteen or twenty miles in length. Both shores are mountainous and thickly covered with the palmy growths of the tropics. All is confusion on board, and I also must prepare to set foot on the land of Brahma, Vishnu and Shiva.

CHAPTER II.

IMPRESSIONS OF BOMBAY.

A Foretaste of India—Entering Bombay Harbor—I Reach the Shore—My First Ride in a Palanquin—Mr. Pallanjee's Hotel—Appearance of Bombay—Its Situation—The First Indian Railroad—English Hospitality—American Consuls and Residents—The Parsees—Sir Jamsetjee Jeejeebhoy—His Family and Residence—Parsee Faith and Ceremonics—Bridal Processions—A Drive to Malabar Hill—Tropical Gardens—Tax on Palm-Trees—A Hindoo Temple—The Jeejeebhoy Hospital—Dr. Bhawoo Dajee.

Before reaching Bombay, I had a slight foreshadowing of Indian life. The servants on the steamer being all Indians, and the passengers mostly belonging to the East India service, many peculiarities of every-day life were already familiar to me. I had mastered the mysteries of curry; I learned to say "tiffin" instead of "lunch;" I became accustomed to being addressed as "sahib," and even ventured so far into Hindustani, as to call out boldly at table: "*pani do!*" (give me water) or: "*saf basan lao!*" (bring a clean plate). Thus the first bloom of the new land was lost to me—all those nameless slight peculiarities which surround you with an enchanted circle when you first plunge yourself into another climate and another race. Nevertheless, there was enough left to make my landing on Indian soil a circumstance of no ordinary character.

We came slowly up the splendid bay, until within half a mile of the town. The shores being low, nothing but an array of brown tiled roofs, and a small Gothic spire, was visible behind the crowd of vessels at anchor. On the other hand, however, the islands of Elephanta and Panwell, and the ranges of the Mahratta Ghauts, were gorgeously lighted up by the evening sun. But little time was allowed for admiring them; the anchor dropped, and a fleet of boats, conveying anxious friends and relatives, gathered about us. The deck was covered with pyramids of baggage, all was noise and confusion, here shouts of joy and there weeping, here meeting and there parting, many scenes of the drama of life enacted at the same moment. Finding myself left wholly to my own resources, I set about extricating myself from the bewilderment, and accepting the first native who addressed me, I embarked for the shore before the other passengers had thought of leaving. "Rupees," said the master of the boat, holding up three of his fingers. "*Ek*," (one) I answered. Up went two fingers. "*Ek*," again; and so I went ashore for one. We came to a stone pier, with a long flight of steps leading down to the water. The top of it was thronged with natives in white dresses and red turbans. Among them were the runners of the hotels, and I soon found the one I wanted. At a small customs office on the pier, my baggage was passed unexamined, on my declaring that I had but two pounds of Turkish tobacco. A line of cabs, buggies and palanquins with their bearers was drawn up on the pier, and in order to be as Indian as possible, I took one of the latter.

It was not a pleasant sensation to lie at full length in a cushioned box, and impose one's whole weight (and I am by no means a feather) upon the shoulders of four men. It is a conveyance invented by Despotism, when men's necks were footstools, and men's heads playthings. I have never yet been able to get into it without a feeling of reluctance, as if I were inflicting an injury on my bearers. Why should they groan and stagger under my weight, when I have legs of my own?—and yet, I warrant you, nothing would please them less than for me to use those legs. They wear pads on the shoulders, on which rests the pole to which the palanquin is suspended, and go forward at a slow, sliding trot, scarcely bending their knees or lifting their feet from the ground. The motion is agreeable, yet as you are obliged to lie on your back, you have a very imperfect view of the objects you pass. You can travel from one end of India to another in this style, but it is an expensive and unsatisfactory conveyance, and I made as little use of it as possible, in my subsequent journeys.

As I was borne along, I saw, through the corners of my eyes, that we passed over a moat and through a heavy stone gateway. I then saw the bottoms of a row of fluted Grecian pillars—a church, as I afterwards found—then shops, very much in the European style, except that turbaned Hindoos and mitred Parsees stood in the doors, and finally my bearers came to a halt in a wooden verandah, where I was received by Mr. Pallanjee, the host of the British Hotel. I was ushered up lofty flights of wooden steps to the third story, and installed in a small room, overlooking a wide prospect of tiled roofs, graced here and there with a cocoa-nut or brab palm. The partitions to the rooms did not reach the ceiling; there were no glass windows, but merely blinds, and every breeze that came, swept through the whole house. The servants were mostly Portuguese, from Goa, but as India is especially the country of servant and master, every person is expected to have one for his own use. I chose a tall Hindoo, with one red streak and two white ones (the signs of caste) on his forehead, who, for half a rupee daily, performed the duties of guide, interpreter, messenger and valet de chambre. Nothing can exceed the respect shown to Europeans by the native servants. They go far beyond the Arab and Turkish domestics of the East, or even the slaves in Egypt. No Russian serf could have a greater reverence for his lord. As a natural consequence of this, they are noted for their fidelity; the ayahs, or nurses, are said to be the best in the world.

Bombay, as a city, presents few points of interest to a traveller. It is wholly of modern growth, and more than half European in its appearance. It is divided into two parts —the Fort, as it is called, being enclosed within the old Portuguese fortifications and surrounded by a moat. It is about a mile in length, extending along the shore of the bay. Outside of the moat is a broad esplanade, beyond which, on the northern side, a new city has grown up. The fortifications are useless as a means of defence, the water of the moat breeds mosquitos and fevers, and I do not understand why the walls should not have been levelled, long since. The city within the Fort is crowded to excess. Many of the streets are narrow, dark and dirty, and as the houses are frequently of wood, the place is exposed to danger from fire. The population and trade of Bombay have increased so much within the last few years, that this keeping up of old defences is a great inconvenience So far are the old practices preserved, that at one particular gate, where there was a powder magazine twenty years ago, no person is permitted to smoke. Southward of the Fort is a tongue of land—formerly the island of Colaba, but now connected by a causeway—on which stands the light-house. To the north-west, beyond the city, rises Malabar Hill, a long, low height, looking upon the open ocean, and completely covered with the gardens and country-houses of the native and European merchants.

The mainland is distant from Bombay about fifteen miles, across the bay. Steamers run daily to Panwell, whence there is a mail-coach to Poonah, the old Mahratta capital, about seventy miles distant. Northward of the Island of Bombay, lies the large Island of Salsette, which is connected with it by two causeways, and Salsette has lately been united to the mainland by a bridge, the strait, at the northern point of the island, being less than half a mile wide. This bridge was built by the Railroad Company, who have already finished thirty-five miles of the great road which is to connect Bombay and Calcutta. The rails were laid as far as Tanna at the time of my visit, and the trains commenced running shortly afterwards. The engineers were occupied in locating that part of the line which crosses the Ghaüts, and which is the most difficult and expensive portion of the road. The East India Company guarantees 5 per cent. annually on the stock, for the period of twenty years, owing to which encouragement, (without which, indeed, the undertaking were impossible,) shares were at a premium.

During my brief stay in Bombay, I made some acquaintances among the English residents, to whom I was indebted for much cordial hospitality. The English in India are said to be the most hospitable people in the world, even to those who bring no letters of introduction. The kindness of my friends, and especially of Capt. R. Baird Smith, of the Bengal Engineers, supplied me with letters for all the principal towns in the interior, so that I had double assurance of a friendly reception. There were no American merchants in Bombay at the time, nor even a Consul. Appointments had been made, and Consuls had gone out, but none of them found the profits of the office equal to its expenses. The last one had appointed Mr. Dossabhoy Merwanjee, one of the principal Parsee merchants, his agent, but the latter had no authority to act in a Consular capacity. The house of Dossabhoy Merwanjee & Co., however, is actively engaged in American trade, most of the vessels which come out from our ports being consigned to it. I was indebted to the members of the firm for much kindness. The only American residents were some missionaries, who have established a school and church, and a Boston ice merchant, who was a man of some importance in such a climate. The ice was preserved in a large stone rotunda, and sold at the rate of four annas (12 cents) the pound. The consumption is increasing, much use of it being now made by the physicians, and with the best effect.

My good fortune in making the acquaintance of Dossabhoy Merwanjee, and other members of the celebrated Lowjee Family, to which he belongs, gave me some insight into native society here—an imperfect experience, it is true, but enough to satisfy me that in few of the English works on India which I have read, has justice been done to the character of the native population. The Parsees, especially, form a community distinguished for its intelligence, enterprise and public spirit. It would be no exaggeration to say that more than half the wealth of Bombay is in the hands of this class. Sir Jamsetjee Jeejeebhoy, the Parsee knight, presents one of the most striking examples of commercial success to be found in the history of any country. This gentleman, whose splendid benevolence has imperishably connected his name with his native city, was the architect of his own fortune. By prudence, economy and intelligence he rose from one success to another, till at present his fortune is estimated at three crores of rupees ($15,000,000.) He has given away in charities of various kinds upwards of $2,000,000, and scarcely a day passes without recording some further evidence of his generosity. Among other works which owe their existence to him—and for which he was knighted by the Queen, being the first native who ever received that distinction—are the Hospital which bears his name, the Causeway from Bombay Island to Salsette (called Lady Jamsetjee's Causeway), and the Aqueduct for supplying the city of Poonah with water. I had a glimpse of him one evening, as his carriage passed me in the street: he was then verging upon his eightieth year, and very infirm. His eldest son, Cursetjee, inherits his enterprise and boldness, and possesses a large fortune of his own making. Another of his sons has distinguished himself as a Persian scholar, and has published a work on the Era of Zoroaster.

Dr. Bhawoo Dajee, a distinguished Hindoo physician kindly accompanied me to Sir Jamsetjee's town residence, a large and elegant mansion within the fort. The old gentleman was absent, but we were received by his son Sorabjee, who inquired after Mr Charles Norton, of Cambridge, and showed me a *North American Review*, containing Mr N.'s biography of Sir Jamsetjee. The residence is very elegantly furnished, in a style combining European comfort with Oriental display. Portraits of the different members of the family occupied the walls, and in the centre of the principal saloon stood a splendid testimonial, in wrought silver, three feet high, presented to Sir Jamsetjee by three of the Bombay merchants.

The Parsees settled on the Malabar Coast about eight centuries ago, after their expulsion from Persia. They are as is well known, followers of Zoroaster, recognizing one Good and one Evil Principle, who contend for the mastery of the Universe. They worship the sun, as the representative of God, fire in all its forms, and the sea. Their temples contain no images, but only the sacred fire, and though they have fixed days for the performance of various rites, they repeat their prayers every morning, soon after sunrise. The dead are neither buried nor burned, but exposed to the air within a walled enclosure, on the summit of a hill. The bodies of the rich are protected by a wire screen, until wasted away, but those of the poor are soon devoured by birds of prey. The children are generally married at from two to five years of age, and brought up together, until of a proper age to assume the duties of married life. Most of the marriages are celebrated in the winter season, and the streets continually resounded with the music of the bridal processions. First came a string of palanquins and carriages, filled with children of both sexes—and very beautiful are the Parsee children—clad in silk bespangled with gold, and with pearl and emerald ornaments in their ears. Then a band of native musicians, generally playing "Lucy Long," or "Carry me back," &c.: after them the bridal dowry, covered with massive extinguish ers of silver, and the procession was always closed by a con course of women, whose loose floating mantles of scarlet, crimson, orange, yellow and purple silk, gleamed in the sun,

> "Like tulip beds, of different shape and dyes,
> Bending beneath the invisible west-wind's sighs."

My friend Cursetjee Merwanjee, accompanied me one afternoon in a drive around the environs of Bombay. After passing the esplanade, which is thickly dotted with the tents of the military and the bamboo cottages of the officers, we entered the outer town, inhabited entirely by the natives. The houses are two or three stories in height, with open wooden verandahs in front, many of which have a dark, mellow old look, from the curiously carved posts and railings of black wood which adorn them. Mixed with the houses are groups of the beautiful cocoa-palm, which rise above the roofs and hang their feathery crowns over the crowded highway. Outside of the town hall is shade and the splendor of tropical bloom. The roads are admirable, and we rolled smoothly along in the cool twilight of embowered cocoa, brab and date palms, between whose pillared trunks the afternoon sun poured streams of broad golden light. The crimson sagittaria flaunted its flame-like leaves on the terraces; a variety of the acacia hung thick with milky, pendulous blossoms, and every gateway disclosed an avenue of urns leading up to the verandah of some suburban palace, all overladen with gorgeous southern flowers. We rode thus for miles around and over Malabar Hill, and along the shores of the Indian Ocean, until the hills of Salsette, empurpled by the sunset, shone in the distance like the mountains of fairy land.

I had thought the Government of Egypt despotic, for taxing the poor Nubias a piastre and a-half (7½ cents) annually for each of their date-trees, but the East India Company exacts from one to three rupees (50 cents to $1.50) on each tree according to its quality. As the principal produce of the trees is *tari*, a kind of palm wine, used only by the natives, such a tax appeared enormous, and gave color to what I had already heard, that the resources of the country are mercilessly drained by the Company, for the purpose of carrying out its expensive system of annexation, and at the same time paying the regular yearly dividend to the stockholders. However, I had determined, on entering India, to clear my mind of all preconceived opinions, and to judge of the effects of British rule as impartially as possible. I shall therefore draw no conclusion at present from this single instance of oppression.

In the course of our excursion we visited a Hindoo Temple on the western shore of the island. It is dedicated to the five principal divinities, each of whom has his separate shrine. We were not permitted to go further than the doors, but the attendants removed the hangings and showed us the figures of the gods. Their names were in the Mahratta language, and I do not remember the Sanscrit appellation of any except Mahadeo. The temple occupied the summit of a small hill, and was approached by ghauts, or flights of steps, of hewn stone. Near it there was a much older shrine, with an image in a dark recess. A tiger, rudely sculptured, sat in the outer porch, facing it. Several bells hung from the roof, and each of the natives who accompanied us rang one of these, both on passing in, and out.

Dr. Bhawoo Dajee took me to visit the Jamsetjee Jeejeebhoy Hospital, the name of which declares its founder. It is a one-story stone building, in the Gothic style, and divided into a number of wards, where the destitute Christian, Jewish, Hindoo, Parsee, or Mahometan invalid is taken in and well cared for. There were about three hundred patients at the time of my visit. The hospital is very clean, kept in excellent order, and the patients appeared to be enjoying as much comfort as was possible, in their condition. Opposite the hospital is the Grant Medical College, an excellent institution, which was then attended by about thirty native students. Bhawoo Dajee himself is a graduate of this College, where he received the gold medal, and was besides awarded a prize of six hundred rupees for an essay on Infanticide. As a physician and surgeon he is among the first of his class in Bombay, and in that refinement and liberality which distinguishes the gentleman and the scholar, he would be a noted man any where. I esteem it a particular good fortune which brought me to his acquaintance.

CHAPTER III.

THE CAVE-TEMPLES OF ELEPHANTA.

Hindoo and Egyptian Antiquities—The Hindoo Faith—The Trinity—A Trip to Elephanta—Scenery of the Bay—Landing on the Island—Front View of the Cave-Temple—Portuguese Vandalism—The Colossal Trinity—The Head of Brahma—Vishnu—Shiva—Remarkable Individuality of the Heads—The Guardians of the Shrine—The Columns of Elephanta—Their Type in Nature—Intrinsic Dignity of all Religions—Respect for the Ancient Faiths—The Smaller Chambers of the Temple—The Shrine of the Sterile—Tamarind Trees—Smaller Cave-Temples—Return to Bombay Island—Sunset in the Botanic Garden.

WHILE in Bombay, I took a step further back into the past, than ever in all my previous experience. In Egypt, you are brought face to face with periods so remote, that they lie more than half within the realm of Fable; yet there the groping antiquarian has pierced the mystery, and leads you down from dynasty to dynasty, on the crumbling steps of hieroglyphic lore. But in India,—the cradle, as many believe, of the Human Race—we have no such helps, and while we gaze upon the tokens of a faith which was no doubt, pre-existent to that of the Pharaohs, science sits down baffled and leaves us to wander in the dark. No Wilkinson or Champollion writes on the altars of the gods: "B. C.— so and so much." The whole backward vista of Time is thrown open, and we are free to retrace the ages, even to the days when there were giants. I no longer marvel at any of the ancient faiths; I only wonder that those vast, strange and gorgeous systems of mythology ever should have disappeared from the religions of the world, while such types of them remain in existence.

The Hindoo faith, in its original and pure form, was a consistent monotheism, and no doubt is still so understood by the more intellectual of its professors. The parent Deity Brehm, was an invisible and Omnipotent God, the maker of Heaven and Earth, and like the Divinity of the Buddhists, too great for mortal comprehension. The three deities who sprang from him may be regarded rather as personifications of his attributes than as distinct personalities. These deities, who form the *Trimurti*, or Hindoo Trinity, are Brahma, the Creator, Vishnu, the Preserver, and Shiva, the Destroyer. Among the emblems of the latter is a new-born infant, showing that Life is continually reproduced from Death. From these three spring a host of inferior deities, who, with their progeny, amount to the number of thirty-three millions, of whom three millions are evil, and the remainder good. Here the preponderance of Good over Evil in the government of the world, and consequently the beneficence of the ruling Deity, is strikingly acknowledged. The original faith has greatly degenerated, as all the old religions have, and among the ignorant millions exists only in the most extraordinary superstitions and the grossest forms of idolatry; but no one can deny the simple grandeur of its first conception.

However, as I am a traveller, and not a theologian, let me return to the subject, which is my visit to the Cave-temples of Elephanta. These celebrated remains are upon the Island of Elephanta, in the bay, and about seven miles distant from Bombay. I was accompanied by the captain of an American bark. We engaged a bunder-boat, a craft with a small cabin, something like the *kangia* of the Nile, embarked at the Apollo pier, and went up the bay with the flood tide. We passed the fort and floated along the shore as far as Mazagaun, where the wind favored us for a run out to the island. The scenery of the bay is beautiful, the different islands rising from the water in bold hills covered with vegetation, while the peaks of the Malabar Ghauts cut their sharp outlines against the sky, on the opposite side. Butcher's Island, which lies between Bombay and Elephanta, is comparatively low and flat, and has a barren appearance, but it contains a number of European bungalows, and seems to be a favorite place of residence. Elephanta, on the contrary, which is about a mile in length, is lofty, and covered with palm and tamarind trees. Its form is very beautiful, the summit being divided into two peaks of unequal height.

The water is shallow on the western side, and as we approached several natives appeared on the beach, who waded out two by two, and carried us ashore on their shoulders. A well-worn foot-path pointed out the way up the hill, and in a few minutes we stood on the little terrace between the two peaks, and in front of the temple. The house of the sergeant who keeps guard over it still intervened between us and the entrance, and before passing it I stood for some time looking across to Bombay and Salsette, enchanted with the beauty of the prospect before me. More than half the charm, I found, lay in the rich, tropical foliage of the foreground.

Turning, I passed around the screen of some banana trees

and under the boughs of a large tamarind. The original entrace to the temple is destroyed, so that it is impossible to tell whether there was a solid front and doorway, as in the Egyptian rock-temples, or whether the whole interior stood open as now. The front view of Elephanta is very picturesque. The rock is draped with luxuriant foliage and wild vines, brilliant with many-colored blossoms, heightening the mysterious gloom of the pillared hall below, at the farthest extremity of which the eye dimly discerns the colossal outlines of the tri-formed god of the temple. The chambers on each side of the grand hall are open to the day, so that all its sculptures can be examined without the aid of torches. The rows of rock-hewn pillars which support the roof, are surmounted by heavy architraves, from which hang the capitals and shattered fragments of some whose bases have been entirely broken away. The Portuguese, in their zeal for destroying heathen idols, planted cannon before the entrance of the cave, and destroyed many of the columns and sculptured panels, but the faces of the colossal Trinity have escaped mutilation.

This, the *Trimurti*, is a grand and imposing piece of sculpture, not unworthy of the best period of Egyptian art. It reminded me of the colossal figures at Aboo-Simbel, though with less of serene grace and beauty. It is a triple bust, and with the richly-adorned mitres that crown the heads, rises to the height of twelve feet. The central head, which fronts the entrance, is that of Brahma, the Creator, whose large calm features, are settled in the repose of conscious power as if creation were to him merely an action of the will, and not an effort. On his right hand is Vishnu, the Preserver, re presented in profile. His features are soft and feminine, full of mildness and benignity, and are almost Grecian in their outlines, except the under lip, which is remarkably thick and full. The hair falls in ordered ringlets from under a cap something between a helmet and a mitre. The right arm which is much mutilated, is lifted to the shoulder, and from the half-closed hand droops a lotus-blossom. The third member of the Trinity, the terrible Shiva, the Destroyer, is on the left of Brahma, and, like Vishnu, his head is turned so as to present the profile. His features are totally different from the other two. His forehead is stern, ridged at the eyebrows, his nose strongly aquiline, and his lips slightly parted, so as to show his teeth set, with an expression of fierce cruelty and malignity. A cobra twists around his arm and hand, which grasps the snake by the neck and holds it on high, with hood expanded, ready to strike the deadly blow.

Nothing astonished me more, in this remarkable group, than the distinct individuality of each head With the exception of the thick under lip, which is common to all three, the faces are those of different races. Brahma approaches the Egyptian and Vishnu the Grecian type, while Shiva is not unlike the Mephistopheles of the modern German school. The group stands in an excavated recess, or shrine, at the entrance of which, on each side, are two colossal statues. They are more rudely executed, and the faces exhibit a grosser type, the nose being broad and slightly flattened, and the lips thick and projecting. The hand holds the lotus-flower, and the eyes are closed, but the expression of the face is that of happy reverie rather than sleep. Had the temple been Buddhist, I should have said that they were meditating their final beatific absorption into the Divine Essence. The same figures are seen in other parts of the temple, and their aspect perfectly harmonizes with the symbols introduced into the purely ornamental parts of its architecture.

This reminds me of the columns supporting the roof, which were unlike any others I had seen. The lower part is square, resting on a plinth, but at about half the height it becomes circular and fluted—or rather filleted, the compartments having a plane and not a concave surface. The capital is a flattened sphere, of nearly double the diameter of the shaft, having a narrow disc, with fluted edges, between it and the architrave. I knew these columns must have some type in Nature, and puzzled myself to find it. On visiting one of the smaller temples on the eastern side of the island, the resemblance flashed upon me at once—it was the poppy-head. The globular capital and its low, fluted crown, are copied almost without change from the plant, and these two symbols—the poppy and the lotus—with the closed eyelids and placid faces of the colossal guardians, give the whole temple an air of mystic and enchanted repose. One involuntarily walks through its dim and hushed aisles with a softer step, and speaks, if he must speak, in an undertone.

There is something in every form of religion worthy of general respect; and he who does not feel this, can neither understand nor appreciate the Art which sprang from the ancient Faiths. Our teachers of religion speak with sincere and very just horror and contempt of all forms of idolatry, yet, under pain of their anathemas, I dare assert, that he who can revile Osiris and Amun-Re, is unworthy to behold the wonders of Thebes. The Christian need not necessarily be an iconoclast: nay more, his very faith, in its perfect charity and its boundless love, obliges him to respect the shrines where the mighty peoples of the ancient world have bowed and worshipped. Besides, there is Truth, however dim and eclipsed, behind all these outward symbols. Even the naked and savage Dinkas of Central Africa worship trees; and so do I. The Parsees worship the sun, as the greatest visible manifestation of the Deity; and I assure you, I have felt very much inclined to do the same, when He and I were alone in the Desert. But let not the reader, therefore, or because I respect the feeling of worship, when expressed in other forms than my own, think me a Pagan.

The walls of the great hall of the temple of Elephanta, are divided into tablets, or compartments, each of which contains, as a central figure, the colossal statue of some god, surrounded by a host of inferior deities. Few of these have escaped the fanatical fury of the Portuguese, but sufficient remains to show the bold and masculine character of the art which produced them. The smaller figures are introduced above and at the sides of the central god, and some of the tablets have a striking resemblance to pictures of the old Italian masters, representing a saint surrounded by a cloud of cherubs. In the absence of all inscriptions, it is impossible to determine at what time the temple was excavated. The architecture, judged by its style alone, appears to be the antecedent of the Egyptian, which would then represent its perfect development, modified somewhat by being transplanted to a different soil. But I believe that most ethnographers now consider that the ancient Egyptians and Hindoos are kindred branches of one stock, whose seat is to be looked for somewhere in Central Asia.

The side chambers of the temple are much smaller, and the walls are covered in the same manner, with sculptured tablets. Some of the figures have been recently smeared with red paint, a sign that they are still worshipped by some of the Hindoo sects. At the foot of a flight of steps which leads to the chambers on the left of the grand hall, two curious figures of dogs seated on their hind legs, which have been very lately excavated, are erected on pedestals. It requires an experienced antiquarian to tell whether they are dogs, lions, or dolphins. There are three or four small inclosed apartments resembling the adyta of the Egyptian temples. In the centre of each is a low pedestal, or platform, upon which stands a stone about three feet high, with a rounded top—the Lingam, which is one of the most ancient as well as common of the Hindoo symbols. One of these, in particular, is still in great repute among the natives, and is resorted to by the Hindoo women, who seat themselves upon it for a certain length of time, as a cure for barrenness. I was told that an English lady of Bombay, whose marriage had not had the desired result, was induced to try the experiment, which, to her great surprise, was successful.

After spending some time in the larger temple, two native boys showed us the way to the two smaller ones, which are higher up the hill, on its eastern side. Other visitors had come in the mean time, and a company of sailors were employed in knocking down the pods of the tamarind trees. The husk incloses a thick paste, wrapped around the seeds, with an intensely acid, but agreeable taste. From the gap between tho two peaks of the islands, we looked down into a lovely little valley on the opposite side, gradually widening to the water, near which was a native hamlet. I longed to pitch my tent in one of its palm-groves, and to spend a week in studying the strange gods in the caverns above.

The smaller temples have been much mutilated. The entrances are nearly filled up with rubbish, and the inner chambers are now the abodes of the jackal and the serpent. They were too dark to be properly seen without torches, which we had not, but I could perceive that many of them contained the upright stone, and the usual sculptured tablets on the walls. The outer courts of both were supported by elegant poppy-headed pillars, a few of which have escaped destruction Excavation would no doubt reveal much that is now hidden, but the Government has no taste for such things, and there are few archæologists in Bombay. The most that has been done is to build a cottage and station a sergeant at the entrance of the great temple, in order to prevent visitors from injuring the sculptures.

The afternoon shadows were growing long by this time, admonishing us to return. The wind had risen, and as it was not entirely favorable, we were obliged to run up the bay, past a point of the Island of Salsette, before we could make a tack for the city. Instead of going on to Bombay, however, we landed at the pier of Mazagaun, and drove to the Botanic Garden, near the Governor's residence, at Parell. The garden is laid out with great taste, and filled with a variety of rare tropical trees, among which are several superb Brazilian palms. I there saw the first banyan-tree, but the specimen was too young to justify its fame. The flaming blossoms of the azalias, pelargoniums and sagittarias first deepened in hue, and then grew dusky and indistinct in the fading flush of sunset, as I wandered through the palmy alleys, breathing of "nard and cassia," and the voluptuous Persian rose. But the short southern twilight sank away, and I rode back to Bombay, with the silvery, meteoric lustre of the zodiacal light gleaming over my path.

CHAPTER IV.

A NAUTCH AMONG THE PARSEES.

New-Years Day—A Tropical Gift—A Parsee Bungalow—Our Reception—Chewing the Betel-Nut—The Nautch-Girls—Their Dances—Supper—Prejudices of Caste—The Bengalee Dance—A Gilded Bridegroom—Piercing Music—Ship-Building in Bombay—Education of the Natives—Their Appeals to Parliament.

The morning of New-Year's Day, 1853, dawned clear and beautiful. Lord Falkland, Governor of the Bombay Presidency, gave a splendid ball at his residence at Parell, on the previous evening. The simple ceremony of calling upon him would have insured me an invitation; but as I carelessly neglected to do this, and therefore missed the ball, I accepted the more readily an invitation to attend a *nautch* at the country residence of my Parsee friends, on the following evening. A servant came to my room early on New-Year's morning, with a tray heaped with fruit, a large bunch of roses, and a polite note from Dossabhoy Merwanjee Wadya and his associates, containing the compliments of the season, and an invitation to be at Parell at half-past nine o'clock. I could not help being struck with the difference between New-Year in Bombay and in New York. While my friends were making their round of calls, muffled in furs, and with red noses and frosty hands, I was sitting on an open verandah, as lightly clad as possible, looking down on the palms and papayas in the gardens below, and listening to the songs of birds gathered on all the house-tops, my New-Year's gift consisting of a pummelow (a fruit resembling the shaddock, but of much finer flavor), a pile of oranges and golden bananas, and a *pawn*, for chewing, wrapped in a gilded betel-leaf.

Three countrymen—all who were in Bombay, with the exception of the Missionaries—were also invited, as well as two Englishmen, but the remainder of the guests were native, Parsee and Hindoo. A pleasant drive of five miles brought us to the country-house, which was built on land granted to the family by the East India Company, on account of the services they have rendered as ship-builders. It was a spacious one-story bungalow, and brilliantly lighted up for the occasion with hanging lamps of cocoa-nut oil, which gives out a very delicate and pleasant perfume while burning. We were ushered into a hall, around the sides of which were couches made in imitation of sofas, and not so lazy and luxurious as the Turkish divan. The floor was carpeted, and the musicians and nautch-girls were seated in a group in one corner.

Dossabhoy, and our friends, Hirjeebhoy, the head builder in the Bombay dock-yard, Jamsetjee and Cursetjee, received us cordially, and immediately on taking our seats, bunches of fragrant roses were presented to us, over which fresh rose-water was sprinkled from a silver vase. Another servant then appeared with a tray of *pawns*, which the Parsees were already chewing vigorously. Indeed, you rarely see a native, of whatever condition, without a pawn in his mouth. They are composed of chips of betel-nut, cardamum seeds and betel-leaf, to which some add lime made from mussel-shells. In order to be like the rest, I commenced chewing, and found the taste very much like sassafras, but more astringent. It is by no means disagreeable, and must be rather conducive to health than otherwise, or it would not have become a universal custom. Both the leaf and nut are excellent tonics.* The juice only is swallowed, but the practice of chewing makes both the mouth and teeth, for the time, of a bright red color. I was quite shocked on landing, to see so many natives (as I thought) spitting blood.

In a short time the musicians had finished tuning their instruments, and the two nautch-girls (bayaderes) took their places on the floor. The word *bayadere* is a French invention and is unknown in India. These girls were about tweny-five years of age, small in stature, dark-brown in complexion, plain in features, and inert and languid in expression. They were far from being as handsome or graceful as the *Almehs* who danced for us in the temple of Luxor. They wore full robes of a gay color, descending nearly to the ancle, but confined by a broad shawl so far below their hips as to restrict the motion

*Prof. Johnston says: "On those who are accustomed to use it, the betel produces weak but continuous and sustained exhilarating effects. And that these are of a most agreeable kind, may be inferred from the very extended area over which the chewing of betel prevails, among Asiatic nations. In the damp and pestilent regions of India, where the natives live upon a spare and miserable diet, it is really very conducive to health. Part of its healthful influence in fever-breeding districts is probably to be ascribed to the pepper-leaf which is chewed along with the betel-nut."

of their feet. They had also shawls around their heads, trowsers of red silk, and slippers. The musicians commenced singing a melancholy, monotonous measure, with a lively accompaniment on their lutes. The girls joined in the singing, occasionally lifting their arms with the utmost deliberation, or slightly shifting the position of their feet. Now one advanced a few steps and as slowly retreated, now the other. I never saw a dance so spiritless and inexpressive.

Some of the songs, on the other hand, pleased me exceedingly. Less wild and barbaric than the Arab chants, they are pervaded with the same expression of longing and of love, and though sung by voices which were occasionally shrill and harsh, still preserved a touching air of tenderness. After witnessing two or three dances, we were called into the other room, to a collation of fruits and sweetmeats, in which the Parsees joined us, contrary to the usual custom of their sect. This restriction, however, does not seem to be a part of their faith, but to have resulted from a long residence among the Hindoos, who maintain such a religious distinction of caste, that to the Brahmin, the mere touch of one of the lower orders is defilement, and can only be removed by bathing and change of apparel. The Mussulmans in India have adopted the same notions, and will neither eat with Christians nor drink from the same vessels.

During the interval, the nautch-girls made a change in the fashion of their dress, by binding their robes in such a manner that they reached only to the knees, and giving their turbans a flattened form, like those worn by the natives of Bengal. In fact, the dance which succeeded was called the Bengalee. It differed little from the preceding, except that the measure was more animated, and the languid shuffling of the feet done in somewhat quicker time. The song which accompanied it was translated to me, and ran thus: "My beloved Nabob, take me to Calcutta: with the howdah on the elephant, the saddle on the horse." This is the style of poetry of which these songs are usually composed, but some of them cannot be so safely translated. There are nautch-girls who have a fame among the natives equal to that of Taglioni or Ellsler in Europe, and who are paid at the rate of five hundred rupees a night, but they are to be found at the Courts of the native sovereigns in Northern India, where the nautches are got up on a grand scale.

The previous evening, on my way home from the Botani Garden, I met a magnificent marriage procession in the streets of the native town. First came a large number of beautiful children in open vehicles, the pearls and spangles of their dresses glittering in the light of torches, which were borne on long poles, and waved in riotous jubilee to the sound of the music. Behind them were boys in jewelled robes, on horseback, with servants holding golden-fringed umbrellas above their heads. The music—a piercing medley of fifes, drums, and lutes—came next, and then the bridegroom, mounted on a white horse. He was a man of about twenty, clad in splendid robes of white silk, embroidered with gold His turban gleamed with pearls, and his cheeks and forehead were covered with gold leaf. He was a living El Dorado, but sat so grave and motionless on his horse, staring straight before him, that he might have been taken for a bedizened statue. A servant, holding a silver screen resembling a fan, walked on each side of him, and behind him came the dowry, borne on men's heads. It was contained in twenty or thirty miniature houses, arranged so as to form a quadrangle, with a temple in the centre.

I passed a number of houses illuminated for marriage festivities, and from one of them there came the sound of a flute more shrill and piercing, I have no doubt, than any other flute in the world. Its tones were so intensely shrill as to become tangible. They were shot out of the open windows like barbed arrows, and whenever any one struck you it was followed by a keen sense of pain. They flew whistling down the street, rattling against the walls, transfixing all civilized ears and torturing all susceptible nerves. I shudder, even now, to think of the smarts I endured while passing that house.

The Wadya family, to which my host belonged, have been for more than half a century the ship-builders of Bombay. The vicinity of the teak forests has occasioned the building of several ships of the line for the British Navy in the dock-yard there. The first of these, the *Minden*, has been in service for nearly fifty years, and her condition still attests the excellence of her construction. It was between her decks, while lying off Fort McHenry, that Francis Key wrote our "Star-spangled Banner." The present head-builder Hirjeebhoy Merwanjee, had on the stocks at the time of my visit, two steamships of eighteen hundred tons each. He was nearly three years in England, studying his profession, and has published a work in English, giving his views of English institutions and society. The Government has done much for the natives in the establishment of such institutions as the Grant Medical College, the Elphinstone Institution, and others, but much still remains to be done. The amount expended for educational purposes in the Bombay Presidency is about £12,500, which is insufficient to support any general system of instruction. The Board of Education consists of three English residents and three natives; in its operation it embraces instruction in the Mahratta and Guzeratee, as well as the English and Hindostanee languages. The Elphinstone Institution has at present about 1,400 scholars, the great proportion of whom are studying in the English department. They are, however, first required to pass in the vernacular languages. The respect in which such men as Mountstuart Elphinstone and Sir Charles Forbes are held by the natives, shows how truly they appreciate every effort for their improvement, and how eagerly they would respond to any measure which had their good in view.

The more intelligent of the natives took advantage of the approaching renewal of the East India Company's Charter (which expired in April, 1854), to form associations and draw up memorials for presentation to Government, in which they represented the disadvantages of the present system in its effect on the native population. The movement was rather too late to be productive of much effect, but it was interesting as showing the temper of the native subjects in India. I saw none of the memorials except that of the Bombay Association, which was drawn up by Dr. Bhawoo Dajee. It was an admirably written document, moderate and respectful, but at the same time firm and dignified in its tone, stating with great clearness the causes of complaint, and suggesting means of redress

CHAPTER V.

THE BANGHY CART.

Preparations for Departure—Warnings—Filial Gratitude—The Banghy Cart—A Night Gallop through Bombay—The Island Road—Ferry to the Mainland—Despotism of the Banghy-Cart—Morning Scenery—The Bungalow—Breakfast—The Sun as a Physician—An Army of Bullocks—Climbing the Ghauts—Natural Pagodas—The Summit—A Kind Sergeant—The Second Day—Resemblance to Mexico—Natives and Villages—The Menagerie Man in Egypt—An English Cantonment—Dhoolia—The Lieutenant and his Hospitality—A Rough Road—Accident—Waiting in the Jungle—The Bullock-Cart—Halt at Seerpore.

As I was bound for China, and could spare but a very short time for my journeys in India, I remained only a week in Bombay. The information given me by my English friends did not furnish a very satisfactory prospect of visiting Delhi and the Himalayas, and reaching Calcutta, within the space of two months, without a much greater expenditure of money than I was prepared to make. The usual mode of travelling had up to that time been by palanquin, a mode as costly as it is disagreeable. The post-road to Agra, however, had recently been made passable for a small cart which carried the mails, and just before my arrival a *banghy-cart* had commenced running from Bombay to Indore, a distance of 375 miles, or about half way to the former city. A *banghy* means, I believe, a package, or something of that sort, and the cart answers to a package-express. Mr. Cowasjee Ruttonjee, the contractor, assured me that the trip would positively be made within six days, travelling day and night. The fare was four annas (twelve cents) per mile, or nearly $47, exclusive of expenses by the way. This, for India, was considered cheap travelling, and I resolved to make a trial of it. I was obliged to give up the idea of taking a servant with me, and to trust entirely to about twenty words of Hindostanee, which I had picked up on board the Achilles. Many were the evil predictions made to me by most of my English friends: "You can never stand the fatigue; you can get nothing to eat; you will be perfectly helpless if any thing happens," etc. But an old officer, who had travelled not only over all India but nearly all the world, wisely comforted me. "Never mind what these people say," said he; "they are accustomed to travel luxuriously, with retinues of servants. Depend upon it, you will get along without the least difficulty."

I sent my heavy baggage by the steamer to Calcutta, limiting myself to two small carpet-bags, which was all that Cowasjee would take in his cart. My Hindoo servant, with the one red and two white stripes on his forehead, procured me a native tailor, who made me several pairs of pantaloons, of a shape so remarkable that I have not been able to wear them, to this day. Perhaps as I grow older, my form will approach nearer to the standard of Hindoo Art, and they will then become serviceable. The striped servant looked very forlorn and disconsolate, as he carried my carpet-bags from Pallanjee's Hotel to the Express Office, on the evening of the

3d of January. "O my master!" he bewailed: 'I am werry sorry to part with you. You are my father, and I am your son. O my father, I shall never forget you!" Considering that he was of a dark-brown complexion, forty years old, and rather ill-favored, I was not anxious to accept the relationship, but, not to be wanting in parental regard, I gave him nearly double the wages agreed upon. Not only did he show no gratitude, but importuned me for more—so little filial affection is there in India!

The banghy-cart was in readiness before Cowasjee's office, when I arrived. It was a square, springless buggy, with a white canvas top, and extremely heavy shafts and wheels. My baggage and the packages for the interior were stowed in the body of the vehicle, the driver and I took our seats, Cowasjee inclined his body and touched his Parsee mitre, and away we dashed into Monument-square. A groom ran at the horse's head till we were fairly under way, and then climbed upon the box behind us. We went out of the gates of the Fort, crossed the esplanade, and entered the busy native town, where we encountered two marriage processions. The red torches glittered on pearls and gold embroidery, on the silver pyramids of the dowry, and the rainbow silks of the women. Our horse, frightened by the noise of the drums and cymbals dashed off furiously, making directly for a blank wall, before which several persons were passing. The driver seemed powerless, and we came instantly upon the wall, catching one of the natives between it and the wheel. I sprang forward, seized the reins and drew the horse around just in time to save the man's life, though not, I fear, to prevent his being badly injured The horse now started at a mad gallop down the street, which was crowded with people. The driver stooped down and raised to his mouth something which, in the darkness, resembled a bottle. He did indeed take a horn—and blew the most terrible blasts, as we careered onwards like Shiva, the Destroyer, the white-robed, ghost-like natives scattering on all sides before us. I grasped the top of the cart tightly and awaited the result, for the horse swerved from side to side in such a manner that a crash seemed inevitable. However, in less time than it has taken to write these lines, we were outside of Bombay, and the cessation of noise and glare restored the animal to his senses.

There was no moon, but we had the brilliant starlight of the tropics, and for an hour after leaving, the zodiacal light stood like a shining obelisk in the west. The road was broad, and as smooth and as hard as a floor, and in less than an hour we reached the first station. Another horse was in readiness, and not less mettlesome than the first, so that we made fully six miles an hour. The road was embowered in mango, sycamore, palm and tamarind trees, whose breath made the night warm and balmy. Our lamps shed transient gleams on the rich masses of foliage, and I was so delighted with the pictures thus brought out of the darkness on either hand, that I reached the end of the gardens and of Bombay Island with regret. A solid stone causeway extends across the shallow strait to the Island of Salsette, whose hills now rose dimly before me. In these hills are the caves and temples of Kenary. During my stay at Bombay I had not time to visit them but I was informed that they are on a much smaller scale than those of Elephanta, though so numerous that the natives reckon their number at nine hundred.

We changed horses twice on the island of Salsette, once at a village of mud and bamboo huts, so thoroughly Egyptian in appearance that I could have believed myself on the banks of the Nile. At midnight we reached the northern end of the island, which is about twenty miles in length. We roused the sleepy ferrymen, who dragged the cart upon a platform laid across two small boats, and slowly rowed us over to the mainland of India. The strait, as well as I could distinguish, is very crooked, and not more than a quarter of a mile in breadth. Up to this time I had not spoken, nor been spoken to, for a very good reason, but no sooner was the cart hauled ashore, than the boatmen came up to me exclaiming: "*kishti-walla: chirramirry!*" (As much as to say; "we are the boatmen, give us a gratuity." I remembered the words, and found them next morning in my vocabulary.) I gave them a small fee, and then the driver came up, saying "Salaam, sahib—*chirramirry!*" So there could be no doubt as to the meaning of "chirramirry."

With a new driver and a new horse I again started forward. The country was more open and undulating, and all signs of gardens and residences disappeared. Now and then we passed a mud village, and about every hour changed horses at a rude station, before reaching which the driver blew furious peals upon his trumpet. In consequence of this, we generally found the horse in waiting, and experienced no delay in changing. The night wore away, the waning moon came up, and then the morning-star; the travelling natives, encamped among the trees, began to bestir themselves, and with the first streak of daylight their heavy ox-wagons were in motion. Now came the horn again into play, and thence forth there was no cessation of its warning blasts. Every thing must give way to the banghy-cart. Woe to the native who, having heard the horn half a mile behind him, still dozed on, allowing his plodding cattle to keep the best track. Down jumped the groom, battering the beasts out of the way, and a touch of the driver's whip not seldom quickened the senses of their masters. No one dared to remonstrate, for the banghy-cart is attached to the Post-Office Department.

Morning showed me an open, rolling country, studded here and there with clumps of trees, and showing occasional signs of cultivation. As it was then the dry season, the grass was brown and withered, and the soil parched. The sea was out of sight, and the broken ranges of the Ghauts before me, seemed near at hand. The road was broad and good, and bridged over the gullies, but so beaten by continual travel, that we swept along in a cloud of dust. I hailed the rising sun with the fervor of a Parsee, for the night had been so cold, that in spite of a thick great-coat, I was chilled to the very bones. I was getting hungry, also, and knowing that we must be approaching a bungalow, I took out Forbes's Hindostanee grammar, and began searching for the words to express my wants. Having prepared a sufficient stock of nouns, and the verbs "bring" and "give," I deemed myself capable of achieving a breakfast.

But first, it is necessary to explain the meaning of a bungalow. I believe it is the general term in India for a residence of the better class, as the English, except in large cities, always speak of their houses as "bungalows." On all the principal lines of road throughout the country, the Government has erected bungalows, at intervals of from ten to twenty miles, for the accommodation of European travellers. The natives have their *serais*, resembling the Turkish khans, and unless travelling by post, are not admitted into the bungalows The latter are plain but substantial cottages, furnished only with tables, chairs, and bedsteads, and generally containing two dining and two sleeping apartments. There are out-houses for the residence of a native servant, called a *peon*, who has charge of the establishment, and for the cooks, or mess-men, who are obliged to procure supplies and prepare meals according to a fixed scale of prices. For the use of the bungalow, each traveller pays one rupee (fifty cents) per day. Were it not for this excellent arrangement, one would be obliged to take tents and all the paraphernalia of a household, and to carry supplies with him from place to place. A register for the names of travellers is kept in each bungalow, and they are requested to note the sums paid, in order to prevent dishonesty on the part of the peons. By nine o'clock we reached the village of Khurdee, sixty-four miles from Bombay. The word "hazree" (breakfast) conveyed my intention to the driver, and he answered: "Achchà, sahib" (very well, sir). I succeeded so well with the messman that in an hour an excellent curry and omelette smoked upon the table. The natives, all along the road, have ingrafted some English words upon the Hindostanee, and frequently use them in a very amusing manner. Whenever I asked for eggs, I was almost sure to be asked in return: "*Half biled* or *mom-let?*" I was provident enough to supply myself with a paper of tea in Bombay, since it is not always to be had on the road.

On getting into the cart, at the last station before reaching Khurdee, the step broke, and as I fell, my knee struck upon a projecting bolt, causing such intense pain as almost to deprive me of my senses By the time we halted again, the joint was so stiff that I could scarcely bend it. The hurt produced such a chilliness that my teeth chattered, and I was fain to sit in the sun while breakfast was preparing. The morning was scorchingly hot, and I soon noticed that the heat seemed to draw out the pain from the injured limb. In fact, after sunning it half an hour I was able to get up and walk as usual, and thenceforth never felt the slightest inconvenience from the injury. This is a case of sun-cure, which I recommend to any one who is anxious to start a new system of healing.

Khurdee lies at the base of the Ghauts, and our road now plunged into a wild, hilly region, covered with jungle. The road was broad, but very rough, and so steep that nothing but the emigrant trail over the Sierra Nevada could equal it. At the worst descents, my conductor called upon the aid of half a dozen bullock-drivers, who seized the shafts and pushed back ward with all their force. Our progress was still further hindered by the endless throng of bullocks which we met. They were laden with bags of rice and of grain, and bales of cotton, and on their way downward to the coast. Between Khurdee and Kussara, a distance of twelve miles, we must have passed from fifteen to twenty thousand of them. They were all heavily laden, and jogging on at a slow, patient walk, which would carry them about ten miles a day. Those, however, who are trained to harness and employed by the natives as draught animals, easily travel twenty-five miles a day, even on a long journey. Though the cow is such a sacred beast in India, there is no end to the labor imposed upon her children, nor is she herself always spared.

We were nearly four hours in making the twelve miles over the pass of Rudtoondee, and then came down upon Kussara, a little village situated in a dell at the foot cf the Tull Ghaut. The highest parapet of the range was now above us and the final ascent to the table-land commenced. The physical formation of this part of India very much resembles that of the Western Coast of Mexico. The summit level is nearly uniform, but instead of presenting a mural front, it thrusts out projecting spurs or headlands, and is cloven by deep gorges. Sharp peaks rise here and there from the general level, formed of abrupt but gradually diminishing terraces, crowned by domes or towers of naked rock. At a distance, they bear an extraordinary resemblance to works of art, and, what is very striking, to the ancient temples of the Hindoos. Is this an accidental resemblance, or did not the old races in reality get their forms of architecture directly from Nature? It is certainly a striking coincidence that all the hills in the Nubian Desert should be pyramids, and all the peaks of the Indian Ghauts pagodas. The word *ghaut* means a flight of steps, as the Ghauts are a succession of terraces descending from the table-land to the sea; and every principal Hindoo temple is approached by a ghaut. The formation of the summits is a characteristic of Indian scenery. Tennyson, who, I believe, has never been in India, describes in two lines the most peculiar aspects of the country:

"And over *hills with peaky tops engrailed,*
And many a tract of palm and rice,
The throne of Indian Cama slowly sailed,
A summer fanned with spice."

There is a splendid artificial road leading up the Tull

Ghaut. As a piece of engineering, it will vie with some of the best roads in Europe. The grade is so slight that we drove all the way on a fast trot, and the windings around the sides of the gorge gave me grand views of the lower terraces of the Ghauts. At the top, we entered on the great table-land of Central India. It was an open, undulating region, much better cultivated than any I had yet seen, and crossed, at intervals of twenty to thirty miles, by high ranges of hills. The air was drier and purer than below, and the setting sun shone broad and warm over tracts of wheat and sugar-cane. We rolled along merrily, through the twilight and into the darkness again, and towards nine o'clock came to the large town and military station of Nassick.

I went directly to the bungalow, for I was quite ready for dinner. An Englishman came out of one of the rooms, and not only assisted me in ordering the meal, but sent his own servant to help get it ready. He evidently took me for an officer (for a traveller is a rare sight in India), and meekly remarked, "I am only a sergeant, in the Engineers Corps. I caught the fever in the jungles at Khurdee, and have been sent up here to recover." I was very much fatigued, and lay down upon the bare bedstead, while dinner was preparing. The sergeant brought his pillow and placed it under my head, and when I awoke after two hours' sleep, I found his cloak carefully wrapped around me and himself tenderly watching, that nothing might disturb my slumbers. It was nearly midnight before the banghy-cart came. I took leave of the kind-hearted sergeant, and we set out at a slow pace. We had already crossed the watershed of India, and soon after leaving Nassick, forded the Godavery, one of the largest streams in the country, which empties into the sea on the Coromandel Coast, not far from Madras. Soon afterwards we entered a large town by a gateway, with a Moorish arch, and threaded the silent streets—a scene which recalled forcibly to my mind, a midnight ramble through the town of Ekhmin, in Upper Egypt.

All the rest of the night we travelled slowly along, through a rolling country, and about nine next morning reached Chandore, only forty-five miles from Nassick. Chandore is a walled town, situated in a hollow at the foot of the Chandore Ghaut. It boasts several Hindoo temples of dark stone, but none of them remarkable for size or beauty. The grotesque idols, their faces smeared with red paint, were visible through the open door. I went to the bungalow for breakfast, and was obliged to wait three hours before the cart came—a delay which enabled me to get a little more sleep. Nevertheless, the heat and glare of the noonday sun so disposed me to drowsiness, that I was several times on the point of tumbling out of the cart. I should have stated that at Khurdee we changed vehicles, and after that I had nothing but a square box on wheels, without springs or cover. We crossed the Chandore Ghaut by a wild pass, half way up which stands a pagoda, so old and black that it might properly belong to the Yezidees, or Devil-Worshippers. Beyond the Ghaut we came upon a waste, hilly region, entirely covered with thorny jungle.

All this part of India reminded me strongly of the table-land of Mexico. There are the same broad, sweeping plains, gashed by deep ravines and gullies; the same barren chains of hills, and the same fertile dips of lowland, rich in corn and cane. I passed through more than one landscape, where, if I had been brought blindfold and asked to guess where I was, I should have declared at once: "This is Mexico." Substitute the words *nulla* for "arroyo," (gully,) *ghaut* for "sierra," nd *jungle* for "chapparal," and you change a description of he Mexican into that of the Indian table-land. I must dmit, however, that, in general, Mexican scenery is on a broader and grander scale than here. We Americans need not envy England the possession of India; for, if we were not a people obstinately opposed to the acquisition of new territory—if we were not utterly blind to "manifest destiny," and regardless of the hints which "Geography" is constantly throwing out to us—we might possess ourselves of Cuba and Mexico, and thus outrival her. Some of my readers may laugh at the absurdity of such an idea; but when a man is travelling alone, among a strange people, he is scarcely responsible for all that comes into his head.

The resemblance to Mexico, however, does not extend to the towns and population, which are rather those of Egypt. The Indian native is darker than the Egyptian Fellah, and has a more acute and lively face, but in his habits and manners he has much in common with the latter. He has the same natural quickness of intellect, the same capacity for deception, the same curious mixture of impudence and abject servility, and the same disregard of clothing. The houses are low cabins of mud and bamboo, or in the larger villages, of mud and unburnt bricks, with mud divans in front, and sometimes thatched verandahs resting on wooden pillars. Nothing can be more miserable than the appearance of the smaller villages, which are even inferior to those of the Nile Delta, and I should like to exhibit them to an original Englishman who went in the same boat with me from Alexandria to Cairo As we were passing one of the villages on the Nile, he came up to me with a horrified expression of face, grasped my arm, pointed to the huts, and exclaimed: "Look there! people actually live there!" "Is it possible?" said I, with as much astonishment as I could command, on such short notice. "Yes," he replied; "Good God, it's dreadful!" This man was a son of a keeper of a menagerie, and was on his way to Central Africa, in search of the Great Hydrocephalus, or some other unknown monster. He was in a furious state of indignation, because Discount & Co., the bankers at Alexandria, had taken four per cent. commission on his letter of credit. "It's only a month since I left England," said he, "and that's four per cent. a month, and that makes forty-eight per cent. a year. Suppose I had been a year on the way, I should have been ruined. If I had money enough to buy the Hydrocephalus, I should not draw a penny, and then they would have to refund the whole of it. But I'll write a letter to *The Times*, and we'll see how much more business of that sort they'll do."

To return to the banghy-cart: we rolled on all the afternoon through alternate jungle and cultivated land, and toward evening reached Mulleigaum, a military cantonment. It is situated in the middle of an open plain, which, although apparently barren, needs but irrigation to make it one vast garden. The neat bungalows of the English officers are embowered in foliage and blossoms, which water alone has coaxed out of the soil. The orchards of bananas dropped their plumy leaves, and the thick hedges of Persian roses, crimson with blossoms, scented the air far and wide. Through the verandahs and open doors I caught glimpses of elegant furniture and pictures within, and once a female figure glided past. I had fancied India to be a place of exile, but nothing could be more cheerful and homelike than these residences. The sepoys were drawn up on the parade-ground for evening review, and a most soldierly appearance they made. We drove to the post-office, and as I had not time to take dinner, I accepted the services of a Portuguese who spoke English, and who offered to procure me supplies for the road. He obtained some biscuits, boiled some eggs, and made me a bottle of strong tea, but refused to accept of the slightest pay for his services.

Thus supplied, I entered on the third night of my journey. It was somewhat cloudy and dark, and I could only observe that our road lay over the same wide uplands, except for a few miles, when passing the Lulling Ghaut. The way was rough and stony, and the thumps I received kept me from falling into the road through drowsiness. An hour past midnight I reached the military station of Dhoolia, 215 miles from Bombay, and was not sorry when the driver informed me that he should go no further that night. Off I started for the bungalow, and on reaching it, was surprised to find the rooms lighted, and a man in English dress on the verandah. He held a small lantern before him, which prevented my seeing his face. "Is this the travellers' bungalow?" I asked. He said nothing, but threw the light of the lamp full upon my face, held it there a few moments, and then cried out: "Why, you're a traveller! Yes. Come in. It's full, but I'll make room for you. I'm just taking a cup of tea: will you take tea, or beer, or brandy-and-water? *Itchoglan*.

bring tea!" There was no resisting such a rapid welcome, and before I had time to put in a word of explanation, I was seated on one end of the table, drinking a cup of tea with the Lieutenant, for such he proved to be. Meanwhile, he was giving orders on all sides. One servant ran for a bedstead; another for a pillow; a third for a quilt. "I'll make you comfortable," said he; "you didn't expect such rough times, did you now? You thought India was like England, didn't you? That's the way. But you want to go to bed. Here, let my servants pull off your boots, and help you undress. You never did that in England, you know, and you won't know how to go about it." And so he ran on, what length of time I cannot tell, for I no sooner lay down, than I fell fast asleep.

I was awakened at sunrise by his servant, with a cup of tea and a plate of biscuit. The Lieutenant walked with me to the Post-Office, and as the cart was not ready, took me to the bungalow of some other officers, who immediately invited me to breakfast. The conversation was so exclusively military, that I did not feel much interested in it. So-and-so, of the 99th, was going to sell out; such-a-one, of "Ours," had applied for two months' leave, etc. Presently the cart came, and I took a cordial leave of them all. The road, after leaving Dhoolia, became indescribably bad. The soil was a soft brown loam, which, after the rains, had been terribly cut up by the heavy bullock-carts, and was now hard and dry. Our horse stumbled slowly along over the ruts, a groom leading him by the head. The country was crossed by deep nullas, or gulleys, many of which were very difficult to pass. The scenery presented no new features, except a singular isolated hill, resembling a fortress, near Soongheer. Beyond this point it was mostly hilly jungle, with few habitations. During the afternoon, we passed three elephants, which were standing in the shade of a large peepul tree, motionless as if ewn out of basaltic rock.

It was already two o'clock, and we had only proceeded about twenty miles from Dhoolia, when the axle suddenly snapped under the repeated jolts, and I was thrown into the road. I escaped with a slight bruise, and sat down in the jungle to await the issue. As I could neither give nor take suggestions, I was silent; but I had with me that exhaustless fountain of patience, a pipe, and soon attained a mood of cheerful indifference as to what might happen. The driver took out the baggage and packages, and sat down with them on the opposite side of the road; the groom took the horse and galloped off. An hour passed by; two hours; and still we sat in silence, watching the procession of Hindoos, Moslems, bullocks, ponies and camels that came and went between us. At last a bullock-cart dashed up on a fast trot, the baggage was packed upon it, I took my seat and away we went, leaving the broken banghy-cart in the road. Was that the last of it? the reader may ask. We shall see.

We reached a place called Seerpore, at dusk, our brave bullocks having made ten miles in two hours. I had supper, a good night's rest, and breakfast, and there was still no sign of the cart. The messman, who was very civil and attentive, informed me that it would be mended by noon. Meanwhile, there was I, I knew not precisely where. I could not find the place on the map. That it was in India I was certain, because there was a handsome Hindoo temple close be side the bungalow, and before the temple an immense ban yan tree, and under the banyan tree two elephants. I made a sketch of the scene, as a memorial of the adventure.

At last a native entered, and with a profound salaam, said: "*Sahib banghy-cart taiyar hai*" (Sir the banghy-cart is ready).

CHAPTER VI.

THE BANGHY-CART, CONCLUDED—INDORE.

Departure from Seerpore—Another Break-down—A Crippled Cart—Palasnehr—Indian Horses and Drivers—Jungle—The Banyan Tree—The Tamarind—The Natives of the Jungle—Military Salutations—The Town of Sindwah—Tokens of Decay—The Sindwah Jungles—A Dilemma—The Vindhya Mountains—The Station of Mhow—Arrival at Indore—The Town—The Rajah's Palace—The Rajah and his History—His Tastes—Hindoo Temples and their Worshippers—The English Residency—Cold Weather.

It was not without some misgivings that I again took my seat in the banghy-cart, and left the place called Seerpore. I was now entering the Sindwah jungles, a desolate region, swarming with tigers, and so unhealthy that from the end of July to the first of January it is impassable. In case of accident there must be detention, and detention in such a case is fraught with danger. However, "nothing venture, nothing win," is the traveller's true maxim. We thumped and bumped along in the noonday heat, making about two miles an hour, and had proceeded five miles, when I saw the axle which I had been watching) suddenly give way again. I jumped out in time to avoid the crash, and once more took my seat in the jungle, in the shade of a thorny bush The groom mounted the horse and rode away; the driver unpacked the baggage and seated himself opposite to me, and thus we sat for three hours. "Patience," after all, is the watchword of life. It may seem incredible, but I was thoroughly patient during all this time.

The groom at last appeared with a new cart—and such a cart! It had been broken so often, that it was a hopeless cripple. The square box had such a pitch forward, and the step was so short, that I could by no possibility keep my seat without holding fast with both hands. By this time it was dusk, and we crept forward gradually, the horse occasionally falling down in the ruts, and coming to a stand-still every fifty yards, until urged forward by repeated cries of "*ai bap! ai bhai!*" (Oh, my father! my brother!) About ten o'clock we reached a village called Palasnchr, only sixteen miles from Seerproe, having been ten hours on the way. The driver succeeded in making me understand that he did not intend to go any further that night. I therefore went to the bungalow, and aroused the sleepy khitmudgra, (butler,) "What can I get for supper?· I asked. "*Kuch na,*" (nothing). So I took a carpet-bag for a pillow, lay down on the bare bedstead, and slept soundly until morning. "Can you get me any thing for breakfast?" I asked again. "*Kuch na.*" And the banghy-cart being ready, I went away hungry from Palasnehr.

The road was a little better, but as we travelled on a trot instead of a walk, the cart lost nothing of its roughness, which, indeed, was rather increased. The labor of holding on taxed me sorely, and as there was no relaxation, except when we stopped to change horses, the muscles of my arms and legs at last became so exhausted that I was ready to double up and sink together in a heap. My wrists and ankles were swollen for several days afterwards, from the effects of that ride. The horses and drivers on this part of the road are probably the worst in the world. The driver's knowledge is confined to holding the reins, and even this he understands very imperfectly. Instead of choosing the smoothest part of the road he takes the roughest, and if a stone is to be seen, his satisfaction is not complete unless the cart runs over it. He frequently swerves some distance from the direct track to effect this object. As for the horse, he is the master, and if any exertion is necessary you may possibly flatter but cannot force him into it. When first harnessed he never starts of his own accord. One groom stands at his head patting and coaxing, while two others push at the wheels until they press him forward. He then backs, and sometimes sits down on his haunches. More force is put to the wheels, until backing becomes a labor to him, and then he goes forward as long as the road is level. But by and by you come to a slight ascent. He knows already where it is, and unless you keep him on a gallop he stops at the bottom. The groom jumps down and runs to his head. "*Tăb di*" (pat him), says the driver, and while the former pats him on the neck, the latter cries out in most endearing tones: "Oh, my father, my brother, my bully, my brave fellow!" Thus encouraged he makes a start, and gets about half way up the rise, when he stops and leisurely backs down again to the bottom. This is repeated three or four times, and finally some of the bullock-drivers are called on to assist. They lay hold on the wheels, and the horse, instead of drawing up the cart, is himself pushed up with it. On one occasion, where there was a rise of about one foot in ten for a hundred yards, I was obliged to wait an hour and a half before we succeeded in passing.

Soon after leaving Palasnehr, the road crossed the Sindwah Ghaut, a range of hills about six miles in breadth and covered with jungle. Beyond them opened the valley of the Nerbudda; the Vindhya Mountains, on the opposite side, though fifty miles distant, were dimly visible. Between lay a wild waste of jungle, almost uninhabited, a reservoir of deadly malaria and a paradise for panthers and tigers. The word "jungle," I should explain, is used to express any kind of wild growth, from a thicket to a forest, whether highland or lowland. The different varieties are distinguished as "close jungle, thorn jungle, wet jungle," etc. About Sindwah the jungle is close, composed of thick clumps of shrubbery and small trees, with here and there a magnificent banyan or peepul tree towering over it. In the valley of the Nerbudda there are many banyans, and some of great size. Few trees present grander masses of foliage than this. Instead of a low roof of boughs, resting on its pillared trunks, as I had supposed, it sends up great limbs to the height of a hundred, or even a hundred and fifty feet, and the new trunks are often dropped from boughs thirty feet high. They hang like parcels of roots from the ends of the boughs, and when broken off and prevented from reaching the earth, continue to increase and become woody like the trunk. I have seen a tree on which huge half-trunks, that had never reached the earth, hung from the branches, like the fragments of shattered pillars, hanging from the roof of an Egyptian rock-temple. The leaves of the banyan are large, glossy and dark-green, and in the winter the foliage is studded with buds of a bright purple color.

The only other large trees that I remarked, were the sycamore (peepul) and the tamarind. The acacia and mimosa are occasionally met with, and the date and brab palms thrive in the valleys. The tamarind frequently rivals the banyan in size, while its foliage is wonderfully graceful and delicate. The leaflets of its slender pinnate leaves are so small, that the Koran could not more forcibly describe the torments of the Mahometan Hell, than when it says that the sinners in the nether fires shall receive, to cool their thirst, just so much water as will lie on one of these leaflets, once in a thousand years. Of the smaller trees and shrubs, there is a great variety, but the tamarind and banyan are the characteristic trees of India, as the palm is of Egypt, and the magnolia and cypress of our Southern States.

From Dhoolia to the Nerbudda, my road was through the District of Candeish, which, two or three weeks previous, was the subject of general attention, on account of the rising of the natives. The disturbance had been quelled, but if I had not had such confidence in the potency of English rule, I should have felt that I was exposed to some danger. We met continually with companies of armed natives—not the mild, abject inhabitants of the cultivated districts, but the tall, fierce sons of the jungle—men with keen eyes, heavy black beards, and a striking expression of courage and defiance in their whole bearing. They did not stoop and touch the earth in humble salutation, as I passed, but looked me full in the face, without a single word of greeting. Some were armed with the long Bedouin guns, some with spears, and all wore sabres. They were nearly all on foot, but a few, who seemed to be men of authority, rode on ponies. I should judge they were mostly Mahometans, from their turbans, and from the cast of their features. It is very easy to distinguish between the followers of the rival religions, without reference to any distinguishing mark of dress, and merely from the expression of the face.

We constantly met long trains of laden bullocks and with numbers of *hackrees*, or native ox-carts. Many of the trains were accompanied by *cheprasses*, or Government servant, (distinguished by a band over the shoulders with an inscribed brass plate upon it), and by sepoys. In all my life I never received half the number of military salutations, as during this journey. Of course I was in the East India Company's service, for nobody else travels there; my brown face showed that I had been a long time in the country, and my habit of never expressing astonishment, when among a strange people, was sufficient, in spite of my ignorance of the language, to certify to the fact. Every sepoy drew himself up, faced right about, gave his right arm a wide sweep and brought his hand to his cap. I made an officer's response, of course, but merely gave a slight nod to the salutations of the peasants, though they sometimes almost prostrated themselves before me. Near Sindwah we passed a small village, where all the male inhabitants rushed out of their houses, ranged themselves in a row beside the road, with the elder or chief at their head, and successively touched the dust and their foreheads. It is not to be inferred that these humiliating tokens of reverence and submission to the English power have been forced upon the people. They learned submission long ago, it is natural to them. The Indian servant not only calls you his father, but his King and his God, and when he wants to ask you a special favor, comes to you with a bunch of grass in his mouth, saying he is your beast.

During the forenoon we passed Sindwah, a miserable village at present, though once a place of some importance, as its massive fortress testifies. There is some cultivation near it, but the country shows marks of neglect and decay. I was told that a large part of Candeish, which is now waste jungle, was a flourishing and well-populated region fifty years ago. I could at first find no adequate reason for these tokens of decay; but I believe that, in most instances, they are owing to a superstition of the natives, which prevents them from inhabiting lands belonging to families that have become extinct. They believe that the spirits of the former owners linger upon the soil, and would visit them with calamity, or death, if they persisted in remaining.

All the rest of the day, and part of the night, we jolted on through the lonely jungles. I was in great hopes of seeing a tiger spring across the road, but had no such luck. Although the ground was baked hard and dry, there was still an exhalation from it, as my shadow appeared with a slight halo around it, such as one sees on a summer morning, when the dew begins to dry. I suffered with a dull headache all day, but the rough road might account for this. Towards midnight we reached Akbarpore, on the Nerbudda, having made fifty-four miles. I was too sore to wait for supper, but went to sleep at once, after ordering breakfast at sunrise, when the cart was to be ready again. Sunrise came, and eight o'clock, but neither cart nor breakfast. At last the driver appeared, and made me a number of remarks for which (in my ignorance of the language) I was none the wiser. "Is the cart ready yet?" I asked. "Yes, it is ready, but"—and here my comprehension ceased. A horrid suspicion flashed through my mind: "Is it gone?" "Yes, it is gone, but"—and he became unintelligible again. "Is there no cart?" again I asked. "Yes, there's a cart, but"— That dreadful "but" completely floored me. I went into the kitchen, took the half-cooked breakfast from the fire, and hurriedly ate it, for I had lived on biscuits for two days. I then went directly to the post-station, but there was no cart there. The people made many observations, but all availed nothing, till at last one of them rose and beckoned me to follow him. We went down to the Nerbudda, which is a beautiful river, a third of a mile wide, crossed the ferry, and behold! there stood a new cart, and there lay a new driver, asleep in the sun!

The road was tolerable, I could now sit without holding on, and thus the journey became pleasant again. The valley of the Nerbudda is very rich and fertile, the soil resembling the black loam of Egypt. We passed many fields of flax, covered with blue and white flowers; wheat, cotton, tobacco and poppies, besides small patches of sugar-cane. All seemed to thrive equally well. But a small proportion of the soil is cultivated, and it is no exaggeration to say, that the valley might be made to support a hundredfold its present population. We now approached the picturesque Vindhya Mountains, one of the summits of which was crowned with a white building—the tomb of a Moslem Saint, as well as I could understand the driver. The road passes the mountains, at a place formerly called Ghara, but now Kintrey's Ghaut, in honor of the engineer. It is, indeed, admirably planned, though somewhat out of repair. The summit, which separates the waters of the two sides of India, overlooks a waste and bleak country. Soon after descending the northern side, we crossed the head-waters of the Chumbul, the largest affluent of the Jumna. At eight o'clock I reached the military station of Mhow, within fourteen miles of Indore, and was so well satisfied that I allowed the driver to stop for the night.

Mhow is a handsome station, the officers' bungalows, surrounded with small gardens, being scattered over an extent of two miles. It stands on a dry plain, 2,000 feet above the sea, and is considered a very healthy place of residence. The highest point is crowned by a large white church, the spire of which may be seen for some distance. The place is included within the limits of the Madras Presidency. I had only a passing glimpse of the town, as I left early next morning. A drive of two hours, over a good road and through a rolling upland country, devoted to the opium culture, brought me to Indore, and I bade adieu to the banghy-cart, hoping I might see no more of it. The journey from Bombay occupied six days and a half, and I accomplished it with less fatigue, though with more bruises than I expected.

Indore is the capital of an independent State, and the station of an English "Resident"—an office which is equivalent to that of an Envoy or Ambassador, except that the Resident meddles rather more in the affairs of the State to which he is accredited. Mr. Hamilton, the Resident at Indore, was absent on a journey, but I was most kindly received by Dr. Impey, the Residency Surgeon, to whom I had a letter. With true Indian hospitality, he took me at once to his house, where both he and his amiable lady did their utmost to make my sojourn agreeable.

Indore is a town of about 60,000 inhabitants, having been much increased within a few years by the tyranny of the Begum of Oodjein, a holy old city about eighty miles distant many of the inhabitants of which have emigrated to the former place. Portions of Indore are well built, reminding me somewhat of Konia, and other places in the interior of Asia Minor. The houses are generally of wood, two stories high, the upper story projecting and resting on pillars, so as to form a verandah below. The pillars and the heavy cornice above them are of dark wood, and very elaborately carved. In the centre of the town is the Rajah's palace, fronting a small square. It is a quadrangle of about four hundred feet to a side, the portion over the main gateway rising to the height of eighty or ninety feet, and visible for many miles around. The architecture is Saracenic, though not of a pure style. The gateway, however, and the balconies over it, are very elegant, and the main court, surrounded by lofty pillars of dark wood, connected by ornate horseshoe arches, has a fine effect. The outer walls are covered with pictures of elephants, horses, tigers, Englishmen and natives, drawn and colored with the most complete disregard of nature.

On our way to the town one evening, we met the Rajah and his suite, just setting out on an excursion into the country. He was attended by a large retinue of persons, soldiers dressed in the European style, officials in gaudy dresses holding spears and flags, and all the paraphernalia of a petty prince. He is very fond of display, but I must confess that the whole show was rather picturesque than imposing. I had a good view of the Rajah, who was a young man of about twenty, tall and stout for his age, and with a good-humored though not remarkably intelligent face. He wore a crimson robe, and a rich silken turban, studded with jewels. His story is quite romantic. Twelve years ago he was a poor shepherd boy in the neighborhood of Mhow. The former Rajah, Hurry Rao Holkar, having died childless, and without any near relatives, the State might have readily fallen into the possession of the East India Company. Instead of taking it, however, search was made for a successor, and the poor shepherd boy was found to belong to a remote branch of the family. He was thereupon invested with the Rajahship, and Mr. Hamilton, the Resident, was appointed Regent during his minority.

Notwithstanding he was educated under English auspices, the Rajah did not seem to have acquired any English ideas, except a taste for horses and hunting. The only public works of his which were pointed out to me, were a small hospital and school, and a bridge across the river, or rather ravine, on which Indore is built. The latter was a very substantial structure, of hewn stone, and cost upwards of $100,000. The finest thing I saw in the place was a well, built by one of the former Rajahs. It was a large square shaft, about forty feet deep, with a broad flight of steps leading down to the water, and cool chambers and balconies of hewn stone, for recreation during the hot weather.

In riding through and around the town, I was struck with the number of small Hindoo temples. The principal temple is adjacent to the Rajah's palace; but as Europeans are not allowed to enter, I saw only the outside. In the suburbs, how ever, there are many sanctuaries erected to the different gods the most of them being open canopies or domes, resting on pillars, and none above twenty feet in height. The idols are generally smeared with red paint, a token that they have recently been worshipped. There were multitudes of beggars, some of whom asked for alms in the name of Vishnu, and others in the name of Allah, the latter being Mussulmen. In one street we passed a house where the piercing shrieks of a fife and the dreadful clatter of a drum announced a marriage festival, and not far off, two women, seated in front of a door, howled incessant lamentation for a corpse within: Destruction and Reproduction, both the attributes of the god Shiva, in whose name a beggar at that very instant demanded charity.

There is a picturesque orchard of mango and date trees on the eastern side of the town, but the soil is too thin on the uplands around it to support much vegetation. The garden of the Resident is artificially made. His residence, which I visited, is a stately stone mansion, with large and lofty rooms, furnished in superb style. He maintains a great state, which he may well do on a salary of £4,000 a year, in a country where labor and the ordinary necessaries of life cost next to nothing. The wages of a field-laborer here are two annas (six cents) a day, he finding his own food. Women receive one and a half annas, and boys one anna daily. House servants are better paid, as they are obliged to wear rather more garments, but, as each has his particular business, eight or ten are required to do the work of a small family.

I found the weather unpleasantly cold, coming from the

latitude of Bombay. During the nights the temperatare was so low that thin cakse of ice frequently formed on shallow pools. From the supplies thus collected, the English residents are furnished with ice during a part of the hot season.

CHAPTER VII.

THE MAIL-CART.

The Mail-Cart—Setting out from Indore—Night Travel—Stupidity of the Natives—Mussulmen—Nearly an Accident—Scenery of the Road—A Polite Englishman—Miseries of the Journey—A Tiger Party—Budjrungurh—Goonah—A Free Use of Hospitality—The Thugs and Robbers—Second Halt—Miss Burroughs—Going On—The Plain of Hindostan—Approach to Agra—A Landmark.

At sunset on the 11th of January, I took leave of my hospitable hosts at Indore, and again ventured upon unknown seas. I had taken passage for Agra in the mail-cart, a vehicle precisely resembling the banghy cart, but with the advantage of greater speed. The distance to be travelled was 380 miles, and the fare 50 rupees, which is considered very cheap in India, but would be very dear in any other country. The average rate of speed is from eight to nine miles an hour, so that the mail reaches Agra in a little more than two days from Indore; but as few mortal frames would be equal to such work, travellers are allowed to make the journey in several stages, by stopping at any of the dawk bungalows on the road and waiting for the next day's mail.

The mail cart is propelled by two horses, one of which is an outrigger. This facilitates the ascent of slight elevations in the road, except when the two animals choose to move in different directions, which is by no means a rare occurrence. However, I found that I could retain my position on the box without holding fast with both hands, and this was a great improvement on the banghy cart. We set off at a full gallop, over a hard, well beaten road, and through a rolling, open country. The twilight died away and the young moon went down before we reached Dewas, twenty-four miles from Indore, and thenceforth we galloped by starlight. Ever the same rolling upland, thinly inhabited and scantily cultivated; broad belts of jungle, more dreary and stunted than in the regions south of the Nerbudda, and crossed by frequent abrupt nullas. Occasionally we passed low ranges of stony hills, where the rate of our speed caused a most intolerable jolting. The native villages, slumbering under the broad arms of peepul and banyan trees, were picturesque enough in the gloom, which hid their dirt and deformity, while the grotesque cones of their temples were the only objects that showed with any distinctness. The silent driver always blew a discordant blast on his horn while passing through these villages, and on approaching the post-stations, which are from five to seven miles apart. We always found a few sleepy grooms in waiting with the fresh horses, which were slowly harnessed to our cart, and after going through their exercise of backing and rearing, sprang forward with a galvanic start, and an impetus which did not cease until we rew up at the next post.

Thus the night wore away. My only amusement was in watching the Great Bear, as he slowly wheeled around the pole-star, for in my previous watches I had learned to measure the nours of the night by his progress. The driver now and then made a remark, very profound, no doubt, if I had understood it. I always assented, to avoid discussion, which would have been embarrassing, and if he addressed a question to me, invariably answered: "I don't know." There is no use in telling these people that you don't understand their language, for they jabber away to you just the same as ever. It is much better to make a short and despotic use of the few words you know, and restrict the conversation to those remarks which are indispensable. As we proceeded northward, I noticed that Arabic words were frequently used. The form of salutation was the usual "salaam aleikoom" of the East, and the driver exclaimed, each time that he mounted the cart: "in the name of the most merciful God." In addition to this, he frequently touched the rim of the wheel and his forehead alternately several times with his fore-finger—probably as a charm to prevent accidents, and I devoutly hoped it might be efficacious, for we had no other safeguard. Had the axle snapped, as in the case of the banghy-cart, I should not have gotten off so easily.

When morning came, there was so little change in the features of the landscape that I could have believed myself still in sight of Indore, and yet we had made more than a hundred miles during the night. I was quite benumbed from the coldness of the air, and began to feel the effects of the jolts I had undergone. Soon after sunrise the driver discovered that one of the linch-pins was broken off, so that the wheel kept its place from mere force of habit. He asked me whether he should proceed, but as I knew he only put the question for form's sake, since the mail could not be detained

I told him to drive on, which he did, "in the name of the most merciful God." Our speed, after this, was more furious than before, and a mad gallop of six miles, during which I constantly kept myself braced in an attitude to spring out, brought us to the next post, where we were fortunate enough to find a substitute for the pin. During the day we passed two mail-carts, lying by the road-side, with their axles broken.

Nothing could exceed the monotony of the scenery, which while the dry season lasts, wears a bleak and desolate aspect. During the rains, when the soil is hidden under a deluge of herbage, and the ragged shrubbery of the jungles starts into new bloom and foliage, it must present a very different appearance. Except in the sheltered hollows, where the palm still flourished, there was no token of a tropical climate. I found more interest in observing the crowds of natives whom we met on the road. In addition to the different Indian races, who had now become tolerably familiar to me, there were occasionally men of taller stature, lighter complexion, and a bold, unsubmissive expression of face, whom I took to be Sikhs or Affghans

About noon we reached a place called Bursud, where there was a traveller's bungalow, occupied by an English family. A lady was standing in the verandah, and I took off my hat to her as we passed. Politeness is its own reward, for no sooner had we stopped to change horses, than the lady's husband made his appearance, and very politely asked me to take some refreshments. The invitation was timely, for the appetite of a hungry man is not satisfied with biscuits (which was all my store), but I had determined to reach Goonah, half-way to Agra, before resting, and could not detain the mail. I only men tion the circumstance as another instance of the hospitality of the English in India.

By this time I was in that feverish and excitable condition which shows that one's powers of endurance are beginning to give way. I was bruised and shaken from head to foot, racked with aches and pains, and above all exquisitely tortured by a small iron rod which ran around the box whereon we sat, to prevent our being thrown into the road. The mark of that rod was imprinted on my flesh for days afterwards. During the afternoon we came into a hilly country where the road was a little better, and I experienced some relief. The hills were covered with jungle, but there was cultivation in the valleys between, especially about the little town of Ragoogurh, which is the residence of a Rajah. It is a walled town of rectangular form, with round towers at the corners, but the walls have tumbled down in various places, making unsightly breaches and disclosing the poverty of the dwellings within.

A short distance further we overtook a large concourse of natives, all of whom carried long bamboo poles in their hands Among them were several cheprassees, or Government servants, and two or three sepoys. They all drew up in a line on each side of the road, making the most profound salaams as I passed between their ranks. I was at a loss to understand this display until, at the end of the concourse, I came upon a magnificent elephant (the largest I ever saw), when I decided that these must be the attendants of the Rajah of Ragoogurh. The whole thing was explained, however, by the appearance of two English gentlemen and some attendants carrying a wild boar. They had been out tiger hunting, and the crowd of natives with bamboos were the "beaters," who are employed in India, instead of dogs, to sweep the jungles and start the beasts from their coverts. One of the gentlemen, I afterwards learned, was one of the most noted tiger slayers in the country, and had just recovered from being dreadfully mangled by a panther, an accident which had lamed him for life. He had suffered fever, lockjaw, paralysis and partial mortification, yet outlived them all, to the amazement of every body and the dismay of the tigers.

At the mouth of a wide bay formed by the hills is the town of Budjrungurh, which, according to an itinerary of the road, is the residence of one of Scindiah's pundits; so that, if I had not the satisfaction of beholding a learned Pundit, I at least saw his habitation. The town is perched on a tongue of land which shoots out from the hills, dropping into a precipice of naked red rock on three sides. With its tottering walls, and the tall, parabolic domes of a cluster of temples on the plain below, it made a striking picture in passing. There was now but one more stage to Goonah, and after passing the shoulder of the hill beyond Budjrungurh, I saw in the distance the goal for which I had been so ardently longing. Its thatched houses, half hidden in groves of tamarind and date-palm, beckoned to me across a broad plain of wheat and poppies, which basked in the warm light of the descending sun. In half an hour I dismounted in the bazaar, having travelled 185 miles in less than twenty-four hours.

The traveller's bungalow was occupied by an invalided officer, who had charge of keeping the post-stations in order. There was a spare room, which I at once appropriated, and throwing myself upon the bare charpoy bedstead, fell asleep

I was aroused by a native, whom I took to be the khitmudgar of the bungalow, and who delivered himself of several unintelligible sentences. I thereupon went to the officer's room, and with an apology for my intrusion, begged him to interpret for me. "Why," said the captain, "he says you have only to order what you like for dinner—beef-steak, mutton chops, sherry, brandy or beer." Here is truly a model bungalow I thought. "Will you tell him," I asked, "to get me the best dinner he can, and a bottle of beer, as soon as possible?" "The dinner is ready," said the servant; which means that you will get it in three hours, and in just that time it was brought to me. But the next day I discovered, accidentally, that the man I had taken for the khitmudgar was the captain's own servant, and that the worthy officer had simply translated his own hospitable message to me!

An English Lieutenant, who was encamped in the village with a company of sepoys, came up and spent the evening with me. He was born in India, and I was the second American he had ever seen. He invited me strongly to stop the next evening at Meeana, where he proposed to encamp, and promised to prepare refreshments for me. He moved away early in the morning, and as I could not stop at Meeana, I saw him no more. The mail-cart came along the next day about two P. M., and as I had spent all the morning in sleep, I felt ready to undertake the latter half of the journey. When I called the true khitmudgar, in order to pay him for my meals, he declared that I owed him nothing, for every thing had been sent to me by the "captain-sahib." I then went to the latter, explained my mistake and apologized for my apparent rudeness, for any other course was out of the question

"Pshaw!" said the Captain, bluntly: "don't say a word. As long as I live in the bungalow, travellers are of course my guests."

My host, moreover, warned me against a frightful nulla, or gully, in which the mail-cart was upset a few days before, and the driver's thigh broken. Night came on before we reached the locailty, but though we crossed a number of deep nullas, I could not discover the scene of the accident. Robbers are plentiful in this part of the country, and even the mail-cart had just been plundered. All the region between Indore and Agra, was once noted as being the principal haunt of the Thugs, or Stranglers. The system is now almost if not wholly extinct; at least, the Thugs no longer dare to practise their horrid trade upon Europeans. This is owing to the vigorous measures adopted by the Government, which has lately taken up the task of suppressing infanticide, and will, it is to be hoped, be equally successful.

Not to tire the reader with too many details of my progress, I will only state that about ten o'clock that evening I reached a village called Tongra, on the banks of a small lake, and was there obliged to halt another day, on account of the seat thence to Agra having been previously engaged by an English officer. The rest was not unwelcome, and the silent and attentive khitmudgar was a capital purveyor. On leaving, I indorsed the opinion of Miss Burroughs, who wrote in the traveller's book that this was the only bungalow worthy of the name. I was pleased to see that all travellers since her time had done the same, for several pages were thickly studded with: "Ditto to Miss Burroughs."

At the same hour on the following evening the mail-cart

came, and away we galloped over rolling uplands, through wastes of jungle, and across umberless nullas. Thus the chill, uncomfortable night passed away. The rising sun showed a barren valley, shut in by brown hills, covered with long grass and and. Climbing out of this valley upon a bleak eminence, I saw like a boundless sea before me, the great Plain of Hindostan—that vast, alluvial level, which extends without a break from Calcutta to the Indus. We now entered on a richer and more cheerful region. The villages were embowered in tamarind and sycamore trees, and with the exception of occasional belts of sand, the plain was well cultivated. We were ferried across the Chumbul, the principal affluent of the Jumna—a shallow river, nearly half a mile in breadth, and flowing at the bottom of a deep bed which it has worn for itself in the sandy soil.

Passing Dholpore, the residence of a Rajah, and Jajow, a picturesque old place, with a handsome mosque and serai, we rapidly approached Agra. I looked forward to the distant belt of trees which hid the city, with the sensation of a man, who, after drifting for days on a dangerous sea, approaches a safe harbor. At last, a snow-white dome stood suddenly on the horizon, and I hailed the renowned Taj Mahal, for I knew it could be none other. There was Agra, the City of Akbar, and I—to borrow the words of Eothen—I had lived to see, and I saw it.

CHAPTER VIII.

THE CITY OF AKBAR.

Akbarabad—The Modern City—The English Cantonments—Rev. Mr. Warren—The Fort of Agra—The Jumma Musjeed—Entering the Fort—Judgment-Seat of the Emperor—The Gates of Somnauth—Akbar's Palace—Splendor of its Decorations—The Palace of Glass—A Cracked Throne—The Pearl Mosque—Tomb of Akbar, at Secundra—An Indian Landscape—Saracenic Art—Mission Printing-Office—The American Missions—The Agra Jail—Dr. Walker's System of Education—Arithmetic in Chorus—Effect of the System.

AGRA is still called by the natives AKBARABAD—the City of Akbar—from the renowned Emperor to whom it owes its origin. All its former splendor grew up under his reign, and all its architectural remains, except the Taj Mahal, date from his time. In this respect it differs from Delhi, which, although still called by the Mohammedans Shahjehanabad, (from Shah Jehan, the grandson of Akbar), is more especially the capital of the Mogul Emperors, and bears the memorials of many successive reigns. Yet I doubt whether their combined feebler lights can equal the sunlike lustre of Akbar's name, and whether their city, with all its stores of historic associations, can so interest and attract the traveller as this, the capital of the greatest man who ever ruled in India

The modern city is not even the shadow of the ancient capital. *That* has wholly passed away, except the Fort—a city in itself—and some ruined palaces on the bank of the Jumna. But for nearly two miles in every direction, the mounds, remains of walls and other indications of habitations are abundant. Much more was to be seen a few years ago than at present, but as the old bricks were constantly taken to construct new buildings, these vestiges gradually disappeared. The population, which once numbered more than half a million, has dwindled to about 70,000, and the native city has little more to interest the traveller than any ordinary Indian town—Indore, for instance. There is one principal street, passing through its whole length to the gates of the Fort, and in this are situated the residences of the wealthier inhabitants, which are generally of brick or red sandstone. The verandahs and hanging balconies, with their exquisite Saracenic arches, carved ornaments and stone lattice-work, remind one of Cairo. The street is also a sort of bazaar, and during the day presents a very busy and animated scene. It is so narrow that two vehicles can with difficulty pass, while all the other streets of the city are only attainable by pedestrians. On the side facing the Jumna there are few striking buildings except the Custom-House, once the palace of a rich native. Stone ghauts, here and there, lead down to the holy stream, which at the time of my visit was so much diminished by the dry season that it did not occupy more than one-third of its bed.

South of the city are the cantonments, divided into the civil and military lines, and occupying a space of five miles in length by nearly two in breadth The bungalows of the English residents are neat, cottage-like buildings of one story, with steep, thatched roofs. Each stands in its own "compound," or enclosure, so that the cantonments present a truly suburban aspect. Broad roads, as smooth and hard as a floor, run in all directions, and offer admirable drives to the inhabitants, whose buggies may be seen at all hours of the day, dashing back and forth. A spacious square, planted with young trees, is called the Park, and beyond this rises the lofty spire of the English Church. The various public buildings —the Bank, the Post-office, the Government House, and others, are distinguished from the private residences by their size, but have little pretension to architectural beauty.

On entering Agra I was taken to the traveller's bungalow, which stands on a waste plat of ground, adjoining the Park. The succeeding day was so cold, dull and rainy, that I remained indoors, and rested my shattered frame. Mr. Thomasson, the Governor of the north-western provinces, to whom I had letters, was absent at Benares, but I was most hospitably received by Rev. Mr. Warren, an American Missionary, under whose roof I sojourned during my stay. Under his guidance, and that of Mr. Hutton, the Editor of *The Agra Messenger*, I visited all the objects of interest in the city and vicinity.

The Fort, which contains the Palace of Akbar, and the celebrated Motee Musjeed or Pearl Mosque, is one of the grandest structures of the kind in India. It is about a mile and a half in circuit, and its stately, embrasured battlement of red sandstone are seventy feet in height. Nothing can be more imposing than the view of this immense mass of masonry, rising high above the buildings of the modern city, and almost overtopping the domes of the Jumma Musjeed (Sunday mosque), which stands without its gates. Its appearance, nevertheless, is very deceptive with regard to its strength, for the walls, impregnable as they look, are mere shells, and would not stand a single day's cannonading.

Before entering the Fort, I visited the Jumma Musjeed. The front of the mosque faces the principal gate, a broad, enclosed square, which is now used as a market-place, intervening between. The mosque stands on a lofty platform, which is reached by a spacious flight of steps. In India all places of worship, except the inner shrines—the holy of holies—are open to the conquerors, who walk in, booted and spurred, where the Hindoo and Moslem put their shoes from off their feet. I should willingly have complied with this form, as I did in other Moslem countries, but was told that it was now never expected of a European, and would be in fact a depreciation of his dignity. The Jumma Musjeed is a melancholy picture of ruin. The walls which enclose the fore-court are tumbling down, and the inlaid inscriptions which surround the façade are falling out, piece by piece. The body of the mosque is divided into a central and two smaller side-halls, each of which opens upon the court-yard by a lofty, arched portal, and is surmounted by a swelling oriental dome, of corresponding proportions. India being east of Mecca, the mosque of course occupies the western side of the court, and at each of the adjacent corners rises a lofty and graceful minaret. This is the plan on which all Indian mosques are built, and they vary in architectural beauty according as the portals, the domes and minarets approach a true artistic proportion.

Crossing by a drawbridge over the deep moat which sur

rounds the Fort, we passed through a massive gateway and up a paved ascent to the inner entrance, which shows considerable taste. It consists of two octagonal towers of red sandstone, inlaid with ornamental designs in white marble. The passage between them is covered by two domes, which seem to rise from accretions of prismatic stalactites, as in the domes of the Moorish Alhambra. This elegant portal, however, instead of opening upon the courts of palaces, ushers you into a waste of barren mounds, covered with withered grass. But over the blank red walls in front, you see three marble domes, glittering in the sunshine like new-fallen snow, and still further, the golden pinnacles of Akbar's palace, and these objects hint that your dream of the magnificence of the Great Mogul will not be entirely dispelled.

But first, let us visit the modern Arsenal, which was once the *diwan*, or Judgment-seat of Akbar. It was formerly an open portico, or *loggia*, the roof resting on three rows of pillars, which were connected by Saracenic arches; but at present, the outer row of arches being walled up, it forms a spacious hall, divided into three aisles. All the weapons of modern warfare, with here and there a crooked scimetar or battle-axe, of ancient times, are ranged round the pillars and between the arches in those symmetrical groupings peculiar to instruments of death. At the intersections of the central arches hang tri-colored banners of red, blue and yellow, with the names of the British victories in India inscribed upon them in English and Sanscrit. The great curiosity, however, is the celebrated gate of Somnauth, which was carried off by that stern iconoclast, Sultan Mahmoud of Ghuznee. Somnauth was a holy Brahminical city on the coast of Goojerat, and noted at that time for the wealth and magnificence of its temples. It is related of Mahmoud, that, after having taken the city and commenced demolishing the idols, the Brahmins offered him immense sums if he would spare the deity of their great temple. Mahmoud was only tempted for an instant. "Truth," he said, "is better than gold," and raising his iron mace, he smote the idol, which, as it split, poured from its hollow body a store of gold and jewels far exceeding what the Brahmins had offered him. This incident has afforded subject for poetry to Rückert, the German poet, and our own Lowell.

The gates were taken by Mahmoud to his capital of Ghuznee, where they remained until the recent invasion of Affghanistan by the English, when that fantastic individual, Lord Ellenborough, bore them off to Agra. They are about twelve feet high, elaborately carved and inlaid, and said to be composed entirely of sandal-wood. On one of the panels, three metal bosses are nailed. According to tradition, they were taken from Mahmoud's shield. In the centre of the hall is the throne whence Akbar pronounced judgment, after the cases had been discussed in his presence. It is a pavilion of white marble, inlaid with jasper and cornelian, in the form of flowers, ornamental scrolls and sentences from the Koran Below it is an immense slab of white marble, on which he was accustomed to seat himself.

Beyond the arsenal, and in that part of the Fort overlooking the Jumna, is the monarch's palace, still in a tolerable state of preservation. Without a ground-plan it would be difficult to describe in detail its many courts, its separate masses of buildings and its detached pavilions—which combine to form a labyrinth, so full of dazzling architectural ef fects, that it is almost impossible to keep the clue. On entering the outer courts, I was at once reminded of the Alhambra. Here were the same elegant Moorish arches, with their tapering bases of open filigree work resting on slender double shafts—a style so light, airy and beautiful, that it seems fit only for a palace of fairies. Akbar's palace is far more complete than the Alhambra. No part has been utterly destroyed, and the marks of injury by Time and battle, are comparatively slight. Here a cannon-ball has burst its way through the marble screen of the Sultana's pavilion; there an inlaid blossom of cornelian, with leaves of blood-stone, has been wantonly dug out of its marble bed; the fountains are dry, the polished tank in the "Bath of Mirrors" is empty, the halls are untenanted—but this is all. No chamber, no window or staircase is wanting, and we are able to re-people the palace with the household of the great Emperor, and to trace out the daily routine of his duties and pleasures.

The substructions of the palace are of red sandstone, but nearly the whole of its corridors, chambers and pavilions are of white marble, wrought with the most exquisite elaboration of ornament. The pavilions overhanging the river are inlaid, within and without, in the rich style of Florentine mosaic. They are precious caskets of marble, glittering all over with jasper, agate, cornelian, blood-stone and lapis-lazuli, and topped with golden domes. Balustrades of marble, wrought in open patterns of such rich design that they resemble fringes of lace when seen from below, extend along the edge of the battlements. The Jumna washes the walls, seventy feet below, and from the balconies attached to the *zenana*, or women's apartments, there are beautiful views of the gardens and palm-groves on the opposite bank, and that wonder of India, the Taj, shining like a palace of ivory and crystal, about a mile down the stream.

The most curious part of the palace is the *Sheesh Mahàl* (Palace of Glass), which is an oriental bath, the chambers and passages whereof are adorned with thousands of small mirrors, disposed in the most intricate designs. The water falls in a broad sheet into the marble pool, over brilliant lamps, and the fountains are so constructed as to be lighted from within. Mimic cascades tumble from the walls, over slabs of veined marble, into basins so curiously carved that the motion of the water produces the appearance of fish. This bath must once have realized all the fabled splendors of Arabian story. The chambers of the Sultanas and the open courts connecting them are filled with fountains. Though the building is an incrustation of gold, marble, and precious stones, water is still its most beautiful ornament. Within these fairy precincts lie the gardens, still overrun with roses and jasmine vines, in the midst of which fountains are playing. There is also a court, paved with squares of black and white marble, so as to form a *pachisi* board. This is a game resembling backgammon, but, instead of ivory pieces, it was played on this colossal board by Akbar and his wives, or eunuchs, with girls, who trotted from square to square as the moves were made.

On an open terrace in front of the *Diwan e'Khaz*, where Akbar sat on great occasions, is his throne, a slab of black marble, about six feet square. It is cracked entirely through, which my old guide accounted for by saying that when the Mahrattas took Agra, the Rajah of Bhurtpore seated himself on the throne, whereupon it not only cracked from side to side, but blood gushed out of its top, in two places. When Lord Ellenborough was Governer-General of India, he also sat upon it, causing it to shed blood a second time. There are two red stains on its surface, which sufficiently attest these miracles to all good Mussulmen. Opposite the throne is a smaller one of white marble, where, if tradition may be relied on, the Emperor's fool, or jester, took his place and burlesqued his master.

Before leaving the Fort, I visited the Motee Musjeed, or Pearl Mosque, as it is poetically and justly termed. It is, in truth, the pearl of all mosques, of small dimensions, but absolutely perfect in style and proportions. It is lifted on a lofty sandstone platform, and from without nothing can be seen but its three domes of white marble with their gilded spires. In all distant views of the Fort these domes are seen, like silvery bubbles which have rested a moment on its walls, and which the next breeze will sweep away. Ascending a long flight of steps, a heavy door was opened for me, and I stood in the court-yard of the mosque. Here, nothing was to be seen but the quadrangle of white marble, with the mosque on its western side, and the pure blue of the sky overhead. The three domes crown a deep corridor, open toward the court, and divided into three aisles by a triple row of the most exquisitely proportioned Saracenic arches. The Motee Musjeed can be compared to no other edifice that I have ever seen. To my eye it is a perfect type of its class. While its architecture is the purest Saracenic, which some suppose cannot exist without ornament, it shows the severe simplicity of Doric art. It has, in fact, nothing which can properly be termed ornament. It is a sanctuary so pure and stainless, revealing so exalted a spirit of worship that I felt humbled, as a Christian, to think that our nobler religion has so rarely inspired its architects to surpass this temple to God and Mohammed.

After visiting the palace, Mr. Warren accompanied me to the tomb of Akbar, at Secundra, about six miles from Agra. Secundra takes its name from Alexander, whose invasion of India has thus been commemorated by the Moguls. The great Macedonian, however, did not penetrate so far as this, his battle with Porus having been fought on the Jhelum, or Hydaspes, beyond Lahore. The road to Secundra is studded with tombs, and there are many remains of palaces on the bank of the Jumna. The tomb of Akbar stands in the midst of a large square garden, which has a lofty gateway of red sandstone in the centre of each of its sides. From these four gateways, which are upward of seventy feet high, four grand causeways of hewn stone converge to the central platform, on which the mausoleum stands. The intermediate spaces are filled with orange, mango, banana, palm and peepul trees. In the centre of the causeways are immense tanks and fountains. The platform of solid stone which terminates these magnificent approaches is about four hundred feet square. The mausoleum, which is square, measures more than three hundred feet on a side, and rises in five terraces, in a pyramidal form, to the height of one hundred feet. Around each of the terraces runs an arched gallery, surmounted by a row of cupolas, resting on small pillars. The material of the edifice is red sandstone, except the upper story, which is of white marble.

A long, descending passage leads from the main entrance to a vaulted hall in the centre of the structure. Light is admitted through a few small openings in the dome, barely sufficient to show you a plain tomb, in the form of a sarcophagus, with a wreath of fresh roses lying upon it. Beneath it is the dust of Akbar, one of the greatest men who ever wielded a sceptre—the fourth descendant in a direct line from Tamerlane, the grandson of Baber, the Conqueror, and the grandfather of Shah Jehan, in him culminated the wisdom, the power and the glory of that illustrious line. I doubt if the annals of any family that ever reigned can furnish six successive monarchs comparable, in the greatness of their endowments and the splendor of their rule, to Baber, Humayoon, Akbar, Jehan Ghir, Shah Jehan and Aurung-Zebe.

On the summit of the mausoleum, which is open to the sky, and surrounded by screens of marble, wrought into patterns of marvellous richness and variety, stands a second tomb, under a pavilion of marble, covered with a gilded dome. This is exquisitely sculptured, containing the ninety-nine names of God, in raised Arabic characters, infolded in elaborate scroll-work. At each corner of the upper terrace are two marble turrets, the domes of which are covered with gilded and emblazoned tiles. The screens of marble filigree around the sides are arranged in panels, no two of which present the same design. There are small openings, at intervals, through which I looked out on the level country watered by the Jumna—yellow sandy tracts near the river, but receding into green wheat-fields and dark mango-groves. Agra was almost hidden from sight by the trees, but above them rose the spires of two Christian churches, the red battlements of th Fort, and farther off the dome of the Taj, a silvery disc, like the gibbous moon, just hanging on the horizon. A warmth and sunny silence, like that of Egypt, hung over the land scape. What I had seen of the splendor of the Moguls and what I then saw, overpowered me like a magnificent dream.

We in America hear so little of these things, and even the accounts we get from English travellers are generally so confused and unsatisfactory, that the reader must pardon me, if in attempting the description, I lose myself in details. I thought the Alcazar of Seville and the Alhambra of Granada had already presented me with the purest types of Saracenic architecture, but I was mistaken. I found, in India, conceptions of Art far nobler and embodiments far more successful There is a Saracenic, as distinctly as there is a Greek and Gothic school of Art—not the inferior, but the equal of these.

At Secundra, the tomb of Akbar's Christian wife, the Begum Mariam, who is believed to have been a Portuguese woman—has been taken by the Church Mission, which has converted it into a printing establishment. It is the largest office of the kind in India, giving employment to about three hundred men, most of whom are natives. Printing is carried on in English, Hindee, Urdoo, Sanscrit and Persian. There is a type foundry connected with it, in whch the casting is done entirely by natives. The wages paid in these establishments vary from $1 50 to $1 per month. Many of the laborers are Christians, there being a native Christian community of about five hundred persons attached to the Secundra Mission. Most of these, however, are persons picked up during the great famine of 1837, when thousands of children, having been deserted by their parents, were taken by the Missionaries and educated in the Christian faith. During that year the Missions prospered exceedingly. The Presbyterian Mission, at the head of which is Mr. Warren, had just established seminaries of education for both sexes, where instruction was furnished at a rate which allowed the poorest of the European and half-caste population to send their children. Native scholars were of course admitted, but were obliged to share in the religious instruction of the European children. These schools were under the charge of the Rev. Mr. Fullerton and his wife. Whether Missions in general repay the vast pecuniary expense and sacrifice of life and talent which they exact, is a question concerning which I have strong doubts; but that they have accomplished good in India, and that their ministers are conscientious, zealous and laborious men, I am well satisfied.

Mr. Warren also took me to visit the Agra Jail, in which a new and interesting experiment is now being tested, The jail there is a sort of general penitentiary, whither prisoners are sent from all parts of the north-western provinces. The number then incarcerated was about 2,800. The jail encloses a space of about forty acres, wherein are numbers of small buildings and manufactories, as the prisoners are all required to labor about eight hours a day. Dr. Walker, the Superintendent, who formerly had charge of the jail at Mynpoorie, introduced a system of prison education, which was so successful, that when he was promoted to the management of the great central jail at Agra, he determined to continue it. At first he experienced great difficulty, the prisoners suspecting that some mysterious Christian doctrine lay covert in the multiplication-table and the spelling-book; but his perseverance so wrought upon them that all of those employed at labor within the jail (700 being kept upon the roads, in fettered gangs), were willing scholars.

Dr. Walker was kind enough to conduct me through the jail, and put the prisoners through their exercises. It was a most remarkable spectacle. Here were hundreds of men seated at their looms, weaving carpets, singing the multiplication table in thundering chorus. "*Twelve times twelve*," sang the monitor, in a shrill *solo*: "*One hundred and forty-four!*" burst out the chorus, in all sorts of voices. We went into the blacksmith s shops where the prisoners, by a refinement of punishment, were made to forge their own fetters, themselves fettered. "*Seven times sixteen*," sang the solo, as he raised his hammer. "*One hundred and twelve*," was roared in answer, drowning the clang and bang of the iron. In the women's department there was a shrill tempest of vulgar fractions; the cooks recited astronomical facts while mixing their rice. Even the hardest cases, confined in solitary cells, were going on with their "*a-b abs*," through a hole in the door, to a monitor standing outside. The murderers, confined for life (of whom there were several hundred), were not exempted, but went through the numerals while they worked at paper-making. I brought away a sheet of paper, made entirely by these wretches, and will present it to King Bomba, whenever he is ready to write his abdication.

There is a monthly examination of the prisoners, and they who can read a short story, and repeat the multiplication table of whole numbers and fractions up to 16x16, $6\frac{1}{2}$x25 and $6\frac{1}{2}$x$6\frac{1}{2}$, are entitled to a visit from their friends or a bath in the Jumna, if Hindoos, and a visit to the Taj, if Moslems. The more advanced scholars are obliged to pass in writing, the facts of astronomy, simple and compound interest, &c. There is great emulation among the prisoners, and their progress is very rapid. As one result of the system, in their moral improvement, it will be enough to state that in 1851, before it was introduced, the number of punishments administered for offences committed within the jail, was 162; in 1852, after its introduction, the number so punished was 18. It is not much to the credit of the Government that it only allows the miserable sum of five rupees ($2 50) a month in support of so important an experiment.

CHAPTER IX

THE RUINS OF FUTTEHPORE-SIKREE

Excursion to Futtehpore-Sikree—The Road Thither—Approach to the Ruins—Their Extent and Grandeur—The Palace of Rajah Beer-Bul—Perfect Condition of the Remains—Shekh Bushàrat-Ali—Age of Futtehpore—The Emperor's Palace—Rooms of the Sultana Mariam—Akbar's Tolerance—The Five Palaces—The Pillar of Council—Profusion of Ornament—The Emperor's Salutation—The Elephant Gate and Tower—The Durgah—Shekh Selim-Chishti—He gives a Son to the Emperor—The Splendor of his Tomb—View from the Gateway—An Experiment—Tiffin in the Palace—The Story of the Rajah Beer-Bul and the Ruby—Last View of Futteh pore-Sikree.

Before leaving Agra I made an excursion to the ruins of Futtehpore-Sikree, which are about twenty-two miles to the west of the city. I had been so strongly counselled to visit the place, as well from its historic interest (having been the favorite residence of Akbar), as from the extent and magnificence of its remains, that I postponed for another day, though reluctantly, my departure for Delhi. Mr. Sherer, one of the Secretaries of Government, kindly offered to accompany me, and through his familiarity with the history of those times, the new desolate spot was peopled for me with the phantoms of its former inhabitants. I have rarely had the Past sc vividly restored, or so completely given myself up to its illusions. The day was one of the whitest in my calendar, and not unworthy to be chronicled beside the memorable Theban days of the previous year.

In order to make the excursion in a single day, I had relays of horses sent out in advance, and took my departure before sunrise, in a light *garree*—a two-wheeled vehicle, resembling a genteel cart. The road was broad and good for the first eight miles, and bordered by stately acacia, peepul and neem trees. I passed two or three large walled gardens, belonging to native Rajahs, and a cleanly little village, with several small temples to Vishnu and Shiva. The road gradually became rougher, though the country still continued level and tolerably cultivated. My horses, inspired by the pleasant morning air, trotted merrily along, and before three hours were over, Futtehpore-Sikree was in view. A low range of red sandstone hills appeared in the west, with here and there a crumbling ruin on the crest. The extremity of this range, about four miles distant, was covered with a mass of walls, terraces and spires, crowned with a majestic portal, which rose high above them, gleaming against the sky with a soft red lustre, as the sun shone full upon it.

As I approached nearer, I found that this part of the hill was surrounded by a lofty wall of red sandstone, with a machicolated or notched parapet, and a spacious gate, through which my road ran. It is almost entire, and upwards of six miles in circuit, enclosing a portion of the plain on both sides of the hill. Driving through the deserted gateway, I was amazed at the piles of ruins which met my eye. Here was a narrow hill, nearly a mile and a half in length, and averaging a hun dred feet in height, almost entirely covered with the remains of palaces, mosques and public buildings, in some places nearly as perfect as when first erected, in others little else than shapeless masses of hewn stones. Innumerable pavilions resting on open arches, cupolas and turrets, shot up from this picturesque confusion; but the great portal, of which I have already spoken, dominated over all, colossal as one of the pylons of Karnak. The series of arched terraces, rising one above another up the sides of the hill, gave the place an air of barbaric grandeur, such as we imagine Babylon to have possessed, and of which there are traces in Martin's pictures. But here there was nothing sombre or stern; the bright red sandstone of the buildings, illumined here and there by a gilded spire, was bathed in a flood of sunshine, and stood, so shadowless as almost to lack perspective, against a cloudless sky. The modern village of Futtehpore at the foot of the hill, was adorned with beautiful trees, and that part of the plain enclosed within the ancient walls was green with fields of young wheat.

I drove through the long, rambling street of Futtehpore, not without considerable risk of destroying the stock of the native merchants, for the space between their shopboards was scarcely wider than my *garree*. Then owing to the stupidity of the groom, who had missed the road, I was obliged to return as I came, and finally climbed the hill on foot. In the palace of Rajah Beer-Bul one of Akbar's Prime Ministers, I found Mr. Sherer, who had come out luring the night in a palanquin. The palace was an exquisite building, quite uninjured, and had been fitted up with tables, chairs, carpets, etc., for the convenience of visitors to the place

There was a table set in a cool, vaulted hall in the second story, and Mr. Sherer's servants were preparing breakfast in the Rajah's kitchen. We took our seats on the massive stone terrace of the palace, to await the meal. The royal residence of Akbar was on our left; the grand Durgah, or tomb of Shekh Selim-Chishti on the right, and the empty quadrangles into which we looked, showed no trace of ruin. The stone pavements were partly overrun with grass, but not a block of the arched corridors surrounding them had tumbled from its place. How like yesterday seemed the Futtehpore of three centuries ago! The palace was deserted, not ruined, and its lord was not dead, but absent. I felt like an intruder in the sculptured chambers of Beer-Bul, and should not have been much surprised had a chobdàr, with his silver mace, made his appearance, to drive me away.

The guardian of the place, a lusty old Mussulman, named Shekh Bushàrat-Ali, came to make his salaam and accompany me over the ruins. He was a stout man of fifty-five, with a gray moustache, and a face expressive of great good-will and good-humor. He wore a white turban and a cotton gown, tied on the left shoulder, so as to expose the left side of a most sleek and capacious chest. The Hindoos and Parsees tie their garments on the right shoulder, in opposition to the Mussulmans. Bushàrat-Ali was a very devout follower of the Prophet, and knew most of the Koran in Arabic. He was greatly delighted when I addressed him in that language, and thereafter was continually repeating prayers and singing passages of the Koran, that I might perceive how much he knew. His knowledge of Futtehpore was much inferior to that of Mr. Sherer, who had carefully studied the history of Akbar's reign, but he was a pleasant companion during our rambles among the ruins, and we suffered him to go through with his stories and traditions as usual.

After breakfast, we set out to make a thorough survey of the place. I should first state that Futtehpore-Sikree was a country residence of Akbar, and stood in the same relation to Agra that Windsor Castle does to London. It was completed in 1571, and for twelve years his court was stationed there. At that time it must have been a populous place, but it is probable that the dwellings of the lower classes of the natives consisted then, as now, of mud huts, for there are very few ruins on the plain surrounding the hill. The existence of a Mint and other public edifices, on a very large scale, shows that it was considered as a temporary capital, rather than as a mere palace of summer resort.

Commencing with the Emperor's palace, we first visited the separate dwelling assigned to his Christian wife. This, unlike other Moslem buildings, is covered with paintings in fresco, evidently by Persian artists. They are said to represent the adventures of the hero Rustum as related in Firdusi's "*Shah Nameh.*" Certain niches, however, over the doors and windows, contain pictures of a different character, and certainly have a religious significance. On one side are the Hindoo gods and goddesses—the elephant-headed Ganeish, Mahadeo, and Lokshmi—and on the other two tablets, almost obliterated, but still sufficiently distinct to show that one of them is intended for the Annunciation. Akbar's latitude in religious matters is well known, but I had not given him credit for so much toleration as this would imply. Among the ornamental designs of this palace, the Greek Cross is not unusual, and it is related that when the Jesuits solicited the Emperor's protection, he replied to them: "What would you have? See! I have more crosses on my palace than you in your churches."

The buildings of the palace cover the crest of the hill, having superb views on both sides, over many a league of the fruitful plain. There is quite a labyrinth of courts, pavilions, small palaces, gateways, tanks, fountains, and terraces, and I found it difficult to obtain a clear idea of their arrangement. Most of the buildings are so well preserved that a trifling expense would make them habitable. For a scholar or poet I can conceive of no more delightful residence. Adjoining the palace of the Christian woman, stands the *Panch-Mahal* (Five Palaces), consisting of five square platforms, resting on richly carved pillars, and rising one above another in a pyramidal form, to a considerable height. Mr. Sherer supposes it to have been a sleeping place for the servants connected with the palace. Beyond it is a court-yard, paved with large slabs of sandstone, and containing a colossal *pachisi*-board, such as I have described in speaking of the Palace at Agra. In one corner of the court-yard is a labyrinthine building, of singular design, wherein the ladies of the Emperor's *zenana* were accustomed to play hide-and-seek. A little further is a sort of chapel, two stories high, and crowned with several cupolas. On entering, however, I found that there was but one story, extending to the dome, with a single pillar in the centre, rising to the height of the upper windows. This pillar has an immense capital of the richest sculpture, three times its diameter, with four stone causeways leading to the four corners of the chapel, where there are small platforms of the shape of a quadrant. Tradition says that this building was used by Akbar as a place for discussing matters of science or religion, himself occupying the capital of the central pillar, while his chief men were seated in the four corners.

In this same court is a pavilion, consisting of a pyramidal canopy of elaborately carved stone, resting on four pillars, which have a cornice of peculiar design, representing a serpent. This pavilion approaches as near the Hindoo style of building, as is possible, without violating the architecture of the palace, which is a massive kind of Saracenic. It was the station of a Gooroo, or Hindoo Saint, whom Akbar, probably from motives of policy, kept near him. The palace of the Sultana of Constantinople is one mass of the most laborious sculpture. There is scarcely a square inch of blank stone in the building. But the same remark would apply to almost the whole of the palace, as well as to that of Beer-Bul. It is a wilderness of sculpture, where invention seems to have been taxed to the utmost to produce new combinations of ornament. Every thing is carved in a sandstone so fine and compact, that, except where injured by man, it appears nearly as sharp as when first chiselled. The amount of labor bestowed on Futtehpore throws the stucco filigrees of the Alhambra quite into the shade. It is unlike any thing that I have ever seen. And yet the very name of this spendid collection of ruins, which cannot be surpassed anywhere, outside of Egypt, was unknown to me, before reaching India!

We paid rather a hasty visit to the *Diwán-e'-khaz*, the *Diwán e'-am*, and the mint. The latter is an immense quadrangle, half blocked up with ruins. In the diwan-e'-am, is the balcony where Akbar usually made his public appearance in the morning, to the crowd waiting in the court to see or petition him. He was greeted on these occasions with the cry of "*Allah akbar!*" (God is great!) to which he invariably replied: *Jilli jellallihoo!*" (May his glory shine!) This was a mode of salutation introduced by himself, because the two phrases contained his name–Jellal-ud-deen Akbar. I have frequently heard a very similar style of address in Bohemia, where the greeting is: "Praised be Jesus Christ!" and the answer: "In eternity. Amen."

On the north side of Beer-Bul's palace, a little further down the hill, is the famous Elephant Gate. Akbar at one time intended to make a fortress of the place, and commenced by building this gate, which is a very noble structure, flanked by two octagonal bastions: but Shekh Selim-Chishti, in whose sanctity the Emperor had great faith, threatened to leave, in case the plan was carried out, and the fortress was therefore relinquished. On each side of the gate is a colossal elephant, on a lofty pedestal, but both the animals have lost their trunks, and are otherwise mutilated. A steep paved road, between gardens, hanging one below the other on arched terraces, interrupted occasionally by the ruins of palaces, leads down the hill to the Elephant's Tower, a minaret about ninety feet high, and studded from top to bottom with the tusks of elephants. There is much discussion concerning its character, but the most plausible supposition is that it was erected by Akbar over the grave of a favorite elephant. It is called by the natives the *Hirun Minar* (Antelope tower).

By this time it was two hours past noon, and I still had the famous Durgah to see. We therefore retraced our steps, and ascended to the highest part of the hill, where the tomb rises like a huge square fortress, overtopping the palace of Akbar himself. We mounted a long flight of steps, and entered a quadrangle so spacious, so symmetrical, so wonderfull in its decorations, that I was filled with amazement. Fancy paved court-yard, 428 feet in length by 406 in breadth, surrounded with a pillared corridor 50 feet high; one of the noblest gateways in the world, 120 feet high; a triple-domed mosque on one side; a large tank and fountain in the centre, and opposite the great portal, the mother-of-pearl and marble tomb of the Shekh, a miniature palace, gleaming like crystal, with its gilded domes, its ivory pillars, and its wreaths of wondrous, flower-like ornaments, inwrought in marble filigree. The court, with its immense gate, seemed an enchanted fortress, solely erected to guard the precious structure within.

Shekh Selim-Chishti was a very holy man, who became known as such by his intimacy with tigers, several of whom lived with him in a cave on the hill where his tomb now stands. His renown reached the ears of Akbar, who, finding him to be a man of apparent sanctity and considerable wisdom, built the palace of Futtehpore-Sikree, it is said, to be near him. He consulted him on all important occasions, and, as the story goes, was finally indebted to him for an heir to his throne. For some time after Akbar's accession, he was without a son, and twice demanded of the Shekh whether he should ever have one. "No," said the latter; "it is not so written." Now he, the Shekh, had an infant son of six months old; for these Moslem saints are the reverse of celibates. Upon Akbar coming to make the demand a third time, and receiving the same answer, this infant, who was present in his cradle during the interview, suddenly spoke although never before had he so much as lisped a syllable. 'Father," said he, "why do you send away the Conqueror of the World, in despair?" "Because," said the Shekh, although he marvelled not a little at this unexpected question; "there is no son written for him, unless another will give up the life of a child destined for him; and who will do this?" "If you permit me, father," said the infant, "I will die, that a son may be born to the Emperor,"—and even before the Shekh signified his consent, he gave up the ghost. That day an heir to the throne was conceived, and in due time was born. There are scandalous persons, however, who say that this is an allegory, veiling a truth, and that the Shekh, in procuring an heir for the Emperor, did, in fact, give up his own son, but without destroying his life. Be that as it may, Jehan-Ghir, the son of Akbar, bore the name of Selim until he ascended the throne.

We are allowed to enter the inner corridor which surrounds the Shekh's tomb, and to look in, but not to cross the threshold. The tomb, as well as a canopy six feet high, which covers it, is made of mother-of-pearl. The floor is of jasper, and the walls of white marble, inlaid with cornelian. A cloth of silk and gold was spread over it like a pall, and upon this were wreaths of fresh and withered flowers. The screens of marble surrounding the building are the most beautiful in India. They are single thin slabs, about eight feet square, and wrought into such intricate open patterns that you would say they had been woven in a loom. The mosque, which is of older date than the tomb, is very elegant, resembling somewhat the Hall of the Abencerrages in the Alhambra, except that it is much larger, and of white marble.

instead of stucco. Bushàrat-Ali informed me that the Durgah was erected in one year, from the wealth left by the Shekh Selim-Chishti at his death, and that it cost thirty-seven lacs of rupees—$1,750,000.

We ascended to the summit of the great gateway, for the sake of the panoramic view of Futtehpore-Sikree, and the adjacent country. It is a vast plain, and our horizon was described by a radius of twenty miles—a circle of fresh wheat-fields, dotted with mango-groves, and now and then the blue gleam of a river or irrigating canal. There were some low hills in the west, and the famous citadel of Bhurtpore, in that direction, was barely visible. The country, though less garden-like, reminded me of the plain of the Nile. A few years ago it was all an uncultivated waste. Mr. Thomasson, the late Lieutenant-Governor of the north-western provinces happening to be at Futtehpore-Sikree one day, heard a native say that in Akbar's time, the country was annually overflowed, so that the palace was in the midst of a lake. "Well," said Mr. T., "I will overflow it, too." And he ordered the banks of a small river, which flows into the Jumna near Bhurtpore, to be cut away, so that, when the rainy season came, the water spread over about twenty square miles of land. That year the natives had crops such as had never been heard of in those parts, but they had also a fever, which carried off eight hundred persons. However, the Governor made his work good, by cutting a canal to take off the inundation, and now the region has regained its health, and kept its big crops into the bargain.

We went back to Beer-Bul's palace, where the servants had prepared tiffin in the mean time. Bushàrat-Ali sang an

Arab love-song, and told us tales of the time of Akbar Some of these could not very well be repeated, as, like most Eastern stories, they were narratives of skilful intrigue; but there was one relating to Beer-bul himself, which I here relate in the Shekh's words, merely omitting some of his endless repetitions of phrases.

"One day," so began the old man, "Akbar-Shah and Rajah Beer-bul were sitting together. Akbar said to Beer-bul, 'What would you do, if a great misfortune fell upon you?' Said Beer-bul, 'I should give myself up to pleasure.' 'How to pleasure,' said Akbar, 'when you were unfortunate?' 'Still,' said Beer-bul, 'I should do it.' The next day Akbar said to Beer-bul, 'Take this ruby, and keep it till I call for it.' Now it was a ruby worth millions of rupees, such as there never was in the world, before nor since. So Beer-bul took the ruby home to his daughter, and bade her keep it carefully, for it belonged to Akbar-Shah; and she locked it up in a chest with three locks.

"Then Akbar sent to the greatest robber in the place, who was condemned to die, and had him brought before him. Robber,' said he, 'I will give you your life, if you can do one thing for me.' 'What is that?' said the robber. 'You must steal from my Minister, Beer-bul, a ruby which I have given him to keep,' said Akbar-Shah. The robber agreed and no sooner had he gone into the city upon this errand, than he sent for a very cunning little old woman. There is now no woman living who is so cunning as she was, although" —interpolated the Shekh, with a sly twinkle of the eye— 'there are still some, who would be a match for Ebliz himself. Well, this little cunning old woman went to Beer-bul's daughter and engaged herself as maid, and she gradually sc won her confidence that Beer-bul's daughter showed her the box with three locks and the ruby. So she filched the keys opened the locks, took the ruby, and gave it to the robber, who brought it to Akbar. Then Akbar threw it into the Jumna, and sent for Beer-bul. 'Bring me the ruby,' said he. 'Very well,' said Beer-bul, and went home to bring it, but behold! it was stolen. 'Well, where's the ruby?' said Akbar. 'Your Majesty shall have it in fifteen days.' 'Very well,' said Akbar, 'but remember that your head is security for it.'

"Beer-bul went home, and said to his daughter, 'We have but fifteen days to live—let us spend them in festivity.' So they ate, and drank, and gave feasts and dances, till in twelve days they had spent many lacs of rupees, and there was not a *pice* left them to buy food. They remained thus two days. On the fourteenth morning, the daughter of a fisherman who fished in the Jumna, said to her father: 'Father, the Rajah Beer-bul and his daughter have had nothing to eat for two days; let me take them this fish for breakfast.' So she took them the fish, which Beer-bul's daughter received with many thanks, and immediately cooked. But as they were eating it, there came a pebble into Beer-bul's mouth. He took it out in his fingers, and, wah! it was the ruby. The next morning he went to Akbar-Shah, and said: 'Here is the ruby, as I promised.' Akbar was covered with surprise; but when he had heard the story, he gave Beer-bul two crores of rupees, and said that he spoke the truth—it was better to rejoice than to grieve in misfortune."

The moral of this story is rather awkwardly brought out,

but the plot is curious, from its resemblance to the 'Ring of Polycrates." It was spun out to a much greater length in the Shekh's narration.

I took leave of Mr. Sherer, who was to go back in the evening by palanquin, shook hands with Bushàrat-Ali, and drove slowly down the hill, and out the gate. I was about two miles distant when the sun went down in a broad crimson glory, and my last view of Futtehpore-Sikree was as a dark band sublime against the deepening brilliancy. But I shall long remember the day I spent in its palaces.

CHAPTER X.

THE TAJ MAHAL.

Distant Views of the Taj—Tomb of Itmun e' Dowlah—The Garden of Rama—Night Worship—The Taj Mahal—Its Origin—The Light of the Harem—Portal and Avenue to the Taj—Its Form—Its Inlaid Marbles and Jewel Work—Tomb of Noor-Jehan—The Dome—Resemblance to Florentine Art—Proofs of Saracenic Design—The Echo under the Dome—Beauty of the Taj—Saracenic Architecture—Plan of Shah Jehan—Garree Dawk—Leaving Agra—Night—Allyghur—The Grand Trunk Road—Distant View of Delhi—Arrival.

I PURPOSELY postponed my visit to the Taj Mahal—the most renowned monument of Agra—until I had seen every thing else in the city and its vicinity. The distant view of this matchless edifice satisfied me that its fame was well deserved. So pure, so gloriously perfect did it appear, that I almost feared to approach it, lest the charm should be broken. It is seen to best advantage from the tomb of Itmun e' Dowlah, the Prime Minister of Shah Jehan, which stands in a garden on the northern bank of the Jumna, directly opposite to the city. I spent an afternoon at this tomb and the Ram Bagh, (Garden of Rama,) two miles further up the river. The former is a mausoleum of white marble, elegantly sculptured and inlaid, standing on a raised platform, from the corners of which rise marble minarets. Its design shows the same purity of taste, the same richness of fancy, which I had previously remarked in the Pearl Mosque, and afterward in the Taj.

The Ram Bagh is a garden which, I believe, formerly belonged to the Mogul Emperors, and is now kept in order as a place of recreation, by the Government. Too much praise cannot be awarded to the British rulers in India, for the care with which they have restored and protected all of these monuments of the past, expending large sums to prevent the mosques, palaces and tombs of the former rulers from falling into decay. On account of the humidity of the soil, and the abundance of insects and reptiles, the Ram Bagh is traversed by raised stone causeways, the principal of which inclose water tanks and fountains. It is a pleasant, shady retreat, with a stone balcony overhanging the rapid Jumna, and commanding a view of many ruined palaces on the opposite bank. There are suites of apartments, comfortably furnished, which are let to visitors at the rate of a rupee per day; but when the applications are frequent, no one is allowed to stay more than eight days, in order to give a chance to others. My friends brought their servants and a handsome tiffin, of which we all partook, in the largest chamber. We returned across the bridge of boats in the evening. The Hindoos had lighted lamps in front of the many little shrines facing the water, and in some of them stood persons waving a torch back and forth before the face of the god, crying out at the same time "Ram, Ram, Ram!" "Ram, Seeta, Ram!" This ceremony, with the pouring of the Jumna water over the image, and decorating it with wreaths of flowers, appeared to be the only form of worship observed. There are more substantial offerings made, but if the god gets them, the Brahmins take care that he shall not keep them.

To return to the Taj—for the reader expects me to describe it, and I must comply, although reluctantly, for I am aware of the difficulty of giving an intelligible picture of a building, which has no counterpart in Europe, or even in the East. The mosques and palaces of Constantinople, the domed tent of Omar at Jerusalem, and the structures of the Saracens and Memlooks at Cairo, have nothing in common with it. The remains of Moorish art in Spain approach nearest to its spirit, but are only the scattered limbs, the torso, of which the Taj is the perfect type. It occupies that place in Saracenic art, which, during my visit to Constantinople, I mistakenly gave to the Solymanye Mosque, and which, in respect to Grecian art, is represented by the Parthenon. If there were nothing else in India, this alone would repay the journey.

The history and associations of the Taj are entirely poetic. It is a work inspired by Love, and consecrated to Beauty. Shah Jehan, the "Selim" of Moore's poem, erected it as a mausoleum over his queen, Noor Jehan—"the Light of the World"—whom the same poet calls Noor-Mahal, "the Light of the Harem," or more properly, "Palace." She is reputed to have been a woman of surpassing beauty, and of great wit and intelligence. Shah Jehan was inconsolable for her loss and has immortalized her memory in a poem, the tablets of which are marble, and the letters jewels:—for the Taj is poetry transmuted into form, and hence, when a poet sees it, he hails it with the rapture of a realized dream. Few persons, of the thousands who sigh over the pages of Lalla Rookh, are aware that the "Light of the Harem" was a real personage, and that her tomb is one of the wonders of the world. The native miniature painters in Delhi show you her portrait, painted on ivory—a small, rather delicate face, with large, dark, piercing eyes, and black hair flowing from under a scarf adorned with peacock's feathers.

The Taj is built on the bank of the Jumna, rather more than a mile to the eastward of the Fort of Agra. It is approached by a handsome road, cut through the mounds left by the ruins of ancient palaces. Like the tomb of Akbar, it stands in a large garden, inclosed by a lofty wall of red sandstone, with arched galleries around the interior. The entrance is a superb gateway of sandstone, inlaid with ornaments and inscriptions from the Koran, in white marble. Outside of this grand portal, however, is a spacious quadrangle of solid masonry, with an elegant structure intended as a caravanseraï, on the opposite side. Whatever may be the visitor's impatience, he cannot help pausing to notice the fine proportions of these structures, and the rich and massive style of their architecture. The gate to the garden of the Taj is not so large as that of Akbar's tomb, but quite as beautiful in design. Passing under the open demi-vault, whose arch hangs high above you, an avenue of dark Italian cypresses appears before you. Down its centre sparkles a long row of fountains, each casting up a single slender jet. On both sides, the palm, the banyan, and the feathery bamboo mingle their foliage; the song of birds meets your ear, and the odor of roses and lemon-flowers sweetens the air. Down such a vista, and over such a foreground, rises the Taj.

It is an octagonal building, or rather, a square with the corners truncated, and each side precisely similar. It stands upon a lofty platform, or pedestal, with a minaret at each corner, and this, again, is lifted on a vast terrace of solid masonry. An Oriental dome, swelling out boldly from the base into nearly two-thirds of a sphere, and tapering at the top into a crescent-tipped spire, crowns the edifice, rising from its centre, with four similar, though much smaller domes, at the corners. On each side there is a grand entrance, formed by a single pointed arch, rising nearly to the cornice, and two smaller arches (one placed above the other) on either hand. The height of the building, from its base to the top of the dome, is 262 feet, and of the minarets, about 200 feet. But no words can convey an idea of the exquisite harmony of the different parts, and the grand and glorious effect of the whole structure, with its attendant minarets.

The material is of the purest white marble, little inferior to that of Carrara. It shines so dazzlingly in the sun, that you can scarcely look at it near at hand, except in the morning and evening. Every part—even the basement, the dome, and the upper galleries of the minarets—is inlaid with ornamental designs in marble of different colors, principally a pale brown, and a bluish violet variety. Great as are the dimensions of the Taj, it is as laboriously finished as one of those Chinese caskets of ivory and ebony, which are now so common in Europe. Bishop Heber truly said: "The Pathans designed like Titans, and finished like jewellers.' Around all the arches of the portals and the windows—around the cornice and the domes—on the walls and in the passages, are inlaid chapters of the Koran, the letters being exquisitely formed of black marble. It is asserted that the whole of the Koran is thus inlaid, in the Taj, and I can readily believe it to be true. The building is perfect in every part. Any dilapidations it may have suffered are so well restored that all traces of them have disappeared.

I ascended to the base of the building—a gleaming marble platform, almost on a level with the tops of the trees in the garden. Before entering the central hall, I descended to the vault where the beautiful Noor-Jehan is buried. A sloping passage, the walls and floor of which have been so polished by the hands and feet of thousands, that you must walk carefully to avoid sliding down, conducts to a spacious vaulted chamber. There is no light but what enters the door, and this falls directly upon the tomb of the Queen in the centre. Shah-Jehan, whose ashes are covered by a simpler cenotaph, raised somewhat above hers, sleeps by her side. The vault was filled with the odors of rose, jasmine, and sandal-wood, the precious attars of which are sprinkled upon the tomb. Wreaths of beautiful flowers lay upon it, or withered around its base.

These were the true tombs, the monuments for display being placed in the grand hall above, which is a lofty rotunda, lighted both from above and below by screens of marble, wrought in filigree. It is paved with blocks of white marble and jasper, and ornamented with a wainscoting of sculptured tablets, representing flowers. The tombs are sarcophagi of the purest marble, exquisitely inlaid with blood-stone, agate, cornelian, lapis-lazuli, and other precious stones, and surrounded with an octagonal screen six feet high, in the open tracery of which lilies, irises, and other flowers are inter wrought with the most intricate ornamental designs. This is also of marble, covered with precious stones. From the resemblance of this screen and the workmanship of the tomb to Florentine mosaic, it is supposed by some to have been executed by an Italian artist; and I have even heard it stated that the Taj was designed by an Italian architect. One look at the Taj ought to assure any intelligent man that this is false—nay, impossible, from the very nature of the thing. The Taj is the purest Saracenic, in form, proportions, and ornamental designs. If that were not sufficient, we have still the name of the Moslem architect, sculptured upon the building.

I consider it extremely doubtful whether any Italian had any thing to do with the work, though it is barely possible that one may have been employed upon the screen around the tombs. In the weekly account of the expenditures for the building of the Taj, there is a certain sum mentioned as paid to "the foreign stone-cutter," who may either have been Italian, Turkish, or Persian. As for the flowers, represented in bas-relief on the marble panels, it has been said that they are not to be found in India. Now these flowers, as near as they can be identified, are the tulip, the iris, (both natives of Persia,) and the lotus. But I noticed a curious feature in the sculpture, which makes it clear to me that the artist was a native. *The flowers lack perspective*, which would never have been the fault of an Italian artist of Shah Jehan's time—about the middle of the seventeenth century. Bishop Heber has declared that he recognized Italian art in the ornaments of the Taj, but he declared also that its minarets have no beauty, that the Fort of Agra is built of granite, and fell into many other glaring errors, both of taste and observation, which I have no time to point out.

The dome of the Taj contains an echo more sweet, pure and prolonged than that in the Baptistry of Pisa, which is the finest in Europe. A single musical tone, uttered by the voice, floats and soars overhead, in a long, delicious undulation, fainting away so slowly that you hear it after it is silent, as you see, or seem to see, a lark you have been watching, after it is swallowed up in the blue of heaven. I pictured to myself the effect of an Arabic or Persian lament for the lovely Noor Jehan, sung over her tomb. The responses that would come from above, in the pauses of the song, must resemble the harmonies of angels in Paradise. The hall, notwithstanding the precious materials of which it is built, and the elaborate finish of its ornaments, has a grave and solemn effect, infusing a peaceful serenity of mind, such as we feel when contemplating a happy death. Stern, unimaginative persons have been known to burst suddenly into tears, on entering it; and whoever can behold the Taj without feeling a thrill that sends the moisture to his eye, has no sense of beauty in his soul.

The Taj truly is, as I have already said, a poem. It is not only a pure architectural type, but also a creation which satisfies the imagination, because its characteristic is Beauty Did you ever build a Castle in the Air? Here is one, brought down to earth, and fixed for the wonder of ages; yet so light it seems, so airy, and, when seen from a distance, so like a fabric of mist and sunbeams, with its great dome soaring up, a silvery bubble, about to burst in the sun, that, even after you have touched it, and climbed to its summit, you almost doubt its reality. The four minarets which surround it are perfect—no other epithet will describe them. You cannot conceive of their proportions being changed in any way, without damage to the general effect. On one side of the Taj is a mosque with three domes, of red sandstone, covered with mosaic of white marble. Now, on the opposite side, there is a building precisely similar, but of no use whatever, except as a balance to the mosque, lest the perfect symmetry of the whole design should be spoiled. This building is called the *jowâb*, or "answer." Nothing can better illustrate the feeling for proportion which prevailed in those days—and proportion is Art.

In comparing these masterpieces of architecture with the Moorish remains in Spain, which resemble them most nearly, I have been struck with the singular fact, that while, at the central seats of the Moslem Empire, Art reached but a comparative degree of development, here, in India, and there, on the opposite and most distant frontiers, it attained a rapid and splendid culmination. The capitals of the Caliphs and the Sultans—Bagdad, Cairo, Damascus, and Constantinople—stand far below Agra and Delhi, Granada and Seville, in point of architecture, notwithstanding the latter cities have but few and scattered remains. It is not improbable that the Moorish architects, after the fall of Granada, gradually made their way to the eastward, and that their art was thus brought to India—or, at least, that they modified and improved the art then existing. The conquest of India by Baber, (grandson of Tamerlane and grandfather of Akbar,) is almost coeval with the expulsion of the Moors from Granada.

But the sun grows hot; it is nearly noon. We have spent

three hours in and around the Taj, and we must leave it. Nothing that is beautiful can be given up without a pang, but if a man would travel, he must endure many such partings. I must add, however, before we go, that on the opposite bank of the Jumna there is an immense foundation-terrace, whereon, it is said, Shah Jehan intended to erect a tomb for himself, of equal magnificence, but the rebellion of his sons, and his own death, prevented it. What the gods permitted to Love, they forbade to Vanity. A shekh, who takes care of the Taj, told me, that had the Emperor carried out his design, the tombs were to have been joined by a bridge, with a silver railing on each side. He told me that the Taj, with its gateways, mosque, and other buildings attached, had cost seven crores of rupees—$35,000,000. This, however, is quite impossible, when we consider the cheapness of labor in those days, and I believe the real cost is estimated at £3,000,000 ($15,000,000), which does not seem exaggerated.

On the same evening, after visiting the Taj, I left Agra for Delhi. My kind host, Mr. Warren, whose hospitality was untiring, gave me letters to his colleagues in other parts of India, and his lady furnished me with the needful provisions for the journey. I went by the *garree-dawk*, which was a great improvement both upon the banghy and mail-carts. There were three rival companies for the conveyance of passengers, by carriages, on the Grand Trunk Road, as it is called, extending from Calcutta to Delhi, a distance of nine hundred miles. Four years ago, there was no other way of travelling, except on horseback or in a palanquin. Progress in India, though slow, is perceptible. The *garree* resembles a cab, with the space between the back and front seats filled up and covered with a mattrass. You provide yourself with a quilt and pillow, stow your baggage into the bottom, and take your ease, as if upon your own bed. Thus you can travel, and even sleep, with a tolerable degree of comfort. There are relays of horses, about six miles apart, and if no accident should happen, the garree rolls on at the rate of seven miles an hour.

I left Agra at eight o clock in the evening. It was a raw, misty, moonlit night, and I found an overcoat indispensable. Indeed, during the week I spent in the place, I suffered continually from cold. We had fires in the morning and evening, and I was fain to get into the sun at mid-day, though warned not to expose myself to his rays. There was no frost, but the making of ice was carried on briskly, and three thousand maunds (120,000 lbs.) were already stored in the ice-house. I sat up to take a last view of the Fort and Jumma Musjeed, paid half a rupee toll at the bridge of boats over the Jumna, and then lay down on my mattrass, to try the effect of my new conveyance. It was really quite agreeable, and except when the horses were changed, or took a fancy to baulk and plunge, I could sleep without difficulty. About three o'clock in the morning, the driver awoke me to announce his *budlee*, or substitute, (a hint for backsheesh,) declaring that we were at Allyghur. This was once a strong fortress, and the scene of a battle between the English and native troops. There is a pillar erected to commemorate it, which pillar I saw in the moonlight, as we drove on towards Delhi.

The morning showed a splendid road, leading over a boundless plain, covered with fields of wheat, barley, mustard and poppies, and dotted with groves of mango or tamarind trees. Its aspect continued unvaried for hours, except that there was once or twice a low red hill in the distance, or a native town, with whitewashed mosques and mouldy Hindoo temples near at hand. The road was crowded with native travellers, with bullock-carts, ponies, and on foot, and other *garrees*, conveying the "*sahib log*" (nobility) of the land, passed me frequently. I noticed a sort of native omnibus, drawn by slow horses, wherein natives, and they only, are conveyed at the rate of one anna (three cents) per mile. This is a recent invention.

The plain gradually lost its mango groves, and assumed a bleak and sterile appearance. I crossed a river by a handsome suspension bridge, then the Eastern Jumna Canal, and in the afternoon, when still twelve miles distant from Delhi, descried its mosques on the horizon. As I approached, the great fortress-palace built by Shah Jehan, (nearly as large as the Fort, at Agra,) rose from the plain. The city, which lies to the west of it, was almost hidden by trees, which belt it around. The superb domes of the great mosque rose above them, and on either hand I could see immense tombs and other ruined edifices, scattered far and wide over the plain. I crossed the Jumna, which is here as broad as at Agra, by a bridge of boats, passed a very old, crumbling fortress, overgrown with trees and bushes, then the Imperial Palace, now occupied by His Majesty, Akbar II., and was finally set down at the dawk bungalow. The first thing I did, on arriving in the capital of the Great Mogul, was to order dinner, and by the time that business was over, it was too dark to see any thing of the city. I had a letter to Mr. Place, of the *Delhi hi Gazette*, and after making many inquiries of the chokedar who finally recognized him as being "Palace Sahib" and the "*chappa-khana-walla*" (printing-office fellow!) procured a guide to his residence. The next morning I shifted my quarters to the shelter of his hospitable roof.

CHAPTER XI

THE CAPITAL OF THE GREAT MOGUL.

Delhi—The Mogul Empire at Present—Ruins of former Delhis—The Observatory—A Wilderness of Ruin—Tomb of Sufdur Jung—The Khuttub Minar—Its Beauty—View from the Summit—Uncertainty of its Origin—The Palace of Aladdin—Ruins of a Hindoo Temple—Tomb of the Emperor Humayoon—Of Nizam-ud-deen—Native Sam Patches—Old Delhi—Aspect of the Modern City—The Chandree Choke—Bayaderes—Delhi Artisans and Artists—The Jumma Musjeed—A Hindoo Minstrel and his Songs—The Palace of Akbar II.—Neglect and Desolation—The Diwan—An Elysium on Earth—The Throne Hall—The Crystal Throne—The Court of Akbar II. —A Farce of Empire—The Gardens—Voices of the Sultanas—Palace Pastimes.

DELHI is the Imperial City of India, having been chosen by the Mogul Conquerors as their capital, which it thenceforth remained, except during the reign of Akbar. After the death of Aurungzebe, the power of the Emperors gradually declined; the Mahrattas and Rajpoots laid waste and seized upon their territories, and finally the English, who found that the shortest way of effecting their object as peace-makers was to become conquerors, took what fragments remained of the Empire. The sovereignty, however, is still acknowledged and treated with the same outward ceremonials of respect and submission, as when the Company owned nothing but a factory in Bengal, and the Mogul was lord of all India. The dominions of Akbar II., the present Emperor, the lineal descendant of the House of Tamerlane and his illustrious suc cessors, are embraced within the walls of his palace, and comprise rather less than a square half mile. The Government allows fourteen lacs of rupees ($700,000) annually for the maintenance of himself, his family, and the princes attached to his Court—a large and hungry retinue, many of whom cannot venture outside of the walls without running the risk of being seized for his debts. They are all in debt, from the Emperor to his lowest menials, and the Government allowance is always conveyed to the Palace under a strong guard, to prevent its being forcibly carried off by the creditors. This pitiful farce of Royalty is all that remains of the Mogul Empire—once the most powerful and enlightened sovereignty in Asia.

The modern City of Delhi is the latest of the name, and having been founded by Shah Jehan, is still called by the natives Shahjehanabad. There were several Delhis, one of the oldest of which is the city built by Toglukh, and called Toglukhabad, the ruins of which lie about fifteen miles to the south of the present city. Another city, now called Old Delhi, built during one of the succeeding reigns, is about two miles distant. It is still surrounded by lofty walls, with circular stone bastions, and has several thousand inhabitants. But all of the country south of the Jumna, for an extent of more than ten miles in every direction, is strewed with the ruins of palaces, mosques, and tombs. Whenever the city was taken and desolated in the early wars, instead of rebuilding it, the inhabitants founded a new one in the vicinity; and afterwards, whenever the caprice of an Emperor prompted him to erect a new palace, the nobles, and after them the common people, gradually shifted their residences, until the location of the city was quite changed; and thus, for centuries, Delhi continued to be a migratory capital. For the last two centuries it has been stationary, and will now probably remain so. But the ruins of the former Delhis cover a much greater space than that occupied by the ruins of Thebes, and had they all belonged to one city, it would have been the greatest in the world.

On the day after my arrival, Mr. Place drove me in his carriage to the Khuttub Minar, the pride and boast of Delhi, as the Taj is of Agra. It is eleven miles distant, in a south-westerly direction. This, again, was a day to be remembered We left at an early hour, and without entering the city, drove along its walls, past the Cashmere and Lahore Gates. It was a balmy morning, with a pure, crystalline atmosphere, such as I had not seen for weeks. The air seemed to be more dry and bracing than at Agra, for though the temperature was lower, I felt the cold much less keenly. At a short distance from the city, we came upon the ruins of a magnificent observatory. The most prominent object was a colossal gnomon, built of stone, and rising to the height of near forty feet. Around this was a circular plane, precisely parallel to that of the ecliptic, and nearly a hundred feet in diameter. There were also two circular buildings, with a double row of narrow slits, or embrasures, around them, and the remains of stone tables in the inside, the circumferences of which were divided into degrees. These buildings were no doubt intended for observing the rising and setting of stars, measuring their distances from each other, and other similar processes. The observatory could only have been used for astronomical observations of a very simple character.

Beyond this all was ruin. The country was uneven and covered in all directions, as far as the eye could reach, with masses of stone and brick, the remains of walls and arches, and the tombs of princes, saints and scholars who flourished during the Mogul dynasty. The tombs were large square buildings, surmounted with domes. Some were merely of brick and mortar, but others of sandstone and white marble, and adorned with very elegant gateways. Grass and bushes were growing out of the rifts of the domes, and the seeds of the peepul tree, taking root in the mortar, had in many places split asunder the strongest masses of masonry. During many miles of our journey, there was scarcely a change in the melancholy panorama. Ruin succeeded ruin, and between and beyond them there were but perspectives of ruin in the distance. The habitations of men were few and scattered, and but little of the soil showed any appearance of cultivation. The wild vulture hovered sullenly over the waste, and the fox and jackal sneaked about the crumbling walls. That beautiful fragment of Persian poetry, recited by Mahmoud the Conqueror, as he entered Constantinople, came into my mind: "The spider hath woven his web in the imperial palaces; and the owl hath sung her watch-song on the towers of Afrasiab."

About six miles from Delhi we came upon the splendid tomb of Sufdur Jung, a prince who was connected with the royal house of Oude. It resembles the Taj in design, but is smaller and built of a mixture of sandstone and marble, the effect of which is very beautiful and pleasing. The present King of Oude has appointed a sum for its repair and preservation, but there are no signs, in the general air of neglect which pervades the place, of any money having been thus ap plied I was quite charmed with the beauty of the architectural details, in this edifice; the arched windows, the vaulted ceilings of the chambers, and the designs of the marble balconies, were among the finest things of the kind which I saw in India.

From the top of the tomb we first saw the Khuttub Minar, and after five more miles of ruin, drew up in the court-yard of a caravanserai near its base. The unusual form of the Khuttub detracts from its height, when seen from a distance, but greatly increases it on a nearer view, by exaggerating the perspective. Hence, unlike some towers which seem to shrink as you approach them, the Khuttub, which at a few miles' distance resembles an ordinary factory-chimney, swells to a sublime altitude when you are in its vicinity. It is a round pillar, of 240 feet in height, the diameter at the base being 35 feet, but gradually diminishing to less than 10 feet at the top. It is divided into five stories, the relative height of which decreases in the same ratio as the diameter of the shaft. Each story has a heavy cornice of the richest sculpture, surmounted by a low stone balustrade. The three lower stories are entirely of red sandstone, fluted, or rather reeded with alternate convex and angular divisions, and belted at short intervals by bands of Arabic inscriptions, sculptured in relief, and of colossal size. The two highest stories are mostly of white marble, without inscriptions, and deviate slightly from the diminishing slope of the pillar, whence it is generally supposed that they were added at a later period. Some English officers, thinking to improve the work, crowned it with a grotesque cupola, which was a ridiculous excrescence on the shaft, until Lord Hardinge ordered it to be taken down.

Such are the dimensions and style of the renowned Khuttub, but they are very far from expressing the majesty of its appearance, or the rich and gorgeous sculpture with which it is adorned. As I stood a short distance from the base, my gaze ravelling slowly from bottom to top, and from top to bottom, Mr. Place declared it to be the finest single tower in the world, and asked me whether I did not think so. I said, "No," for just then I had Giotto's Florentine Campanile and the Giralda of Seville in my mind, and could not venture to place it above them; but the longer I looked, the more its beauty grew upon me, and after spending three or four hours in its vicinity, I no longer doubted. It *is*, beyond question, the finest shaft in the world.

We mounted to the summit by a winding staircase of 378 steps, which became so narrow, as the diameter of the shaft diminished, that some of my corpulent friends could never have reached the top. The view was very extensive, and on such a bright, warm day, very beautiful, in spite of its desolation. On all sides there was a brown, undulating waste, dotted with ruins, but enlivened by an occasional garden or wheat-field. Low, red hills in the south and west, a glimpse of a blue lake in the distance, the massive battlements of the deserted City of Toglukh in the south-east, and the domes of Delhi in the north, made up the panorama. When the air is very clear, the crests of the Himalayas, two hundred miles distant, can be discerned on the horizon.

There is a difference of opinion as to whether the Khuttub is of Hindoo or Moslem origin. Nothing positive is known concerning the date or design of its erection. Some suppose it to have been a watch-tower, others a monument others a minaret, others again a gigantic symbol of Shiva. Both the Hindoos and the Moslems claim it, the former alleging that the Arabic inscriptions were subsequently added by the conquerors. A short distance to the north there is the base of a tower similar in design, but of much grander dimensions, the building of which was relinquished after it had been raised about fifty feet from the ground. This, the Hindoos say, was commenced by the Moslems, in order to surpass the Khuttub, which they found impossible. Without entering into a discussion for which I am not prepared, I may venture to say that the three lowest stories appear to me to be of Hindoo construction, both from the singular manner in which the shaft is reeded, and from the absence of arches in the openings for air and light. The arch (which was first introduced into India by the Moslems) appears in the upper stories, and it is generally admitted that they were added at a later period. Some of the Arabic inscriptions refer to the repair of the shaft, and date from the reign of Feroze Shah, about four and a half centuries ago.

The Khuttub stands in the midst of a wilderness of ruins. There are the arcades of what was once a splendid Hindoo temple, changed into the court-yard of a mosque which was begun on a magnificent scale, but never finished, and the conflicting styles are mixed together in the most incongruous manner. A college of marble and sandstone, in the later Moorish style, stands on one side of it, and a few hundred paces in an opposite direction, lie the ruins—fancy such a thing, if you can—of the palace of Aladdin! The genii have taken back their windows of ruby and pearl, the gold and ivory have disappeared, and there are now only a few shapeless chambers, tottering to their fall. The remains of the Hindoo temple show that it must have been one of the finest in this part of India. The arcades are supported on several hundred columns, scarcely any of which are similar. They are covered, from cap to pedestal, with elaborate sculpture, including figures of the gods, of dogs, horses, monkeys and elephants, of the chain and bell, the pomegranate, and other religious emblems. The domes at the corners of the quadrangles are not vaulted, but formed by flat stones laid diagonally across and overlapping each other, as in the Cyclopean remains of Italy. In the court stands a pillar of iron about eighteen feet high, and called by the natives "Feroze Shah's Walking-Stick." It bears an inscription in a very ancient character, which long puzzled the scholars, but was finally deciphered by Mr. Prinsep. The column appears to have been set up in token of victory, by a king who flourished about a century before the Christian Era. There are others, similar to it, in other parts of India.

There was not sufficient time to visit Toglukhabad—the ruins of which, indeed, are only remarkable for their massive masonry; so, after peeping into Sir Theophilus Metcalf's elegant country residence, which was made out of one of the old tombs, we drove back to Delhi, taking the tomb of the Emperor Humayoon by the way. This lies to the south-east of the city, adjoining a walled palace or fortress, which is still inhabited. The tomb is on a grand scale, rising to the height of one hundred feet, from a noble terrace of solid masonry, but has a most wretched, forlorn air. The floors are covered with litter and filth, the marble screens broken and battered, the dome given to bats and owls, and the spacious garden has become a waste of weeds. From the terrace, I counted upwards of fifty similar palaces of the dead, several of them, if not on a scale of equal grandeur, yet even superior in design and in the richness of their decoration.

There was an old porter, who attended for the sake of a trifle, by way of backsheesh, and on our leaving, urged us to visit the tomb of Nizam-ud-deen. I was beginning to feel tired of so much decayed splendor, but my friend said that the place was really curious, and so we drove back about half a mile Here there was a small native village—perhaps a remnant of one of the old Delhis—crowded in among the tombs. Nizam-ud-deen had truly a splendid mausoleum, of white marble with gilded domes, and there was an inclosure of marble fretwork of great beauty, surrounding the tomb of a daughter of the present Emperor. It was a labyrinth of a place, with a dark, deep tank in the midst, surrounded by high walls on three sides, with a flight of steps leading down to the water, on the fourth side. While we were looking into it, three or four half naked boys made their appearance on the high roofs overhanging the tank, and offered to jump down, for a few annas apiece. I accordingly agreed, hardly thinking they would dare such a thing, when three of them boldly sprang from the highest platform, about seventy feet above the water. The fearful picture they made in descending quite took away my breath, and there was a sound when they struck the surface, as if they had fallen upon stone. They soon rose again, and came scrambling up the steps to get their money, complaining, with chattering teeth, of the coldness of the water.

In returning to the city, we passed around the walls of Old Delhi, which are upward of eighty feet high. I was anxious to see the interior, but it was then too late, and another opportunity did not afterwards occur. Mr. Place, who had resided in Delhi for ten years, told me that he had never been inside the walls.

Modern Delhi was the largest and most picturesque native city I had then seen. The houses are of brick and stucco, painted in gay colors, and very few of them less than two stories in height. They have tiled roofs, which gives the place, when seen from a minaret, a strong resemblance to Smyrna, and other large Turkish towns. It covers an extent of about two square miles, but is very compactly built, and the population is reckoned at near 200,000 souls. Most of the European residents have their bungalows on the heights outside of the Cashmere Gate, and near the military cantonments. There is an aqueduct of hewn stone traversing the city, which supplies the inhabitants with drinking water, brought from a distance of seventy-five miles, the water of the Jumna being strongly impregnated with natron, and injurious to health. The palace, which is surrounded by a deep moat, has a massive gateway and barbican in the centre of its western front. An open space intervenes between it and the city, and exactly opposite the gateway begins the Chandnee Choke—the Broadway of Delhi, which runs directly through the centre of the city, to the Lahore Gate. It is a noble avenue, somewhat resembling a Parisian *boulevard,* having a small aqueduct, fringed with trees, on each side of the main highway, and separating it from the paved sidewalks. The houses are made picturesque by their wooden galleries and balconies, and some of them are very pretty specimens of architecture.

When the heat of the day has subsided, and the afternoon shadows are growing long and cool, all the natives of any standing or pretension repair to the Chandnee Choke. Then broad as it is, it can scarcely contain the gay throngs that parade up and down its whole extent. There are Princes of the Emperor's Court, mounted on brilliantly caparisoned elephants; country Chiefs on horseback, with a fierce air, and weapons in bundance; Hindoo Baboos, with the symbol of their caste painted on their foreheads; *hackrees*, drawn by bullocks, and resembling pagodas on wheels, behind whose tassels and dusty red curtains sit the discreet ladies of the land; travelling merchants, slowly pacing along on camels; Sikhs, with forked black beards; long-locked Affghans, with bright, treacherous eyes; and Persians, grave as the maxims of Saadi, besides a vast retinue on foot, exhibiting the most brilliant combinations of color in their garments. The ordinary dress is pure white, but here you see in addition, caps and scarfs of the most vivid shades of crimson, blue, green, yellow and orange, with a profusion of gold fringe and spangles. The merchants sit cross-legged in their shops, looking out on the array, and chatting cheerfully with passing acquaintances, while from the balconies above, the Bayaderes, clad in their most attractive finery, play the part of sirens to the crowd below.

Here, as in Egypt, only females of this class are allowed to show their faces unveiled, and one has no other authority for forming an opinion regarding the beauty of the sex. Among the many faces I saw while passing through the Chandnee Choke, there were but two which were really beautiful, while most of them were so coarse and repulsive that I should think there was little danger of their drawing many victims into their toils. But there was scarcely a house, the upper story of which was not occupied by these creatures. A native court in India, with its army of pensioned idlers, is a hot-bed for all forms of vice, and Delhi is only surpassed in this respect by Lucknow and Hyderabad.

In addition to the manufacture of shawls and scarfs, in which its artisans are only inferior to those of Cashmere and Umritsir, Delhi is celebrated for its jewelry. The gold and silver smiths produce articles of exquisite workmanship, and occasionally very fine jewels are to be met with. Those of a secondary value, such as agate, onyx, cornelian, topaz, carbuncle and moon-stone, are very plentiful, and may be had at a trifling rate. The bed of the Jumna abounds in beautiful cornelians, sards and agates. In rambling among the shops I saw several natives of Cashmere, who were exceedingly handsome men, with skin as fair as a European's and soft brown hair. They belonged evidently to the pure Caucasian stock. A native miniature painter showed me the portrait of a Cashmerian Sultana, which was a vision of perfect loveliness. The features were like those of a high-born English beauty, but with an enchanting touch of Southern languor in the dark eye, the drooping, fringed lid, and the full, crimson lip. He had also a portrait of Tootee Beegum, a Sikh princess, whose style of beauty was thoroughly Oriental—a brilliant, passionate face, capable of expressing the extremes of firmness and tenderness. The delicacy of touch and artistic truth of these native artists is extraordinary. I know of but few miniature painters in America who could equal them. In landscapes they are not so successful for though the pictures are very laboriously finished, and show fair idea of perspective, they lack color and atmosphere.

The Jumma (or Jooma) Musjeed at Delhi is a noble structure, equalled only, as a mosque, by the Motee Musjeed at Agra. It is on a much larger scale than the latter. It stands in the middle of the city, at the meeting of four of the prin cipal streets, and is raised on a grand platform of masonry twenty feet high, with broad flights of steps leading up on each side. The material is sandstone and white marble, the three superb domes being built of both, disposed in vertical bands, or stripes. At a distance, when softened by the haze, they resemble huge balloons of striped silk, hovering over the city. We were allowed to walk rough-shod through the court-yard, and to climb one of the minarets, but two Hindoo pilgrims from Ajmere were ignominiously driven out, on attempting to enter. We inquired the reason of this, and were told that the "sahib" had ordered it so, on account of recent fights which had occurred between the rival sects. The two religions, nevertheless, are blended in some degree among the low and ignorant classes, the shrines and sacred places of each being held in common reverence by them. The two Rajpoots whom we saw ejected, seemed very much mortified that they were not allowed to visit this sanctuary of the Mussulmen.

A very curious illustration of Progress in India was furnished to me one day, during my sojourn with Mr. Place. We were dining together in his bungalow, when a wandering Hindoo minstrel came along with his mandolin, and requested permission to sit upon the verandah and play for us. I was desirous of hearing some of the Indian airs, and my host therefore ordered him to perform during dinner. He tuned the wires of his mandolin, extemporized a prelude which had some very familiar passages, and to my complete astonishment, began singing: "Get out of the way, Old Dan Tucker!" The old man seemed to enjoy my surprise, and followed up his performance with "Oh, Susanna!" "Buffalo Gals," and other choice Ethiopian melodies, all of which he sang with admirable spirit and correctness. I addressed him in English, but found that he did not understand a word of the language, and had no conception of the nature of the songs he had given us. He had heard some young English officers singing them at Madras, and was indebted entirely to his memory for both the melodies and words. It was vain to ask him for his native Indian airs: he was fascinated with the spirit of our national music, and sang with a grin of delight which was very amusing. As a climax of skill, he closed with "*Malbrook se va-t-en guerre*," but his pronunciation of French was not quite so successful. I had heard Spanish boatmen on the Isthmus of Panama singing "Carry me back to ole Virginny," and Arab boys in the streets of Alexandria humming "Lucy Long," but I was hardly prepared to hear the same airs from the lips of a Hindoo, in the capital of the Great Mogul.

It only remains for me to describe my visit to the Emperor's Palace. Mr. Place having previously sent a messenger to announce the visit, we found two chobdars (beadles) with silver maces, waiting for us outside of the great gate. We were allowed to drive through, the sentinels presenting arms, into a small court, through a second bastioned gateway, and down a stately, vaulted passage, to a large, open quadrangle, where we dismounted and proceeded on foot. The vaulted gallery must have once been an imposing prelude to the splendors of the palace, but it is now dirty and dilapidated, and the quadrangle into which it ushers the visitor resembles a great barn-yard, filled with tattered grooms, lean horses and mangy elephants. The buildings surrounding it were heavy masses of brick and sandstone, and were rapidly falling into ruin

But there was another gate before us, and I hastened through it, hoping to find something which would repay the promise of the magnificent exterior. There was, indeed, the Palace of Shah Jehan, but in what condition! Porticoes of marble, spoiled by dust and whitewash, exquisite mosaics with all the precious stones gouged out, gilded domes glittering over courts heaped with filth, and populated with a retinue of beggarly menials. This was all that was left of the Empire of Tamerlane and Akbar—a miserable life-in-death, which was far more melancholy than complete ruin.

The only parts of the palace I was allowed to see were the *diwan*, the throne-hall and the mosque—all of which bear a general resemblance to the palace of Akbar, at Agra, but are more wantonly despoiled. The diwan is an elegant arcade formed by three rows of arches, with a pavilion of the purest marble in the centre, inlaid with gold and precious stones. Over this pavilion is the inscription in Persian, which Moore has introduced in his "Light of the Harem,"—"If there be an Elysium on Earth, it is here—it is here." What an Elysium at present!

The throne-hall is a square canopy resting on massive square pillars. It is constructed entirely of white marble, very highly polished, the pillars being inlaid with cornelian and bloodstone, and the ceiling richly gilded. In the centre of this once stood the famous peacock throne, which has recently been removed, and we were unable to get a sight of it. By persevering, however, we succeeded in seeing the crystal throne of the Great Mogul, which is four feet in diameter by two in height, and the largest piece of rock crystal known to exist. The bases of the pillars in this splendid hall were painted with roses and tulips, the colors of which were very well preserved. The mosque—an imitation of that in the palace at Agra—did not appear to have heard a prayer for years.

Akbar II. has reigned in this little dominion since 1805 and is now upward of eighty years of age. He was the last of the line, but having four sons, the succession will be continued. He devotes his time to literature, amusements and sensuality. The Mussulmen speak highly of his literary acquirements, and his poems in the Persian language are said by those who have read them to possess considerable merit. There is a Court newspaper, entitled *The Lamp of News*, published within the palace, but its columns are entirely devoted to the gossip of the city, and private scandal. Until recently the law administered within the palace bore a resemblance to the bloody rule of former days. Persons who had incurred the royal displeasure had their hands, ears or noses cut off, and were then thrust out of the gates. Finally the English Resident at the Court hinted to his Majesty that these things were very disagreeable and ought to cease. "What!" said the descendant of Tamerlane; "am I not King in my own palace?" "Undoubtedly," blandly replied the Resident; "your Highness is the Conqueror of the World and the Protector of Princes; but such a course is not pleasing to the Governor-General, and it would be a great evil to the world if the friendship of two such mighty and illustrious Sovereigns were to be interrupted!" The forms of respect to the phantom of the old authority being thus preserved, the Emperor instituted a milder regimen.

We finished our visit by a walk in the gardens. Here, the old trees, rankly overrun with parasitic plants, with an under growth of wild and unpruned rose-bushes, afforded a pleasant relief to the decay of the imperial halls. But the garden-pavilions were tumbling down, the pools and fountain-basins were covered with a thick green scum, and rank weeds grew in all the walks. We lingered for some time under the windows of the *Zenana*, listening to the clatter of female voices, and trying to draw therefrom some inference as to the features of the Sultanas. Alas! the tones were all too shrill to have come from beautiful lips. On our way out, several sentinels belonging to the Emperor's boy-corps stood at the interior gates and made very respectful salaams as we passed. The poor little half-starved, half-clothed wretches are obliged to exercise daily, and often four hours at a time. Most of the male inmates of the place were perched upon the roofs, engaged in flying flocks of pigeons, which they made to advance or recede, separate and unite again, by uttering a peculiar cry and waving a long rod with a little flag on the end of it. At the gate we dismissed the chobdars with a gratuity, and I went home.

"The spider hath woven his web in the imperial palace."

CHAPTER XII

JOURNEY IN A PALANQUIN.

Departure for the Himalayas—"Laying a Dawk"—Last View of Delhi—A Rainy Night—Quarters at Meerut—The Dawk Agent—Hindoo Punctuality—Meerut—Palanquin Travelling—Tricks of the Bearers—Arrival at Roorkhee—Adventures in Search of a Breakfast—First View of the Himalayas—A Welcome Invitation—Roorkhee—The Ganges Canal—Its Cost and Dimensions—Method of Irrigation—The Government and the People—Aqueduct over the Sclanee River—Apathy of the Natives.

At the close of my stay in Delhi, I found that precisely half the time which I had allotted for my transit through India had expired, and but a single month remained. However, although nearly a thousand miles from Calcutta, I determined to push on to the Himalayas, and get a glimpse of the highest mountain in the world. Once on the Grand Trunk Road, on my return, I could depend on making a hundred miles a day by the *garree-dawk*, without excessive fatigue, and there were few points of interest, except Allahabad and Benares, to detain me on the way to Calcutta. I therefore made arrangements —"laid a dawk" is the Indian expression—for a trip to Landowr, the highest point in the Himalayas, which can be conveniently reached during the winter season, by way of Roorkhee and Hurdwar. The distance of Landowr from Delhi is nearly two hundred miles, and there is no carriage dawk beyond Meerut, fifty miles from the latter city. I was therefore obliged to travel by *palkee dawk*, or palanquin. A statement was drawn up of the different places I intended to visit, with the length of my stay at each, and a messenger dispatched to summon the bearers to be in readiness at the proper time, at the different stations along the road. Twelve days were allowed for the trip to Landowr and back to Meerut. The expenses of the dawk, including the hire of the palanquin amounted to nearly $60.

The garree, or carriage, for Meerut called for me on Wednesday afternoon, the 26th of January, and I took leave of Mr. Place, after having been most hospitably entertained by him for four days. The weather was dark, raw and lowering, and I had not crossed the tedious bridge over the Jumna, before the rain began to fall. My last view of Delhi was dull and misty; the palace of Shah Jehan loomed up more grandly than ever, but the domes and minarets of the Jumma Musjeed, which need to be touched with sunshine, on a background of blue sky, lost half their airy grace. I had a comfortable cart, with a mattress on the bottom, and disposed my carpet-bags in such a way as to make it as easy as an arm-chair. The rain increased, however, the roads became wet and slippery, and the plain had a dull November look, which was very dreary. I was delayed by the obstinacy of the horses, who finding the cart a little heavier than usual, did their best to disable it. Night soon came on, the rain rattled on the roof, and drawing my quilt around me, I lay down and slept until aroused by the driver, asking where he should take me, for we had reached Meerut. I directed him to go to the "*punch ghur*" (punch house), as a hotel is termed, in this part of India. There I found consummars, chokedars, and the other varieties of servants usually attached to a bungalow, but no one who spoke English. I did my best to get a note conveyed to the person who was to furnish me with a palanquin and bearers the next morning, but found the thing quite impossible.

I arose betimes, and set out to find the agent, for seven o'clock was the time appointed for starting. After endless questions and a walk of three miles, I was finally directed to a mean house, in the door of which stood one of the meanest individuals in appearance, that I ever beheld. He was a half-caste, of a dirty complexion, unwashed, pitted with the small-pox, limping, and dressed in a vile cloak covered with grease and patches. He informed me that the bearers were ready, and pointed to the palanquin, which was standing in the verandab. The man's appearance made me suspicious, and though there was really a palanquin, I feared that before travelling far I should find it to be a little buggy. He promised to send it to the hotel, whither I hastened, expecting to find breakfast ready as I had ordered. Vain hope! There is no equivalent for "punctuality" in the Hindostanee tongue. I waited an hour; the palanquin arrived; I stormed in English, for, unfortunately, I knew no anathemas in their language, but the cooks were miracles of calmness and deliberation. When breakfast finally came, I was obliged to eat a few mouthfuls hurriedly and depart, lest I should give the bearers along the road a chance to claim demurrage.

Meerut resembles the other Indian cantonments in most

respects. It has a number of handsome bungalows, besides a church with a very ambitious spire. Owing to an abundance of good water, its gardens and orchards are much more luxuriant than those of Agra and Delhi. It must be both an agreeabe and healthy place of residence. The sky was clear, after the rain of the previous day, and the air delightfully cool and bracing, though colder than I desired. I rode with the palanquin windows open, and found that by propping myself against a carpet-bag, I could get a tolerable view of the country on both sides. There was little variety in the scenery, as I was still on the great Plain of Hindostan. I noticed, however, some change in the vegetation; the tamarind and taree-palm were but rarely to be seen; the peepul and saul were the principal trees. The wheat was much more backward than in the warmer plains about Agra.

I had eight bearers, four of whom only carried the palanquin at one time. They relieved each other every half-mile, and all of them gave place to a new set, at the end of the stage, which varied from eight to ten miles. There was, besides, a mussalchee, or torch-bearer, who, during the day, carries the superfluous garments of the bearers, and demands backsheesh when they are changed. The amount given is four annas (12½ cents), to each set of bearers. They usually average about four miles an hour on good roads, carrying the palanquin along on a slow, sliding trot, every step of which they accompany with a grunt. I do not know a more disagreeable method of travelling. It is as necessary to preserve a nice equilibrium as in a Turkish caique, and as you lie at full length in a narrow box, you cannot turn your cramped limbs without thrusting your body too far on one side or the other. The jolting motion of the palanquin is unpleasant, and the measured grunts of the bearers give you the idea that they are about to drop you, through fatigue, while nothing can be more annoying than their constant stoppage to shift the pole from one shoulder to another. Sometimes they groan out, "*julaee jào!*" (go quickly!) and when they meet any body in the road, they cry: "Take care! we have a great Lord inside!"

Thus I jogged on all day, through a tame and monotonous country. I looked continually to the north, for a glimpse of the Himalayas, and once thought I saw some sharp white peaks, but they gradually moved together and changed their forms. Toward evening my bearers stopped at a village, which they said was the end of their *chokee* (stage), but that the new bearers, who ought to have been in waiting, had gone on to another village, about a mile distant. To avoid the delay of waiting their return, they offered to take me on to the village for an additional backsheesh; and I consented. When I arrived, however, and found the new bearers in readiness, I asked them: "Is this the beginning of your *chokee*, or the village behind us?" "This is the place," they all exclaimed; whereupon the others were quite abashed at finding their trickery exposed, and their expected backsheesh lost. At sunset I passed through Mozuffernuggur, a large town about thirty-six miles from Meerut. At the next *chokee* beyond it, I was delayed an hour and a half by the non-appearance of the bearers. My men began to shout, and the cries were taken up by one person and another, till they seemed to radiate through the whole country, and fill the air, far and near. The men were at last gathered together, and we went on by torch-light The night was clear and cold, and I lay muffled up, cramped and shivering, until we arrived at the station of Roorkhee, three hours past midnight.

There was a Government bungalow, to which the bearers conveyed me, awoke the sleepy chokedar, kindled a cocoa-nut amp, and left me. I removed every thing from the palanquin o the room, fastened the doors, and then lay down upon the charpoy (bedstead), where I slept until morning. On awaking, my first sensation was that of hunger, for I had fasted twenty-four hours, so I summoned the chokedar, and ordered him to get breakfast for me. "*Bohut achchà*," (very well,) said he, and then went on to make some statement, the most prominent words of which were "*ghurreeb purwar.*" I asked him for tea, for eggs, for fowls, but though he always replied "very well," there was sure to follow something about "ghurreeb purwar." At last I decided that these words referred to some necessary article, without which he could not provide breakfast. I thought of the Arabic words *gurra*, a gourd, and *georboh*, a water-skin, and it was quite plain that "ghurreeb purwar" must mean either a tea-kettle or a frying pan. "Well," said I, when he had repeated the words for the twentieth time, "I have no ghurreeb purwar; you must get one. Go and borrow one from the Sahibs!" The man stared at me in a wild way, and went off, but not to provide breakfast. I learned afterwards that "ghurreeb purwar" was a title addressed to myself, and means "Protector of the Poor." It is addressed to all Europeans in these parts, and no exclusive honor is meant thereby, as Bishop Heber supposed, when he wrote in his Journal, that the people, on account of his kindness to them, had bestowed upon him the title of "Protector of the Poor."

While anxiously waiting for breakfast, I amused myself by reading a list of the books in the Library of the Ganges Canal at Roorkhee, which hung upon the wall. Who would have guessed that an humble author, in scrambling about the world, should find one of his works in the furthest corner of India, at the very foot of the Himalayas? Yet so it was; and the fact made the place less inhospitable, in spite of my hunger. Where my words have already been, I thought, shall not my body find nourishment? and while trying to reason myself into the impression that there was a breakfast somewhere in Roorkhee, which it was destined that I should eat, I walked out upon the verandah.

It was about eight in the morning: an atmosphere of crystal, and not a cloud in the sky. Yet something white and shining glimmered through the loose foliage of some trees on my right hand. My heart came into my mouth with the sudden bound it gave, when, after plunging through the trees like one mad, tumbling into a ditch on the other side, and scrambling up a great pile of dirt, I saw the Himalayas before me! Unobscured by a single cloud or a speck of vapor, there stood revealed the whole mountain region, from the low range of the Siwalik Hills, about twenty miles distant, to the loftiest pinnacles of eternal snow, which look down on China and Thibet. The highest range, though much more than a hundred miles distant, as the crow flies, rose as far into the sky as the Alps at forty miles, and with every glacier and chasm and spire of untrodden snow as clearly defined. Their true magnitude, therefore, was not fully apparent, because the eye refused to credit the intervening distance. But the exquisite loveliness of the shadows painted by the morning on those enormous wastes of snow, and the bold yet beautiful outlines of the topmost cones, soaring to a region of perpetual silence and death, far surpassed any distant view of the Alps or any other mountain chain I ever saw. As seen from Roorkhee the Himalayas present the appearance of three distinct ranges. The first, the Siwalik Hills, are not more than two thousand feet in height; the second, or Sub-Himalayas, rise to eight or nine thousand, while the loftiest peaks of the snowy range, visible from this point, are 25,000 feet above the sea. Far in the north-west was the Chore, an isolated peak, which is almost precisely the height of Mont Blanc, but seemed a very pigmy in comparison with the white cones beyond it.

I had a letter to Col. Cautley, the Superintendent of the Ganges Canal, and hastened to deliver it in time to share his breakfast. He was not in Roorkhee, as it happened; but I learned from the servant that there was a "sahib" living in the house, and sent the letter in to him. The "sahib" did just what I had hoped, that is, he came out and asked me in to breakfast with him—which I was but too ready to do. The letter was forwarded to Capt. Goodwyn, the next in command, and before the meal was concluded I received a kind note from that officer, offering me a room in his house.

Roorkhee has suddenly risen into note from being the head-quarters of the Engineers employed on the Ganges Canal. A large workshop is in operation, and the Government has just established a College for educating Civil Engineers. The Europeans are comparatively few, and the native town is inhabited almost entirely by the workmen employed on the Canal. It is a pleasant, healthy place, scattered over a rising ground, overlooking the Valley of the Ganges, and enjoys one of the finest prospects of the Himalayas to be had from any part of the plains. A very handsome Gothic Church (designed by Mr. Price, the gentleman to whom I was indebted for a breakfast) had been recently erected, and this, with the open, turfy common in front of the town, and the absence of tropical trees, reminded me strongly of England.

The Ganges Canal is one of the grandest undertakings of the present day. It has been constructed under the direction and at the expense of the Government, mainly for the purpose of irrigating the level, fertile tracts between the Ganges and Jumna, but also to afford the means of transporting the productions of the country to the head of navigation on the former river, at Cawnpore. The labor of more than ten years had been expended on it at the time of my visit, and four or five years more were considered necessary to complete it.* It will be eighty feet wide, varying in depth according to the season, but probably averaging eight feet, and, including its numerous branches, will have an extent of eight hundred miles! It taps the Ganges at Hurdwar (eighteen miles to the north-west of Roorkh), and returns to it again at Cawnpor, a distance of more than four hundred miles. The total cost, when completed, will not fall much short of £2,000,000, but it is expected to yield a return of £500,000 annually. This calculation is based on the success of the East and West Jumna Canals, which are comparatively on a small scale. The former of those was finished in 1825, since when it has paid all the expense of construction, together with an annual interest of 5

* The water was let into the main trunk of the Ganges Canal in the summer of 1854, and the work, so far as it has gone into operation, is perfectly successful.

per cent thereupon, and £320,000 clear profit. The latter, finished a few years since, has paid the cost and interest, with £30,000 profit.

The use of the water for irrigation is not obligatory upon the inhabitants, but they are generally quite willing to avail themselves of it. There are three ways in which it is furnished to them: First, by villages or companies of cultivators contracting for as much as they want; secondly, by a fixed rate per acre, according to the kind of grain, rice being the most expensive and cotton the cheapest; and thirdly, by renting an outlet of a certain fixed dimension, at so much per year Along the Jumna Canals the people do not wait, as formerly, to see whether the crops will be likely to succeed without irrigation, but employ it in all seasons, and are thereby assured of a constant return for their labor. The Ganges Canal will be of vast importance in increasing the amount of grain produced in Hindostan, the design of the Government being to *render famine impossible.* It is to be hoped that such a dreadful spectacle as the famine of 1838, when hundreds of thousands perished from want, will never again be witnessed in India. That such things have happened is the natural result of the tenure by which land is held and cultivated. The Government is the proprietor, and the *zemindars*, or tenants pay 75 per cent. of the assessed value of the products. The land is sub-let by the zemindars to the *ryots*, or laborers, and these, the poor and ignorant millions of India, of course gain little or nothing beyond a bare subsistence. If the crops fail, they have nothing at all. The Ganges Canal will therefore, to a certain extent, prevent famine, by assuring perennial crops. It will enrich the Government, because, in addition to the sale of the water, it will increase the rent of the lands as they become more productive, but it will very slightly mitigate the condition of the ryots.

The greatest modern work in India is the Canal Aqueduct over the Selanee River, at Roorkhee. It is entirely constructed of brick, and, including the abutments, is about a quarter of a mile in length, by a hundred and eighty feet in breadth. There are sixteen arches, of about seventy feet span, and rising twenty feet above the river, the foundations of the piers being sunk twenty feet below the bed. The arches are four feet thick, in order to support the immense pressure of such a body of water. Hundreds of workmen were employed on the structure, and a small railroad had been laid down for bringing the materials. A locomotive was imported from England, but, through the neglect of the native firemen, soon became a wreck. During the short time it was in operation a great number of accidents occurred. It was found almost impossible to keep the natives off the track. Their stupidity in this respect is astonishing. If you have a hard heart you may run over as many as you like in a morning's ride, for they will assuredly not get out of your way unless you force them to it.

CHAPTER XIII.

HURDWAR AND THE GANGES.

Native Workmen at Roorkhee—Their Wages—Departure for Hurdwar—Afternoon View of the Himalayas—Peaks visible from Roorkhee—Jungle-grass—Jowalapore—Approach to the Siwalik Hills—First View of the Ganges—Ganges Canal—Prediction of the Brahmins—An Arrival—The Holy City of Hurdwar—Its Annual Fair—Appearance of the Streets—The Bazaar—A Himalayan Landscape—Travel in the Jungle—A Conflagration—The Jungle by Torch-Light—Arrival at Dehra.

Before leaving Roorkhee I paid a visit to the workshops, where I was much struck with the skill and aptness of the natives employed. The shops are instituted for the purpose of constructing the implements used on the Canal works. The machinery is driven by steam and conducted entirely by natives under European superintendence. One of the departments is devoted to the construction of mathematical instruments, which are fully equal to those of English manufacture. "The natives," to use the words of the Superintendent, "learn in one sixth of the time which an English workman would require." Their imitative talent is wonderful, but they totally lack invention. This makes them a people easily improved, as they are anxious to learn, but never knowing more than is taught them, never using their knowledge as a lamp to explore the unknown fields of science or art. These workmen are paid from four to eight rupees a month, according to their skill, but the ordinary laborers on the Canal, though hired at four ($2), do not, owing to their indolence, generally receive more than two rupees per month, out of which they find themselves. It is said that one rupee (fifty cents,) monthly, covers all their necessary expenses.

After two days at Roorkhee, I summoned the bearers to be in readiness at sunrise, the next morning. Capt. Goodwyn was kind enough to see that all the arrangements were complete, besides ordering me an early breakfast, and his amiable lady provided me with a tiffin, which I was to eat in Col. Cautley's bungalow at Hurdwar. The morning was bright and cold, and as I was borne down the bank to the Selanee River, I noticed that a light rime lay upon the grass. The bearers shivered as they waded through the chill water, though their bare legs were nearly as tough and leathery as an elephant's. I opened the palanquin so that I might look on the Himalayas, as I lay, but their cold morning gleam was not so beautiful as the warm red flush which had lain on them during the previous afternoon and evening. I had accompanied my hosts to the cricket-ground, where there was a match between the military and the civilians. The game was explained to me, and politeness required that I should take an interest in its progress; but my whole soul had gone off to the Himalayas, and I could see or think of nothing else. I was most struck with their exquisite beauty of form and coloring. The faintest pink of the sea-shell slept upon the steeps of snow, and their tremendous gulfs and chasms were filled with pale-blue shadows, so delicately pencilled that I can only compare them to the finest painting on ivory. When I reflected that each of those gentle touches of blue was a tremendous gorge, ' where darkness dwells all day ; " that each break in the harmonious flow of the outline on the sky—like the break in a cadence of music, making it sweeter for the pause—was a frightful precipice, thousands of feet in depth and inaccessible to human foot, I was overpowered by the awful sublimity of the picture But when their color grew rosy and lambent in the sunset, I could think of nothing but the divine beauty which beamed through them, and wonder whether they resembled the mountains which we shall see in the glorified landscapes of the future world.

The snowy chain visible from Roorkhee extends from Nepaul to the borders of Cashmere, and includes some of the highest peaks, though not the very highest, in the Himalayas. In front rise the Gungootree and Jumnootree, the sources of the Jumna and Ganges, about 25,000 feet high; further to the eastward, Buddhreenath, a little lower; and in the distant north-east, the summit of Nundidevi, which has an altitude of nearly 26,000. Dwalagheri, Chumalari, and a third peak which, according to recent measurements, is fully 30,000 feet above the sea, are further to the eastward. There is generally much cloud and mist upon them during the winter season, and at Roorkhee they told me there had not been so fine a view of them for two months, as on the morning of my arrival.

After crossing the Selanee River, I was carried on through a low tract, at first covered only with long jungle grass, ten feet high, but afterward studded with picturesque topes, or groves, of mango and peepul trees. Being sheltered by the Siwalik Hills, and inundated by the overflow of the Ganges, the vegetation was very luxuriant, and had more of a tropical character than upon the plains. In the dense jungles along the Ganges, about fifteen miles from Roorkhee, there is an abundance of tigers, leopards and wild elephants. The deer, antelope and wild boar are also frequent. On my way to Hurdwar I passed through Jowalapore, a queer old town which appeared to have some share in the sanctity of the neighboring city. I sat up in the palanquin to have a better view of the place and people, as I was borne through its tortuous streets. There were a number of temples and caravanserais, and the roofs of the houses were tenanted by sacred apes, whose posteriors were painted of a bright crimson color. The inhabitants looked at me with curiosity, and some of them made very respectful salaams. There was a bazaar and market in full operation, which were almost an exact counterpart of those of the smaller Egyptian towns. Among the crowd I noticed two handsome, fair-skinned Cashmerians.

The road now approached the Siwalik Hills, which were steep and covered with jungle to the summit. The gorge through which the Ganges forces its way at Hurdwar made an abrupt gap in their chain, revealing a striking view of the second or Sub-Himalayas, which now completely hid the snowy peaks. It was nearly noon by this time, and the day was warm and summer-like. The bearers threaded the shade of the mango topes, crossed the canal, passed, without entering, the town of Khunkhul, and finally set me down at Col. Cautley's bungalow, at Myapore. This is a little village about half a mile from Hurdwar, at the point where the canal leaves the Ganges. The bungalow—a thatched cottage, pleasantly embowered in trees—was comfortably furnished though untenanted. I took possession for the time; the servant set about making tea for me, and sent word for the new bearers to be ready in two hours.

Meanwhile I strolled out to see the head of the canal. In ten minutes I stood on the lofty banks of the Ganges, looking down on his clear blue stream. The gorge lay open before me; the hills rose on either hand covered with a wilderness of jungle; the white pinnacles of the temples of Hurdwar shone over the top of a belt of trees; the sacred ghauts led down to the water; but beyond all, crowning the huge blue bulk of the Sub-Himalayas, towered the snowy cone of Gungootree. It was an impressive scene. Here was the river beneath my feet; there one of his most sacred cities; and in the remote distance the snows wherein he is cradled. I went down the bank, and there, at the last gate of the Himalayas, where they let him out upon the plain of Hindostan, drank of the Holy River.

The dam across the Ganges at the head of the Canal was of course postponed until the remainder of the work should be finished, but the abutments and a regulating bridge of red sandstone were already completed. The canal was expected to take away nine tenths of the river at this place—a prospect which spread terror among the Brahmins. They declared that the goddess Gangajee had announced to them in a vision, that she would never lie quietly in any other than her accustomed bed. If the English turned her out of it she might be forced to go a few miles, but she would assuredly break loose and return. The Brahmins, therefore, predicted the total failure of the Canal. The removal of so much water will be a disadvantage to those who inhabit the banks, but Col. Cautley supposes that the loss will be supplied by springs in the river-bed.

While I was preparing to leave, a garree drove up, out of which descended a ruddy, powerful man, a lady and two fat and rosy children. The gentleman, who had charge of the operations at Mapyore, immediately addressed me in the most cordial manner. He had just brought his family down from Landowr in the Himalayas, to spend a few days, and I learned from him that the snows were fast melting. He had been five years in America, and professed himself delighted to meet a citizen of that country. I would willingly have prolonged my stay, but the bearers were waiting, so we shook hands and I was carried on to Hurdwar.

This is one of the most curious cities in India. It lies on the western bank of the Ganges, exactly in the gorge formed by the Siwalik Hills. There is but one principal street, running parallel to the water, and crossed by others so steep as to resemble staircases. Broad stone ghauts descend to the river, to allow the pilgrims facility of bathing. Between them, upon platforms of masonry of various heights, are temples to the Hindoo gods, principally to Ganeish and Shiva. The emblem of the latter divinity, the *lingam*, or symbol of the Phallic worship, is seen on all sides. Its signification, however, would never be guessed by a stranger, nor is there any thing indecent in the ceremonies with which it is worshipped. The temples are from twenty to fifty feet high—none, I think, of greater altitude—and generally built of gray sandstone. There is great similarity in their design, which is a massive square shrine, surmounted by a four-sided or circular spire, curving gradually to a point, so that the outline of each side resembles a parabola. All parts of the building are covered with grotesque but elaborate ornaménts and many of the spires are composed of a mass of smaller ones, overlapping each other like scales, so that at a distance they resemble slender pine-apples, of colossal size. There are fifty or sixty temples in and about the city, some of them being perched on the summit of cliffs rising above it. Most of them are whitewashed, and have a new and glaring appearance; but there are others, enclosed in large courtyards, which are very black and venerable, and seem to be regarded with more than usual reverence. I could see lamps burning before the idols, in the gloomy interiors, but was not allowed to enter. There is a great annual *mela*, or fair, held at Hurdwar, which is sometimes attended by a million and a half of persons. I believe there are never less than five or six hundred thousand present. The natives flock from all parts of Hindostan and Bengal, from the Deccan, the Punjàb, from Cashmere, Affghanistan, Tartary and Thibet, some as religious devotees, some as worldly tradesmen. For miles around the place it is one immense encampment, and all the races, faces, costumes, customs and languages of the East, from Persia to Siam, from Ceylon to Siberia, are represented. Buying and selling, praying and bathing, commercial fleecing and holy hair-cutting, and all kinds of religious and secular swindling, are in full operation; and Hurdwar, which is at other times a very quiet, lonely, half-deserted, out-of-the-way nook, is then a metropolis, rivalling London in its tumult. Some of the missionaries usually attend on such occasions, in the hope of snatching brands from the burning, but the fires are generally so hot that they do little more than scorch their fingers for their pains.

As I passed slowly through the streets, I was much entertained by the picturesque and filthy appearance of the town Its holiness was apparent at a glance. It reminded me of one of those naked *fakeers*, covered with dirt and ashes, who by gazing steadfastly upon their navels, attain the beatitude of saints. The streets were narrow, very dirty and enclosed by high black houses. Blacker and more dirty were the temples. On the low, thatched verandahs in front of the shops, sat groups of sacred monkeys, with painted posteriors, like those of Jowalapore. They were silent and contemplative, but the sacred bulls, who blocked up the streets below them, exhibited a cool impudence, which nothing but a human being could surpass. The inhabitants were all engaged in plaiting bamboo splits into baskets. I could not imagine what all this basket-making was intended for, until I reflected that the time of the Fair was approaching, and that the Brahmins would need them as depositories for their spoils. Another part of the Bazaar was entirely filled with a display of beads; a still larger department was devoted to the sale of idols, hundreds of whom squatted cross-legged on both sides, staring at me with marvellously good-humored faces. Ganeish looked so comical with his elephant's ears and trunk that I felt tempted to give the latter member a tweak. But in the remaining portion of the bazaar was stowed nothing but assafœtida, which is brought over from Thibet. It must have been of good quality, for the fragrance was overpowering My bearers hurried through, crying out, as they had done since entering the town: "Make way for the Maharajah!"

Passing around the hill, the road began to descend, and a superb view of the Dehra Dhoon—a large valley enclosed between the Siwalik Hills and the Sub-Himalayas—presented itself to my view. Before me lay the Ganges, its waters glittering in the sun, as it spread them out in the valley, after forcing a pass through a deep, dark gap in the mountains before me. These mountains, the Sub-Himalayas, stretched far to the west, point lessening and fading beyond point, till the magnificent perspective of the Dhoon was closed by the distant Chore, the twin brother of Mont Blanc. Snow sparkled on all the summits, though the main range was quite out of view. On my left the rich, woody undulations of the Siwalik Hills swept into the distance, and the great valley below, as far as my eye could reach, appeared to be a boundless forest. I was now fairly within the Himalayas, and this view gave a splendid promise of the scenery which they infold.

The jungle grew more dense as we advanced, and the signs of habitation less and less frequent. The forests were the finest I had seen in India, composed principally of saul trees, with clusters of bamboo in the hollows. In some places they were so laced together with vines, which had in turn become trees, that their recesses were almost impenetrable. Hundreds of bright-green parrots chattered on the boughs, and flowers of brilliant colors gleamed in the foliage. My bearers trotted rapidly through these beautiful solitudes, for tigers are plentiful, and the carcass of a cow, covered with vultures, which lay near the road, hinted of them. There were at least fifty huge birds, shrieking and fighting for the morsels which remained, and some of them, who were already gorged, could with great difficulty get out of the way of my men. Toward evening, I was startled by a roaring sound, resembling a high wind advancing through the forest. But soon dense volumes of white smoke became visible, and occasionally streamers of flame shot above the tree-tops. A turn in the road discovered an open tract at the foot of the hills, covered with tall jungle-grass, which the natives had set on fire. The grass was very thick, and from eight to ten feet high, so that the conflagration was on a grand scale. The flames, of a brilliant scarlet color, pressed along the slope with the fury of a charging battalion, and their deep roar, with the incessant snapping and crackling of the grass, made a noise truly awful. I was strongly reminded of my unlucky attempt at burning out lions, on the White Nile, a year previous. The fire had just leaped over the road, and my bearers passed in safety.

We were obliged to cross several spurs of the Siwalik range. The same forest still spread its thick fold over them, and the turnings of the road as it rose or descended, gave it the appearance of a labyrinth. Sunset came on as we were traversing the crest of a long ridge, whence there was a fine view over the leafy wilderness below me, and while I was borne along by the silent bearers, looking down on the darkening valley or watching the last flush fading from the Himalayan snows, I felt that there might be times when palanquin travelling was agreeable. I was a little startled, on being carried into a gloomy glen, to see a dozen men burst out of the thickets, but it appeared that they were travelers, who had taken a nearer path, known only to themselves.

When it grew dark, the mussalchee lit his torch and walked beside the palanquin, waving the light to and fro, that the bearers might see where to put their feet. The red glow illuminated, with splendid effect, the masses of foliage on either hand, and I lay watching it for hour after hour, till I fell from reverie into sleep. I was awakened once when the bearers were changed, and a second time, when, two hours after midnight they set me down at the hotel in Dehra.

CHAPTER XIV.

THE HIMALAYAS.

Reception by Mr. Keene—We start for the Himalayas—The Dehra-Dhoon—Morning View of the Sub-Himalayas—Leopards—Rajpore—Wilson, the "Ranger of the Himalayas"—Climbing the Mountain—Change of Seasons—The Summit of the Ridge—Village of Landowr—Snow-Drifts—The Pole and the Equator—Rev. Mr. Woodside—Mast-Head of the Sub-Himalayas—View of the Snowy Peaks—Grand Asiatic Tradition—Peculiar Structure of the Himalayan Ranges—Scenery of the Main Chain—The Paharrees—Polyandry—The Peaks at Sunset—The Plain of Hindostan—A Cloudy Deluge.

On visiting Mr. Keene, the Deputy Magistrate of Dehra, the morning after my arrival, I was at once installed as an inmate of his house during my stay, and invited to accompany him to Mussooree and Landowr, on the following day. The invitation chimed so thoroughly with my own plans, that I accepted it, together with his hospitality. Mr. Keene is one of the few persons in the East India Company's Service, who have devoted their leisure to literary pursuits. He is one of the main props of *Saunders' Magazine*, a very creditable monthly periodical, published at Delhi; and I do not betray a secret, when I state that he is also the author of the frequent poems signed "H. G. K.," which appear in *Blackwood.*

We rose early the next morning, and after a cup of tea, set off in Mr. K.'s buggy for Rajpore, at the foot of the mountains. The town of Dehra is situated near the centre of the Dhoon, or Valley, of the same name, which is a tract about seventy miles in length by fifteen in breadth, between the Siwalik Hills and the Sub-Himalayas, and extending from the Ganges to the Jumna. Protected alike from the hot winds of the plains, and the cold blasts of the hills, it is one of the most fertile regions in India, and one of the most beautiful which I saw. From Dehra, the whole extent of the magnificent valley is visible. The curves of the Himalayan range fill up its vistas, on either hand, with views of the loftier summits, and thus it appears completely shut out from the world. The vegetation is much more luxuriant than upon the plains, and owing to its sheltered position, most kinds of tropical fruits thrive well, although it lies between 30° and 31° N.

The morning was mild and cloudless, the road excellent, and we rattled along merrily between clumps of bamboo and groves of mango-trees, occasionally looking up to the snows that sparkled six thousand feet above us. The houses on the very summit of the mountain were distinctly visible The vast sides and shoulders of the range were scantily clothed with jungle, through which showed the dark-red hue of the soil, softened to a lurid purple by distance. Toward their bases the jungle was dense and green, except where the soil had been cleared and formed into terraces for cultivation. The surface of the valley presented a charming alternation of grain-fields, groups of immense mango trees, and patches of woodland, resembling, in its general aspect the Midland Counties of England. Mr. Keene pointed out a hill to the eastward, as the scene of a bloody battle during the war with the Goorkhas, or hill-tribes, and the spot where Gen. Gillespie fell. The fortress, which formerly crowned the hill, has been entirely demolished. The jungles in the valley abound with wild beasts. Only two weeks before, a lady who was taking an afternoon ride to Rajpore, saw two full-grown leopards lying in a field, not more than fifty yards from the road. The beasts gazed at her very complacently, as well-bred leopards might, but attempted no familiarities.

In an hour we reached Rajpore, which sits upon the lowest step, or foundation stone of the mountain. On some fine wooded knolls to the west of it there are several handsome bungalows, the summer residences of invalided or furloughed officers. There is also a little hotel, whither we drove, in order to hire ponies for the climb of seven miles to Landowr. A tall, heavy-featured weather-beaten gentleman of forty-five or fifty, was standing in the verandah. He had a red Scotch complexion, gray eyes, and yellow hair on the sides of his head, the crown being bald. There was something indolent and phelgmatic in his air, and I was greatly surprised when Mr. Keene pointed him out to me as Wilson, the noted "Ranger of the Himalayas," as he is generally called. We entered into conversation with him at once. He had come down from Landowr that morning on his way to Dehra, but would be back in the hills in a few days. He has lived almost exclusively among the upper ranges of the Himalayas for more than ten years, and know every pass (so he informed me), as far as Cashmere. His wanderings have extended as far as Ladak, or Leh, in Thibet, the capital of a state which is at present tributary to Goolāl

Singh, the Rajah of Cashmere. He said there was no difficulty in reaching either Cashmere or Ladak, and if I had had two months more—but one cannot see every thing. Wilson has much influence over the *pahàrrees*, or mountaineers, and his services are in great request during the summer, when sporting tours are made in the upper Himalayas. In addition to the ibex, bear, and mountain sheep, there are abundance of superb golden pheasants and other magnificent specimens of the feathered race, the skins of which he preserves, and which, when sent to Calcutta for sale, produce him a handsome return.

I hired a pony for two rupees, and we immediately set out for Landowr. Mr. Keene, being the Deputy Magistrate of the Dhoon, was escorted through the town by the local police, who took their departure with profound salaams. The road, which was merely a narrow path for horses, notched along the abrupt side of a spur of the mountain, commanded a striking view of a deep gorge on the right hand, the sides of which were terraced and covered with a luxuriant crop of wheat. As we ascended further, the Dhoon extended below us, checkered with forests and fields, while the white fronts of houses dotted its verdurous map. I was reminded of the view from Catskill Mountain-House, but missed the clearness and brilliancy of our American atmosphere. Here there was a film of blue vapor on the landscape, like a crape over my eyes, through which the more distant objects glimmered in indistinct and uncertain forms. The further we climbed, the dimmer became the scene, until there remained but a vapory chaos—the mere ghost of a world below us, out of which rose the summits of the Siwalik Hills as if upheaved by the subsidence of the agitated elements.

The road was excessively steep, and only wide enough to admit of two horsemen passing each other. In many places it overhung descents which were so nearly precipitous that a stone flung out would strike the earth many hundreds of feet below. The jungle became more scanty, and the wild flowers ceased. Patches of snow appeared on the heights on either side, and gushes of a cold wind, sweeping through gaps in the range, now and then blew in our faces. At length we reached the top of a ridge, an outlying spur from the summit upon which Landowr is perched. The road became more level, and when skirting the tremendous gulf separating the branches of the range, was protected by a balustrade. A gateway cut in the rock admitted us to the north side of the ridge we had ascended, and the passage through it introduced us to a scenery of such a different character, that it might well be called the Gate of the Seasons. Behind us the sun shone warm, the grass was green and a few blossoms still kept their places on the trees; but around and before us were beds of snow, bare, brown patches of sward, and leafless boughs. Only the oak —an evergreen variety, with a leaf resembling the beech—and the rhododendron, retained their foliage. The height before us was sprinkled with one-story bungalows, which clung to such narrow ledges of the mountain over such abrupt and frightful gulfs, that they seemed to have been dropped and lodged there. The precipitous village and the houses scattered along the irregular summit is called Landowr. The place has an extent of a mile and a half, and half the inhabitants, at least during the summer, are English. On one of the highest points, is a large military hospital. About two miles to the

West of Landowr is Mussooree, which is scattered in like manner, over a ridge nearly a thousand feet lower.

The street of the native village through which we passed was covered with snow to the depth of three feet, and owing to the constant thaw which was going on, our horses had some difficulty in getting through. The roofs were in many places broken by the weight of snow which had fallen upon them. However we reached Mr. Keene's bungalow without accident, where his tenant, Lieut. B., anticipated our wishes by ordering tiffin to be got ready. I had now reached the summit of the second range of the Himalayas, 8,000 feet above the sea. The cottage where we were quartered was perched on a narrow shelf, scooped out of the side of the mountain. From the balcony where I sat, I could have thrown a stone upon the lowest house in the place. For the first time in several weeks, the thermometer was above freezing-point, and the snows with which the roof was laden poured in a shower from the eaves. Around me the heights were bleak and white and wintry, but down the gorge below me—far down in its warm bed—I could see the evergreen vegetation of the Tropics. Buried to the knees in a snow-drift, I looked upon a palm-tree, and could almost smell the blossoms of the orange-bowers in a valley where frost never fell. It was like sitting at the North Pole, and looking down on the Equator.

I had a letter to Mr. Woodside, an American Missionary who lived upon the highest point of Landowr, and Mr. Keene and I visited him during the afternoon. We had still half a mile to climb before reaching the summit of the mountain, which I found to be a sharp, serrated crest, not more than ten yards in breadth. Mr. Woodside's house commands a view of both sides of the Sub-Himalayas; and a natura mound beside it has been ascertained, by measurement, to be the loftiest spot in this part of the range. The house and mound were purchased by a benevolent Philadelphian, as a sanitarium for Missionaries—a thing much needed by that class. I suggested to Mr. Woodside the propriety of planting a tall flagstaff on the mound, and running up the national colors on certain anniversaries.

The view from this point best repaid me for my journey to the hills. The mound on which we stood was conical, and only twenty feet in diameter at the summit. The sides of the mountain fell away so suddenly that it had the effect of a tower, or of looking from the mast-head of a vessel. In fact, it might be called the "main truck" of the Sub-Himalayas. The sharp comb, or ridge, of which it is the crowning point, has a direction of north-west to south-east (parallel to the great Himalayan range), dividing the panorama into two hemispheres, of very different character. To the north, I looked into the wild heart of the Himalayas—a wilderness of barren peaks, a vast jumble of red mountains, divided by tremendous clefts and ravines, of that dark indigo hue, which you sometimes see on the edge of a thunder-cloud —but in the back-ground, towering far, far above them, rose the mighty pinnacles of the Gungootree, the Jumnootre, the Budreenath, and the Kylâs, the heaven of Indra, where the Great God, Mahadeo, still sits on his throne, inaccessible to mortal foot. I was fifty miles nearer these mountains than at Roorkhee, where I first beheld them, and with the additional advantage of being mounted on a footstool, equal to one third of their height. They still stood immeasurably above me, so cold, and clear, and white, that, without knowledge to the contrary, I should have said that they were not more than twenty miles distant. Yet, as the crow flies, a line of *seventy* miles would scarce have reached their summits!

Though not the highest of the Himalayas, these summits form the great central group of the chain, and contain the cisterns whence spring the rivers of India, Thibet and Burmah. The snows of their southern slopes feed the Jumna and Ganges; of their northern, the Sutledj, the Indus and the Brahmapootra. Around this group cling the traditions of the Hindoo Mythology. Thence came the first parents of the race; there appeared the first land after the deluge. And upon the lofty table-lands of Central Asia, whereon those peaks look down, was probably the birth-place of the great Caucasian family, from which the Hindoos and ourselves alike are descended. Far to the north-west, where the Altay, the Hindoo Koosh (or Indian Caucasus), and the Himalayas, join their sublime ranges, there is a table-land higher than Popocatapetl, called, in the picturesque language of the Tartars, the "Roof of the World." Under the eaves of that roof, on the table-land of Pamir, if we may trust Asiatic tradition, dwelt the parents of our race. I fancied myself standing on the cone of Gungootree, and looking down upon it. The vast physical features of this part of the world are in themselves so imposing, that we are but too ready to give them the advantage of any myth which invests them with a grand human interest.

There is a peculiarity in the structure of the Himalayas,

of which I had not heard, until I visited them. At their north-western extremity, on the frontiers of Cashmere and Affghanistan, the lower or Sub-Himalayas are lofty, and so separated by deep valleys from the higher or snowy range, as almost to form a parallel chain. As we proceed eastward, however, the relative height of the two ranges gradually changes. The peaks of the Upper Himalayas increase in height, while those of the Sub-Himalayas decrease. A little to the east of the Dhoon, the Siwalik Hills cease entirely. The Sub-Himalayas gradually dwindle away toward Nepaul, becoming more narrow and broken as they approach the termination of the chain. Dwalagheri, in the main Himalayan chain, once supposed to be the highest mountain in the world, is in Nepaul. But further to the *east*, is Chumalari, which is still higher, and recent measurements have discovered that another peak, still further eastward, in the former province of Sikim, is higher than Chumalari. This regular increase of altitude in the Himalayas, as you proceed eastward, is very curious. The height of Dwalagheri is estimated at 27,000 feet; Chumalari, a little more than 28,000, and the third peak, the name of which I forget, fully 30,000 feet! The Rev. Mr. D'Aguilar, whom I saw at Roorkhee, penetrated to the glaciers of Jumnootree. He informed me that in ascending the Himalayas, the productions become not only of the temperate zone, but English in their character; the flowers, fruit and shrubs being almost identical with those of England. In the valleys, however, is found the *deodar*, or Himalayan cypress, which grows to a height of more than 200 feet. There is a temple near the source of the Ganges, but owing to the danger and difficulty of the journey, comparatively few pilgrims reach it. The air of the mountain is pure, fresh and invigorating, and the *pahar-rees* are said to be both physically and mentally superior to the inhabitants of the plains. Mr. D'Aguilar considered them as a strikingly honest and faithful race. Owing to the difficulty of procuring subsistence, and the necessity of restricting the increase of population, Polyandry has existed among them from time immemorial. The woman and her husbands live together harmoniously, and the latter contribute each an equal share to the support of the children. Among these people the saying will particularly apply: "It's a wise child that knows its own father." Another of their customs is still more singular. Their ideas of hospitality compel them to share not only their food, but their connubial right with the stranger, and no insult is so great as a refusal to accept it. While in Landowr, I saw several of them walking bare-legged through the snow, which troubled them as little as it would a horse. They were handsome, muscular fellows, with black eyes, ivory teeth and a ruddy copper complexion.

I spent the afternoon with Mr. Woodside, and at sunset went again upon the mound, to witness the illumination of the Himalayas. Although there were clouds in the sky, the range was entirely unobscured, and the roseate glare of its enormous fields of snow, shooting into flame-shaped pinnacles, seemed lighted up by the conflagration of a world. It was a spectacle of surpassing glory, but so brief, that I soon los the sense of its reality.

I was called, however, to witness another remarkable phenomenon. Turning from the fading hills, I looked to the south. The Dehra Dhoon was buried under a sea of snow white clouds, which rolled and surged against each other sinking and rising, like the billows of an agitated sea. Where we stood, the air was pure and serene; but far away, over that cloudy deluge—which soon tossed its waves above the peaks of the Siwalik Hills—more than a hundred miles away —and high in air, apparently, ran a faint blue horizon-line, like that of the sea. It was the great plain of Hindostan, but so distant that the delusion was perfect. The great white billows rose, and rose, whirling and tossing as they poured into the clefts of the hills, till presently we stood as on a little island in the midst of a raging sea. Still they rose, disclosing enormous hollows between their piled masses; cliffs, as of wool, toppled over the cavities; avalanches slid from the summits of the ridges and slowly fell into the depths; and as I looked away for many a league over the cloudy world, there was motion every where, but not a sound. The silence was awful, and as the vast mass arose, I felt an involuntary alarm, lest we should be overwhelmed. But to our very feet the deluge came, and there rested. Its spray broke against the little pinnacle whereon we stood, but the billows kept their place. It was as if a voice had said: "Thus far shalt thou come, and no further: and here shall thy proud waves be stayed."

CHAPTER XV.

SCENES IN THE DEHRA DHOON

Return to Dehra—The Dhoon—System of Taxation—The Tea-Culture in India—Tea-Garden at Kaologir—Progress by Force—Ride to the Robber's Cave—A Sikh Temple—A Sunny Picture—Sikh Minstrelsy—Rajah Loll Singh—English Masters and Native Servants—Preparations for Departure.

We returned from Landowr on Wednesday afternoon, the 2d of February. Lieut. B. urged us to remain another day, but the Himalayas (which I had gone up the mountain at sun rise to see) were half covered with clouds, the snow was melting on all sides, and the paths were almost impassable from mud and slush. There was said to be a specimen of the *yak*, or Tartar cow, at Mussooree, which I should have seen, but for three miles of sloppy road. As it was, I was glad to escape from the dreary though sublime heights of Landowr, and return to Dehra, with its groves and sunny gardens. The air was still more hazy than on the preceding day, but as we descended, the phantom valley flushed into form and color, and in an hour and a half from the time my pony tumbled down in a snow-drift, I reined him up under a palm-tree.

Dehra, as I have already stated, is one of the loveliest spots in India. Judging from the number of handsome bungalows in and around the town, the Anglo-Indians are of a similar opinion. As much of the valley is entirely given up to jungle, parts of it, which are marshy and undrained, are considered unhealthy, but a little attention would make it one of the healthiest, as it is one of the most fertile, districts in Northern India. A small irrigating canal has been carried through the central part, but it does not even pay the expenses, so feeble and defective is the agriculture of the Dhoon. There are reckoned, within its limits, a hundred villages, but the population must be very scanty, since the revenue obtained by Government only amounts to 22,000 rupees. When I state that the tax imposed upon the *zemindars*, who hold the land as Government tenants, amounts to 75 per cent. of the estimated value of the products, it will be seen how trifling the actual yield must be. The *ryots*, or peasants, to whom the land is sub-let by the zemindars, are only able to eke out a bare subsistence, so that here, where thousands of acres of the best land are lying waste, the greater part of the inhabitants are in a state of extreme poverty. This system, by which the East India Company is the virtual proprietor of all the territory under its exclusive control, must necessarily be a check to the prosperity of India and the civilization of its people; but when I expressed such an opinion to the English residents, I was generally met by the remark (the same often used by Americans, apologetic of Slavery): "We did not make it—we found it so."

The introduction of the Tea Culture into India is an interesting experiment—if, indeed, it can still be considered an experiment. The Government, within the past ten years, has devoted much attention to it. All the principal varieties of the tea-plant have been imported, experimental gardens laid out, at different points in the Himalayas, from Assam to the north-western frontier of the Punjaub, and Chinese workmen procured to teach the preparation of the leaves. Mr. Fortune, whose travels in China, on his mission to effect these objects, have excited considerable notice, had been dispatched a third time to that country, to procure fresh supplies of plants and workmen. The Tea Plant was first introduced into Assam, a district north of Bengal and lying on the Brahmapootra River. A company was formed about fifteen years ago, for the cultivation and manufacture of Tea; but through ignorance and inexperience, it was for some time a losing concern. At present, however, it has so far succeeded as to produce 300,000 pounds of Tea, and to pay 10 per cent. annually to the Company. The experimental gardens in the northern and western parts of the Himalayas have been established more recently, and the natives are now beginning to take up the cultivation of the plant.

One of the gardens is at Kaologir, about three miles from Dehra, and I visited it in company with Mr. Keene. Mr. Fortune considers that a level alluvial soil, like that of the Dhoon, is not so well adapted for tea as the hilly country about Almorah and in the Punjaub, and if he be correct I did not see the plant in its greatest perfection; though I should think it difficult for any plantation to present a more flourishing appearance than parts of that at Kaologir. It consists of three hundred acres of level gound—a rich, dark loam, mixed with clay—and contains plants in every stage of growth, from the seedling to the thick, bushy shrub, six feet high. It was then the blossoming season, and the next crop of leaves would not be gathered before May. The plant bears some resemblance to the ilex, or holly, but the leaf is smaller, of a darker green, and more minutely serrated. The blossom is mostly white—in some varieties a yellowish-brown—and resembles that of the wild American blackberry. The plants were set about three feet apart, in rows four feet from each other, with small channels between, for the purpose of irrigation. Mr. Fortune, however, considers that irrigation is rather injurious than otherwise.

Mr. Thomson, the Superintendent of the plantation, assured me that the average yield of the plants, after they had reached a proper growth for plucking, might be set down at 1 cwt. per acre, though, under favorable circumstances, it could be increased to 200 lbs. At present, the Dehra and Almorah teas sell for purely fancy prices, being bought up with avidity at the annual sales, at from two to three rupees a pound. Dr. Jameson, who has charge of all the Tea plantations in the north-west, estimates that when the culture shall have become general, Tea can be profitably produced at six annas (18 cents) the pound. The zemindars, who are with difficulty brought to accept of the slightest innovation, are very reluctant to undertake the culture, although the Government not only releases them from all tax upon land planted with Tea shrubs, but binds itself to buy from them, at a remunerative price, all the Tea they can produce. It is now proposed to *command* every zemindar who leases property beyond a certain number of acres, to cultivate five acres of the Tea plant Those who know the natives best say that this is the only way in which Tea Culture can be rapidly extended; the natives being perfectly willing to obey any commands, although they may be immovable to all persuasion. I have been told that when urged to introduce certain improvements into their system of agriculture, they often answer: "If you really want us to do so, why don't you give us the *hookm* (command)?" There would seem to be some reason, then, in such a despotic mode of introducing the Tea Culture. I drank of both the Dehra and Almorah Teas, which were deliciously pure and fragrant, though much stronger than the adulterated Teas exported from China.

The garden at Kaologir was kept in fine order, the fields being perfectly clean and free from weeds, and separated from each other by hedges of Persian roses, of the deepest crimson dye and intensest summer perfume. We passed through the plantation, and struck across an open tract of country toward the tents of Mr. Thornhill, the Magistrate of the Dhoon. He received us hospitably under the shade of his patriarchal mango-trees, and lent us two horses, to take us to the Robber's Cave, which was three or four miles distant, among the hills at the base of the Himalayas. We had a charming ride through alternate groves, jungles and grain-fields. The great mountains before us lay warm and red in the afternoon sun, and away to the west, like a soft, white cloud, the Chore lifted his snowy head. The peasants were at work in the fields, and boys, clad only in the *dhotee*, or breech-cloth, tended the cows as they browsed along the edges of the jungle.

Finally the path brought us to the brink of a deep sunken glen, the sides of which were walls of magnificent foliage. It extended before us for nearly a mile, narrowing as it approached the hills, two of which overhung and finally blocked it up. Our horses scrambled down with some difficulty, and we followed the course of a clear mountain stream, which issued from the further extremity. As the glen grew narrower, its sides became more steep and lofty, yet so thoroughly draped with shrubs and pendant vines, that scarcely a particle of soil was visible. The foliage rolled down in gorgeous masses, on either hand, dipping its skirts in the clear, bright stream, that flowed at the bottom. But the glen at length became a ravine, the ravine a crevice, and the hills closed, leaving only a split, as of an earthquake, for the passage of the water. A cold wind blew continually from the opening. We rode within it a short distance to notice the splendor of the leafy, sunlit glen, seen through the black jaws of the gloomy passage. The rock is a coarse conglomerate of limestone, whence I suspect that the "Cave," as it is called, is a natural grotto, and not a crevice produced by an earthquake, as some persons suppose. By wading in the bed of the stream, you can pass entirely through the hill, a distance of nearly a mile, emerging into a similar glen on the opposite side. I was struck with the resemblance of the place to the famous "Annathal," near Eisenach, in Germany.

One morning I made a visit to a Sikh temple, of great sanctity, which stands at the further end of the town. It is connected with the tomb of a Gooroo, or Saint, and is about two hundred years old. It is enclosed in a spacious court, and appears to have been built on the site of some older edifice, as a portion of the gateway is evidently of much earlier date than the tomb. One of the buildings, now used as a habitation, has a portico of very grotesque design, covered with paintings representing events in the Saint's life, and, singularly enough portraits of some of the Hindoo gods. The religion of the Sikhs is a compromise between Islam and Hindooism, rejecting all the minor divinities of the latter and accepting, in their stead, the One God of the Moslems, without the full recognition of Mahomet as his Prophet. They abjure caste, but, probably out of regard for the feelings of their converts, abstain from eating cow's flesh. Their moral code is very similar to that of the Hindoos and Moslems. One of the pictures in the portico illustrates a miracle which happened to the Sikh Saint, during a visit which he made to Mecca. Being directed by the Moslem priests to sleep with his feet to the Kaaba, he refused, and lay down with his head towards it, but during the night it turned around in a marvellous manner, and presented itself to his feet!

A second gateway admitted us into a garden, containing the tomb of the Saint, and the tombs of his four wives. The former stands in the centre, the latter in the four corners of a paved court, and are connected with each other by narrow stone causeways. The Saint's tomb is covered with a lofty dome, and surrounded with a cloister, richly enamelled and painted, in the style of the Mogul tombs about Agra and Delhi. It has no pretensions to architectural beauty, but was a most picturesque object, with its white dome, its deep shadowy arches, and the brilliancy of its colors half touched with sunshine, half buried in the shade of two massive peepul trees. Over the corner of the platform rose the stems of the palm and Italian cypress, and beyond the garden-wall appeared the tufted tops of some clumps of bamboos. It was a picture ready for the sun-steeped pencil of Cropsey.

But after we had passed around to the front, another picture, not less beautiful, was speedily formed. A blind Sikh fakeer, who had pilgrimed his way thither from the Punjaub, lay in the sun, half-propped against one of the pillars with a *sitar*, or Indian violin, in his hand. We asked him to play for us, whereupon he slowly tuned the strings, took up a short bow, and began playing one of those passionate melodies of love and languishment, which you only hear in a southern clime. The body of the violin was of wood, curved and ribbed so as to resemble a crooked gourd, or a segment of a fossil ammonite. It had a short neck, and four strings of catgut, under which were eight very slender wires, out of the reach of the bow, but tuned so as to give out a spontaneous accord to the notes produced upon the strings. The tones were like those of an ordinary violin, but very pure, sweet and ringing. I should think the instrument capable, in the hands of a master, of producing the most exquisite musical effects. In the Sikh's hands, it spoke truly the language of Southern love, now passionate, now imploring, but falling always into the same melting cadences, which were too beautiful to be monotonous. He sang, like the Arabs, in a succession of musical cries. Around him were Sikh priests and a knot of half-naked boys, some basking in the full glare of the sun, some seated under the arches of the tomb. They were all necessary parts of the picture Would the music have had the same meaning, if the Sikh had been seated under a pine, on the Catskill?—No; that same pine is not more different from the palm which I saw while listening to the song, than is Man, in the North, from Man, in the South.

On our return home we called at the house of the Rajah Loll Singh, a Sikh Chieftain, to whom the English are indebted in a great measure for the conquest of the Punjaub But, having been treacherous to his countrymen in the first place, he was afterward accused of meditating treachery to the English, and had only recently been released from temporary imprisonment at Agra. He had a pension of 1,000 upees a month from the Government, with which he rented a handsome bungalow, and was living in considerable style He had a great passion for dogs, and was something of a *shikarree*, or sportsman. The guards at his residence presented arms as we rode up, and we were soon afterwards received by the Rajah himself. Loll Singh means "Red Lion," and the name well suited his stout, muscular figure, heavy beard and ruddy face. He was richly dressed in a garment of figured silk, with a Cashmere shawl around his waist, and a turban of silk and gold. Rings of gold wire, upon which pearls were strung, hung from his ears to his shoulders. His eye was large, dark and lustrous, and his smile gave an agreeable expression to a face that would otherwise have been stern and gloomy. As he spoke no English, my conversation with him was confined to the usual greetings, and some expressions of admiration respecting a favorite spaniel, which he called "Venus." He spent the same evening at Mr. Keene's, appearing in a very rich and elegant native costume, with an aigrette of large diamonds and emeralds attached to his throat.

I was much amused by noticing the opinions of different English residents, respecting their native servants. Som praised their honesty and fidelity in high terms; others denounced them as liars and pilferers. Some trusted them implicitly with their keys, while others kept their cupboards and closets carefully locked. Nearly all seemed to agree however, that one can never wholly depend on their truthfulness. There are laws prohibiting the master from beating his servants, and indeed blows are of no effect. The punishment now adopted, is to fine them, which has been found very efficacious. They care little for being reproved, if in their own language, but are greatly annoyed by the use of English terms, which they do not understand. Thus, to address a man as: "You wicked rectangle!" "You specimen of comparative anatomy!" &c., would be a much greater indignity than the use of the vilest epithets, in Hindostanee.

After having enjoyed Mr. Keene's hospitality for five days, I ordered my bearers to be ready on Saturday for the return to Meerut. The day, however, brought a thunder-storm and rain in torrents, obliging me to postpone my departure until the following morning. Rajah Loll Singh offered me his elephant, for the ride through the Siwalik Hills, and as my kind host proposed to take me across the Dhoon in his buggy, I sent the palanquin and bearers on in advance, to await me at Mohun, on the other side of the pass

CHAPTER XVI

JOURNEY TO MEERUT AND CAWNPORE.

Ride to Shahpore—The Rajah's Elephant—The Pass of the Siwalik Hills—I Resume the Palanquin—The Large Punch-House—Saharunpore—The American Mission—The Botanic Garden—A Dreary Journey—Travellers—Salutations—Return to Meerut—A Theft—Journey over the Plains—Scenery of the Road—The Pollution of Touch—Fractious Horses—Arrival at Cawnpore—Capt. Riddell—The English Cantonments.

I LEFT Mr. Keene's pleasant residence at Dehra on Sunday morning, the 6th. The thunder-storm had passed away, the sky was blue and vaporless, the verdure of the beautiful valley freshened by the rain, and the heights of the Sub-Himalayas were capped with new-fallen snow. My host and I took a hasty breakfast, and then set off for Shahpore in his buggy. The distance was nine miles, the road muddy, full of deep pools left by the rain, and ascending as we approached the hills, so that we made but slow progress. From the mouth of the pass I turned to take a last view of the lovely valley. Just within the opening is Shahpore, a native hamlet, consisting of about a dozen bamboo huts. Mr. Keene was here met by one of the native police, who engaged to send a cheprassee with me to Mohun, for the purpose of seeing that my bearers were ready.

The Rajah had kept his promise, and his big she-elephant had already arrived. She knelt at the keeper's command, and a small ladder was placed against her side, that I might climb upon the pad, as I had been unable to borrow a howdah. I had a package of bread and cold roast-beef, to serve me as a tiffin, but was careful to conceal it from the driver, otherwise himself and the elephant, with all her trappings, must have undergone purification on account of the unclean flesh. I took a reluctant leave of Mr Keene, seated myself astride on the pad, with the driver before me, on the elephant's neck, and we moved off. The driver was a Sikh, in a clean white and scarlet dress, and a narrow handkerchief bound around his head. His long, well-combed hair was anointed with butter, and, as his head was just under my nose, I was continually regaled with the unctuous odors. He carried a short iron spike, with which he occasionally punched the elephant's head, causing her to snort and throw up her trunk, as she quickened her pace. I found the motion very like that of a large dromedary, and by no means unpleasant or fatiguing. Though walking, she went at the rate of about five miles an hour. I noticed that the driver frequently spoke to her, in a quiet, conversational tone, making remarks about the roads and advising her how to proceed—all of which she seemed to understand perfectly, and obeyed without hesitation.

After leaving Shahpore, the road ascended through a wild gorge of about half a mile, where it reached the dividing ridge and thence descended into a winding glen, which showed traces of having been worn through the hills by the action of water Our path followed the bed of the stream for the distance of eight miles, where the pass opens upon the great plain. The scenery is very wild and picturesque, the hills being covered to their very summits with jungle, the abode of the tiger and wild elephant. None of the peaks are more than 1,000 or 1,200 feet above the bottom of the glen, yet in their forms they have a striking similarity to the great Himalayan range. They are sharp and conical, frequently with a perpendicular front, like a bisected cone, and are divided by deep and abrupt chasms. I was quite charmed with the succession of landscapes which the windings of the pass brought to view, and nothing was wanting to complete my satisfaction but the sight of a tiger. The jungle was filled with parrots, a bird with plumage blue as a turquoise, and flocks of wild peacocks. The plumage of the latter bird is much more brilliant than that of the domesticated fowl, although the body is smaller. Near the entrance of the pass, a large congregation of monkeys, each seated on a huge boulder left by the floods, gravely watched me as I passed.

At Mohun I found my palanquin standing in front of the Police office, which was a bamboo hut. The cheprassees were very obsequious in their offers of service, and immediately called together my bearers. I sent back the elephant, seated myself cross-legged in the palanquin, and made a very fair tiffin out of the prohibited cow's-flesh and bread. Saharunpore was twenty-nine miles distant, and it was already noon. I therefore urged on the bearers, in the hope of arriving before dark. The plain was very monotonous, swept by cold winds from the hills, and appeared like a desert, by contrast with the luxuriant Dhoon. The sun went down, and I was still stretched in the tiresome palanquin, but about dusk the mussalchee (torch-bearer) came and asked where they should take me. I supposed there was a hotel in Saharunpore, and answered; "to the *punch ghur*" (punch-house or hotel). "Which one?" he again asked. At a venture, I answered: "the *burra* (large) punch-ghur." Away they went, and in a quarter of an hour, the palanquin was set down. "Here is the punch-house," said the mussalchee. I crept out, and found myself at the door of the Station Church! There happened, however, to be some natives passing through the enclosure, who directed me to the dawk bungalow, as there was no hotel. I called on the Rev. Mr. Campbell, an American Missionary, in the course of the evening, and he at once quartered me in his house.

As my bearers were engaged to start for Meerut the next morning, my kind host arose before sunrise and took me in his buggy to see something of the place. The cantonments are scattered over a wide space, and have not the comfortable air of those at Meerut. The lanes are lined with the *casurena* or Australian Pine, a lofty, ragged looking tree, with very long and slender fibres, which gives the place the air of an English or German country town. The native city has a population of about 80,000 inhabitants, and appeared to be an industrious and flourishing place. The American Mission at Saharunpore is supported by the Presbyterian Board. The Missionaries have erected a handsome church, two spacious dwelling-houses, and a school house, all within the same enclosure, besides an agency in the native town for the distribution of books, and the dis cussion of religious matters with any of the natives who choose to come forward. Mr. Campbell was sanguine as to the ultimate success of Missions in India. Their schools of education (embracing also religious instruction) are certainly doing much to enlighten the race; but so far as I could learn, very few scholars change their faith, though educated as Christians. They look upon the Christian Doctrine very much as we look upon the Greek Mythology. They are interested in it, they admire portions of it, yet still go on worshipping the lingam, and keeping up the distinctions of caste. I have no doubt that *caste* is at the bottom of all this, and that many who are convinced in their own hearts of the truth of Christianity, dare not avow it, on account of the ban of excommunication from their friends and kindred, which would immediately follow.

Mr. Campbell took me to the Botanic Garden, where I had the pleasure of meeting Dr. Jameson, who has charge of the Tea Culture in the north-west. The Garden is one of the finest in India. It is laid out with great taste, and contains nearly all the indigenous trees and plants, besides many exotics. I there saw, for the first time, a cinnamon tree, the large glossy leaves of which were redolent of its spicy blood. The cinnamon is brother to our native sassafras. It is of so refined and dainty a nature, that there are but few parts of the world where it will grow.

I left Saharunpore at ten o'clock, congratulating myself, as I entered my palanquin, that it was the last journey I should make in such a disagreeable vehicle. It was a veiled, cool and dreary day; the plains had even a wintry look, and nothing could be more monotonous. I was heartily sick of the journey before night. The Himalayas were so obscured that nothing but a large leaden-colored mass was to be seen on the horizon. The road was crowded with people among whom were several Englishmen in their palanquins, on their way up to the hills. Numbers of native women also passed, some in the *hackree*, or bullock-cart, and others borne in a *dhoolie*, a rude sort of palanquin made of bamboo, and covered with a cotton cloth. These are the "ferocious Dhoolies," who, according to Sheridan, in one of his Parliamentary speeches, "carried off the unfortunate wounded" from the field of battle—the orator, ignorant of Hindostanee, supposing that the "dhoolies" were a tribe of savage people.

At dusk I reached a station where the bearers were not on hand, but such vigorous search was made for them that I was not detained more than half an hour. The native salutation in these parts is "Ram, Ram!" and the answer the same—as if one should say, in English, "God, God!" instead of "Good morning." I was no longer addressed as "Protector of the Poor," but received the Persian title of *Khodawend*, which signifies "My Lord." About nine o'clock I reached Mozuffernuggur, only half way to Meerut. I rolled myself in my quilted *rezaya*, closed the palanquin, except when the bearers cried out for backsheesh, and so slept, dozed, and waked alternately through the long, chilly night. The first streak of dawn showed me the buildings of Sirdhana (the former residence of the famous Begum Somroo), on the right, and just as the sun rose the shivering bearers set me down at the hotel in Meerut.

I visited the unwashed individual of whom I spoke in a

former chapter, returned him his palanquin, and then engaged a garree to Cawnpore. The distance was 273 miles, and the cost of a comfortable garree, with relays of horses, about $16. In order to rest, and to allow time for the necessary preparations to be made, I did not leave until evening—a delay which enabled the native servants at the hotel to steal from me a handsome box of Cashmere manufacture—the present of a friend—containing several beautiful Delhi miniatures. I did not discover the loss until reaching Cawnpore, and was the more annoyed at it, as there was then no chance of replacing the miniatures.

The night of leaving Meerut, I again passed Allyghur, much to my regret, for I desired to see the famous pillar of Coel. Morning dawned on the plains of Hindostan. There is almost as little variety in the aspect of these immense plains as in that of the open sea. The same fields of wheat, poppies, grain and mustard alternate with the same mango or tamarind groves; the Hindoo temples by the roadside are the same dreary architectural deformities, and the villages you pass, the same collections of mud walls, thatched roofs and bamboo verandahs, tenanted by the same family of hideous fakeers, naked children, ugly women (who try to persuade you that they are beautiful, by hiding their faces), and beggars in every stage of deformity. But I noticed, as I proceeded southward, spacious caravanserais, built of burnt brick, though ruined and half deserted; richer groves of tamarind and brab palm; and the minarets and pagodas of large towns which the road skirted, but did not enter. I stopped at the bungalow of Etah for breakfast, which was ready in an hour. The bungalows on this road are much superior to those in other parts of India. The floors are carpeted, and there are mattrasses and pillows on the charpoys. The rooms have a neat, homelike air, and are truly oases in that vast wilderness—for such India still is, except where the European hand has left its trace. The day passed away like other days on the plains It was warm during the mid-hours, and the road was very dusty, in spite of the recent rains. It is a magnificent highway, and would not suffer by comparison with any in Europe. The amount of travel is so great, that from sunrise until sunset, I beheld an almost unbroken procession of natives of all descriptions, from the Affghan and Sikh, to the Goorkha of the hills and the Mahratta of the Deccan, with tattoos (as the little country ponies are called), camels, elephants, Persian steeds, buffaloes, palanquins, dhoolies, hackrees, bullock trains, and the *garrees* of luxurious travellers like myself. I can, however, feel neither the same interest in, nor respect for, the natives of India, as for the Arab races of Africa and Syria. The lower castes are too servile, too vilely the slaves of a degrading superstition, and too much given to cheating and lying. One cannot use familiarity towards them, without encouraging them to impertinence. How different from my humble companions of the Nubian Desert!

About noon I passed Mynpoorie, a civil and missionary station, though not, I believe, a military cantonment. Towards evening I stopped for an hour at another bungalow, to take dinner, and then started for Cawnpore. The driver was changed again at dusk, and as I was very thirsty, I asked him to get me a drink of water, before giving him his backsheesh. Unfortunately, I had forgotten to bring a glass with me, and the people refused to let me touch one of their brass drinking-vessels, as this would occasion them a violent scouring, if not the destruction of the article. After some search, a clay vessel of the rudest description was found, with a spout like a tea-pot, and I was allowed to drink by holding it above my head and pouring the stream down my throat. I had learned the trick of this on the Nile, or it might have been a strangling matter. To such an extent are the accursed laws of caste carried, that where the English have ruled for nearly a century, their very touch is defilement. On my trip from Bombay to Agra, being ignorant of the practical operation of these laws, I frequently helped myself to the cups of the natives, when they refused to furnish me with drink. In this way, very innocently, I occasioned the destruction of considerable crockery.

We had several fractious horses during the night, but I had learned patience by long experience, and so lay still and let the beast take his course. I think we must have been detained in one spot nearly half an hour, by a horse that *would* dash from side to side, obstinately refusing to go forward. In the traveller's book at the bungalow where I dined, I read the memorandum of a gentleman who had been left in the lurch by the driver and groom, after they had taken the bits out of the horse's mouth. He was run away with, and narrowly escaped being dashed to pieces. I feared, once or twice, that I might have the same driver and groom, and the same wicked tattoo. At last, when the Great Bear (my nocturnal dial) had passed his occultation, and I knew that the dawn would appear in half an hour, I was set down at the Cawnpore Hotel. Shortly after I arrived, a salute of nineteen guns announced the departure of the Governor of the North-West.

Looking out of the window of my room, after sunrise, I saw the Ganges flowing beneath it—not a sparkling mountain stream, as at Hurdwar, but a deep, muddy river, lined with barges. The opposite bank was a beach of white sand, which glared painfully in the sun. After a visit to a half-blood, or *Eurasian* banker, I went to the Joint Magistrate, Capt. Riddell, whom I found dispensing justice to the natives, under the shade of a huge umbrella tent, in the midst of his own umbrageous compound. He received me very courteously, and insisted on my removing to his house but as I had made arrangements to leave the same evening for Lucknow, I could only promise to spend Saturday morning with him after my return.

Cawnpore is a pleasant spot, though it contains nothing whatever to interest the traveller. It is one of the largest cantonments in the Mofussil (the Anglo-Indian term for the rural districts), and the scattering bungalows of the civil and military residents extend for five miles along the western bank of the Ganges, which is high and steep. The town is shaded with neem trees of great size. In walking past the bungalows, I noticed many elegant and well kept gardens, and was more than once greeted with the delicious odor of violets in bloom. Close beside the beds of this humble Saxon flower hung the scarlet buds of the Syrian pomegranate, or the tattered plumes of the tropical banana. The residences are large, but their enormous roofs of thatch contrast oddly with verandahs supported by Ionic pillars

The Church is a large Gothic edifice, English from turret to foundation stone, and an exile, like those who built it. A Gothic building looks as strangely among palm-trees, as an Oriental palace on the shores of Long-Island Sound.

CHAPTER XVII.

A DAY AT LUCKNOW.

Crossing the Ganges—Night-Journey to Lucknow—Arrival—A Mysterious Visitor—A Morning Stroll—The Goomtee River—An Oriental Picture—The Crowds of Lucknow—Col. Sleeman, the Resident—Drive through the City—The Constantinople Gate—Architectural Effects—The Imambarra—Gardens and Statues—Singular Decorations of the Tomb—The Chandeliers—Speculation in Oude—Hospital and Mosque—The King's New Palace—The Martinière—Royalty Plundered—The Dog and the Rose-Water—Destruction of the King's Sons—The Explosion of a Fiend—Misrule in Oude—Wealth of Lucknow—A Ride on a Royal Elephant—The Queen-Dowager's Mosque—Navigating the Streets—A Squeeze of Elephants—The Place of Execution—The Choke—Splendor and Corruption.

THE post-garree for Lucknow called for me in the evening, at the hotel. There is a good road from Cawnpore to the former place, with communication twice a day, and the distance, fifty-three miles, is usually made in seven hours. In a few minutes after leaving, we reached the bridge of boats over the Ganges, where I, as the passenger, was obliged to pay half a rupee at each end. This is a regulation peculiar to the Cawnpore bridge, distinguishing it from all others in the world. After crossing the river, we came upon a long plank causeway, extending over the sandy flats on the opposite side. The night was dark and damp, and I closed the panels on each side and disposed myself to sleep. The country between the two places is an extension of the great plain, and there is nothing on the road worth seeing.

On awaking out of a sound sleep, about three o'clock in the morning, I found the garree standing before the door of the dawk bungalow and post-office, which are both in one building. The drowsy chokedar showed me into a room with *eight* doors, containing a table and charpoy covered with a rude mattrass. I tried to fasten the doors but four of them, which led into other parts of the building, had no locks. I then half undressed and lay down on the mattrass to finish my night's rest. It might have been an hour afterward, as I was lying in that dim condition betwixt sleeping and waking, when I heard a slight noise at one of the doors—a muffled vibration, as if it had suddenly opened to a gentle pressure. Listening intently, with all my senses preternaturally sharpened, I heard a very slow and cautious footstep upon the matting, and was trying to ascertain in which direction it moved, when I distinctly felt the gentlest touch in the world, as if some one had passed his hand down my side. I sprang up in some alarm, uttering an involuntary exclamation, but could neither see nor hear any thing, nor did any thing appear until I became fatigued with watching, and fell asleep again But, from the fact that several attempts at robbery were made the same night, I have no doubt whatever that it was an artful thief in search of plunder, and probably one of those adroit scamps to be found only in India, who will take the clothes off a man's back while he is asleep, without awaking him.

After an early cup of tea, I started off on a solitary stroll, postponing my visit to Col. Sleeman, the English Resident, until after breakfast. I set out at random, but soon ascertained the direction in which the principal part of the city lay, by glimpses of its fortress walls, domes and airy minarets. I did not feel inclined, however, to plunge into its depths without a guide, but followed the course of a bazaar, which was filled with venders of fruit, vegetables and firewood. Crowds of people passed to and fro, the gaudy dresses of many of the natives betraying, as at Delhi, the presence of a native court. Some were borne in palanquins, some mounted on elephants, and a few on fine horses of Arabian blood. They looked at me with curiosity, as if an Englishman on foot was an unusual sight. On the way I passed several small mosques, which showed an odd mixture of the Saracenic and Hindoo styles, a hybrid in which the elegance of Saracenic architecture was quite lost. Whichever way I looked, I saw in the distance, through the morning vapors, the towers of Hindoo temples, or the bulbous domes of mosques, many of them gilded, and flashing in the rays of the sun.

The street I had chosen led me to a bridge over the river Goomtee, which here flows eastward, and skirts the northern side of the city. The word *Goomtee* means literally, "The Twister," on account of the sinuous course of the river. Looking westward from the centre of the bridge, there is a beautiful view of the city. Further up the river, which flowed with a gentle current between grassy and shaded banks, was an ancient stone bridge, with lofty pointed arches. The left bank rose gradually from the water, forming a long hill, which was crown ed with palaces and mosques, stretching away into the distance, where a crowd of fainter minarets told of splendors beyond. The coup d'œil resembled that of Constantinople, from the bridge across the Golden Horn, and was more imposing, more pictu- esque and truly Oriental than that of any other city in India. The right bank was level, and so embowered in foliage that only few domes and towers were visible above the sea of sycamores, banyans, tamarind, acacia, neem and palm-trees. I loitered on the bridge so long, enjoying the refreshing exhilaration of such a prospect, that I am afraid the dignity of the great English race, in my person, was much lessened in the eyes of the natives.

The picture, so full of Eastern pomp and glitter, enhanced by the luxuriance of Nature, was made complete by the character of the human life that animated it. Here were not merely menials, in scanty clothing, or sepoys undergoing daily pillory in tight coats and preposterous stocks, but scores of emirs, cadis, writers, and the like, attired in silken raiment and splendidly turbaned, continually passing to and fro, with servants running before them, dividing the crowds for the passage of their elephants. The country people were pouring into the city by thousands, laden with their produce, and the bazaars of fruit and vegetables, which seemed interminable, were constantly thronged. At first I imagined it must be some unusual occasion which had called such numbers of the inhabitants into the streets; but I was told that they were always as crowded as then, and that the population of Lucknow is estimated at 800,000 inhabitants! It is, therefore, one of the most populous cities in Asia, and may be ranked with Paris and Constantinople, in Europe. Its length is seven miles, the extreme breadth four miles, and the central part is very densely populated.

After breakfasting at the bungalow, I called upon Col Sleeman, the East India Company's Resident, whose works on India, combined with his labors for the extirpation of the Thugs or Stranglers, have made his name known in Europe and America. The Residency is a large and lofty building, deserving the name of a palace, and surrounded by beautiful gardens. I had no letter to Col. Sleeman, but took the liberty of asking his advice relative to the things best worth seeing in Lucknow, as I had but a day to spare. Nothing could exceed the prompt and kind response of that gentleman. He immediately ordered his carriage, and as he was personally occupied, sent one of his native secretaries to conduct me through the city. I entered the bazaar again in grand style, with postilion, grooms and footmen, who ran in advance to clear a way, and obliged even the elephants to stand on one side. Nevertheless the streets were so densely crowded, that we proceeded very slowly. After threading the masses of the populace for about a mile and a half, between rows of three-story native houses, mosques, and caravanserais, we reached what appeared to be the heart of the city. A spacious gateway spanned the street, over which a forest of tall minarets and gilded domes rose in the distance. Passing through the arch, we entered an open square, with a large mosque and hospital on the left side, and a magnificent gate of white marble beyond. This is called the *Roomee Derwazee* or Constantinople Gate, from an idea that it is copied from a gate in that city, but I have no recollection of any gate there which even remotely resembles it.

After passing the Roomee Derwazee, I was startled by the unexpected splendor of the scene. I was in the centre of a group of tombs, mosques and pavilions, all of which were of marble or covered with white stucco, and surmounted with swelling Oriental domes, which shone like solid gold—fitting crowns to the slender arches, and the masses of Saracenic filigree and fretwork, from which they sprang. A huge stone tank, with flights of steps descending into it on all sides, occupied the foreground of the picture. Around its banks, and between the dazzling pavilions, ran a boskage of roses in full bloom, in the midst of which a few tall palms shot up into the sunshine. It was nearly noon, and the sun, now almost vertical, poured such an unrelieved glare upon the scene, that my eyes were not strong enough to endure it for more than two or three minutes.

On the left was the gate of the Imambarra, or tomb of Azuf ed-Dowlah, one of the former Nawabs of Oude, and here the carriage drew up. I alighted, and entered a quadrangle surrounded by the same dazzling white architecture, with gilded domes blazing against the intense blue of the sky. The enclosed space was a garden, in which stood two beautiful mausoleums of marble. Several feeble fountains played among the flowers, and there was a long pool in the midst, with a bridge over it, and grotesque wooden figures of sepoys, of the size of life, standing guard at each end. Scattered about the garden were also several copies in plaster of classical statues, and one in marble of Actæon and his hounds. Although Lucknow is a thoroughly Moslem city, most of the inhabitants, as well as the royal family, belong to the sect of Sheeahs—the descendants of the partisans of Ali—who do not scruple to make pictures or models of living things. This is a cause of great annoyance and sorrow to the Sonnees, or orthodox Mussulmen, who hold it to be a sin in the sight of God. The idea originated, no doubt in the iconoclastic zeal of the Prophet and his immediate successors.

On ascending the marble steps leading to the edifice at the bottom of the garden, I imagined for a moment that I beheld a manufactory of chandeliers. Through the open marble arches nothing else was at first visible. The whole building was hung with them—immense pyramids of silver, gold, prismatic crystals and colored glass—and where they were too heavy to be hung, they rose in radiant piles from the floor. In the midst of them were temples of silver filigree, eight or ten feet high, and studded with cornelians, agates and emeralds. These were the tombs. The place was a singular jumble of precious objects. There were ancient banners of the Nawabs of Oude, heavy with sentences from the Koran, embroidered in gold; gigantic hands of silver, covered with talismanic words; sacred shields, studded with the names of God; swords of Khorassan steel, lances and halberds; the turbans of renowned commanders; the trappings of the white horse of Nasr ed-Deen, mounted on a wooden effigy; and several pulpits of peculiar sanctity. I had some difficulty in making out a sort of centaur, with a human head eyes of agate, a horse's body of silver, and a peacock's tail, but was solemnly informed that it was a correct representation of the beast Borak, on which the Prophet made his journey to Paradise. The bridle was held by two dumpy angels, also of silver, and on each side stood a tiger about five feet long and made of transparent blue glass. These, I was told, came from Japan.

I had some difficulty in believing that this curiosity shop was the tomb of the Poet-King, Azuf ed-Dowlah; but so it was The decorations are principally due to the taste of the present king who is silly almost to imbecility, and pays the most absurd sums for his chandeliers and glass tigers. The two finest chandeliers cost him $50,000 each; but it is not to be supposed that all this money went into the pocket of the merchant. The Grand-Vizier, and other officers of Court, had their shares, down to the eunuchs. The King gave a small garden-palace to one of his wives not long ago. A wall was necessary to screen a part of the garden from the view of the public, and a mason was called upon to undertake the work. On being asked to state the cost he at first said 100,000 rupees, but, calculating afterwards, that of this sum the Grand-Vizier would keep the half, the Minister of the Treasury 20,000 rupees, and various other privileged bloodsuckers a proportionate share, while the building of the wall would actually cost 5,000 rupees, he gave up the contract, as a losing job! No description can fully illustrate the corruption of the Court of Oude. It is a political ulcer of the most virulent kind, and there is no remedy but excision. For the sake of Humanity, the East India Company would be fully justified in deposing the monarch and bringing the kingdom under its own rule.

Returning through the Constantinople Gate, I entered the large building adjacent, which was formerly a hospital, and still contains the tomb of its royal founder. Its architecture is purer than that of the Imambarra. The proportions of the halls are admirable, and the deep embroidered arches of the portico have the finest effect. Adjoining this edifice is a mosque built upon a lofty platform of masonry. It is an ambitious work, but falls behind those of Delhi, and the minarets are so large as to be out of all proportion. On the return to Col. Sleeman's, I passed under the walls of an old palace, which were lined with massive buttresses. I was told that it is used as a retreat for the wives of former kings.

Capt. Sleeman (the Resident's nephew), who has charge of suppressing the Dacoits, or organized robber-bands of India, took me upon the flat roof of the Residency, whence there is a fine panorama of Lucknow. Two-thirds of the city are as completely buried in foliage as the suburbs of Damascus. To the east, at a short distance, was the king's new palace, where he at present resides—a line of white walls and terraces, about half a mile in length, and topped with a mass of gilded towers and domes. Permission to visit it is not given without application two or three days previous, so that I was obliged to be content with an outside view. Near it is the palace of Feroze Buksh another cluster of gilded domes, and in the distance the marble tower of the Martinière. This is a college founded by General Martine, a French adventurer, who came out to India as a common soldier, entered the service of the King of Oude, and died a millionnaire. The building, which is of marble, and in a style of architecture resembling nothing on Earth (nor, I should hope, in Heaven), was erected by him during his lifetime, as a palace for the King. The latter, however, refused to take it off his hands, secretly resolving to seize upon it as soon as the old General was dead. Martine, who knew much more of human nature than of architecture, determined to block this game of the King, and when he died, had himself buried in a vault made under the foundation of the building, where he still lies, with a company of soldiers in effigy, keeping guard over his remains. No Mussulman will sleep in a house where any one is buried and the King was obliged to respect the General's will.

which devoted the building to a college, under the name of the Martinière.

To such an extent are the Kings of Oude plundered that a French cook, who spent some years in the service of a former monarch, is reported to have gone home with a fortune o $350,000. It was recently discovered that one of the parasites of the Court had been receiving two seers (four lbs.) of rose-water and a jar of sweetmeats daily for thirty years—and for what service? The father of the present King was annoyed, thirty years ago, by the barking of a dog. He sent for the owner, and commanded him to silence the animal. "Your Majesty," said the man, "nothing will stop his barking, unless he has two seers of rose-water and a jar of sweetmeats given him every day." "Take them, then," said the King, "only let us have no more noise." The knave took his rose-water and sweetmeats daily, and had lived luxuriously upon the proceeds for thirty years.

The present King is even more foolish and credulous, although he has received a good literary education, and has the Persian poets at his tongue's end. Although not more than forty years old, his excesses have already reduced him to a state of impotence. Nevertheless, his wives and eunuchs flatter him that he has begotten a large number of children, who are carried off by a demon as soon as they are born. About once a week (so I was informed) the Chief Eunuch rushes into his presence, exclaiming in great apparent joy, "O Lord of the World a son is born unto you!" "Praise be to God!" exclaims the happy King; "which of my wives has been so highly honored?" The eunuch names one of them, and the King rises in great haste to visit her and behold his new offspring. But sudden ly cries and shrieks resound from the women's apartments. A band of females bursts into the room, shrieking and lamenting 'O great King! a terrible demon suddenly appeared amongst us. He snatched your beautiful son out of the nurse's arms and flew through the window with a frightful noise." And so this trick is repeated from week to week, and the poor fool continually laments over his lost children.

Not long since a Portuguese mountebank happened to hear of this delusion. He repaired to the King, told him that he had discovered the nature of the demon that had molested him, and would destroy him, for a certain sum. The King agreed to the terms, and in a few days, the people of Lucknow were startled by seeing a great body of workmen engaged in digging trenches in a meadow near the river. After several days' labor, they threw up a rude fortification of earth, in the centre of which they buried several barrels of powder. The Portuguese declared that he was in the possession of charms, which would entice the demon into the fort, whereupon the train should be fired, and instantly blow him to atoms. A favorable night was selected for the operation, and the inhabitants of the city were shaken out of their beds by a terrific explosion, followed by a salvo of 121 guns, as a peal of rejoicing over the slaughter of the demon. But alas! the scattered fragments of the fiend reünited, and he has since then carried off nearly a score of the King's new-born progeny.

This weakness of character, it may readily be imagined, is the prime cause of the evils under which Oude is groaning. The Grand-Vizier is an unprincipled tyrant, and to such a degree of resistance have the people been driven, that the revenues are collected yearly with cannon, and a large armed force

Oude is the garden of India, and though now so waste and exhausted, from a long course of spoliation, yields a revenue of three crores of rupees ($15,000,000), only one third of which reaches the King's hands. The rest is swallowed up by the band of venal sycophants who surround him. An officer who knew Oude in the reign of Saadet Ali, forty-five years ago, told me that he remembered the time when all the country from Lucknow to Benares bloomed like a garden and overflowed with plenty. Now it is waste, impoverished, and fast relapsing into jungle. Thousands of people annually make their escape over the frontier, into the Company's territories, and at Cawnpore it is not unusual to see them swimming the river under a volley of balls from their pursuers. Great numbers of males of the lower classes enlist as sepoys, in the Company's regiments and it is estimated that of 200,000 natives from all parts of India who now serve in the army, 40,000 are from Oude alone.

Nevertheless, there is far more life, gaiety and appearance of wealth in Lucknow than any other native city in India. This is principally accounted for by the large sums that flow into the city from other quarters. The former monarchs of Oude, fearful of revolutions which might thrust their families from the succession, were in the habit of lending large sums to the East India Company, at an interest of five per cent., for the purpose of securing some property for their posterity, in case of trouble. Of late years the Company has declined to receive any more such loans, but still continues to pay interest on £6,000,000. At present many of the rich men of Oude invest their surplus funds in the Company's paper. There are besides many pensioners of the Government residing in Lucknow, and it is estimated that in addition to the interest paid, 120 lacs of rupees ($6,000,000), come into Oude yearly from the Company's territories.

In the afternoon, Capt. Sleeman kindly offered to accompany me on a second excursion through Lucknow. We were joined by one of his friends, and mounted on three of the King's largest elephants. With our gilded howdahs, long crimson housings, and the resplendent dresses of the drivers and umbrella-holders who sat behind us, on the elephants' rumps, we made as stately a show as any of the native princes. It was the fashionable hour for appearing in public, and, as we entered the broad street leading to the Roomee Derwazee, it was filled with a long string of horses and elephants, surging slowly through the dense crowd of pedestrians. We plunge boldly into the tumult, and, having the royal elephants, and footmen gifted with a ten-man power of lungs, make our way without difficulty. It is a barbaric pageant wholly to my liking, and as I stare solemnly at the gorgeous individuals on the elephants that pass us, I forget that I have not a turban around my brows. We duck our heads involuntarily, as we pass through the great gates, though the keystone is still twenty feet above them.

We pass the Imambarra, and a long array of other buildings and at last halt in front of the new mosque, which the King's mother is having built. It is large and picturesque, but shows a decline in architecture. The minarets are much too high. They have fallen down twice, and one of them is going to fall again. The domes are troubled with the same weakness, and, although the devout old lady has already spent $5,000,000 on the mosque, I doubt whether she will ever be able to finish it.

Turning back, we plunge into the heart of the city—into

the dark, narrow, crooked old streets of the Lucknow of last century. The houses are three stories high, projecting so that the eaves almost touch, and exhibit the greatest variety in their design and ornament. My attention is divided between looking at them, and watching my elephant. The street is so narrow and crooked that we run some risk of crushing our howdahs against the second-story balconies, but the beast, with his little, keen, calculating eye, knows precisely how far to go without striking. We pass several elephants safely, and are getting accustomed to the novel and intricate by-way, when up comes an enormous beast, ridden by a human elephant, in a green silk robe. The animal looks puzzled, and the man looks sullen, and vouchsafes us no greeting. He is a Cadi's secretary, it is true, but our elephants, being royal, take precedence of his. Neither beast will advance, for fear of wedging themselves together. At last my driver encourages his elephant; he tells him to press close against the wall and slip past; my howdah shoots under a balcony, but I bend profoundly and escape it. We press through, one after another, and the fat gentleman in the green silk gets awfully squeezed. Now we devote our attention to prying into the second stories of the houses, but the windows are all latticed, and there are sparkles through the lattices, which we take to be the flash of eyes.

"Here is the gate where the heads of malefactors are exposed," says one of my companions, and I look up with a shuddering expectancy, thinking to see a bloody head spiked over the arch. But there is none at present, and we pass on to the place of execution—a muddy bank overhanging a sewer, filled with the drainage of the city. Here the heads of the condemned are struck off, after the death-warrant has been thrice made out and signed by the king. This is a custom peculiar to Oude, and wisely adopted to prevent the ruler from shedding blood without due reflection. The first and second orders which the executioner receives are disregarded, and the culprit is not slain until the command is repeated for the third time.

We return through the Choke, the main street of the old city, after having penetrated for two miles into its depths. There is a crush of elephants, but the street has a tolerable breadth, and no accidents happen. We are on a level with the second-story balconies, which are now tenanted (as those in the Chandney Choke of Delhi) by the women of scarlet, arrayed in their flaunting finery. We see now and then an individual of another class, which I should name if I dared—but there are some aspects of human nature, which, from a regard for the character of the race, are tacitly kept secret. But see! we have again emerged into the broad street and begin to descend the slope towards the river. The sun is setting, and the noises of the great city are subdued for the moment. The deep-green gardens lie in shadow, but all around us, far and near, the gilded domes are blazing in the yellow glow. The scene is lovely as the outer court of Paradise, yet what deception, what crime, what unutterable moral degradation fester beneath its surface!

CHAPTER XVIII.

ALLAHABAD, AND A HINDOO FESTIVAL

Return to Cawnpore—An Accident—The Road to Allahabad—Sensible Pilgrims—Morning—Beauty of Allahabad—The American Missionaries—The Hindoo Festival—The Banks of the Ganges—Hindoo Devotees—Expounding the Vedas—The Place of Hair—A Pilgrim Shorn and Fleeced—The Place of Flags—Venality of the Brahmins—Story of the Contract for Grass—Junction of the Ganges and Jumna—Bathing of the Pilgrims—A Sermon—The Mission—Subterranean Temple—The Fort of Allahabad.

I LEFT Lucknow at nine o'clock on the evening of the 11th, in the garree for Cawnpore. I was unable to sleep, from toothache, and was lying with shut eyes, longing for the dawn, when there was a jar that gave me a violent thump on the head, and one side of the garree was heaved into the air, but after a pause righted itself. The horse started off at full speed, dragging the wreck after him, but was soon stopped, and I jumped out, to find the spring broken, and the hind wheels so much injured that we were obliged to leave the vehicle in the road. The driver had no doubt fallen asleep, and the horse, going at his usual rapid rate, had hurled the garree against a tree. Leaving the groom to take charge of the remains, the driver took the mail-bag on his head, my carpet-bag in his hand, and led the horse toward Cawnpore. I followed him, and we trudged silently forwards for an hour and a half, when we reached the Ganges, at daybreak. It was lucky that the accident happened so near the end of the journey

The same afternoon I left Cawnpore for Allahabad, in a garree, as usual. Still the same interminable plains, though the landscape became richer as I proceeded southward, except when the road approached the Ganges, where there are frequent belts of sandy soil, worn into deep gullies by the rain. The fields of barley were in full head, the mustard in blossom, and the flowers of the mango-tree were beginning to open. The afternoon was warm and the road very dusty. I passed the town of Futtehpore at dusk, but experienced an hour's delay during the night, which I was at a loss to account for until I found the next morning that the driver had taken two natives on the roof of the garree, as passengers to Allahabad. They were pilgrims to the Festival, and were thus depriving themselves of the greatest merit of the pilgrimage, which consists in making the journey on foot. There is now quite a sharp discussion going on among the learned pundits, as to whether the *merit* of a religious pilgrimage will be destroyed by the introduction of railroads. That railroads will be built in the course of time, is certain; that thousands of pilgrims will then make use of them, is equally certain; a prospect which fills the old and orthodox Brahmins with great alarm.

I passed a dreary night, martyred by the toothache. When the sun rose I saw the Ganges in the distance, and the richness and beauty of the scenery betokened my approach to Allahabad. The plain was covered with a deluge of the richest grain, fast shooting into head, and dotted with magnificent groves of neem and mango trees The road was thronged with pilgrims, returning from the Festival, and the most of them, women as well as men, carried large earthen jars of Ganges water suspended to the ends of a pole which rested on their shoulders. In spite of the toils of the journey and the privations they must have undergone, they all had a composed, contented look, as if the great object of their lives had been accomplished.

In two hours I reached the Allahabad Cantonments, but failing to find the residence of Mr. Owen, of the American Mission, I directed the driver to take me to the hotel. On the way we passed through the native town, which abounds in temples and shrines. Flags were flying in all directions, drums beating, and several processions could be discovered marching over the broad plain which intervenes between the town and the fort. The day was gloriously clear and balmy, and the foliage of the superb neem and tamarind trees that shade the streets, sparkled in the light. I remembered the story of the Mohammedan Conquerors, who were so enchanted with the beauty of the country, and so well satisfied with the mild and peaceable demeanor of the inhabitants, who gave up the place without striking a blow, that they named it Allahabad—the City of God. Its original name was Priàg, a Hindoo word signifying "the Junction," on account of the confluence of the Ganges and the Jumna.

The first face I saw at the hotel was that of a fellow-traveller across the Desert, whom I had last seen at Suez. He had just come up from Calcutta, on his way to Lahore. I saw but little of him, as Mr. Owen insisted on my taking a room at his house, where I was again on American soil, on the banks of the Jumna. I have rarely passed a day more agree ably than in his pleasant family circle, which was enlarged in the evening by the presence of his colleagues, the Rev. Messrs. Shaw and Hay. The American Missionaries in India, wherever I have met them, were to me what the Latin monks in Palestine were, but not like the latter, with a latent hope of reward. They are all earnest, zealous and laborious men, and some of them, among whom I may mention Mr. Owen, and Mr. Warren, of Agra, are ripe scholars in the Oriental languages and literature.

Mr. Owen had an appointment to preach to the natives in the afternoon, and I accompanied him to the scene of the festival, on the banks of the Ganges. The climax of the occasion was past, and the great body of the pilgrims had departed for their homes, but there were still several thousands encamped in and around the town. On the plain, near the Ganges, stood an extempore town, consisting of streets of booths, kept by the native merchants, who took care of their temporal and spiritual welfare at the same time, with a dexterity which would have done credit to a Yankee. Upon mounting a dyke which had been erected to restrain the water of the Ganges during inundations, I again beheld the Holy River and its sandy and desolate shores. It was indeed a cheerless prospect—a turbid flood in the midst, and a hot, dreary glare of white sand on either side. The bank of the river, from the point where we stood to its junction with the Jumna—a distance of nearly half a mile—was covered with shrines, flags, and the tents of the fakeers, which consisted merely of a cotton cloth thrown over a piece of bamboo There were hundreds of so-called holy men, naked except a single cotton rag, and with their bodies covered with ashes or a yellow powder, which gave them an appearance truly hideous. Their hair was long and matted, and there was a wild gleam in their eyes which satisfied me that their fanatical character was not assumed. Many of them were young men, with keen spirited faces, but the same token of incipient monomania in their eyes. Some few were seated on the ground, or in the shade of their rude tents, rapt in holy abstraction, but the most of them walked about in a listless way, displaying their disgusting figures to the multitude.

The shrines, of which there were great numbers, were tawdry affairs of tinsel and colored paper, with coarse figures of Mahadeo, Ganeish, Hanuman and other deities. Many were adorned with flowers, and had been recently refreshed with the water of the Ganges. I was struck with the figure of an old grey-bearded saint, who was expounding the Vedas to a Brahmin, who, seated cross-legged under a large umbrella, read sentence after sentence of the sacred writing. The old fellow showed so much apparent sincerity and satisfaction, and was so fluent in his explanations, that I was quite delighted with him. Indeed, there was not the slightest approach to levity manifested by any one present.

We threaded the crowd of ghastly Jogees, Gosains and other ashy fakeers, to the Place of Hair-Cutting—an enclosed spot, containing about an acre and a half of ground. Here the heads and beards of the pilgrims are shorn, a million of years in Paradise being given by the gods for every hair so offered up. The ground within the enclosure was carpeted with hair, and I am told that on great occasions it is literally knee-deep. There were only two persons undergoing the operation, and as I wished to inspect it more closely, I entered the enclosure.

When the repugnance which the Hindoos have toward destroy ing animal life is understood, the reader will comprehend that I did not venture among so much hair without some hesitation. A fellow with a head of thick black locks and a bushy beard had just seated himself on the earth. We asked him who he was and whence he came. He was a Brahmin from Futtehpore, who had made a pilgrimage from Hurdwar, where he had filled a vessel with Ganges water, which he was now taking to pour upon the shrine of Byznath, beyond Benares. In reward for this a Brahmin who was standing near assured us that he would be born a Brahmin the next time that his soul visited the earth. The barber took hold of a tuft on the top of his head, which he spared, and rapidly peeled off flake after flake of the bushy locks. In less than five minutes the man's head and face were smooth as an infant's, and he was booked for fifty thousand million years in Paradise. But the change thereby wrought upon his countenance was most remarkable. Instead of being a bold, dashing, handsome fellow, as he at first appeared, his physiognomy was mean, spiritless, and calculated to inspire distrust. I should not want better evidence that Nature gave men beards to be worn, and not to be shaven.

As soon as the shearing was finished, three Brahmins who had been hovering around carried the subject off to be fleeced They were sharp fellows, those Brahmins, and I warrant they bled him to the last *pice*. The Brahmins of Allahabad are not to be surpassed for their dexterity in obtaining perquisites. They have apportioned India into districts, and adjoining the Place of Hair they have their Place of Flags, where there are upwards of two hundred flags streaming from high poles. The devices on these flags represent the different districts

The pilgrim seeks the flag of his district, and there he finds the Brahmin licensed to take charge of him. There is no fixed fee, but every man is taxed to the extent of his purse. One of the Rajahs of Oude, who had been shorn a short time previous to my arrival, gave the fraternity six elephants and the weight of a fat infant son in Cashmere shawls and silver.

In justice to the Brahmin caste, I should remark that those who serve as priests in the temples are not to be confounded with the secular Brahmins, many of whom are fine scholars, and enlightened and liberal-minded men. But the priesthood is perhaps more corrupt than any similar class in the world. They do not even make a pretence of honesty. An acquaintance of mine bargained with some Allahabad Brahmins to supply him with grass for thatching his house. They showed him a satisfactory sample, and he agreed to pay them a certain price. But when the grass came it was much worse than the sample, and he refused to pay them full price. The matter was referred for arbitration to three other Brahmins, who decided in the gentleman's favor. But the contractors declared they would have the full price. "Why do you not bring me good grass, then?" said the gentleman. "Because we have it not," they answered. "Why then did you send me such a sample?" "To make you contract with us," was the cool reply. "You may take the quarrel into Court, for I shall not pay you," declared the gentleman. "We shall not go to Court, for we shall certainly lose the cause," said they; "but we *will* have the money." Thereupon they went to the carpenter who was building the house, and who was a Hindoo related the case, and called upon him to make up the full sum. The astonished victim declared that it was no affair of his. "No matter," said they, "if you don't pay it, one of us will commit suicide, and his blood will be upon your head"—this being the most terrible threat which can be used against a Hindoo. The carpenter still held out, but when the oldest of the Brahmins had decided to kill himself, and was uncovering his body for the purpose, the victim was obliged to yield, and went off in tears to borrow the money. Truly, this thing of caste is the curse of India.

Passing the Place of Flags, where the streamers were of all imaginable colors and devices, we descended to the holiest spot, the junction of the Ganges and Jumna. According to the Hindoos, *three* rivers meet here, the third being the Seriswattee, which has its source in Paradise, and thence flows subterraneously to the Ganges. There were a number of bamboo platforms extending like steps to the point where the muddy waters of the Ganges touched the clear blue tide of the Jumna. [In this union of a clear and a muddy stream, forming one great river, there is a curious resemblance to the Mississippi and Missouri, and to the Blue and White Niles.] Several boats, containing flower-decked shrines, with images of the gods, were moored on the Jumna side, the current of the Ganges being exceedingly rapid. The natives objected to our getting upon the platforms, as they were *kana*, or purified, and our touch would defile them, so we stood in the mud for a short time, and witnessed the ceremony of bathing. The Hindoos always bathe with a cloth around the loins, out of respect for the Goddess Gungajee. There were about a dozen in the water, bobbing up and down, bowing their heads to the four points of the compass, and muttering invocations. Others, standing upon the bank, threw wreaths of yellow flowers upon the water. On our return to the encampment of the fakeers, we visited a pit-shrine of Ha numan, the monkey god, who helped Rama in his conquest of Ceylon. He lies on his back in a deep hole, and is a hideous monster, about twelve feet long, carved out of a single piece of stone. Several natives were prostrating themselves in the dust, around the mouth of the pit.

Mr. Owen preached for half an hour in the mission tent among the fakeers. A number of natives flocked around, listening attentively, and made no disturbance, though two or three of them were Jogees of the most fanatical kind. They were apparently interested, but not touched. Indeed, so deeply rooted are these people in their superstitions, that to awake a true devotional feeling among them must be a matter of great difficulty. In the evening I attended Divine service in the Mission Church, and was much pleased with the earnest and serious air of the native converts. They were all neatly dressed and behaved with the utmost propriety. The Missionaries have instructed four natives, who were ordained as ministers, under the names of Paul, Thomas, George and Jonas. The mission school was attended by three hundred pupils, the most of whom were natives, and all received religious instruction. There is also a printing office under the charge of the Rev. Mr. Hay, in which, during the previous year, six millions of pages, in the Hindoo, Urdoo, and Persian languages had been printed. The Lieut. Governor of the Northwest, during his visit to Allahabad, spoke in public in the highest terms of the labors of the American Missionaries.

On my way to the fort the next morning, with Mr. Owen, we met one of the Ameers of Scinde, who was a prisoner at large in Hindostan. In the fort three princes of Nepaul were kept in very strict confinement, on account of having been engaged in a conspiracy. The most remarkable thing in the fort is a subterranean temple, evidently of great antiquity. It consists of a single low hall, supported by square pillars, and contains many figures of Mahadeo in niches around the walls, and a quantity of lingams scattered over the floor. There is a narrow passage issuing from it which has not been explored. Some of the Brahmins say it leads to Benares, and others to Hell. In the centre of the fort stands a column of red sandstone, resembling the iron pillar at Delhi, and with an inscription in the Pali character. The arsenal, which occupies part of the *zenána* of the Emperor Akbar, is the largest in India. In other respects the fort is not remarkable, though, having been repaired by the English, it is in better condition to stand an attack than the immense shells which tower over Agra and Delhi.

CHAPTER XIX

THE HOLY CITY OF INDIA.

Crossing the Ganges—Pilgrims Returning Home—Vagaries of the Horses—Benares—Prof. Hall—The Holy City—Its Sanctity—The Sanscrit College—Novel Plan of Education—Village of Native Christians—The Streets of Benares—Sacred Bulls—Their Sagacity and Cunning—The Golden Pagoda—Hindoo Architecture—Worship of the Lingam—Temple of the Indian Ceres—The Banks of the Ganges—Bathing Devotees—Preparations for Departure.

AT noon, on Monday, the 14th, I left the hospitable roof of Mr. Owen, at Allahabad. On reaching the Ganges, I found the drawbridge open, and a string of upward bound vessels passing through. There were thirty-nine in all, and so slowly were they towed against the stream, that full two hours elapsed, and I still sat there in the heat, contemplating the white and glaring sand-flats of the opposite shore. There was an end of it at last; my garree was pushed across, and over the sands, by a crowd of eager coolies, and having attained the hard, macadamized road, shaded by umbrageous peepul and neem trees, I whirled away rapidly toward Benares. My road lay along the northern bank of the Ganges, through a very rich and beautiful country. The broad fields of wheat and barley just coming into head, were picturesquely broken by "topes" of the dark mango or the feathery tamarind, and groves of the brab palm. It was a land of harvest culture, with all the grace of sylvan adornment which distinguishes a park of pleasure.

The road was thronged with pilgrims returning from the great *mela*, or fair, of Allahabad. During the afternoon I passed many thousands, who appeared to be of the lowest and poorest castes of the Hindoos. They all carried earthen jars filled with the sacred water of the Junction (of the Ganges and Jumna), which they were taking to pour upon the shrines of Benares or Byznath. At the stations where I changed horses, they crowded around the garree, begging vociferously: "O great Being, an alms for Shiva's sake!" One half-naked, dark-eyed boy of ten years, accosted me in fluent Arabic, exclaiming: "O great lord, may Peace repose upon your turban!" with such a graceful and persuasive air that he did not need to ask twice. But for the others, it was necessary to be both blind and deaf, for there was no charm in the serpent-armed Destroyer to extort what had been given in the sacred name of Peace. As night approached, the crowds thickened, and the yells of my driver opened a way through their midst for the rapid garree. They moved in a cloud of dust, of their own raising, and I had no comfort until the darkness obliged them to halt by the roadside and around the villages, after which the atmosphere became clearer, and the road was tolerably free from obstruction.

The horses, however, gave me no peace, and every change, at the relay stations, seemed to be for the worse. After balking at the start, they would dash off in fury, making the body of the garree swing from side to side at every bound, till a crash of some kind appeared inevitable. One of these careers was through a long and crowded village, in which a market was being held. I did not count how many times my flying wheels grazed the piles of earthenware, and the heaps of grain and vegetables, but I know that there were screams of alarm, gesticulations, fright and confusion, from one end of the village to the other, and how we ran the gauntlet without leaving a wake of ruin behind us, is a mystery which I cannot explain. I gradually became too weary to notice these aberrations of the propelling force, and sinking down into the bottom of the garree, fell into a sleep from which I was awakened at midnight by the driver's voice. I looked out, saw a large Gothic church before me, in the moonlight, and knew by that token that the goal was reached.

The next morning I called upon my countryman, Mr. Fitz-Edward Hall, to whom I had letters, and, according to Indian custom, immediately received the freedom of his bungalow. Mr. Hall, who is a native of Troy, New York, is Professor of Sanscrit in the Sanscrit College at Benares, and enjoys a high and deserved reputation throughout India for his attainments, not only in the classic language of the Brahmins, but also in the Hindoo and Urdee tongues. With his assistance I was enabled to take a hasty but very interesting survey of Benares, within the two days to which my stay was limited.

Benares, the Holy City of the Hindoos, and one of the most ancient in India, lies upon the northern bank of the Ganges, at the point where it receives the waters of the two small tributaries, the *Burna* and *Arsee*, from whose united names is derived that of the town. All junctions of other rivers with the Ganges are sacred, but that of the Jumna and the invisible

Scriswattee at Allahabad, surpasses all others in holiness Nevertheless, Benares, from having been the spot where Maha deo (if I am not mistaken), made his last *avatar*, or incarnate appearance on the earth, is so peculiarly sanctified that all persons who live within a circuit of five miles—even the abhorred Mussulman and the beef-eating English—go to Paradise, whether they wish it or no. According to the gospel of the Brahmins, the city and that portion of territory included within the aforesaid radius of five miles, is not, like all the rest of the earth's bulk, balanced upon the back of the great Tortoise, but up held upon the points of Shiva's trident. In this belief they boldly affirmed that though all other parts of the world might be shaken to pieces, no earthquake could affect the stability of Benares—until 1828, when without the least warning towers and temples were thrown down, hundreds of persons buried in the wreck, and half built quays and palaces so split and sunken, that the boastful builders left off their work, which stands at this day in the same hideous state of ruin. This mundane city, however (they say), is but a faint shadow, a dim reflection of the real Benares, which is built upon a plain half-way between Earth and Heaven.

The English cantonments encircle the old Hindoo city. Owing to the deep, dry beds of the small rivers, scarring the rather arid level which it covers, the settlement has not the home-like, pleasing features of others in Hindostan. There are a few handsome private mansions, a spacious church, and the new Sanscrit College, which is considered the finest modern edifice in India. To those who are familiar with the East India Company's efforts in this line, such an opinion will not raise very high expectations. The College is o Gothic cross—

a reminiscence of Oxford, and beautiful as it is in many respects, we should prefer something else, to project against a background of palms and tamarinds. It is built of the soft rose-colored sandstone of Chenar, and the delicate beauty of its buttresses and pinnacles, wrought in this material, make us regret that the architect had not availed himself of the rich stores of Saracenic art, which the mosques and tombs of the Mogul Emperors afford him. Gothic architecture does not, and never can be made to harmonize with the forms of a tropical landscape.

The plan of this College is unique and has of late been the subject of much criticism. It was established by the East India Company sixty-three years ago, for the purpose of instructing the children of Brahmins in the Sanscrit Philosophy and Literature, and since the construction of the new building, the English College has been incorporated with it. The Principal, Dr. Ballantyne, who is probably the profoundest Sanscrit scholar living, has taken advantage of this junction to set on foot an experiment, which, if successful, will produce an entire revolution in the philosophy of the Brahmins. The native scholars in the English College are made acquainted with the inductive philosophy of Bacon, while the students of Sanscrit take as a text-book the Nyaya system, as it is called, of Guatama, the celebrated Hindoo philosopher. There are many points of approach in these two systems, and Dr. Ballantyne has been led to combine them in such a way as finally to place the student, who commences with the refined speculations of Guatama, upon the broad and firm basis of the Baconian system. The latter is thus prepared to receive the truths of the physical sciences, a knowledge of which must gradually, but inevitably overthrow the gorgeous enormities of his religious faith.

After visiting Mr. Reid, the Commissioner of the District, Mr. Hall accompanied me to the Mission establishment of the English Church. Here there is a small village of native Christians, whom I could not but compassionate. Cut off for ever from intercourse with their friends, denounced as unclean and accursed, they showed their isolation by a quiet, patient demeanor, as if they passively sustained their new faith, instead of actively rejoicing in it. There was, however, a visible improvement in their households—greater cleanliness and order, and the faces of the women, I could not but notice, showed that the teachings of the missionaries had not been lost upon them. I wish I could have more faith in the sincerity of these converts; but the fact that there is a material gain, no matter how slight, in becoming Christian, throws a doubt upon the verity of their spiritual regeneration. If lacking employment, they are put in the way of obtaining it; if destitute, their wants are relieved; and when gathered into communities, as here, they are furnished with dwellings rent-free. While I cheerfully testify to the zeal and faithfulness of those who labor in the cause, I must confess that I have not yet witnessed any results which satisfy me that the vast expenditure of money, talent and life in missionary enterprises, has been adequately repaid.

I spent a day in the streets and temples of Benares. As a city it presents a more picturesque and impressive whole than either Delhi or Lucknow, though it has no such traces of architectural splendor as those cities. The streets are narrow and crooked, but paved with large slabs of sandstone; the houses are lofty, substantial structures of wood, with projecting stories, and at every turn the eye rests upon the gilded conical domes of a Hindoo temple or the tall minaret of a Mohamme dan mosque. It is a wilderness of fantastic buildings, in which you are constantly surprised by new and striking combinations and picturesque effects of light and shade. I should have been content to wander about at random in the labyrinth, but my companion insisted on going at once to the Golden Pagoda, or great temple of Mahadeo, and thither we accordingly went.

The narrow streets were obstructed, in the vicinity of the temple, with numbers of the sacred bulls. Benares swarms with these animals, which are as great a nuisance to the place as the mendicant friars are to Rome. They are knowing bulls, perfectly conscious of their sacred character, and presume upon it to commit all sorts of depredations. They are the terror of the dealers in fruits and vegetables, for, although not always exempted from blows, no one can stand before their horns —and these they do not scruple to use, if necessary to secure their ends. Sometimes, on their foraging expeditions, they boldly enter the houses, march up stairs and take a stroll on the flat roofs, where they may be seen, looking down with a quiet interest on the passing crowds below. From these eminences they take a survey of the surrounding country, calculate its resources, and having selected one of the richest spots within their circles of vision, descend straightway, and set off on a bee-line for the place, which they never fail to find. When the fields look promising on the other side of the Ganges, they march down to the river banks, and prevent any passenger from going on board the ferry-boats until they are permitted to enter. They cross and remain there until the supplies are exhausted, when they force a passage back in the same manner. The gardens of the English residents frequently suffer from their depredations, and the only effectual way of guarding against them is to yoke them at once, and to keep them at hard labor for a day or two, which so utterly disgusts them with the place that they never return to it. It is also affirmed that they carefully avoid the neighborhood of those butchers who supply the tables of the English, having observed that some of their brethren disappeared in a mysterious manner, after frequenting such localities.

We were fortunate in our visit to the Golden Pagoda, for it was one of the god's festival days, and the court and shrines of the temple were thronged with crowds of worshippers. The most of them brought wreaths of flowers and brass vessels of Ganges water, to pour upon the symbols of the divinity. The Pagoda is built of red sandstone, which seems to have grown darker and richer by age, and by contrast with the blazing gold of its elaborate spires, has a wonderfully gorgeous appearance. The style of architecture is essentially the same in all Hindoo temples. The body of the structure is square and massive, enclosing the shrine of the god. From a cornice of great breadth, and often covered with sculptured ornaments, rises a tall spire, of parabolic outlines, which has the look of being formed by an accretion of smaller spires of similar form. It has a general resemblance to a pine-apple or rugged pine-cone. Where the temple is enclosed within a court, as in this instance, there are usually a number of separate shrines, and the clusters of spires and small ornamental pinnacles, entirely covered with gilding, form a picture of barbaric pomp not unworthy the reputed wealth "of Ormuz or of Ind" The shrines stood within dusky recesses or sanctuaries, lighted by lamps filled with cocoa-nut oil. They were in charge of priests or neophytes, who offered us wreaths of jasmine-blossoms, fragrant, and moist with Ganges water. I was about to accept some of them, but Mr. Hall requested me not to do so, as the act was one of worship, and would be looked upon as showing respect to Mahadeo.

The body of the temple abounded with stone images of the *lingam*, on all of which lay wreaths of flowers, while the worshippers, male and female, poured over them the water of the sacred river. The worship was performed quietly and decently, with every outward appearance of respect, and there was nothing in the symbols themselves, or the ceremonies, to give foundation to the charges which have been made, of the obscenity or immorality of this feature of the Hindoo faith. The *lingam* is typical of the creative principle, and by no means to be confounded with the Priapus of the Greeks; it rather points to the earlier phallic worship of the Egyptians, with which it was no doubt coeval. There is a profound philosophical truth hidden under the singular forms of this worship, if men would divest themselves for a moment of a prudery with regard to such subjects, which seems to be the affectation of the present age. So far from the Hindoos being a licentious people, they are far less so than the Chinese on one hand or the Mussulmen on the other, and from what I can learn, they are quite as moral as any race to which the tropical sun has given an ardent temperament and a brilliant vitality of physical life.

I also visited the temple of Unna-Purna—one of the names of the Goddess Bhavani, the Indian Ceres. It stands on a platform of masonry, surrounded by a range of smaller shrines. Hundreds of worshippers—mostly peasants from the surrounding country, were marching with a quick step around the temple, with their offerings in their hands. The shrine of the Goddess was so crowded that I had some difficulty in obtaining a view of her dusky figure. The gay, cheerful aspect of the votaries, with their garlands of flowers and brazen urns of water, recalled to my mind the Eleusinian Festivals of Greece, and the words of Schiller's Hymn flashed into my memory:

"Windet zum Kränze die goldenen Æhren!"

We afterwards went down to the Ganges, and wandered along, past shattered palaces, sunken quays, temples thrown prostrate, or leaning more threateningly than the belfry of Pisa, through a wilderness of fantastic and magnificent forms, watching the crowds bathing in the reeking tanks, or the open waters of the river. Broad stone ghauts (flights of steps) covered the bank, rising from the river to the bases of stately buildings, fifty or sixty feet above. The Ganges here makes a broad bend to the northward, and from these ghauts, near the centre, we saw on either hand the horns of the crescent-shaped city, with their sweeps of temples, towers and minarets glittering in the sun. A crowd of *budgerows*, or river boats, were moored all along the bank, or slowly moved, with white sails spread, against the current. The bathers observed the same ceremonies as I had noticed at Allahabad, and were quite decorous in their movements, the men retaining the *dhotee*, or cotton cloth twisted about the loins. The Hindoos are greatly shocked by the English soldiers, who go naked to the embraces of the Goddess Gunga,—not from that circumstance as connected with bathing, but as a want of respect to the holy stream I finished my visit to the city, by taking a boat and slowly floating down the Ganges in front of it, until its confused array of palaces, and ghauts, and golden spires was indelibly daguerrotyped upon my memory.

The necessity of reaching Calcutta in time for the Hong Kong steamer of the last of February, obliged me to refuse an invitation to a week's tiger-hunting in the jungles of the Vindhya Hills—a prospect which I did not relinquish without some bitter regrets. I thereupon made preparations for my last "garree-dawk" of 430 miles, with a pleasant prospect of a bruised head or broken bones, for after so many narrow escapes, I decided that I either bore a charmed life, or my share of injury was near at hand.

CHAPTER XX.

THE ROAD FROM BENARES TO CALCUTTA.

Moonlight on the Ganges—The Unholy River—Scenery of the Plains—Egyptian Landscapes—Sasseram—Mountains near the Soane River—View of the Ford-Crossing—The Second Day's Journey—The Hills of Behar—Meeting with an Acquaintance—Wild Table-Land—Sunset—A Coolie Trick—The Aborigines of India—Triumph of the Red-haired Lady—Horse Gymnastics—The Lady Defeated—Mungleporo—An Eccentric Night-Journey—The City of Burdwan—Tropical Scenery—Wrecked on the Road—A Wrathful Delay—Wrecked again—Journey by Moonlight—Another Wreck—An Insane Horse—The Hoogly River—Yet Another Accident—A Morning Parade—The End of "Garree-Dawk."

It was nearly midnight, on the 16th of February, when I left a genial company of Benares residents, and started on my lonely journey to Calcutta. My conductor did not pass through the city, but drove around it to Raj Ghaut, five miles distant. The horse was unharnessed, the carriage dragged down the bank by coolies, and deposited on a ferry-boat. I stretched myself comfortably on the mattress, propped against a carpet-bag, and looked out on the beautiful moonlit river. No spice-lamps, set afloat by amorous Hindoo maidens, starred the silvery smoothness of the tide. Alas, I fear that the poetry of the Indian world is in a rapid decline. There was no sound during our passage but the light dip of oars, and the shores, faintly touched by the rays of the setting moon, were wrapped in the hush of slumber. Thus, with a solemn, scarcely perceptible motion, I was ferried across the sacred river.

A plank road led over the sandy flats on the opposite side, and my horse required the assistance of half a dozen coolies, to reach the level of the cultivated land. We rolled on at a lively pace through the night, and the rising sun found me at Durgowtee, thirty-six miles from Benares.. Here a handsome suspension bridge crosses the river Karamnasa, the waters of which are so unholy as to destroy the whole merit of a journey to Benares, should they touch the pilgrim's feet. The bridge was built by a late Rajah of Benares, to prevent the thousands of pilgrims who pass along this road, from forfeiting the reward of their devotion. Notwithstanding this act of pious charity, the Rajah was so unpopular among his people, that they considered it very unlucky to mention his name before breakfast. The country was still a dead level, and though dry at this season, is marshy during the rains. The last season had injured the road greatly, so that for a distance of twenty or thirty miles, but little of it was passable. A rough temporary track had been made beside it, and hundreds of workmen were employed in constructing bridges over the nullas, and repairing the embankments. The country, at first almost bare of trees, and covered with but moderate crops, gradually became warmer and richer in its aspect. The vegetation increased in luxuriance, and the profusion of the brab palm spoke of the neighborhood of the tropics. The villages were shaded with huge banyans, peepuls and other umbrageous trees. The Vindhya Mountains appeared blue and distant in the south-west, and a nearer range in front marked my approach to the Soane River.

The landscapes reminded me more of Egypt than any other part of India. There was the same summer richness in the foliage of the trees, the same vivid green in the broad fields of wheat and barley, then fast ripening, and the same luxury of color in the patches of blossoming poppy. But the air, instead of the crystalline purity of the Egyptian atmosphere, was steeped in a glowing blue vapor—softened by a filmy veil of languor and repose. The sun poured down a summer glow, though a light breeze now and then ran over the fields, and rolled along the road in clouds of whirling dust. Notwithstanding my lazy enjoyment of the scenery, I found my appetite gradually becoming sharper, and was not sorry to reach the large town of Sasseram, where I halted at the bungalow long enough to procure an afternoon breakfast. Resuming my journey, I reached the banks of the Soane River about five o'clock. The mountains on the left, which follow its course, cease at the distance of some miles from the road, whence they have the appearance of a long bluff promontory, projecting into the sea. In advance of the last headland rises an isolated peak with a forked top, precisely as I have seen a craggy island standing alone, off the point of a cape. There is no doubt that Central and Southern India at one time constituted an immense island, separated from the main land of Asia by a sea whose retrocession gave to the light the great plains of Hindostan and the Indus.

The Soane is believed to be the Erranoboas of the old Greek geographers, and at his junction with the Ganges they located the great city of Palibothra. He has a royal bed in which to roll his waters, which were then shrunken to a shallow flood by the dry season. Standing on the western bank, the channel stretched away before me to a breadth of nearly four miles—a waste of bare yellow sand, threaded by the blue arms of the river. Here and there companies of men and oxen dotted its surface, and showed the line of the ford. The tents of those who were waiting to cross on the morrow were pitched on the bank, and the gleam of fires kindled near them shone out ruddily as the sun went down. It was a grand and impressive scene, notwithstanding its sombre and monotonous hues. Such, I imagine, must be the fords of our own Nebraska, during the season of emigration. I paid an official of some kind two rupees, after which my horse was unharnessed, and three yoke of oxen attached to the garree. Descending to the river bank a short distance above, the garree was put upon a ferry-boat, to be taken across the deepest part, while the bullocks were driven through to await us on the other side. The main stream is about half a mile wide, and beyond it lie alternate beds of sand, and small, fordable arms of the river We moved at a snail's pace, on account of the depth of the sand. While in the midst of one of the deepest channels, the water reaching to the body of the garree, one of the oxen twisted his head out of the yoke and darted off. There was great plunging and splashing on the part of the natives for a few minutes, but they succeeded in recovering him, and at length, after a passage of more than two hours, we attained firm earth on the opposite side.

In spite of the lovely moonlight, I shut up the garree, and courted slumber. I passed a tolerable night, and at daybreak reached Shergotty, one hundred and thirty miles from Be nares. The country, for ten miles after leaving that town, was level and gloriously rich. The wheat and barley were taking on their golden harvest hue, and the plantations of poppy sparkled in the sun like sheets of freshly-fallen snow. The villages were frequent, thickly settled, and had a flourishing air. The road still swarmed with Hindoo pilgrims, returning from Benares and Allahabad, almost every one carrying his two jars of Ganges water. At the stations I was assailed by clamorous beggars of all ages and sexes. The troops of coolies on the road were also annoying, by laying hold of the garree at the difficult places, running with it half a mile, and then demanding backsheesh. They made a ridiculous feint of pushing with all their strength, although I could see that there was not the least strain on their muscles, and constantly cried out, with much energy. "Push away there — a great lord is inside!"

I was now in the hilly province of Behar, where the country becomes more undulating, and the cultivation more scanty. A chain of mountains which had been visible for some time in front, began to enclose me in their jungly depths. The road still continued good, the ascents being gradual, and the nullas crossed by substantial bridges. The hills were covered with jungle to their very summits, and the country on either hand, as far as I could see, was uncultivated. The people had a wild, squalid look, and showed evidence of different blood from the race of the plains. I halted in the afternoon at the bungalow of Dunwah for my single daily meal, and while waiting for it, a garree drawn entirely by coolies came up the road from the Calcutta side. The traveller, it seemed, had intentions similar to mine, for his coolies brought him to the bungalow, and I soon heard his voice in the next room, ordering tea and "*moorghee grill*" (broiled chicken). When I was employed on my own meal, he came in to see who I was, and we were both surprised to find that we had been fellow-passengers on board the Haddington, and had parted company at Suez, more than two months before.

Leaving Dunwah, I had two chokees of gradual ascent, among hills covered with jungle, and then reached, as I thought, the dividing ridge, and anticipated a corresponding descent; in place whereof, a level table-land, dotted with detached mountain groups, opened before me as far as the eye could reach. Though thinly inhabited, the soil appeared to be fertile, and the air was purer than on the plains of the Ganges. It was a wild, romantic region, and gave me the idea of a country just beginning to be reclaimed from a state of nature. One would scarcely expect to find hundreds of miles of such land, coëxistent with the dense population of other parts of India. Yet, during my travels, I saw a vast deal of waste and uncultivated territory. Were all its resources developed, the country would support at least double its present population.

The sunset was beautiful among those woody ranges, and the full moonlight melted into it so gently that it seemed to arrest and retain the mellow lustre and soothing influences of twilight. At a chokee which I reached soon after dusk, the people represented to me that the road beyond was mountainous, and that two coolies would be necessary, in addition to the horse. "Well," said I, "let two of you come." I waited in vain for the hills, however, for we went forward at a full gallop, the whole distance. Looking behind to see whether this increase of speed was occasioned by the coolies, I discover ed those two gentlemen comfortably seated on the rumble, with their legs dangling in the air, while every few minutes they uttered cries of such energy, that one would have supposed they were straining every nerve with the violence of their efforts. When we reached the station, they came up boldly and demanded their pay, whereupon I retorted by asking pay of them for their conveyance. They slunk away, quite chop-fallen at my discovery of their trickery.

At dawn the next morning, I reached a town called Topeechanchee. Beyond this point the mountains gradually receded on either hand, and at last appeared only as isolated peaks, rising from the plain. Near Gyra, there is a lofty single peak, celebrated as being the sacred hill of the Jains, who are said to have five temples on the summit. None of them are visible from the road. The natives I met in this part of Behar differed considerably in appearance from the Hindoos of the plains, and probably belonged to the aboriginal tribes who are still found among those hills. The head is much larger and longer, in proportion to the size of the body, which is short, thick and muscular. Several German missionaries have located themselves in this region, and are said to have had considerable success in their labors for the conversion of these wild tribes.

During the forenoon I was overtaken by a green garree, in which sat two ladies. As it approached, I heard a shrill voice urging on the driver, who lashed his horse into a gallop, and as the vehicle passed, the elder lady thrust her head out of the window, and nodded to me with an air of insolent triumph. She had a decidedly red face, diversified with freckles, keen gray eyes, a nose with a palpable snub, and a profusion of coarse hair, of a color, which I will charitably term auburn. It was rather humiliating to be passed in the race by a female of that style of beauty, but I did not dispute her triumph. After leaving Gyra I journeyed all the afternoon over an undulating upland, covered with jungle and crossed by broken chains of hills, which sank into long, regular, surfy swells, as I approached the plains of Bengal. Thus far, beyond a few balks and harmless gymnastics, I had slight cause to complain of the horses furnished to me; but here my troubles commenced in earnest. The initiative was taken by a vicious animal, which bolted away from the station, dashed off the road, and after hurling the garree within six inches of a pit ten feet deep, was recovered, and with much persuasion induced to go forward. I was comforted, however, by passing in my turn, the green garree, but the red-haired lady this time turned her face steadfastly away from me, while a scowl of ill-humor added to the upward tendency of her nose. I looked out and nodded triumphantly, but she only sneered with more freezing contempt. She overtook me again at Burdwan, the next morning, but after that I kept the lead, and saw no more of her.

As night approached, I reached the boundary of the hills; an unbroken level extended to the horizon. The air was exceedingly mild and balmy, and the moonlight so delicious that I sat up for hours, enjoying it. At Munglepore, which I reached about eight o'clock, I met a gentleman and lady, on their way to the North-West, in a private carriage, drawn by coolies. I had a pleasant half-hour's talk with them, and on leaving, the gentleman gave me his name as Major——, of the

——th, and asked me to visit him if I ever came to the Punjaub. The horses, that night, deprived me of all sleep Sometimes the garree was planted firmly for half an hour in one spot, and then with a sudden impulse it shot forward with flying speed, swerving from one side of the road to the other, until a collision of some kind seemed inevitable. Once, the horse ran away, and was only brought up by dashing against the abutment of a bridge; and at another time, being awakened by an unusual movement of the garree, I looked out and found it on the steep side of a hill, with three natives holding on to the uppermost wheels, to prevent it from overturning. Notwithstanding all these perils, we succeeded in reaching Burdwan, seventy-two miles from Calcutta, by daybreak.

This is a large town, and the residence of a Rajah. It is a beautiful place, about two miles in length, and has a large number of European residences. Here I was first struck with the difference between the vegetation of Bengal and the north-western provinces. Instead of those level Egyptian plains, with their topes of mango and tamarind, here were the gorgeous growths of the West Indies, or the Mexican *tierra caliente.* In the gardens of the Europeans, the *Poinsettia* hung its long azure streamers from the trees, and the *Bougainvillia* raised its mounds of fiery purple bloom; the streets were shaded with lofty peepul trees, mixed with feathery groups of the cocoa palm; the native huts were embowered in thickets of bamboo, over which towered the cotton tree, with its bare boughs and clusters of scarlet, lily-shaped blossoms. I arrived at Burdwan at such an early hour, and the new garree and horse were gotten ready for me with so little delay, that there was no time to procure breakfast, before leaving the town. I set out with the expectation of arriving at Calcutta the same evening, but had not proceeded more than five miles, when the horse began to plunge, struck his hind feet through the front of the garree, snapped the axle, and left me stranded on the road.

I dispatched the driver with the horse, back to Burdwan, to bring another vehicle, and took my seat on the ruins to watch over my baggage. Two hours thus passed away; three hours; the sun stood high and hot in the heavens, and at last my pipe, to which I invariably turn for patience, failed of its effect. Twenty-four hours had elapsed since I had eaten, and the pangs of fasting were superadded to the wrath of deceived hopes. Another hour elapsed and it was now high noon; I hailed the natives who passed, and tried to bribe them to drag my carriage back to the town, but they either could not understand, or would not heed me. Still another hour, and with it, finally, the new conveyance came. My wrath was too great for words, but if looks could have affected him, the driver would have crumbled to ashes on the spot. Now, thought I, the Fates are satisfied, and I shall be allowed to pursue my journey in peace. But, after making a mile or so of the second stage, the horse, perceiving two empty wagons by the road-side, dashed up against them with the garree, and there remained. Neither blows nor entreaties would induce him to budge a step, and the driver finally unharnessed him and went back for another. This time I only waited *two* hours, and I neither smoked nor spoke, for I was fast approaching the apathy of despair. Toward sunset I reached a bungalow and achieved a meal, after which, somewhat comforted, I continued my journey.

As the road approached the Hoogly River, the country became more thickly settled, and the native villages were frequent. The large mansions, gleaming white in the moonlight, the gardens, the avenues of superb peepul trees and groves of palm, spoke of the wealth and luxury of the inhabitants. The road was shaded with large trees, between whose trunks the moonshine poured in broad streaks, alternating with darknesses balmy with the odor of unseen flowers. I became tranquil and cheerful again, deeming that my trials were over. Vain expectation! While passing through the very next village, the horse ran madly against a high garden wall on the right hand, and there stuck. He was unharnessed, the garree dragged into the middle of the road, harnessed again, and we started. The same thing happened as before; he gave two frantic leaps, and dashed us against the wall. If ever there was an insane animal, that was one. Six times, as I am a Christian, he dashed me against that wall. The driver's whip was soon exhausted, and I, beside myself with anger, having nothing else at hand, took my long cherry-wood pipe, and shivered it to pieces over his flanks. But he was inspired by the Fiend, and I was obliged to send him away and hire coolies to drag the vehicle as far as the Hoogly, six miles distant, where I arrived shortly after midnight.

I was ferried across the river, took another horse, and having only two stages to Calcutta, confidently lay down and went to sleep. I was awakened in half an hour by the stopping of the garree. Will it be believed that *that* horse, too, had come to a stand? Yet such was the plain Truth—Fiction would never venture on such an accumulation of disasters—and once more the driver went back for another animal, leaving the garree, with myself inside, in the middle of the road. I slept, I knew not how long, until aroused by the sharp peal of volleys of musketry. The sun was up; I rubbed my eyes and looked out. There I was, in the midst of Barrackpore, in front of the parade-ground, where some four or five thousand Sepoys were going through their morning drill. I watched their evolutions, until the last company had defiled off the field, for the driver, probably surmising my fondness for military spectacles, did not make his appearance for another hour.

And now we sped down the grand avenue, which, straight as an arrow, and shaded by giant banyans and peepuls, leads from Barrackpore to Calcutta. Gradually palace-like residences, surrounded with gardens, made their appearance on either side of the road. These, in turn, gave place to bamboo huts, with thatched roofs. Presently, a muddy moat appeared, and having crossed it, I felt that I was at last inside of the Mahratta Ditch, and that my perils were over. In half an hour afterwards I was quartered at Spence's Hotel; my journey of 2,200 miles in the interior of India was finished, and I bade adieu—for ever I trust,—to "garree-dawk."

CHAPTER XXI.

CALCUTTA—THE BRITISH EMPIRE IN INDIA.

Impressions of Calcutta—The Houses of the Residents—Public Buildings and Institutions—Colleges—Young Bengal—Museum of the Asiatic Society—The Botanic Garden—Calcutta at Sunset—Scene on the Esplanade—English Rule in India—Its Results—Its Disadvantages—Relation of the Government to the Population—Tenure of Land—Taxes—The Sepoys—Revenue of India—Public Works—Moral Changes—Social Prejudices.

I REACHED Calcutta on the 21st of February, and embarked for Hong Kong, on the 28th. My stay was consequently too short to justify me in attempting more than a general description of the city, and the impression which it made upon me. After the glowing accounts I had heard in the Provinces, of its opulent social life and architectural magnificence, I confess to a feeling of disappointment. It is the London, or rather the Paris, of India, and the country magistrate, after years of lonely life in the jungles, or in some remote cantonment, looks forward to a taste of its unaccustomed gayeties, as one of the bright spots in his life of exile. But it by no means deserves to arrogate to itself the title of the "City of Palaces," so long as Venice and Florence, or even Cadiz and La Valletta, remain in existence. It is not a city of palaces, but—the European portion at least—a city of large houses; and the view of the long line of mansions on the Chowringhee Road, extending northward to the Government Palace and the City Hall, as seen from the banks of the Hoogly, is certainly an architectural diorama, which would not disgrace any capital in Europe. Beyond this view, which, as it is the first that strikes the eye of a stranger arriving by sea, explains the unbounded admiration of many travellers, there is little to satisfy one's expectations. It is a fair outside, a frontispiece of wealth and parade, concealing the insignificance and poverty of the interior. Penetrate the thin crust, which hints of greater splendors behind it, and you are soon lost in winding, dusty avenues, lined with the mean and narrow dwellings of the lower classes of the native population.

The houses of the European residents, and of the wealthy native Baboos, are all built on the most spacious plan. The chambers are very large and lofty, for the purpose of coolness, and the open, arched verandas of the exterior throw a little grace around the large, blank masses of building. The material employed is brick and mortar only, which is plastered and painted white or cream-colored. On account of the damp, hot atmosphere of Bengal, the painting must be renewed every year, otherwise it becomes mildewed. The upper stories display a great quantity of windows, with green jalousies before them. These mansions are mostly furnished in a rich and elegant style, though straw matting takes the place of carpets, and broad *punkas* (for creating an artificial current of air) hang from the ceiling. A large retinue of servants—varying from ten to thirty—move about in their long white garment and flat turbans, hearing your commands with folded hands and a profound inclination of the head. The style of living is sumptuous, but rather too closely modelled after London habits. Perhaps there is no community in Europe which lives in a style of equal luxury, this being the headquarters of the General Government, and the seat of many of the best offices in its gift.

Calcutta has little to show, in the way of architecture. The Government Palace is said to be a very cool and comfortable residence, which, in that climate, compensates for many defects; but let the reader picture to himself five immense cubes of masonry, touching each other precisely like five black squares on a chess-board, with a low dome over the central one, and he will have a correct picture of it. The City Hall, a semi-Greek structure, is to my eye the finest building in the place. It has a noble hall, supported by two rows of Corinthian columns. The Metcalfe Hall, with a Corinthian portico, the new Hospital, Hare's Hindoo College, the Medical College, and other edifices, are proud testimonials of the public spirit and liberality of the citizens of Calcutta, and their architectural excellence is a matter of secondary importance. The new Cathedral, however, which has lately been erected at a cost of $150,000, reflects little credit on its projectors. It is Gothic, of an impure and disproportionate character, and being planted at one of the most prominent points on the Chowringhee Road, must be a perpetual eyesore to such of the residents as cherish a taste for Art. Several flourishing colleges have been established, of late years, for the improvement of the native population. That which was founded by the late David Hare, Esq., ranks among the first. I received an invitation to attend a performance of *Hamlet*, in English, by a company of Hindoo students, within its walls. Another philanthropic citizen had just completed a college for females, the success of which is doubted, as the Hindoo girls are betrothed very early, and after that ceremony, kept in strict seclusion. There are two mission schools, under the patronage of the Church of Scotland, in each of which there are more than a thousand pupils. Although the conversions to Christianity are comparatively few, the enlightened influence of Education, and, more especially, of European society, is making itself felt among the intelligent native families, and a party which styles itself "Young Bengal" is rapidly increasing its ranks. The young men, whose faith in the absurdities of the religion of their fathers is destroyed, have just entered the stage of utter scepticism, through which they must pass in order to reach the true Gospel. Their scorn and irreverence is manifested in eating the flesh of the sacred cow, making themselves tipsy with the forbidden blood of the grape, and disregarding the awful limits and restrictions of caste. Many Europeans are shocked at these proceedings, but I think they are hopeful signs. You cannot tear the deep-rooted faith of ages out of the heart of a race without tearing up with it all capacity for Faith. But a new soil gradually forms, and the seed of Truth, if dropped at a happy moment, takes living hold therein

During my stay in Calcutta, I enjoyed the hospitality of my countryman, Mr Barstow, and his partner Mr. Ashburner, a Scotch gentleman. Here, as every where throughout India, every door is opened to the stranger, with a spontaneous and generous hospitality which is equalled in no other part of the world. Mr. Chas. Huffnagle, the American Consul, to whom I was indebted for many kind attentions, accompanied me to the Botanic Gardens, and to the Museum of the Asiatic Society. The latter embraces a fine library, including many rare works in Oriental languages, a large zoological and mineralogical collection, and a number of Hindoo antiquities, gathered from different parts of India. Among the latter is a stone covered with Pali characters, from which Mr. Prinsep, the distinguished scholar and antiquarian, obtained his clue to the reading of inscriptions in that language. The Museum, however, is evidently suffering from neglect; the statues and sculptures taken from ancient temples, are scattered about the grounds, and exposed to the action of the weather, and many of the specimens of natural history have been injured by the ravages of the white ants. The Botanic Garden, which is on the opposite bank of the Hoogly, three or four miles below the city, is a beautiful spot, and contains an unusually rich collection of the trees and plants of the Tropics. The banyan tree, with its 110 trunks, is considered a great lion, but I had seen specimens of more than double the size in the valley of the Nerbudda. Among the ornamental plants, I was most struck with the *Amherstia nobilis*, a native of Burmah, with glossy green foliage, and long, pendent spikes of scarlet flowers; the *Bougainvillia spectabilis*, one broad sheet of purple bloom and the *Poinsettia*, whose sky-blue clusters, ten to fifteen feet in length, hung like streamers from the trees on which it leaned.

From half an hour before, until an hour after sunset, Cal cutta is to be seen in its greatest glory. Then, all who can procure an equipage, drive on the esplanade, an open space of three or four miles in length by nearly a mile in breadth, extending along the banks of the Hoogly, from the Government Palace to Fort William, and still further, to the country sub urb of Garden Reach. All the splendor of Chowringhee Road fronts on this magnificent promenade, and I forgave the pride of the Calcuttanese in their city, when I joined the brilliant stream of life in the main drive on the banks of the river, watching hundreds of lordly equipages passing and repassing, while on the other hand, the three miles of stately residences —palaces, if you insist upon it—shone rosy-bright in the face of the setting sun. The Parsee, the Hindoo and the Mussulman mingled in the ranks of the pale Englishmen, and reclined in their carriages, or drove their mettled Arabs with as much spirit as the best of their conquerors. Their Cashmere shawls, their silks and jewels, and the gay Oriental liveries of the syces and footmen, gave the display an air of pomp and magnificence which threw Hyde Park and the Champs Elysées into the shade. The fine band from Fort William, playing lively airs on the green, gave the crowning charm to the hour and the scene. The languor of the Indian day was forgotten, and the rich, sensuous life of the East flashed into sudden and startling vividness. I shall try to retain the impression of these sunset views of Calcutta, for they belong to that class of memories which are but enriched by time.

Here, on the eve of my departure from India, is a fitting occasion to say a few words on the character and the results of the English rule. The Government of the East India Company presents an anomaly to which there is no parallel in history. It is a system so complicated and involved, embracing so many heterogeneous elements, and so difficult to grasp, as a whole, that the ignorance manifested even in the English Parliament, with regard to its operations, is scarcely to be wondered at. From the rapidity of my progress through the country, and the disconnected and imperfect nature of my observations, I feel some reluctance in venturing upon the subject, and the reader must be contented to receive a few general impressions, instead of a critical dissection of the system, which, indeed, would occupy too much space, even if I were competent to undertake it.

My previous notions of English rule in India were obtained chiefly from the articles on the subject in the progressive newspapers of England, and were, I need hardly say, unfavorable. The American press is still more unsparing in its denunciations, though very few of the writers have any definite idea of the nature of the wrongs over which they grow so indignant. That there are wrongs and abuses which call for severe reprehension, is undeniable; but I have seen enough to satisfy me that, in spite of oppression, in some instances of the most grinding character, in spite of that spirit of selfish aggrandizement which first set on foot and is still prosecuting the subjugation of India, the country has prospered under English Government. So far from regretting the progress of annexation, which has been so rapid of late years, (and who are *we*, that we should cast a stone against this sin?) I shall consider it a fortunate thing for India, when the title of every native sovereign is extinguished, and the power of England stretches, in unbroken integrity, from Cashmere to Cape Comorin. Having made this admission, I shall briefly refer to some of the most prominent evils and benefits of the system.

It is the misfortune of India that it is governed by a commercial corporation, which annually drains the country of a large proportion of its revenues. It is true that the amount of the dividend on the East India stock is fixed by Parliament and cannot be exceeded; but that stock, with the debts incurred, by various expensive wars, amounts to upwards of $225,000,000, to meet the interest on which requires an annual expenditure of $15,000,000. Besides this, a large amount of money passes out of the country in the form of salaries and pensions (the Civil Service being much better paid than any other service in the world), so that a constant system of depletion is carried on, which would have greatly impoverished the country by this time, had not its effects been partially counteracted by other and compensating influences in the Government. The governing machinery is also very unwieldy and lumbering, fettered by a system of checks, which, as some of the departments are seven thousand miles apart, renders it extremely difficult to introduce new measures, no matter how urgent may be the necessity for their adoption. Parliament in this instance adheres to the old maxim of *quieta non movere*, and although the charter of the East India Company comes up for renewal once every twenty years, few steps have been taken to lop off the old excrescences and simplify the action of its executive powers.

The relation of the Government to the laboring millions of India is one that has been frequently condemned. It was inherited from the former rulers, but has since undergone considerable modification, and not, I am sorry to say, for the better. It is substantially that of landlord and tenant, the Government holding all the land as its own property, and leasing it to the inhabitants according to a certain form of assessment. In some instances it is leased directly to the laborers, in others to *zemindars*, or contractors on a large scale, who sub-let it to the former at an advanced rate, and practise tyrannical extortions upon them, in order to increase their own profits. The worst feature of this system is, that the rents increase in proportion to the productiveness of the land, so that it discourages the laborer from endeavoring to improve his portion. I have been informed that the amount received by Government averages about 75 per cent. of the value of the produce. The consequence is that the laborers, whether leasing from the *zemindars* or directly from the Government officers, make but a bare subsistence from year to year. In almost any other country they would be kept permanently at starvation point, but in India their wants are so few and their habits of life so simple, that the amount of positive distress is comparatively small. For a common laborer, such as are employed by Government on roads and canals, four rupees a month, or $24 a year, is considered good wages, and there are millions who manage to subsist on half this sum.

In Bengal and Madras the condition of the laboring population is most unfavorable, on account of the peculiar land systems which have been adopted in those presidencies. In Madras, where what is called the Ryotwar system is in force, a general assessment of all produce and property is made every year, and the rents fluctuate according to this standard, within the limits of a maximum rate, fixed by Government. But in order to carry out this system, the assistance of a large number of petty native officials is required, and the abuses which are perpetrated under it are said to be absolutely monstrous In the north-west provinces, where an assessment is only made every thirty years, and the occupation and cultivation of a tract of land constitutes a sort of claim to the renewal of the lease, the country is in a much more flourishing state. The soil is under excellent cultivation, and the inhabitants are thrifty and contented, while in the neighboring kingdom of Oude, grinding taxes are extorted every year by the force of an armed soldiery, districts which twenty years ago blossomed as a garden, are now waste and deserted, and thousands of oppressed subjects annually escape into the Company's territories, where they find at least security of life and property. Despotic as the Company's government certainly is, it is a well-regulated despotism, and its quiet and steady sway is far preferable to the capricious tyranny of the native rulers.

It speaks well for the Government that its military service is popular among the natives. There is no conscription, the Sepoy regiments being raised entirely by voluntary enlistment, and could be increased to any extent, if desired. The military force amounts to about 240,000 men—larger, one would suppose, than is actually needed, since it entails a great expense upon the country. The men are well fed and clothed—with the exception of the tight coats and stiff leather stocks in which they are tortured daily—and receive a liberal pay. They make excellent soldiers, and when placed on the flanks of a European battalion, march to battle as bravely as any in the world. For discipline, drill and soldierly appearance, some of the regiments would be noted anywhere.

The land revenue is of course the main source of supply to the Government, but there are some other taxes which are almost as severely felt by the population. The manufacture of opium is a Government monopoly, which yields a nett annual revenue of $15,000,000. The duty on salt is enormous, and as this is an article of universal consumption, is very severely felt. It amounts in some parts of the country to two rupees ($1) the maund, while in the territories of native princes the article may be bought for six annas (twenty cents) the mauna. The internal customs which formerly existed have been abolished, and a gradual amelioration of the burdens under which the native population has been weighed down, seems to be taking place. Though very slow to expend any money in public works, the Government still moves forward in this direction—and lately by guaranteeing to the holders of stock in the India Railroad Companies five per cent. for twenty years, gave a powerful impetus to an undertaking which will in time change the whole aspect of the country. The Grand Trunk Road, extending from Calcutta to Delhi, a distance of 900 miles, and now being carried on to Lahore, is one of the finest highways in the world. The Ganges Canal, which will cost $10,000,000 when finished, will cover with perpetual harvests the great peninsular plain between the Ganges and Jumna, and render famine impossible in the north of India. There is scarcely a large city in the Company's dominions without its schools, its colleges and its hospitals, supported mainly by Government bounty.

The moral changes which have been wrought within the last hundred years, or since the battle of Plassy laid the true foundation of the present vast commercial appanage, are even greater than the physical. The Civil Service, though liable to objection, from the favoritism practised in the appointment of its officers, and their promotion by seniority, without regard to talent or capacity, still secures to the native a more just and equitable administration of law than he could obtain from magistrates of his own race. The horrid practice of *suttee*, or widow-burning, has been totally suppressed; the confederation of Thugs, or Stranglers, which extended throughout all Central India, has been broken up, and the Dacoits, or robber bands, which are still in existence along the Ganges, and in the hilly country at the foot of the Himalayas, are gradually becoming extinct. With few exceptions, order and security reign throughout the whole of India, and I doubt whether, on the whole, there has been less moral degradation and physical suffering at any time since the power of the Mogul Emperors began to decline.

There is one feature of English society in India, however, which I cannot notice without feeling disgusted and indignant I allude to the contemptuous manner in which the natives, even those of the best and most intelligent classes, are almost invariably spoken of and treated. Social equality, except in some rare instances, is utterly out of the question. The tone adopted towards the lower classes is one of lordly arrogance, towards the rich and enlightened, one of condescension and patronage. I have heard the term "niggers" applied to the whole race by those high in office; with the lower orders of the English it is the designation in general use. And this, too, towards those of our own Caucasian blood, where there is no instinct of race to excuse their unjust prejudice. Why is it that the virtue of Exeter Hall and Stafford House can tolerate this fact without a blush, yet condemn, with pharisaic zeal, the social inequality of the negro and the white races in America?

My visit to India occupied only two months, and consequently some of my conclusions may be too hastily drawn. I have never made a more interesting, or instructive journey, or visited a country better worthy of thorough and conscientious

12*

study. The historical problem which it presents is yet distant from its solution, and it is one which no member of the Anglo-Saxon race can contemplate with indifference.

CHAPTER XXII.

FROM CALCUTTA TO HONG KONG.

Departure from Calcutta—Descending the Hoogly River—An Accident—Kedgeree—The Songs of the Lascars—Saugor Island—The Sandheads—The Bay of Bengal—Fellow-Passengers—The Peak of Narcondan—The Andaman Islands—Approach to Penang—A Malay Garree—Beauty of the Island—Tropical Forests—A Vale of Paradise—The Summit—A Panorama—Nutmeg Orchards—The Extremity of Asia—The Malayan Archipelago—Singapore—Chinese Population—Scenery of the Island—The China Sea—Arrival at Hong Kong.

THE steamship *Pekin* was advertised to leave Calcutta at daylight on the 28th, so I drove down to Garden Reach, where she lay, the evening previous, and passed the night on board. When I went on deck, the sun was rising broad and red between the tall Australian pines on the bank; steam and smoke were jetting out of the steamer's funnels; crowds of natives, with a few Europeans, were gathered on the shore, and all the confusion of letting go cables, bringing baggage at the last moment, shouting from the paddle-boxes, and ringing bells on the forecastle, showed that we were about to start. The steamer's head was swung around by the tide, then running at the rate of seven or eight knots an hour; we ran upon two buoys placed near the shore, broke some floats from the port wheel, and then started for the sea. A little below our anchorage we passed the

Bishop's College, on the western bank of the Hoogly. It consists of several detached buildings, in the hideous Indo-Gothic style introduced by the English. It is an ostentatious institution, and of little practical use in a religious point of view.

We swept too rapidly past the beautiful residences on both banks of the Hoogly—spacious white mansions standing in lawns shaded with the mango, the cocoa-palm and the Australian pine, overgrown with jungle creepers, and surrounded with gardens gay with the crimson *Bougainvillia* or the long white chalices of the *Datura*, fringing the water's edge. Two miles further these evidences of taste and luxury disappeared, and the scattered villages of the natives, with a few patches of corn and cane around them, kept back the primeval jungle. Turning the angle of Garden Reach, we lost our distant view of the Ochterlony Monument, the beacon of Calcutta, though the numbers of native and foreign craft, with steam-tugs, ascending and descending the river, still showed our proximity to a mart of commerce. For some distance along the western bank the people are brick-makers, and their quaint pyramids of yellow clay frequently rise above the tops of the cocoa trees. The Bengalees live in thatched bamboo huts, directly on the water's edge, with a dense rank wilderness behind them. The cocoa-nut palm is the principal tree, though the mango also flourishes, and the graceful *areca* is sometimes seen. The cotton tree, with its showers of scarlet, lily-shaped blossoms, is a most brilliant object, and splendidly stars the deep green background of the jungle. Tigers are abundant in these parts, and the river abounds with crocodiles, but I left India without having seen either of those beasts. The green parrot screamed from the tops of the palms, brown vultures swept lazily through the air, and a few sea-gulls skimmed the waves, but no more ferocious animals met my eyes.

About thirty miles down the river, we ran into a handsome three-masted schooner, carrying away her bow-sprit and cutting in twain one of our quarter-boats. We went more slowly after this, for the navigation was becoming intricate, on account of the breadth of the river and the frequency of sand-banks. The shores being a dead level, and the jungle with which they are covered not very lofty, they soon sank to a low green line on either side, and the native villages ceased. As far as Diamond Harbor, about sixty miles below Calcutta, there is a good road on the eastern bank, and telegraph stations at intervals. The river is here four miles broad, and gradually widens as we approach the sea. We dropped down to Kedgeree, on the western bank, about sunset, and there halted until the next morning at ten, in order to cross St. James's Bar with the flood tide. As we were hoisting anchor, the smoke of a steamer was descried in the offing, and on nearer approach she proved to be the *Tenasserim*, returning from Rangoon with Lord Dalhousie, the Governor General, and suite on board.

While listening to the songs of the Lascars, and Chinamen, as they were getting up the anchor, I was struck with the resemblance of one of their refrains to one of the songs of the Nile boatmen. The rhythm was trochaic trimeter, with a redundant syllable, precisely like the "*Ed-dookkan el-liboodeh fayn?*" of the Arabs. The chorus of these Lascars was '*Panch sepparree Bombay-ka*'" (Five betel-nut palms of Bombay.) They sang in perfect accord, and the air was really very sweet and melodious. The rhythm was marked by a strong accent on the long syllables, which seems to be a gen eral custom of Eastern singers. Another simple and common measure with the Hindoos is: "*Hathee-par howdah, ghora-par jeen*" (the howdah on the elephant, the saddle on the horse), which corresponds to that of Motherwell's ballad:

> "Home came the saddle,
> He nevermore!"

We crossed the mouth of the river to Saugor Island, quite sinking the western shore, and after running past its solitary light-house and dreary tiger jungles, stood out for the Sand-heads. The extreme point of Saugor Island is believed by the Hindoos to mark the junction of the Ganges with the sea, and they accordingly esteem it as one of the holiest spots in India. At a certain season of the year they flock thither in great numbers, for the purpose of bathing and offering sacrifices. This was my last view of India, for, although we were threading the channels of the Sandheads and surrounded by the muddy waves of the Gunga, for two or three hours afterwards, no land was visible. About noon we discharged the pilot, and having fairly entered on the broad Bay of Bengal, headed for Penang.

The voyage across the bay was remarkably pleasant. There was a profound calm in the air and on the water, and our progress through it created but a faint semblance of a breeze. The mercury ranged from 80° to 85°, the temperature at which indolence becomes a luxury. I had been so bruised, jolted, shaken and excited by my journey through India, that the sweetness of the air, the repose of the sea, and the quiet movement of our vessel, were exceedingly grateful and refreshing. There were only six other passengers, and each of us possessed an entire state-room—a great advantage in a voyage in the tropical seas. The captain, a red-haired giant in appearance, was one of the frankest, heartiest and most genial of commanders, and the other officers were quiet and gentlemanly in their manners. Among the passengers were Sir Lawrence Peel, Chief Justice of Bengal, and Mr. Dorin, Secretary of the Board of Directors of the East India Company.

After sailing two or three days across the Bay, towards the Burmese coast, we passed one night through the Cocos Islands, off the northern point of the Great Andaman. The next day we saw the island of Narcondan—a single volcanic peak, which rises from the water to the height of 2,500 feet. Its summit was hidden in clouds, and its sides completely covered with the richest vegetation. It is singular that so little should be known of the Andaman Islands, which lie high up the Bay of Bengal, almost on the route between Calcutta and Burmah. The larger island is about a hundred miles in length, and has a splendid harbor at its northern extremity. The East India Company at one time attempted to make a settlement there, but failed on account of sickness among the colonists. The natives of the islands are believed to be similar to the Papuans, though some consider them a branch of the African race. It is said that they are cannibals, but very little is known of their habits and modes of life.

Approaching the promontory of Malacca, we caught a distant view of the island of Salanga, and then stood in nearer the eastern shore. On the morning of the 6th of March, we made the island of Penang, which is separated from the peninsula by a strait less than a mile in width. The town of Penang lies on the inner side, where the narrowness of the strait forms a secure harbor for vessels. The eastern half of the island is nearly level, rising to the west into a group of lofty mountains, clothed to the summits with forests. A strip of silver beach along the shore, divided the pale emerald of the sea—a hue which betrays a floor of coral—from the darker tint of the forests of cocoa palm, which rose behind. Here and there a picturesque Malay village crouched in the shade, and numbers of small fishing craft dotted the surface of the water. A Chinese junk, with sails of matting, divided into a score of reefs, and with a great black eye on each side of her square bows, moved slowly past us on her way to Singapore. The morning wind, blowing off the land, fanned us with spicy odors, and hinted of the groves of nutmeg and clove-trees, for which Penang is celebrated.

When the steamer came to anchor, and we were informed that seven hours was the limit of our stay, I determined to visit the signal-station on the summit of the highest peak of the island, about eight miles distant, and set off at once, in company with one of the officers. We landed at a little wooden jetty, where a number of light garrees, with a pony harnessed to each, were collected, in anticipation of employment. One of the passengers, who was stationed at Penang, engaged two saddle-ponies for us, and dispatched them in advance, to await us at the foot of the mountain, while we proceeded thither in a garree. The road was admirable, and the Malay groom, running at the pony's head, propelled him forwards even too fast for our liking. The purity of the air, the cloudless beauty of the day, and the glorious groves of balm and bloom—of deep green shades, and glossy lustres, and gorgeous coloring—

through which we drove, have never been surpassed, in all my experience of the tropics. I thought then, and I think so still, that Penang is the most beautiful island in the world. The dwellings of the English residents are large, airy bungalows, embowered in gardens, and surrounded by groves of cocoa and areca palm, the nutmeg and bread-fruit trees. The native town, inhabited by Chinese and Malays, is small, and lies close upon the water, but for miles around it extends a succession of beautiful residences and rich plantations, reaching to the foot of the hills. The Chinese houses, scattered along the road, with their great red hieroglyphics, and the queer, solemnly-stupid yellow faces of their inmates, catch the eye of the traveller from the west, and tell him that he has at last reached the borders of the Far East.

After a drive of four miles, we entered a little dell, where a stream of water, stealing through the woods, fell over the rocks in a miniature cascade. Several lithe Malay youths were bathing in the shallow pool at its foot, and their glowing brown bodies glistened in the sun. Here we mounted our ponies, and commenced the ascent. The path wound backwards and forwards through dense thickets, between banks covered with gigantic fern, till it attained a ridgy spur of the mountain, which it followed upward to the central heights. We soon entered the forests, which gradually became so dense and dark as to shut out every ray of the sun. Trees of thick, glossy foliage, mingled their tops a hundred feet above our heads, and in their shade arose a luxuriant undergrowth. Ferns, whose fronds were frequently from ten to fifteen feet in length, bent their arching plumes above our heads; strange plants, of new and graceful form, clustered on either hand, and birds of bright plumage darted in and out of the foliage There was one, hidden in thickest shades, whose clear, prolonged, bell-like note, rang continually through the forest—a wild, wizard call, which overflowed all the air, and was taken up in one spot as soon as it ceased in another.

We had advanced in this way about two miles, when an opening in the trees disclosed a view to the south, into the heart of a valley of more than Arcadian loveliness. It might have been three miles in length by less than a mile in breadth, and the orchards of palm, orange and spice-trees which covered its lap, almost concealed the dwellings of the planters. It lay between hills of billowy green, which, uniting at the farther end, formed a gorge or gateway of forests, through which shone the dark-blue sphere of the sea. It was a landscape from the paradise of dreams, basking in the light of its own serene and perfect beauty. As I looked down on it from that window of the region of shade, I could have believed that I stood on the Delectable Mountains, and that the valleys of the Land of Beulah were at my feet.

Again we plunged into the depth of the forest, and after two miles more of climbing, which moistened every hair in the coats of our sturdy little ponies, reached the flag-staff, 2,500 feet above the sea. Here there is a summer residence of the Governor, and half a dozen private bungalows. The pure air of the heights, with the refreshing temperature, which stands at from 70° to 75° during the whole year, make this a most delightful place of resort. I climbed to the cross-trees of the flag-staff in order to get an uninterrupted view of the wide summer panorama. The lowland of Penang, with its orchards and gardens, lay at my feet; across the strait stretched many a league of forest, divided here and there by the gleaming windings of rivers, and far back in the vapory distance arose the mountain spine of the Peninsula of Malacca. To the south and west, over scattered island-cones of verdure, curved a great hemisphere of sea, behind which, hidden by the warm noonday haze, were the mountains of Sumatra. That part of the peninsula lying opposite to Penang has been acquired by the East India Company, and erected into a province, with the title of Wellesley; further south, Malacca and Singapore are English dependencies; the gap between Arracan and Tenasserim has been filled up by the recent annexation of Pegu, and now, of two thousand miles of coast line between Calcutta and Singapore, there are not more than two hundred, to which the English title is still wanting. The Anglo-Indian Empire stretches from Beloochistan to the China Sea. They now talk of the *natural* boundaries of Burmah as obviating the need of further annexation to the Eastward; but when did their lust of aggrandizement ever heed any natural boundary except the sea?

On our return to the ship we visited a nutmeg plantation. The trees, which are from twenty to thirty feet in height, are planted in rows, at intervals of about twenty feet. The leaf is dark green and glossy, resembling that of the laurel, and the fruit, at a little distance, might be taken for a small russet-colored apple. When ripe the thick husk splits in the centre, showing a scarlet net-work of mace, enveloping an inner nut, black as ebony, the kernel of which is the nutmeg of commerce.

The clove-tree, not then in its bearing season, has some resemblance to the nutmeg, but the leaf is smaller, and the foliage more loose and spreading. As we drove through the orchard, the warm air of noon was heavy with spice. The rich odors exhaled from the trees penetrated the frame with a sensation of languid and voluptuous repose. Perfume became an appetite, and the senses were drugged with an overpowering feeling of luxury. Had I continued to indulge in it, I should ere ong have realized the Sybarite's complaint of his crumpled rose-leaf.

In the Strait of Malacca, the heat was rather oppressive, the thermometer standing at 88° in the coolest part of the ship We ran down within sight of the peninsula, and on the after noon after leaving Penang, had a distant view of the town of Malacca. The next morning I went on deck, just in time to see the southern extremity of the Continent of Asia. The Peninsula of Malacca tapered away to a slender point, completely overgrown with palm and mangrove trees, which rose in heavy masses from the water's edge. At the end, a single cocoa-palm stood a little in advance of its fellows, leaning outward, as if looking intently across the Southern Sea. The water was smooth and glassy, and belts of a paler green betrayed the hidden banks of coral. Island after island arose in the distance, until we were inclosed in an archipelago of never-fading verdure. They were tenanted entirely by the Malay races; some were hilly and irregular in appearance, while other rose like green cones from the tranquil sea. The Island of Singapore, which we were approaching, was comparatively ow, but not without a picturesque beauty in the irregularity of ts shores. The strait through which we sailed resembled an inland lake rather than a part of the ocean, for the islands were so crowded together in the distance as quite to intercept the sea-horizon. Presently we entered what seemed a river—the narrow strait between Singapore and a small adjacent island, and halted alongside a large wooden pier, in what is called the New Harbor.

The town of Singapore is three miles distant, but as the steamer remained twenty-four hours to coal, we embarked in garrees drawn by Malay ponies, and were carried straightway to the "London Hotel," where we remained until next day. The town is purely commercial, and has grown up principally within the last ten or fifteen years. The population is estimated at 40,000 or 50,000, the greater part of whom are Chinese. There are several of their pagodas in the place, and three large burying-grounds, densely populated, in the vicinity. This was my first sight of a large Chinese community, and the impression it left was not agreeable. Their dull faces, without expression, unless a coarse glimmering of sensuality may be called such, and their half-naked, unsymmetrical bodies, more like figures of yellow clay than warm flesh and blood, filled me with an unconquerable aversion. The scowling Malay, with his dark, fiery eye, and spare but sinewy form, was ennobled by the comparison, and I turned to look upon him with a great sense of relief.

The Island of Singapore is hilly and undulating, although no part of it rises more than 500 feet above the sea. On the eastern side of the town is the English suburb, which contains a number of pleasant residences. The Governor's mansion is delightfully situated on a hill above, commanding a fine view of the harbor, and the large island of Bintang in the distance. The hills around it are covered with turf as fresh and green as that of England. The temperature of the island, which lies in 1° 18′ N., is healthy and agreeable, and scarcely varies throughout the whole year. The vegetation is kept constantly fresh and luxuriant by frequent showers. The interior of the island is covered with plantations of pepper and nutmeg. The depredations committed by tigers are said to be frightful, since in spite of a government bounty for their destruction, more than three hundred persons are annually devoured by them.

We left Singapore on the morning of the 9th, and after passing the island of Bintang, entered the China Sea. Notwithstanding it was the season of the north-east monsoon, we were favored with calm weather and clear skies. During the first two days we passed Pulo Aor, and the barren groups of the Anambas and Natunas, after which nothing occurred to break the monotony of the voyage, until the morning of the 16th, when in the midst of a thick and rainy gale from the north, which came up suddenly during the night, we made the rocks called the Asses' Ears, off the Ladrone Islands, at the mouth of the Gulf of Canton. We got shelter from the heavy swell under the lee of the Lemma Island, and as the clouds broke away a little, saw before us the barren hills of Hong Kong In two hours more we were at anchor in the harbor.

CHAPTER XXIII.

VOYAGE UP THE COAST OF CHINA.

Trip to Macao—Attached to the U. S. Embassy—On Board the Steam-frigate Susquehanna—Departure from Macao—The Coast of China—The Shipwrecked Japanese—Their Address to the Commissioner—The Eastern Sea—The Archipelago of Chusan—The Mouth of the Yang-tse-Kiang—The Steamer Aground—Rumors of the Rebels—Arrival at Woosung—Entering the Woosung River—Chinese Junks—Appearance of the Country—Approach to Shanghai—Arrival.

On arriving at Hong Kong, one of my fellow-passengers entered my name at the Club House, a part of which was fitted up as a hotel. The weather was cold, raw and cloudy, and I spent the greater part of my time in-doors, reading the late files of European journals. The U. S. steam-frigate *Susquehanna* was lying in the harbor, ready to sail for Macao, and as I desired to visit Canton, I accepted Capt. Buchanan's invitation to cross in her to the former place, whence I could take the Canton steamer. She left Hong Kong on the morning of the 20th, and after a pleasant run of four hours anchored in Macao Roads. I went ashore, expecting to proceed to Canton on the morrow: but no one knows what a day may bring forth. Upon calling on the U. S. Commissioner, the Hon. Humphrey

Marshall, to whom I had letters, he generously offered to attach me to the Embassy, that I might be able to accompany him to the seat of war in the North. So rare an opportunity of seeing the most interesting portion of China during the present remarkable crisis in the history of the Empire was not to be neglected; and on the following morning I again found myself on board the Susquehanna, listening to the thunders of the salute which welcomed the Commissioner. It was worth all my long wanderings in foreign lands and among strange races, to experience the pride and satisfaction of walking the deck of a national vessel, and hearing again the stirring music of our national airs. One must drink deep of absence and exile to learn the tenderness of that regard for his native land, which at home lies latent and unsuspected at the bottom of his nature. I want no man for a friend, whose heart will not beat more warmly at the sight of his country's banner floating on a distant sea.

The handsome stern-cabin of the Susquehanna was appropriated to the use of the Commissioner, and his suite, consisting of Dr. Peter Parker, Secretary of Legation, Mr. O. H. Perry, Private Secretary, and myself. We found in Capt. Buchanan, the Commander, all that his reputation as a gentleman and a brave and gallant officer, led us to anticipate; while the officers under his command justified the high opinion I had formed of our naval corps, from the few whom it had previously been my good fortune to meet. Under such auspices, our voyage up the coast of China was one of the most agreeable I ever made.

We left Macao, about nine o'clock on the morning of the 21st, and stood outward to sea, past the Lemma Island. The day was warm and calm, and the barren Chinese coast was unobscured by cloud or vapor. It is a bold, rugged shore, indented with small bays and estuaries, and bounded by a fringe of lofty island-rocks, which are for the most part uninhabitable. In its general features, it resembles the coast of California, but is in reality more sterile, though hardly more so in appearance. Towards evening we saw the promontory called Breaker Point in the distance, and during the night passed within half a mile of the Lamock Islands. The next morning was dull and overcast. We were already within the Straits of Fu-kien, or the Formosa Channel, as it is now called, and had a strong head-wind. During the day we had occasional glimpses of the islands and promontories of the coast, on our left, but too dark and indistinct to be satisfactory. About noon, we passed the headland of Quemoy, north of the Bay of Amoy, which is one of the five ports opened to foreigners by the English war. Its commerce, however, is next to nothing, nearly all the foreign trade being concentrated at Canton and Shanghai.

On Monday afternoon the thirteen shipwrecked Japanese sailors, who, having been picked up at sea and taken into San Francisco, were sent to China by the order of our Government, and placed on board the Susquehanna, were summoned in a body upon the quarter-deck to pay their respects to the "big mandarin," as they termed Col. Marshall. They made a very profound inclination of the head, removing their caps at the same time. Dr. Parker addressed them in Chinese, which they did not understand when spoken; but as the Chinese characters are known to the Japanese (the same character signifying the same word in both languages), he was enabled to communicate with them. They appeared cheerful and in good condition. They were nearly all dressed in sailor costume, with clothes which the officers and men had given them. It was curious to note the variety of feature, form and expression among these men, all of whom belonged to the same class There was one with an unusually broad face and dark complexion, who corresponded to Golownin's description of the Kurile inhabitants of the northern portion of the Empire. They wore their hair short upon the crown and front of the head, but hanging loose and long at the back and sides, which Dr. Parker declared to have been the former Chinese custom, shaven heads and long tails having been introduced by the Mantchow Dynasty. The features of these Japanese were much better than those of the corresponding class of Chinese. The day following their presentation a note written in Chinese characters was addressed by them to Col. Marshall. It was very fragmentary and laconic, owing, no doubt, to the small stock of characters in the writer's possession. It was addressed on the envelope: "To the American King—from thirteen Japanese," and the contents were as follows: "We, thirteen Japanese men, have fathers, mothers, young brothers, old brothers, wives, children. You go to Shanghai: go to Japan!"

On Wednesday we continued to advance against a strong head-wind, catching but few and cloudy glimpses of the coast. During the day we passed the mouth of the estuary of Foo-chow-foo, another of the five ports. Before night, we had passed through the Formosa Channel, and were in the Tong-hai, or Eastern Sea, which is bounded by China, Corea, the Japanese Island of Kiusiu, and the Lew-Chew Archipelago. The next morning we were off the province of Che-Kiang. Soon after sunrise we made a small island called the Straw-Stack, and still further, a headland called Mushroom Peak, from its shape, the sides being perpendicular, and the summit slightly projecting over them. At the other extremity of the same promontory there was a tall isolated rock resembling a pagoda. The afternoon was raw and foggy, and as there was a large number of fishing junks off the coast, our steam-whistle was blown repeatedly, as a signal for them to get out of the way.

On Friday there was a dense fog, with frequent showers of rain, and we saw no land until evening, when we made the rocks called the Brothers, at the eastern end of the Archipelago of Chusan. We had had no observation for a day or two, but when the fog lifted and showed the rocks, we were not a milo from our supposed position. The night set in dark and stormy, and as the tides and currents, which prevail in this part of the Archipelago, are very uncertain, we felt our way in the fog into a strait between the islands of Chusan and Chinsan, and came to anchor under the lee of the latter. It blew violently during the night, but the gale had the effect of clearing away the fog, so that we were able to get under way again at daylight.

We rounded the eastern point of Chinsan, and running in a north-west course, soon made the two groups called the Rugged Islands and Parker's Islands. The water became yellow and muddy, showing that we were already within the influence of the great Yang-tse-Kiang River, and when scarcely abreast the southern entrance, it was as turbid as the Mississippi at New Orleans. The volume of water brought down by the river must be enormous; the southern mouth, which comprises about two thirds, or less, of the main stream, is thirty miles in breadth. Parker's Island was green and beautiful, and appeared to be cultivated. Most of the other islands were lofty;

rugged, as their name denotes, and hopelessly barren. The smaller ones were mere rocks, cleft and divided by deep chasms, like those on the western coast of Scotland. The wind was keen, cold, and strong from the north, and the thermometer down to 60°. The sky was a cool, pale blue, veiled with haze, but the sun shone cheerily at intervals. As we approached our destination, the Japanese desired another interview with the Commissioner. It was intimated that they wished to land at Shanghai, make their way to Chapoo, the Chinese port of communication with Nagasaki, and embark in a junk for the latter place. Chapoo is south of Shanghai, on the Bay of Hang-Chow, and about ninety miles distant.

At noon we reached Gutzlaff Island, at the mouth of the Yang-tse-Kiang (Son of the Sea), and commenced the difficult navigation of the river. The island is a round, rocky hillock, rising 210 feet from the water. From its prominence, and position at the mouth of the river, it is a valuable landmark for vessels. The Yang-tse-Kiang is here about twenty miles broad, flowing between the mainland of China, and the large island of Tsung-Ming. Both shores are a dead level, dyked to prevent inundation, like the banks of the lower Mississippi, and not to be seen from the narrow channel in the middle of the river, which is lined on both sides by extensive sand-banks. We had a strong wind and tide against us, and did not lose sight of Gutzlaff Island until near four o'clock. The water became more dense and yellow as we proceeded, and the paddles of the steamer stirred up large quantities of the soft mud of the bottom. The depth of the stream varied from four to five fathoms.

At six o'clock, as the crew was beaten to quarters, it was

noticed that the engines moved sluggishly, and soon afterwards the ship refused to obey her helm. She was immediately stopped, and a careful sounding showed only two and three quarter fathoms. The previous sounding had been disturbed by the wake of the wheel, and the sinking of the lead into the oose mud, so that we had run about half a mile upon the South Shoal before being aware of it. The engines were backed, but the strong northern gale and ebb tide kept us stationary for about an hour, after which the ship began to move by fits and starts. The guns were run forward to lighten her stern, and the tide setting in her favor, she worked herself off by nine o'clock, and came to anchor in deep water.

We started again the next morning, with the flood tide. The day was crystal-clear, and a bracing wind blew from the north-east. In an hour or two we were hailed by an American pilot, who had been taking a French vessel out of the river. He startled us with the news that the rebels had invested Nanking with an army of 200,000 men, captured all the Chinese war-junks in the Yang-tse-Kiang, and cut off supplies from the beleaguered troops—with many other particulars, which, like all rumors afloat at that time, were greatly exaggerated. In another hour the mainland of China was visible on our left—a low shore, covered with trees, and dotted with the houses of the natives. Numbers of junks were anchored along the beach, and the wreck of a European vessel told of the dangers of the navigation. The island of Tsung-Ming was barely visible to the east. We reached the mouth of the Woosung River about noon, and cast anchor a mile from the shore, to wait for a tide to carry us over the bar. On making signals, a junk came out for the mails, with which she started at once for Shanghai. The mouth of the river was crowded with vessels, the greater part of which were native junks. The stream is about half a mile in breadth, and is protected by two batteries, the northern one having 126 guns. The shore is well wooded, and the trees, with their thin texture and the greenish-gray hue of their budding leaves, showed that we had again reached a climate where spring is known.

Mr. P. S. Forbes, U. S. Consul at Canton, and Mr. Cunningham, Vice-Consul at Shanghai, who had ridden down to Woosung in expectation of the Susquehanna's arrival, came on board shortly after we dropped anchor. At 4 P. M., the tide being again flood, we stood into the river through the fleet of junk sat its mouth. It was a delicate piece of manœuvring, but the vessel minded her helm admirably, and threaded the mazes of the crowded anchorage without touching one of the craft. The tide carried us safely over the bar, and we kept on up the river at nearly our full speed. The stream was covered with junks lying at anchor or sailing up and down. Our steam-whistle warned them to clear the track, and they obeyed with alacrity, the crews gathering upon the high poops to survey us as we passed. Most of the junks had inscriptions across the stern and along the sides of the hull. Some, which Dr. Parker read, denoted that the vessel was in Government service: others had fantastic names, such as "The Favorable Wind," "Happiness," &c. All the larger ones had four masts, each mast carrying a single oblong sail, made of very closely woven matting, crossed with horizontal slips of bamboo. so that it could be reefed to any extent required. The people had a lighter complexion and more regular features than the natives of the southern provinces, and in lieu of, the umbrella hat wore the round black cap of the Tartars.

The country on both sides of the river is a dead level of rich alluvial soil, devoted principally to the culture of rice and wheat. The cultivation was as thorough and patient as any I had seen, every square foot being turned to some useful account. Even the sides of the dykes erected to check inundations were covered with vegetables. These boundless levels are thickly studded with villages and detached houses, all of which are surrounded with fruit-trees. I noticed also occasionally groves of willow and bamboo. The country, far and wide, is dotted with little mounds of earth—the graves of former generations. They are scattered over the fields and gardens in a most remarkable manner, to the great detriment of the cultivators. In some places the coffins of the poor, who cannot afford to purchase a resting-place, are simply deposited upon the ground, and covered with canvas. The dwellings, but for their peaked roofs, bore some resemblance to the cottages of the Irish peasantry. They were mostly of wood, plastered and whitewashed, and had an appearance of tolerable comfort. The people, who came out to stare in wonder at the great steamer as she passed, were dressed uniformly in black or dark blue. Numerous creeks and canals extended from the river into the plains, but I did not notice a single highway. The landscape was rich, picturesque and animated, and fully corresponded with what I had heard of the dense population and careful agriculture of China. I was struck with the general resemblance between the Woosung and the lower Mississippi, and the same thing was noticed by others on board.

Before sunset, we discovered in the distance the factories

and flagstaffs of Shanghai. The town had a more imposing appearance than I was prepared to find. The river makes a sharp bend to the south-west at this point, and over the tops of the trees on the southern bank, we could see a forest of masts, a mile in length, belonging to the native junks. The number of foreign vessels anchored before the factories did not exceed twenty. Rounding the point, we swept between the shipping, past the stately row of tall European residences, and a neat church (Gothic), to the reach in front of the American Consulate, one of the largest and handsomest buildings on the river. The English war-steamers Hermes and Salamander, and the brig Lily, lay anchored there, and the French war-steamer Cassini, a little further up the stream. Beyond them commenced the wilderness of junks, packed side by side in one unbroken mass. As the anchor dropped our band struck up "Hail Columbia" followed by the English and French national airs.

Mr. Cunningham invited the Commissioner and his suite to take rooms at the Consulate, where that splendid hospitality which distinguishes the foreign communities in China is practised to its fullest extent. We found various and contradictory rumors afloat with regard to the Chinese rebels, but it was generally believed that Nanking had fallen into their hands. The merchants were in hourly expectation of hearing that the great city of Soo-Chow, the capital of the silk-growing district, and only seventy miles from Shanghai, had been invested.

CHAPTER XXIV.

AN ATTEMPT TO VISIT NANKING

The Commissioner decides to visit Nanking—Preparations for the Voyage—Departure of four Japanese—The Susquehanna leaves—Woosung—Bush Island and Tsung-Ming—We strike the Blonde Shoal—The Chinese Pilots—Escape of a Boat—Off the Shoal—Mr. Bennett's night cruise after the Boats—Unfavorable Reports—The Return—End of the Expedition—Successful Trip of the Susquehanna in the Summer of 1854.

THREE days after our arrival, the Commissioner decided to start for Nanking. The near approach of the rebel forces to the foreign settlement of Shanghai, the uncertainty with regard to their views towards foreigners, and the utter impossibility of obtaining reliable accounts from the seat of war through the Chinese authorities, led him to this step. The visit was projected with the sole view of obtaining information, that he might best know how to guard the interests of American citizens in China. Like the representatives of England and France in Shanghai, he determined on preserving the strictest neutrality during the civil war then raging in the North. But if, as all accounts concurred in representing, Nanking had already fallen, it was a matter of importance that the rebel leaders should be assured of this neutrality and of the necessity, on their part, of respecting the rights of foreign citizens. The adoption of this course was rendered still more imperative by the falsehoods which the Chinese authorities, and especially the Taou-tai (Governor) of Shanghai had published and circulated concerning the enlistment of foreign aid.

Two hundred tons of coal were taken on board the Susquehanna, and application was made to the Taou-tai for native pilots who knew the river. These he readily furnished, hoping perhaps that our appearance off Nanking would be interpreted to the advantage of the Imperialists. Hundreds of Chinese continued to visit the Susquehanna up to the hour of her departure. Several of the American residents made application to accompany us on the voyage, but, with the exception of Mr. Forbes, no other passenger was taken on board. Previous to sailing, four of the Japanese left our ship. One of their countrymen—one of those who were turned back from Japan in the Morrison, in 1837—was then residing in Shanghai, and he promised to assist them. Neither Capt. Buchanan nor the Commissioner had any authority to keep them on board. They desired their countryman, Otokitchi, to say that they thanked the officers and men of the ship from their hearts, and would never forget their kindness toward them. Two of them wept like children when they left.

We started at floodtide, on the afternoon of the 1st of April. The *bund*, or quay, of Shanghai was crowded with spectators of our departure. We were two hours and a half reaching Woosung. The rich plains on either hand were greener and more beautiful than they appeared on the passage up. The willow trees planted along the numerous little canals intersecting the country were rapidly bursting into leaf. In spite of these tokens of spring, a keen, benumbing wind blew from the north-east, and the cabin was not comfortable without fire. There is perhaps no other part of the world where spring is so tardy. We crossed the bar without difficulty, but afterwards had to thread a fleet of junks, filling up a reach of more than half a mile. This feat was admirably managed, without running afoul of any of the craft, though the winding channels between them were scarcely broader than our beam. The Susquehanna obeyed her helm as readily as a ferry-boat. We anchored for the night in the main channel of the Yang-tse-Kiang, a mile from shore.

At daybreak, the ten Chinese boats which had been engaged for the purpose of going ahead to feel the channel, started in advance. We hove anchor and left at seven o'clock. The four Chinese pilots were on deck, seemingly confident of their ability to carry us through. Just above Woosung, we passed Bush Island; the large island of Tsung-Ming, separating the northern and southern mouths of the Yang-tse-Kiang, was visible beyond it in the distance. Both of these islands have been formed from the alluvial deposits of the river, and are yearly increasing in size. Capt. Potter (an American pilot, who accompanied us) informed me that ten years ago there was but one bush on the smaller island (whence its name), and not an inhabitant. At present it is covered with trees and thickly studded with cottages. Tsung-Ming, a century ago, was a sand-bar; at present it supports a population of six hundred thousand. The immense deposits brought down by the Yang-tse-Kiang, the Hoang-Ho, and other rivers must in the course of time entirely fill up the mouth of the Yellow Sea.

Our mosquito fleet was still visible, running rapidly ahead with the monsoon filling their square sails, and I was looking through a telescope at the clusters of Chinese who were watching us from the shore, when the ship suddenly struck upon a shoal. She was only going at half-speed, and the engine was stopped soon enough to prevent her jamming very hard upon the sand. Still, there she stuck, and as the ebb-tide had just commenced, every effort was made to get her off before the water fell. There were fourteen feet at the bows, and three and one fourth fathoms at the stern: the bottom hard sand. The wheels were backed and a hawser sent out over the stern, to warp her off, but without avail. The place where we struck proved to be the Blonde Shoal, twelve or fifteen miles from Woosung. The accident was entirely owing to the carelessness or treachery of the principal Chinese pilot. We had boats enough to have sounded out for us all the shoals as far as Harvey's Point, but he insisted on sending them ahead, saying that he was perfectly familiar with the channel, and did not require their services for a hundred *li* (thirty miles) further. He put on an offensive, stately air, and carried his head high until chastised by Mr. Cunningham's comprador, who accompanied us as interpreter and commissary. The latter, on receiving an impertinent reply to a question which he had asked by command of Capt. Buchanan, immediately struck the pilot in the face, and brought him to his knees in supplication.

When it was found we could not get off, Capt. Buchanan determined to send the Chinese bum-boat, which accompanied us, ahead to the other boats, with one of the pilots. But the men, instead of keeping up the river, immediately made all speed for the shore. One of the brass field-pieces was hauled to the stern, brought to bear on her, and a few shots fired across her bows, in order to bring her back, but she continued to make away, although the balls ploughed up the sea just beyond her. It happened that the pilot was not on board, as was supposed, but had remained with us, though in great fear for his life. Mr. Bennett, Master of the Susquehanna, was then sent off for the pilots, in one of the ship's cutters At ebb-tide we had but eight feet water under our bows and seventeen under the stern.

At midnight on Saturday night it began to blow very violently from the north, so that about five o'clock, when the tide had risen a few feet, the vessel seemed to be slowly working herself loose. The foresail was bent on, and she immediately gave evidence of feeling it. A few backward strokes of the wheels urged her clear of the shoal, and she hung buoyantly in deep water. But in the distance of a few ship's lengths the water suddenly shoaled again, and she was brought to anchor in five fathoms, with some little difficulty. The utter inefficiency of the pilots was again displayed by their declaring that the channel was on the right of the shoal, when our own soundings the day previous had shown that it was on the left side.

About eight o'clock, Mr. Bennett made his appearance in the cutter. He and his crew were benumbed with cold, having passed the whole night on the river. After running about twenty miles, he stood in toward Harvey's Point, at the northern extremity of Tsung-Ming, where the fleet was to have waited; but on inquiring of some fishermen, learned that it had gone further up the river. About ten miles further, he found the junks at anchor in a creek, on the southern bank

By the time they were collected together, it was ten o'clock at night. Capt. Potter and the comprador went on board the boats, which were ordered to follow the cutter, and return to the Susquehanna. They all got under way at the same time, but in the darkness of the night the cutter soon lost sight of them. She grounded repeatedly on the shoals, and finally got entangled among the bamboo fishing-stakes. The sea continuing to rise, and the gale to blow more violently, she was obliged to come to anchor until morning, when she put off again and beat down to us. Capt. Buchanan and the Commissioner decided, on hearing Mr. Bennett's report, that it was expedient to return to Woosung. The necessity of putting back was keenly regretted by all on board, but the extreme peril to which the vessel was exposed, in case the voyage was continued, left no other alternative. We were obliged to wait for the first of the flood-tide, to run down to Woosung, which detained us until four o'clock. In the mean time, Capt. Potter and the comprador arrived with the other boats. The former reported that no dependence could be placed either on the chart or the Chinese pilots, and that the only way in which the Susquehanna could go up the river, would be to resurvey and buoy out the channel—a work which could not be accomplished in less than two weeks. The failure of our undertaking, the results of which promised to be of great interest and importance at the time, is another proof of the unfitness of large steam frigates for the service required in Chinese waters. Two small, active steamers, such as the English possessed in the Hermes and Salamander, would do more work than a score of unwieldy leviathans.

We returned down the river the way we came, but on ap

proaching Woosung were again exposed to danger through the ignorance of the pilots. The water suddenly shoaled, in spite of their assertion that we were in the deep channel, and our hull touched just as the engines began to back water. We got off barely in time. The command having been given to let go the starboard anchor, a seaman, who was standing upon the port anchor, mistaking the order, and thinking it was about to drop with him, sprang into the river. He was picked up, however, with no other injury than a good drenching.

The next morning we were delayed for some time in crossing the bar, by a large fleet of grain-junks, bound outward on their way to Pekin. A Portuguese *lorcha*, bearing the flag of the Taou-tai, passed us on her way up the Yang-tse-Kiang. The Susquehanna's hull touched on the bar, in two and three quarter fathoms, but the engines dragged us safely over. Within the bar lay a still larger fleet of junks, ready to proceed to Pekin. Each of them had the words "*Kiang-nan*" on the stern,—literally "South of the River," *i. e.*, the Yang-tse-Kiang. A handsome outward-bound junk bore the poetical name of the "Ocean Star." At noon we were again at Shanghai, and dropped anchor in the old position, in front of the American Consulate.

So ended the expedition to Nanking.

NOTE.—The *Susquehanna* made a second attempt to reach Nanking in the summer of 1854, after her return from Japan. She had on board the Hon. Robert M'Lane, successor to Col. Marshal, as U. S. Commissioner to China. On this occasion, the small steam-tug *Confucius* was employed to run in advance of the *Susquehanna* and sound out the channel. After passing

Blonde Shoal no serious difficulty was experienced, a depth of from eight to seventeen fathoms having been found in the Yang-tse-Kiang, as far as Nanking. After the Commissioner had communicated with some of the rebel chiefs, and the object of the voyage was accomplished, a further exploration of the river was made as far as Wu-hu, a large town sixty miles above Nanking. No foreign vessel had ever before advanced beyond the latter city. The river was found to be everywhere broad and deep, flowing through superb valleys; the soil was fertile and capable of supporting an immense population. The current was very swift, and the *Susquehanna*, on her return, frequently ran at a speed of sixteen or seventeen knots. Her appearance, especially in the regions beyond Nanking, created the greatest astonishment among the Chinese, thousands of whom crowded the banks as she passed. The voyage was completed with entire success, no accident of any kind having occurred

CHAPTER XXV.

A SHANGHAI JOURNAL.

Life in Shanghai—The Rebels Expected—My Journal—The Fall of Nanking—The Grain Trade—Soo-Chow Threatened—Barbarities at Nanking—Rumors Concerning the Rebels—Capture of Lorchas—Threats towards Foreigners—Alarm of the Taou-tai—A Rebel Proclamation—Imperial Rewards and Pardons—Col. Marshall's Proclamation—Nanking Besieged by the Imperial Army—Flight from Shanghai—Sir George Bonham—Meetings of the Foreign Residents—Ransom for Shanghai—Soo-Chow not Taken—Uncertainty—Mr. Meadows at Soo-Chow—Defensive Works Commenced—Trouble with the Men of Foo-Kien—Maranders in the Country—Burning of Thieves—The Foo-Kien Grave-yard—Desertion of the City—A Rumored Battle—Death of Tien-teh—Mr. Meadows—Various Rumors—Return of the *Science*—Destruction of Chin-kiang-foo—The Excitement Subsides.

After our inglorious return, the Embassy was again shifted to the American Consulate, and we became once more the guests of our kind friend, Mr. Cunningham. I was supplied with a room and the services of a young Chinese valet, and having, as etiquette prescribed, made the first calls upon the American and English residents, received in due course of time invitations to dinner in return. The presence of the *Susquehanna*, with a fine band of music on board, was the occasion of a round of festivities, which were kept up with more or less energy, during the remainder of my stay. The presence of both the American and English Commissioners, and of five vessels of war at once, was an unusual event for Shanghai, and in spite of the rumored approach of the rebels, the ignorance of their disposition towards foreigners, and the anticipation of an assault, society there had never before been so gay and animated.

During the first fortnight of April, we were in almost daily expectation of the appearance of the vanguard of the rebel army. Each hour brought a new rumor, and each day led to conclusions and conjectures which the morrow proved to be unfounded. Although the true rebellion did not commence until some months afterwards, and the recollection of those days has doubtless been obliterated from the memories of the foreign residents of Shanghai, by the more stirring events which followed, they were sufficiently exciting and interesting at the time. I know no better way of giving a picture of the uncertainty of all news in China, than by transcribing a few pages from a journal which I kept at the time:

April 5th, 1853.

At length we have positive news that Nanking has fallen. The Taou-tai of Shanghai admits it, which is a certain sign of its correctness. The information was received yesterday by M. de Montigny, the French Consul, through the Catholic Missionaries at Nanking, but the fact was doubted by most of the merchants here until the Taou-tai confirmed it. In the final assault, 20,000 Tartars were slain. The streets were blocked up with corpses, and 1,000 *cash* each was paid by the victors for their removal. Twenty thousand rebel troops were left to garrison the city, and a body of 40,000 was dispatched to intercept the imperial troops on their way from Pekin, to raise the siege. The rebels, it is said, will establish their capital at Nanking, and for the remainder of the year will content themselves with consolidating their power in the South and West.

One circumstance, which has operated in their favor, is the almost total destruction of the grain trade between the South and North, by means of the Grand Canal. This has been caused within a few years by inundation between the Yang-tse-Kiang and the Hoang-ho, which have damaged the Canal to such an extent as to render it impassable for the larger class of vessels. The immense transportations of grain, for the supply of the northern portion of China, which were formerly made entirely through this channel, are now transferred to the coasting-junks, which sail at this season from Shanghai, Chapoo and Ningpo.

The city of Soo-Chow, it is said, has paid a ransom of 700,000 taels, to be exempted from capture and pillage. There seems to be no doubt of this, as business is beginning to revive there, and several Soo-Chow families, who had fled to this place, returned last night to their homes. It is not yet known whether a descent on Shanghai is meditated, but word reached us yesterday that Tien-teh does not intend to interfere in any way with foreigners in China.

April 6th.

Yesterday Mr. Forbes conversed with a native, who returned in one of the Taou-tai's *lorchas* from Nanking. The man is known to the Americans here, who place full reliance on his communication. He states that, after the taking of Nanking, the city was given up to sack and slaughter, during three days and 20,000 Tartars—men, women and children—were massa-ered. The Viceroy was quartered and his remains nailed to the four gates of the city. Previous to his death his veins were opened and his blood made to flow into a large vessel of water which the conquerors drank. His daughter, a girl of nineteen, was stripped in the public square, bound upon a cross, and her heart cut out. Many of the Tartar officers were thrown into boiling oil, or tied to stakes surrounded with bundles of oiled straw, and slowly roasted to death. The recital of these atrocities has aroused the utmost horror and indignation among the foreign residents. They were previously, almost to a man, disposed to rejoice at the success of the rebels.

That the Viceroy has been slain, is beyond a doubt. Col. Marshall has received the news officially, through the Governor of Soo-chow, upon whom the functions of Viceroy now devolve, and who is supposed to possess the seals; though another account says they were lost at Nanking. The ransom paid by the merchants of Soo-Chow only exempts the city from pillage. The rebels announce their determination to attack it, and the gates have been closed for several days.

The rumors afloat to-day are still more alarming. The rebels are stated to be marching to Hang-Chow, a large city about midway between here and Ningpo, at the head of the intervening gulf. Their proclamations have been received by the Governor of Soong-Keang, a city only forty miles from this place, and it is also supposed that they have been privately sent here, to the native merchants. Tïen-teh was to have been formally inaugurated as Emperor yesterday, at Nanking Among the tribute sent from Soo-Chow were 1,000 pieces of yellow sillk to be used on the occasion.

The Taou-tai this morning sent word that twenty of the

lorchas which he had dispatched to the relief of Nanking had fallen into the hands of the rebels; who, he feared, having the papers in their possession, would attempt to pass the Custom House at Woosung under false colors, and gain possession of that port. A lorcha, which he had sent up a week ago with $100,000, came back with an acknowledgment of its reception, signed by one of the rebel chiefs. It is reported that the captain, or supercargo, quietly delivered the money and took the receipt, thinking it was all right. The merchants here hinted to the Taou-tai that the sooner all his grain-junks were cleared for Pekin, the better, and he acted upon this suggestion. The river to-day was crowded with sails, and at least sixty or seventy junks dropped down to Woosung. There are still upwards of a thousand in port, and the foreigners are anxious that they should all be removed. In case of an attack they would undoubtedly be fired by the rebels, and set adrift to float down upon the foreign shipping.

Mr. Meadows, the interpreter of the British embassy, has been informed by a Chinese banker that the rebels have addressed the native inhabitants of Shanghai, bidding them be assured, as it is not them, but the foreign population, whom they intend to attack. After the rumors of T'ien-teh's Christianity and his pacific intentions towards foreigners, this news is rather startling, but there may be some reason for crediting it. The fact that the foreigners here have received no communication from the rebels is in itself suspicious—the custom of the latter having invariably been to send the proclamations in advance of their coming. Those who write upon their doors the word "*Obedience*" are saved from pillage.

April 7th.

This has been a day of excitement. About noon we received intelligence that an attack would certainly be made on Shanghai There were rumors of a proclamation which stated that the Chinese inhabitants had nothing to fear, but that the Taou-tai must be given up, as they intended to punish him for sending supplies to Nanking. The foreign residents would not be interfered with, provided they gave security not to carry on the opium trade. There are now vessels lying at Woosung, laden with opium to the amount of $3,000,000. This rumor, if true, would stir up the English to more active measures, Sir George Bonham's avowed policy at present being a masterly inactivity.

The Taou-tai is alarmed. He called to-day upon the English and American Consuls. He denies that Soo-Chow is fallen, says his wives and treasures are still in the city, but that, on the approach of danger, he will remove them to the Custom House, in the midst of the foreign settlement. About three o'clock several English officers imagined they heard the report of cannon at Woosung. I mounted to the roof of the Consulate, whence the shipping at that port is discernible, but could perceive no signs of firing. However, the English deemed it expedient to land 140 men with three or four field-pieces, and had companies of armed sailors patrolling the streets in the evening.

A document has at last been procured, which was taken from one of the gates of Soo-Chow. It is issued in the name of two of the rebel generals, declaring their intention to take Chin-Keang-foo, Soo-Chow, Hang-Chow, Soong-Keang and Shanghai. The Mantchows, it says, are utterly annihilated, and as for the foreigners, they are not human beings. The inhabitants of the three first-named cities have nothing to fear but all good Chinese residing in the two last should immediately remove to the distance of 100 *li* (33 miles), until the army has passed through, as it is by no means certain that there will not be fighting at Shanghai. This document explains the great panic of the Chinese to-day, and their hasty emigration from the city, which has been going on without interruption, from sunrise to the present hour (11 P. M.). The streets are crowded with porters, carrying off chests and boxes of valuables.

Mr. Taylor, an American Missionary, showed me some translations from the *Pekin Gazette*, from which it is evident that the Imperial Court is in great consternation. The Emperor declares his anxiety is so great that he can neither eat nor sleep. The capture of Woo-Chang-foo and Ngan-King is announced, but no mention is made of the siege of Nanking. The Taou-tai of this place is to be promoted for his loyalty. Several Generals, *who were slain by the rebels*, are promoted to the rank of Governor, and others who ran away, but *died afterwards*, are, on that account, absolved from the punishment due to their cowardice! So imbecile and absurd a Court as that of China never before governed a great Empire. Its duration or overthrow is a matter of complete indifference.

Col. Marshall drew up a proclamation this evening, to be issued by the representatives of France and America, since Sir George Bonham refuses to co-operate. It is a brief but forcible paper, declaring that, security of life and property having been assured to the citizens of both countries on the faith of treaties with the Emperor of China, no invading army could be permitted to occupy the foreign settlement here, or exact a tribute from the inhabitants. Furthermore, that the pillage of Shanghai would endanger the foreign residents, and would be resisted. With regard to the contest now waging, a strict and impartial neutrality would be preserved. It is proposed to forward this proclamation to the rebels to-morrow.

April 9th.

Yesterday a dispatch was received, to the effect that Nanking had been invested by the Imperial troops, and that the rebel forces had gone back from Soo-Chow for its relief. It was addressed to the Taou-tai by Heang-Yung, a Tartar General who appears to have acted bravely at the taking of Woo-Chang-foo. According to the proclamation of the Taou-tai, this general arrived before Nankin on the 31st of March, in advance of the main body of the Imperial troops. He calls upon the inhabitants of the province not to be alarmed, as the rebels will be exterminated to a man. Now the proclamation of Lo and W'ang, the two rebel generals, states that Tïen-teh was crowned Emperor at Nanking on the 31st of March, and it is unlikely that both events occurred at the same time. Notwithstanding the proclamation of the Taou-tai the emigration from the city, yesterday, was more active than ever. The *bund* (quay) and streets were crowded with porters, conveying the goods and treasures of the wealthy class, who are flying for refuge to the villages in the country.

No proclamation has yet been issued by the foreign representatives. Sir George Bonham yesterday sent around the draft of one, which differed in no material point from that of Col. Marshall, except that it was more diffuse, and carefully avoided speaking of the rebel forces. In order to secure the consent of all to a single declaration, Col. Marshall amalgamated the two but Sir George still refuses to co-operate. M. de Montigny has subscribed to the American proclamation, which will probably be issued this morning. The English still keep a body of armed sailors on shore, and on board all the vessels of war the usual drill with small arms is carried on every day.

Yesterday afternoon the English and American residents met at their respective Consulates to adopt measures of defence Twenty-seven Americans came together and discussed the matter, in true American style: each one wanted to have his own way, and only ten subscribed to Mr. Cunningham's proposals that a company should be formed, armed and exercised. Several of the Missionaries were quite ready to enter into this arrangement, and one of them, who is a graduate of West Point, offered to undertake the task of drilling them. The English acted with more unanimity, and the most of them subscribed their names to a similar proposal.

The Chinese merchants of Shanghai have made up the sum of $340,000 for the ransom of the city. Yesterday a deputation from them was sent off to Tien-teh, to remain with him as hostages for the payment, until the city shall be taken. It is said that the Taou-tai himself subscribed largely to the sum. Several of the "long-haired rebels" are reported to be in the city, and there is no doubt that their spies are already here. Fifteen hundred desperadoes from the province of Foo-Kien are waiting the moment of attack, to commence pillaging; but the Chinese who now remain have the impression that the Americans and French will defend the city.

April 10th.

We have now come to the conclusion that for the present we have no reason to fear an attack on Shanghai. The army which was marching upon Soo-Chow has not yet made its appearance before that city, having probably gone back to raise the siege of Nanking. Since the Taou-tai's proclamation no further news has been received, but the foreign residents are satisfied that they are safe for at least ten days longer. The Chinese continue to flock out of the city, though not to such an extent as during the previous two days. Now, since the alarm has subsided, the English have begun to adopt active measures of defence. Yesterday afternoon they had forty or fifty sailors at work, throwing up a three-gun redoubt, at the northern end of the race-course. The sailors and marines were drilled in artillery practice at the same time, on the green in the centre of the course.

To-day the news of the advance of the Imperial army upon Nanking is confirmed. Mr. Meadows left here last night at midnight, for the rebel camp, disguised as a Chinaman. He took along a European dress, to wear after arriving, and is understood to possess an order from the Taou-tai to the local authorities on the road, to facilitate his progress.

April 13th.

We are still in the same delightful state of uncertainty, in regard to the future. The rebels and the Imperial forces commanded severally by Tien-teh and Heang-Yuen, have met, and, according to Chinese custom, appointed day before yesterday for the battle: so that we may expect to hear *something* in two days more—but it is too much to hope that we will get the truth, or any thing near it. On Monday evening, a letter was received from Mr. Meadows, who has reached Soo-Chow He found the city perfectly tranquil. The deputation of merchants commissioned to take the ransom to Tïen-teh, had returned after proceeding as far as Chin-Kiang-foo, where they found a body of the Imperial troops. They were obliged to hasten back, to prevent the ransom from falling into the wrong hands. This corroborates the report of the rebels having retreated from Chin-Kiang-foo and fallen back upon Nanking, in order to concentrate their strength for an encounter with Heang-Yuen's army.

Meanwhile the work of defence goes on. The English have taken it upon themselves to construct a double ditch from Soo-Chow creek across to the north-western angle of the city wall, covering the rear of the foreign settlement. An attack, if made at all, will most probably be made from the native city, across a creek which is commanded by the big guns of the *Susquehanna*. At a meeting held at the English Consulate yesterday, the resident merchants decided to bear the expenses of the work. Several hundred coolies have been employed upon the ditch, which is a slight affair, that would not resist a charge of European cavalry, but may prove sufficient against Chinese. The breastwork runs directly across the race-course, and to-day has reached the graveyard of the men of Foo-Kïen, a body of whom came to stop proceedings. The Chinese have a great regard for the graves of their ancestors, which, indeed, are the only objects for which they exhibit the least reverence. These Foo-Kïen people are a fierce, disorderly set, and the natives of Shanghai are in great dread of them. The assistant Engineer of the English steamer *Salamander* mysteriously disappeared two days ago, and has not returned When last seen on Monday night, he was quarrelling with some Foo-Kien boatmen, and it is now surmised that they murdered him. Several dead bodies have floated down the river within a few days.

We hear already of bands of marauders in the vicinity. The magistrates of the different districts have formed a league for their protection, and have resolved to burn alive any man who is caught plundering. Two cases have occurred within a few days. On Monday a band of forty robbers entered a village about two miles from here and demanded a quantity of rice from the inhabitants—which was paid. Two of the men, however, lingered behind, and demanded of one of the villagers that they should be paid 20,000 *cash* (about $14). The man said he had but 8,000 cash in the house, which he would give them. While pretending to get it he found means to whisper to a coolie, who went out and summoned the people. The house was surrounded, the robbers taken and condemned to be burned. One of them was placed beneath the pile, and securely bound. The other was laid upon the top, and several times burst the cords which held him and sprang from the flames. He was relentlessly dragged back, until all power of resistance was lost. In a village about ten miles from here, four Canton men were found plundering a pawnbroker's shop, and suffered the same horrible fate. In every village is suspended a gong, which is to be sounded in case of an attack.

It is from these bands of desperadoes that the older residents anticipate trouble. The Mission Establishment beyond Soo-Chow creek has been furnished with arms by Capt. Buchanan, and its inmates keep up a watch at night. Mr. Yates, of the

Baptist Mission, who had placed his family on board one of the merchant vessels, has returned to his house. In passing through the city yesterday, I noticed many streets which were almost entirely deserted. Mr. Shortrede, the Editor of the *Friend of China*, who came down from the hills two days ago, met two hundred boats on their way to Soo-Chow, laden with people and property.

April 15th.

The difficulty with the Foo-Kïen men has not yet been settled. On the Chinese coolies being prevented by a band of them from digging up the graves, the English brought a field-piece, loaded it, and threatened to fire in case they did not retire. For a time they dispersed, but soon returned in much greater numbers. It is now said that they have decided to allow the breastwork to be thrown up, in case pledges are given by the English, that when the danger is over the earth shall be restored to its former place. This demand will be complied with and the work will proceed, but as the embankments are made upon the line of a proposed road which the merchants have been endeavoring to open, it may be doubted whether the latter will keep faith with the men of Foo-Kïen. On my visit to some American Missionaries in the city yesterday, I was struck with its air of desolation. There are streets where hardly a house is inhabited. Where we found crowds on our first arrival, there is now scarcely a single soul to be seen. I have no doubt that 50,000 persons have emigrated from the city within the past two or three weeks.

News reached us yesterday, that a battle had been fought

before the walls of Nanking, in which the advantage rested with the Imperial troops. Great numbers were slain on both sides, and the revolutionary army had retired within the walls. A letter was also received from Mr. Meadows, who is still at Soo-Chow, where he intends remaining. He repeats the stories which had already reached us, with the additional fact that Tien-teh is actually dead, as was surmised by some, and that the name of the present chief is Tae-ping. Mr. Meadows ap pears in European costume, and has received no molestation. He has put himself in connection with the mandarins, and expects to be protected. The celebrated pagodas on Golden Island in the Yang-tse-Kiang, opposite Chin-Kiang-foo, are said to have been entirely destroyed by the rebels, and all the Buddhist priests beheaded. If this be true, the library of Chinese Literature on the island—one of the most valuable in the Empire—has probably perished also.

April 17th.

Flying rumors from Nanking, favorable to the rebels, now begin to reach us. It is quite evident, from the tenor of the various reports, that the Imperialists have at least gained no success. An intelligent Chinaman, who was on board one of the Taou-tai's lorchas, in the neighborhood of Nanking, states that the accounts we had received of the valor of Heang-Yuen, the Tartar general, are without foundation. The people have unbounded confidence in the rebels, whom he represents as just and humane in their dealings with them. Heang-Yuen, he says, keeps aloof and avoids giving battle. A native messenger dispatched by the Rev. Mr. Taylor, about two weeks ago, re turned yesterday, having succeeded in reaching Nanking. His account is greatly exaggerated; he says there are 500,000 Tartar troops around Nanking, and an equal number of rebels within the walls. The latter never intended to have advanced upon Shanghai, and the report of their march towards Soo-Chow after the taking of Nanking was occasioned by the flight of the Imperial troops in that direction.

The American bark *Science*, despatched by the Taou-tai to the relief of the Imperial fleet, arrived at Woosung on Thursday night, and Capt. Roundy was here at breakfast yesterday morning. He only ascended the Yang-tse-Kiang seventy-five miles, and attributes his difficulties entirely to the Chinese pilots. There is water enough for the largest vessels in the channel, which, however, is narrow and tortuous. A letter was received last night from Capt. Bush, of the schooner *Dewan*, which had reached Chin-Kiang-foo. He states that he had landed and walked through the city, which was entirely deserted—not a soul to be seen. The inhabitants had all gone to Nanking, but under what circumstances, he does not inform us. A letter was also reeeived from Mr. Meadows, who had been deserted by all his servants, and was unable to procure a boat to proceed further.

The foreign residents now no longer apprehend an attack, but the native merchants are still in a state of alarm.

The period covered by these extracts from my journal was the most exciting portion of my residence at Shanghai. After the first alarm had subsided, the fugitive Chinese returned, trade resumed its usual course, and the place enjoyed several months of comparative quiet During the following year

1854, however, all that we had anticipated in the spring of 1853 actually came to pass. The city fell into the hands of the rebels, and the defence the foreign merchants had thrown up as a protection against them, served, singularly enough, to protect themselves from the assaults of the Imperialists.

CHAPTER XXVI

A CHINESE PROMENADE.

Chinese and Foreigners at Shanghai—Situation of the City—A Chinese Promenade—Burying-Grounds—Money for the Dead—A Baby Tower—The Ningpo House—Coffins—Chinese Gypsies—A Street of the Suburbs—The City Gate—A Chinese Pawnbroker's Shop—A Temple—The Statue of Boodh—A Priest at his Devotions—Stenches of the Streets—Beggars—Shops—View of the Tea-Garden—Chinese Gamblers—An Artistic Mountebank—The Baptist Chapel—Scene from its Tower—The Hills—Fanciful Signs—Missionary Labors in China—Apathy of the People—A Chinese Residence—The Library—The City Prison—Torture of the Prisoners—A Bath House—Character of the Mongol Form—The Tutelar Deity of Shanghai—Boodh at Sunset—Kite Flying.

During the two weeks chronicled in the foregoing journal notwithstanding the warlike excitement which was more or less shared by all, I devoted several days to visiting the Chinese city and the points of interest in its environs. Unlike Canton and the other cities of the South, Shanghai is thrown open without restriction to the foreigner, and he may even wander unmolested for a distance of thirty or forty miles into the interior. The natives there, instead of despising the "outside barbarians," look up to them with profound respect; the cry of "*Fan-kwei!*" (foreign devil!) which pursues you in Canton, is never heard in the streets; the stupid faces of the populace are turned towards you with an expression of good will, and there is no hindrance whatever to your studies of the peculiarities of Chinese character and habits. I was soon quite satisfied with the extent of my observations. Superficial as they were, I found nothing in the subject sufficient to tempt me into a further endurance of the disgusting annoyances of a Chinese city. I shall ask the reader's patience during the promenade on which I propose to take him, since it is for the first and last time. The scenes we shall witness are curious, in spite of their disagreeable features, and a conscientious traveller must describe things as he sees them. But, first let me give some necessary details of the topography of Shanghai.

The city lies upon the right bank of the Whang-po (or, as it is called by foreigners, the Woosung) River, about fourteen miles above its junction with the Yang-tse-Kiang. The river here makes a sharp bend to the south, so that the city faces the east. The Chinese town, which is walled, is in the form of a semicircle, with its chord upon the river. It is about five miles in circumference, and contains a population of 300,000. To the north of this, and separated from it by a small creek, is the foreign settlement, which extends along the river for three-quarters of a mile. The houses are large and handsome, frequently good examples of the simpler forms of the Palladian style, and surrounded by gardens. Along the water is a broad quay, called the "*bund*," (from an Indian word,) which is the evening resort of the residents, and the great centre of business and gossip. The foreign community, exclusive of the missionaries, consists of about 170 persons, 14 of whom are ladies. It is, beyond dispute, the most cheerful, social and agreeable community in China.

I was greatly indebted to the Rev. Charles Taylor, of the Methodist, and the Rev. M. T. Yates, of the Baptist Mission, for pilotage through the mazes of Shanghai, and explanations of the many curious scenes we witnessed by the way. Although it required several short excursions to make me familiar with the objects which most interest the stranger, I hope, in the course of one extended walk, to bring them all under the reader's notice, so that there will be no necessity for again taking him within the city walls.

Leaving the American Consulate, we proceed westward along the banks of a little creek, lined with willow trees. Beyond the limits of the settlement we come upon extensive burying-grounds, where rank grass and weeds hide the tombstones, centuries old. These places are sacred, and though the dead have long been forgotten, and their families become extinct, no one dares to interfere with the soil under which they rest. In the midst of one of these neglected cemeteries, stands a horse, of the natural size, sculptured in gray granite. On many of the tombs are heaps of silvered paper, made into the form of ingots of *sycee* silver, which are carried there and burnt, for the purpose of paying the expenses of the dead, in the other world. The usual order of things is reversed in this case, and what is merely the shadow here, becomes the substantial silver there. Judging from the quantities consumed, the dead must live in a most extravagant style. Between the graves and the city wall stands a low building, in a clump of cedar trees. This is one of the "Baby Towers," of which there are several near the city. All infants who die under the age of one year are not honored with burial, but done up in a package, with matting and cords, and thrown into the tower, or rather well, as it is sunk some distance below the earth. The top, which rises about ten feet above the ground, is roofed, but an aperture is left for casting in the bodies. Looking into it, we see that the tower is filled nearly to the roof with bundles of matting, from which exhales a pestilent effluvium.

Some distance further, near the north-western angle of the city wall, we reach the "Ningpo House," as it is called, a beneficial institution of an interesting character. It was built and is supported by a club of Shanghai merchants and traders, who are natives of Ningpo, for the purpose of affording relief to those of their countrymen who may become destitute, and taking charge of the bodies of those who die. It is a collection of low buildings, principally of stone, and separated by paved court-yards into the different departments which it embraces. In one part we find the aged and infirm furnished with food and shelter, both of the plainest kind; in another we enter what appears to be a great coffin warehouse, but is in fact a repository of dead bodies. The ponderous coffins of poplar or sycamore plank, stained of a dark red color, and covered in some instances with gilded hieroglyphics, are ranged in compartments, according to the sex and time of decease of the occupant. They are thus kept for three years, when, if not reclaimed by their relatives at Ningpo and transported thither for burial, they are deposited in a cemetery adjoining the buildings. The bodies are firmly packed in fine lime, which prevents any exhalations from the coffins. We should not suspect that in the warehouse through which we pass there are upwards of a hundred corpses, some of which have been there nearly the whole of the allotted time There are several other beneficial institutions of a similar character in Shanghai, and their provisions appear to be carried out with fidelity and conscientiousness. In each of the establishments there is a hall hung with lanterns, and usually containing the idol of one of their gods, wherein the Directors meet, to smoke, drink tea, and discuss their affairs.

Not far from the Ningpo House, there is a camp of Chinese Gypsies. These outcasts have little in common with the Gypsies of Europe and the East. They are of pure Mongolian blood, and only resemble the former in their wandering habits, their distinct social government, and their mendicity, which constitutes, in fact, almost their only means of support. Their degradation is almost without parallel, and I doubt if there be any thing in human nature more loathsome than their appearance. Here they are, on this bleak hillock, over which a few stunted cedars are scattered. Their lairs—for they cannot be called tents—of filthy matting are not more than four feet high, and barely large enough to contain two persons. They are built upon the cold, wet earth, with perhaps a little straw to protect the bodies of the inmates. Two or three stones and a heap of ashes, on the side of the hill, are all their domestic appliances. As we approach, a wild head, with long, tangled hair, and deep-set, glaring black eyes, is thrust out from each of the lairs. Some lie still, merely following us with their gaze, like a beast surprised in his den; others crawl out, displaying garments that are dropping to pieces from sheer rottenness, and figures so frightfully repulsive and disgusting, that we move away repenting that we have disturbed this nest of human vermin

We now enter an outer street, leading to the northern gate of the city. It is narrow, paved with rough stones, and carpeted with a deposit of soft mud. The houses on either hand are of wood, two stories high, and have a dark, decaying air. The lower stories are shops, open to the street, within which the pig-tailed merchants sit behind their counters, and look at us out of the corners of their crooked eyes, as we go by. The streets are filled with a crowd of porters, water-carriers, and other classes of the laboring population, and also, during the past week or two, with the families and property of thousands of the inhabitants, who are flying into the country, in anticipation of war. At the corners of the streets are stands for the sale of fruit and vegetables, the cheaper varieties of which can be had in portions valued at a single *cash*—the fifteenth part of a cent. A bridge of granite slabs crosses the little stream of which I have already spoken, and after one or two turnings we find ourselves at the city gate. It is simply a low stone arch, through a wall ten feet thick, leading into a sort of bastion for defence, with an inner gate. Within the space is a guard-house, where we see some antiquated instruments, resembling pikes and halberds, leaning against the wall, but no soldiers. A manifesto issued by the Taou-tai—probably some lying report of a victory over the rebels—is pasted against the inner gate, and there is a crowd before it, spelling out its black and vermilion hieroglyphics.

Turning to the left, we advance for a short distance along the inside of the wall, which is of brick, about twenty feet thick, with a notched parapet. Carefully avoiding the heaps of filth and the still more repulsive beggars that line the path, we reach a large, blank building, about two hundred feet square. This is a pawnbroker's shop—for the Chinese are civilized enough for that—and well worth a visit. The front on trance admits us into the office, where the manager and his attendants are busily employed behind a high counter, and a crowd of applicants fills the space in front. We apply for permission to inspect the establishment, which is cheerfully granted; a side-door is opened, and we enter a long range of store-houses, filled to the ceiling with every article of a Chinese household or costume, each piece being folded up separately, numbered and labelled. One room is appropriated wholly to the records, or books registering the articles deposited. There are chambers containing thousands of pewter candlesticks; court-yards piled with braziers; spacious lofts, stuffed to the ceiling with the cotton gowns and petticoat-pantaloons of the poorer classes, and chests, trunks, boxes and other cabinetware in bewildering quantities. At a rough estimate, I should say that there are at least 30,000 costumes; when we asked the attendant the number, he shrugged his shoulders and said: "Who could count them?" There are three or four other establishments, of nearly similar magnitude, in the city. They are regulated by the Government, and are said to be conducted in a fair and liberal spirit.

At the next angle of the wall stands an old Boodhist temple, before the door of which lie two granite lions, broken and overthrown. Squatted on a pedestal within is a gilded idol, about five feet high, while in recesses on either hand are the guardians or watchers of the temple—gigantic figures, armed with swords, and glittering with the gaudiest colors of the Chinese pallet. We pass through this vestibule and ascend a flight of steps to an inner temple, where the god appears in colossal form, and in spite of his slack hands fallen on his knees, his heavy, hanging abdomen, his bloated cheeks, and the good-humored silliness of his face, his appearance is at least respectable. Any colossal representation of the human body, if not an intentional caricature, is to a certain degree majestic and impressive; and though the Chinese Boodh stands, in rank of idolship, far below the Indian Brahma and the grand Egyptian Amun-Re, one cannot flout him to his face. In a chamber adjoining this we find a female divinity—the Queen of Mercy—whose Chinese title I forget. Hearing a continual thumping noise in the room beyond, we push open the door and surprise a Boodhist priest at his devotions. He is seated at a table with a book open before him, from which he is chanting prayers with a monotonous, drawling tone, while with one hand he thumps incessantly with a small wooden hammer upon a hollow drum of the same material. This drum is called by the same name as the great fish upon which the earth rests, and which its sound soothes into quiet. When, at any time, even for a minute, there is no drum beaten throughout the whole world, the fish at once becomes uneasy, and his contortions occasion earthquakes. The priest wears a yellow robe, his skin is yellow, his head is shaven bald, his face is puckered with wrinkles, and altogether he is one of the oddest and funniest old men that ever was seen. He looks up, nods, with a queer twinkle in his eyes, looks down again, and up again, but never once pauses in his chanting or his thumping.

We now take a street which strikes into the heart of the city, and set out for the famous "Tea Gardens." The pavement is of rough stones, slippery with mud, and on one side of the street is a ditch filled with black, stagnant slime, from which arises the foulest smell. Porters, carrying buckets of offal, brush past us; public *cloacæ* stand open at the corners, and the clothes and persons of the unwashed laborers and beggars distil a reeking compound of still more disagreeable exhalations. Coleridge says of Cologne:

> "I counted two and seventy stenches,
> All well defined—and several stinks;"

but Shanghai, in its horrid foulness, would be flattered by such a description. I never go within its walls but with a shudder and the taint of its contaminating atmosphere seems to hang about me like a garment long after I have left them. Even in the country, which now rejoices in the opening spring, all the freshness of the season is destroyed by the rank ammoniated odors arising from pits of noisome manure, sunk in the fields. Having mentioned these things, I shall not refer to them again; but if the reader would have a correct description of Shanghai, they cannot be wholly ignored.

It requires some care to avoid contact with the beggars who throng the streets, and we would almost as willingly touch a man smitten with leprosy, or one dying of the plague. They take their stations in front of the shops, and supplicate with a loud, whining voice, until the occupant purchases their departure by some trifling alms; for they are protected by the law in their avocation, and no man dare drive them forcibly from his door. As we approach the central part of the city, the streets become more showy and a trifle cleaner. The shops are large and well arranged, and bright red signs, covered with golden inscriptions, swing vertically from the eaves. All the richest shops, however, are closed at present, and not a piece of the celebrated silks of Soo-Chow, the richest in China, is to be found in the city. The manufactures in jade-stone, carved bamboo, and the furniture of Ningpo, inlaid with ivory and boxwood, are still to be had in profusion, but they are more curious than elegant. Indeed, I have seen no article of Chinese workmanship which could positively be called beautiful, unless it was fashioned after a European model. Industry, perseverance, and a wonderful faculty of imitation belong to these people; but they are utterly destitute of original taste.

The "Tea Garden" is an open space near the centre of the city, devoted to the recreation of the populace. In the midst of a paven square is a pool of greenish, stagnant water, in which stands a building of two stories, with the peaked, curved, overhanging roofs, which we always associate with Chinese architecture. It is reached by bridges which cross the water in curious zigzag lines, so that you walk more than double the actual distance. On the opposite side are several similar buildings, surrounded by masses of artificial rock-work, but the only token of a garden is a pair of magnolia trees, clothed in the glory of their fragrant, snowy blossoms. Every body remembers the old-fashioned plates of blue Liverpool ware, with a representation of two Chinese houses, a willow tree, a bridge with three Chinamen walking over it, and two crows in the air. These plates give a very good representation of the Tea Garden, which is a fair sample of what is most picturesque in Chinese life. The buildings are tea-houses, and on entering we find them filled with natives of all classes, drinking strong decoctions of the herb, and smoking their slender pipes of bamboo, with bowls about the size of a lady's thimble. The tea is prepared in enormous pots suspended over furnaces of clay. The master of the house shows us a vacant table, but we decline his hint, and pass out to view the crowds in the square.

Here is a man leading a white goat with only three legs, which he wishes to sell, but on a careful examination we perceive that one of the fore legs has been neatly amputated while the animal was young. There are half a dozen gaming tables, each surrounded by its crowd of players and spectators. The Chinese are inveterate gamblers, and as the stakes at many of these tables are as low as a single cash, few are so poor that they cannot make a venture. One of the methods has some resemblance to the "little jokers," so well known at our race courses. The player has three sticks, the ends of which are thrust through his fingers. There is a hole through each of the other ends, which are held in his hand; a cord is passed through one of them, and the play consists in guessing *which* one, as the cord may be transferred from one to the other by a quick movement of the fingers. I put a "cash" on the board, make a guess, and win a cake of suspicious-looking candy, which I give to the nearest boy, to the great merriment of the bystanders. There are also stands for the sale of pea-nuts, reminding us of the classic side-walks of Chatham street, and for the sake of Young America, we must invest a few cash in his favorite fruit. But here is an entertainment of an entirely novel character. A man seated on the pavement, holds in his hand a white porcelain tile, about a foot square. This he overspreads with a deep-blue color, from a spongo dipped in a thin paste of indigo, and asks us to name a flower I suggest the lotus. He extends his fore-finger—a most remarkable fore-finger, crooked, flexible as an elephant's trunk, and as sharp as if the end had been whittled off—gives three or four quick dashes across the tile, and in ten seconds or less, lo! there is the flower exquisitely drawn and shaded, its snowy cup hanging in the midst of its long swaying leaves. Three more strokes, and a white bird with spread wings, hovers over it; two more, and a dog stands beside it. The rapidity and precision of that fore-finger seem almost miraculous. He covers the tile with new layers of color, and flower after flower s dashed out of the blue ground.

The Chapel of the Baptist Mission is in a street near the Tea Garden, and its tower, about seventy feet high, affords an excellent panoramic view of the city and surrounding country. Looking down upon the city, we see nothing but a mass of peaked roofs, covered with tiles which are blackened by age, and here and there the open courts and heavier architecture of temples. The serrated line of the wall surrounds it, and the rich alluvial land extends wide beyond, dotted with villages, clumps of cedar, groves of fruit-trees, or the mounds of ancient cemeteries. The broad river winds through the centre of the landscape, and the number of junks gliding over its surface with their square sails spread to the east wind, give animation to the scene. In front of the city they are anchored in a dense mass a mile in length, and numbering not less than two thousand. The din of gongs and drums and the sputtering of fire-crackers, burnt to secure the aid of the water-gods, reaches us at this distance. Eight or nine miles up the river stands a tall pagoda, and as the air is clear to-day the summits of "The Hills," as they are cal ed by the foreign esidents, are faintly visible in the west. These hills, which are a favorite resort of foreigners during the hot season, are twenty-five miles distant. They are the first range which breaks the vast level of the plains, and command a view of the large town of Soong-Keang in the interior, and the country stretching toward Soo-Chow.

Looking to the river, our eyes are attracted by a large tea warehouse, on the wall of which are painted four enormous characters. Our missionary friend interprets them as signifying "The Place of Heavenly prepared Leaves." In the fanciful and figurative character of their signs, the Chinese remind us of the Arabic races. There is a shop for the sale of *samshoo*, or rice-whiskey, in Hong-Kong, which bears over its door the following inscription: "The joys of Paradise are nothing but a state of perpetual intoxication!" The announcements of vessels up for California are headed with the enticing call: "To the Golden Mountains!"

Notwithstanding the efforts of many zealous and devoted missionaries who have been sent to China, the number of genuine converts is very limited. The Chinese nature appears to be so thoroughly passive, that it is not even receptive. A sort of listless curiosity leads them to fill the chapels of the missionaries, and to gather in crowds around those who preach in the public places, but when the exhortation is finished, away they go, without the least ripple of new thought in the stagnant waters of their minds. The mental inertia of these people seems to be almost hopeless of improvement. Even while the present rebellion is going on—a struggle which, one would suppose, would enlist their sympathies, if a single spark of patriotism or ambition remained—the great mass of the people maintain the most profound apathy. Some advocate of universal peace has cited China as the example of a nation which has successfully pursued a pacific policy; but I say, welcome be the thunder-storm which shall scatter and break up, though by the means of fire and blood, this terrible stagnation! Wh would not exclaim with Tennyson:

"Better fifty years of Europe than a cycle of Cathay."

But we are curious to inspect the dwelling of a Chinaman of the better class, and our friend, who is fortunately able to assist us, conducts us to the house of a wealthy old merchant. It is a stone building, recently erected, and every thing about it indicates great neatness, and an approach to taste in the owner. In the open verandahs are boxes of the *mau-tan*, or rose-scented peony, with gorgeous white and crimson blossoms, and the *lan-whei*, a water-plant of an orchideous nature, with a long spike of yellowish-green flowers. The *mau-tan* also decorates the rooms, which are hung with lanterns of stained glass. The furniture is of wood, of a stiff, uncomfortable pattern, but elaborately carved. The owner, an urbane, polite old gentleman, regales us with cups of stewed tea, whose delicate aroma compensates for the absence of milk and sugar, and asks us up stairs into his library. The shelves are covered with Chinese works, bound in their wooden covers, and in the centre of the room stands a bronze frame, with three apertures at the top, and a bundle of arrows. The latter are the implements of a game which the host explains to us, by taking the arrows to the further end of the room, seizing one by the tip of the shaft with his thumb and fore-finger, and throwing it so as to fall into one of the small circular openings of the frame. We try a game, whereof the victory, owing to his more extensive practice, remains with him.

Toward the northern side of the city is the prison. On each side of the outer gate is painted the figure of an avenging divinity, whose black face and glaring eyeballs strike terror into the minds of the natives. This gate gives admittance to a quadrangular court, surrounded by ranges of cages or cells, wherein the prisoners are subjected to different degrees of punishment, according to their crimes. Some are in chambers divided by strong bamboo gratings; others at large, with heavy shackles fastened to their legs; and the more criminal cases are confined separately in narrow cages, which bind them in the smallest and most cramped space, with their knees drawn up to their chins. Their heads project through holes in the top, and as we pass, their faces are turned to us with a wild, haggard look of suffering. Some of them have been kept for weeks, immovable in those frames of torture, and their condition is too horrible for description. The cell adjoining that in which they lie, and divided from it only by some bamboo stakes, is the one appropriated by the Chinese authorities for foreign prisoners. On the beams are carved a number of names, principally German, and probably those of refractory sailors. The English Government, in those ports where the Consul possesses judicial authority—as in China, Turkey, and the Barbary States—always erects a separate prison for the confinement of English subjects. Our Government, however, from an admirable economy, prefers thrusting its citizens into these loathsome dens, the condition and associations of which increase tenfold the horrors of imprisonment. A few days ago the entire crew of an Amerian vessel in port passed a night in the very cell before us.

On our way to the city wall we pass one of the public baths, and curiosity induces us to step in. The building is low, damp and dirty, and filled with a rank, steamy, unclean atmosphere. It consists of three apartments, in one of which the bathers undress, bathe in the next, and lounge smoking on the benches, in an unembarrassed state of nudity, in the third. As it is towards evening, they belong mostly to the lower classes, and look quite as filthy after the bath as before. The water is not changed throughout the day, and its appearance and condition may perhaps be imagined. The small tank is filled in the morning, and kept heated by a furnace under it. The price of a bath diminishes in proportion as the water gets dirty, until, in the evening, it falls to a single cash (the fifteenth part of a cent). By holding my breath, I remain in the dark, reeking den, long enough to see two yellow forms immersed in the turbid pool, and then rush out stifled and nauseated. Among the bathers in the outer room there are several strong, muscular figures, but a total want of that elegant symmetry which distinguishes the Caucasian and Shemitic races. They are broad-shouldered and deep-chested, but the hips and loins are clumsily moulded, and the legs have a coarse, clubby character. We should never expect to see such figures assume the fine, free attitudes of ancient sculpture. But here, as every where, the body is the expression of the spiritual nature. There is no sense of what we understand by Art—Grace, Harmony, Proportion—in the Chinese nature, and therefore we look in vain for any physical expression of it. De Quincey, who probably never saw a Chinaman, saw this fact with the clairvoyant eye of genius, when he said: "If I were condemned to live among the Chinese, I should go mad." This is a strong expression, but I do not hesitate to adopt it.

Before terminating this long and, perhaps, wearisome ramble, let us enter the great temple of the tutelar divinity of

Shanghai. The obese idol, cross-legged, and with his hands upon his knees, is fifteen feet high, and seated upon a pedestal of about twelve feet. He is gilded from head to foot, and looms grandly through the dusk of the lofty hall. On each side are the gilded statues of nine renowned Chinese saints and sages—eighteen in all—of the size of life. The sacred drum, four or five feet in diameter, and raised on a prop of heavy timbers, stands on one side of the entrance, and the great bell—a universal feature of Boodhist temples—on the other. We beat the drum and strike the bell with a mallet, until the temple rings with a peal of barbaric sound. The priests look on, smiling, for the act is not one of irreverence, but of devotion, in their eyes, and while we are amusing ourselves, we do homage to the great Boodh. The broad interior of the temple is dusky with the evening shadows, when the last red beam of sunset, falling through an upper window, strikes full upon the golden face of the god, lighting that only, so that the large features blaze upon us out of the gloom, as if moulded in living fire. It is as if Boodh had asserted his insulted majesty, and while he is thus transfigured we own that he is sublime.

On our return to the foreign settlement, we hear loud, humming noises in the air, and looking up, see a strange collection of monsters hovering in the sky. An enormous bird, with outspread wings of red and gold, is soaring directly over our heads; a centipede, twenty feet long, is wriggling yonder; a fanciful dragon shoots hither and thither; and a mandarin, in his robes of state, makes his airy *ko-tows*, or salutations, to the gazers below. The natives are indulging in their national amusement of kite-flying, and as long as there is light enough left they will continue. with the eagerness of children, to manœuvre their painted toys. We draw a long breath of relief when we have passed the wall and the muddy creek, and as we walk homeward, mentally revolve the question, whether it is worth satisfying one's curiosity at the expense of so much annoyance and disgust.

CHAPTER XXVII.

EARTHQUAKES AND OFFICIAL VISITS.

An Earthquake—Sensations it Produced—Its Effects—Additional Shocks—The Bowling Alley—Hairs in the Soil—A Shower of Sand—Visit of the Taou-tai to Col. Marshall—Chinese Visiting Cards—The Taou-tai's Appearance—Reception of the Dignitaries—A Chinese Military Review—The Soldiers and their Equipments—Their Discipline—Uncouth Weapons—Absurdity of the Parade—The Commissioner visits the Taou-tai—Reception—The Taou-tai's Residence—Chinese Refreshments—Departure.

OUR attention was for a time diverted from the alarm and excitement occasioned by rumors of the approach of the rebels, through the unexpected visitation of an earthquake, which occurred on Thursday night, the 14th of April. On that evening, M. de Montigny, the French Consul, entertained Col. Marshall at dinner. Capt. Buchanan and Purser Barry, of the Susquehanna, Mr. Cunningham, Capt. de Plas, of the French steamer Cassini, and several other gentlemen were present. About a quarter past 11 o'clock, as the guests were taking leave, some of them being still in the passage, putting on their overcoats, for it was a dark, drizzling night, there was a sudden, violent noise, the timbers of the house cracking and the walls swaying to and fro. I was standing just under the eaves at the time, and my first impression was that the building was tumbling down upon me. I made a spring into the court, with a strange feeling of bewilderment, for every thing was reeling and unsteady. All this was the work of an instant. There was a cry from the ladies within, and they came rushing out in great terror, exclaiming: "an earthquake! an earthquake!" We stood in the open court-yard, awaiting a second shock. The earth continued to heave with a slow, regular motion, gradually diminishing, until the throbs ceased. It produced a slight giddiness and nausea in some of us. Immediately after the shock passed away, a wild outcry arose from the Chinese city, and the large wooden drums in the temples were heard sounding far and near. The object of this was to soothe the great fish upon which the earth rests, and by whose uneasiness the earthquake was caused.

On reaching the Consulate, we found that everybody in the house had felt the shock, and the chandeliers in the drawing-room were still vibrating from it. Mr. L., one of the clerks, stated that his attention was first called to it by seeing several doors which had been locked, fly open without any apparent agency. In the other house belonging to Russell & Co., a chimney was thrown down, and one of the joists drawn from its socket and forced through the ceiling. About fifteen yards of a high brick wall around Mr. Nye's house was overthrown, and a large Chinese warehouse in the city almost entirely destroyed. The dogs (of which there is no scarcity in Shanghai) howled dismally while the motion lasted. The direction of the wave was from north-east to south-west, and the extent of its motion was, I should judge, about two feet. Shanghai is subject to slight shocks, but this was the most severe which had been felt for several years. The nearest volcanoes are in the Japanese island of Kiusiu, about six hundred miles distant.

About midnight two additional shocks were felt, but they were much lighter than the first. On retiring to rest, we found that a number of articles in the rooms had been thrown upon the floor. In the morning I walked up to the northern part of the settlement, where the shock appeared to have been much more violent than at the southern end. In Mr. Nye's *godown* (warehouse) the heavy bales of goods were hurled from their places. Several chimneys were sprung and walls cracked, but the nature of the soil on which Shanghai stands—an elastic, clayey loam, two hundred feet in depth—saved the place from greater injury. In company with some friends I went to the bowling-alley, the walls of which had previously showed a disposition to give way, and were supported on one side by props. After playing an hour or two, we noticed that the southern wall had suddenly sunk outwards more than six inches, and was cracked from top to bottom. There had been, in fact, another smart shock at that very time, and we had not perceived it. The props alone prevented the whole building from coming down upon our heads.

The Chinese servants stated in the morning that hairs were always found in the earth after an earthquake, and brought up two or three gray horse-hairs—or what appeared to be such—which they professed to have found in the yard. Several of the gentlemen immediately went down and commenced searching, and to their astonishment found numbers of gray filaments from four to ten inches long. They projected two or three inches from the soil, and were most abundant among the grass. They were strong, like a coarse hempen fibre, and were readily drawn out without breaking. After a careful examination with a powerful magnifying glass, it was found that they had not the tubular structure of hair, but what they were and whence they came, was a mystery. Some of the profane summarily accounted for them by declaring that the shock of the earthquake caused the earth's hair to stand on end, from fright. They were picked up in nearly all the gardens in town. The Chinese say they are only found for three days after a shock, which, so far as I could learn, also proved correct.

Another circumstance attending the earthquake, was the shower of fine dust, which fell for two or three days afterwards. The same thing was noticed after the earthquake of 1846, which was less violent. The wind was from the north-west, and the sand, which some suppose to come from the great Desert of Kobi, in the interior of China, was so fine as to be impalpable, yet filled the air to such an extent that the sun was covered with a yellow film, and the view obscured as by a thick haze. The Chinese reported that a town about thirty miles distant had been entirely swallowed up, and that a tract of land a mile square had sunk, and had been replaced by a deep lake. We decided at once to pay a visit to the spot, but on inquiry found so many contradictory stories regarding it, that it was quite impossible to discover where the town was. There were three or four slight shocks afterwards at intervals of two or three days.

On the 9th of April, the Taou-tai of Shanghai paid an official visit to Col. Marshall, and to the frigate Susquehanna. He had given notice of his intention two days before, and came in state, attended by four mandarins, and with a long retinue of scarecrow followers. A little in advance of their arrival, the cards of the dignitaries were sent to the Commissioner. They were long slips of crimson paper, inscribed with rows of glaring hieroglyphics, and enclosed in crimson envelopes, The Taou-tai's ran thus: "Woo-keen-chang, of the Ta-Tsing Empire, by Imperial appointment Salt Commissioner, Intendant of the Circuit of the Prefectures of Soo-Chow, Soong-Keang and Tae-Tsung, in the province of Keang-nan, holding the rank of Judge, promoted five degrees, &c., presents his compliments." One of the others was still more remarkable: "Lan-wei-wan, of the Ta-Tsing Empire, Haefung of the Prefecture of Shanghai, in the province of Keang-soo, and *expectant* of the office of Prefect, knocks his head and presents compliments." How titles would multiply in America, if all the "expectants" of office adopted this plan! We should be overrun with such characters as—Hon. Elijah Pogram, Expectant Minister to Russia; Jedediah Peabody, Expectant Collector of Sag-Harbor—and so to the end of the chapter.

The Taou-tai was received with all due distinction, and his interview with the Commissioner lasted about an hour. He was a small man, near fifty years of age (his mustache denoting a grandfather); his complexion was a pale, bloodless yellow, his eyes lively and piercing, and his rather contracted features expressed a keen, shrewd and unscrupulous character. He was formerly a hong merchant of Canton, and is still best known to foreigners by his old name of Sam-qua. He spoke the "pigeon English," or commercial jargon, with tolerable fluency, though the conversation was partly carried on in Chinese, by Dr. Parker. He was dressed in robes of a rich, stiff silk, embroidered with the insignia of his office, and wore a cap with the single peacock's feather and opaque red button of a mandarin of the third class. In his suite was the Colonel of the regular troops stationed at Shanghai—a tall, dignified old mandarin, who conducted himself with a grave and courteous dignity, beside which the Taou-tai, with his fidgety and undecided manners, showed to disadvantage. On entering the room where the Commissioner received them, they all performed the *Ko-tow*, or national salutation, by clasping their hands in front of their breasts, and bowing profoundly with a shaky motion, like those porcelain mandarins with which we are all familiar. They were regaled with tea, champagne and port, and took wine with great gravity, rising and bowing profoundly when they drank. After leaving the Commissioner they went on board the Susquehanna, where Capt. Buchanan received them with a salute of nine guns. They all expressed the greatest astonishment and admiration at the size and strength of the vessel.

During the visit, Col. Marshall expressed a wish to witness a review of the Chinese garrison of Shanghai, and the Taou-tai at one promised to make a public display of the troops, in order to exhibit his military resources to the foreign community. Accordingly, as we were entering the city the next afternoon, a frightful clamor of gongs announced the approach of some unusual spectacle, and we soon became aware that the Taou-tai was fulfilling his promise. First came half-a-dozen old six-pounders, mounted on clumsy carriages, which made a frightful clatter as they rolled over the rough pavement. They were followed by porters bearing chests of ammunition, slung from bamboo poles; then a company of soldiers in dark blue dresses, with a circular coat-of-arms on the breast and back, armed with long spears; another company, with ginjalls, a long, heavy stock, mounted on a tripod when it is fired, and carrying a ball about the size of a grape-shot; afterwards, more spearmen, alternating with companies of matchlocks, and followed by more lumbering six-pounders, chests of ammunition, gongs, yellow banners, covered with hieroglyphics, and other curious and fantastic objects—the procession rushing along without order or organization, shouting and laughing, or brandishing their arms in the most uncouth and barbaric style. Such a display never was witnessed in Shanghai before. There were about four hundred regular soldiers, some of whom were exceedingly well-formed, lusty men, and clothed in an appropriate costume—a short tunic girdled around the waist, full trowsers gathered at the knees, and tight leggings—but the greater portion were evidently porters and peasants, hired for the ocasion, to swell the ranks of the soldiery, and produce an impression of the Imperial power.

There were in the procession some very curious weapons, which I do not suppose any other army in the world can exhibit. In addition to pikes for sticking the enemy, poles for punching them, clubs for beating them, and flails for threshing their heads, I saw some wooden beams about five feet long with handles at each end, the use of which is—*to push them out of the way!* When part of the procession was retarded at any point, the companies behind them made up the loss, by rushing down the street at full speed, leaping in the air as they went, charging with their lances, swinging their flails and shaking their clubs, with cries which were meant to be terrific, but which were ludicrous in the extreme. Among the officers who rode on shaggy native ponies, we recognized the venerable Colonel, who bowed to us with a touch of pride in passing, Last of all, preceded by yellow banners and a deafening tempest of gongs, came the Taou-tai himself, in his green sedan chair, followed by the Government executioners, in red dresses and high conical caps, decorated with the long tail-feathers of the pheasant. The grave and self-satisfied air of the high official was most amusing. The whole thing was like a Chinese travesty of Don Quixote. After parading through the principal streets of the foreign settlement, the procession returned to the city, which it entered by the western gate.

A few days afterwards, Col. Marshall returned the visit of the Taou-tai, at his official residence within the city. He was accompanied by Dr. Parker, Secretary of Legation, and Mr. Cunningham, Vice-Consul. The party set out in sedan chairs, crimson cards having been sent in advance, according to Chinese custom. Along the way—a distance of a mile or more—the Taou-tai had stationed attendants with gongs, which were direfully beaten, as we passed. It was a raw, rainy day, and the streets had more than their usual quantity of mud and filth. After entering the city gate, I, who was last in the procession, was rather startled at finding my chair suddenly dropped in the mud. Looking out, I found the bearers deliberately bargaining at a stall for new straw-sandals, which they purchased and put on their feet leisurely enough, before they picked me up again. On reaching the Taou-tai's residence, the salute of three guns had been fired, and the discordant noises of a dozen dire instruments were dying away. I was carried through a wooden portal of a dark-red color, across a paved court-yard, and finally deposited in a portico or verandah, where the Taou-tai had just formally received the Commissioner and the rest of his suite. The attendants made a loud announcement of some kind as I passed the portal, which was repeated from one to the other, till it reached the Taou-tai at the same time with myself.

We were conducted through a plain but spacious hall, open on two sides to the air, across a small inner court, and into another hall, or audience-room, partially closed by movable screens. It was gaudily furnished, but without an extravagant show of wealth. The predominant color was dark-red, and the walls were relieved with painted tablets of light-blue or green, containing long inscriptions. The floor was covered with a red felt cloth, and straight-backed chairs of camphor-wood were placed around small tables of the same material, containing boxes of sweetmeats. The Commissioner was conducted to a raised divan in the centre, covered with red cloth, upon which he and the Taou-tai seated themselves, with refreshments between them. The latter was more at his ease than on the former occasion, and did the honors of his mansion with more grace than I had anticipated. The conversation was animated, and principally of a general nature, though he made occasional reference to the rebellion. After his manifestoes concerning the success of the Imperialists, I did not consider his expressions on the subject as worthy of much attention, and the commencement of the material part of the entertainment soon gave me a more interesting field of observation.

Cups of birds-nest soup were presented to us, together with porcelain spoons and chop-sticks of ivory and silver. This curious dish fully justifies the taste of the Chinese; it is exceedingly delicate and nutritious. The Chinese wine, served warm, in square silver cups, was also quite palatable, and there was a preparation of almonds, sugar, and rice flour, boiled into a paste, to which we all did full justice. It was, however, a light collation rather than a regular meal, and the greater part consisted of dried and candied fruits, such as oranges, dates, citrons and various kinds of nuts. At the conclusion segars were offered to us, while the Taou-tai took his bamboo pipe. There was a host of attendants, all prompt, silent, and respectful. Sam-qua was too long a resident of Canton, not to have taken some hints from the habits of the foreign merchants there.

At our departure, he accompanied the Commissioner to the outer court. Three guns were fired off as the chair of the latter passed through the portal; the musicians, stationed in a gallery on the side of the court, struck up a horrible discord, which made the gongs that sounded along our homeward march melodious by contrast. The curious natives thronged the streets, to stare at us, and it was a relief when we reached the foreign suburb of Shanghai.

CHAPTER XXVIII.

INCIDENTS OF LIFE IN SHANGHAI.

Spring at Shanghai—Appearance of the Country—Crops—National Conveyance of China—Houses of the Lower Classes—Sail on the River—The Pagoda—Village Market—Sweetmeats and Children—Showers of Cash—Chinese Horticultural Exhibition—The *Lan-whei*—Chinese Love of Monstrosity—Moral Depravity of the Race—Landscape Gardening—A Soldier and his Drill—The Cangue—Visit of the *Hermes* to Nanking—The Rebels—Their Christianity—Condition of the City—Arrival of the U. S. Steam-Frigate *Mississippi*—Commodore Perry—Col. Marshall's Chinese Dinner—Mr. Robert Fortune.

Spring, at Shanghai, comes slowly. When we arrived, at the close of March, the trees were budding into leaf, but did not attain their full foliage before the middle of May. The weather during April was dull and showery, with a lower temperature than would be looked for elsewhere in the same latitude. There was scarcely an evening when fire was not necessary to our comfort. Until all the summer crops had been planted, and for a week or two afterwards, there was little satisfaction in going into the country, where the vernal odors of grass and flowers were wholly lost in the intolerable stench arising from pits of manure. But towards the end of April, when the rumors of war became less frequent, when the shocks of earth quakes had subsided, and the sun made his appearance from time to time, I took many afternoon strolls in various directions, and became familiar with the country life of the Chinese.

There is nothing striking or picturesque in the scenery of this part of China. The country is a dead level, watered with sluggish creeks, and intersected with ditches and canals. It is studded far and near with shapeless mounds of earth erected over obsolete natives; sparingly dotted with clumps of dark cedar-trees or plantations of the inestimable bamboo, and enlivened by occasional hamlets, which, shaded with bushy willows, have a pleasant, rural aspect when seen from a distance, but are mostly disgusting when you draw near. The soil is a very rich clayey loam, and yields abundant crops of rice, wheat, sweet potatoes, beets, beans, pea-nuts, and the other staples of Chinese food. Much of it must have been originally marsh land, which has been drained by canals and the gradual rise of the coast, from the deposits of the Yang-tse-Kiang. The paths from village to village are on narrow dykes, winding between the fields, and crossing the ditches by bridges formed of single large slabs of granite, which are brought down from the hills. Occasionally you see a highway, six or eight feet broad, paved with blocks of stone, laid transversely, but I doubt whether a carriage could go in any direction further than two or three miles from the city. I sometimes met a Chinaman of the better class mounted on a sturdy little pony, and once encountered a traveller from Soo-Chow in the national conveyance of China—the wheelbarrow! He was seated sideways, with his legs dangling below, while his baggage, placed on the opposite side, served to trim the vehicle. It was a one-horse wheelbarrow, propelled by a stout coolie, with a strap over his shoulders, and made a doleful creaking as it passed The persons whom I met showed every sign of civility and respect, and had time permitted, I might have extended my strolls to a distance of thirty or forty miles, without meeting any hindrance. In the villages I frequently entered the houses of the people, to which they made no objection, but seemed rather gratified at the distinction. The domestic arrangements were very simple; the dwellings were all of one story, rarely having more than two rooms, and containing only the rudest appliances of a household. The beds were usually of matting, with bamboo pillows, but the poorer natives slept upon coarse mats laid upon the earth, with wooden stools under their heads. It is not advisable to be too curious, or to spend much time in inspecting Chinese dwellings, on account of their abundant vitality. For the same reason, many features of domestic life among the lower classes must be passed over in silence.

We made an excursion one morning to the pagoda, which stands on the left bank of the Whang-po River, about eight miles above the city. The wind was fair, and Mr. Cunningham's fleet clipper-yacht soon carried us past the thousand junks and notched brick walls of Shanghai. It was in the beginning of May, and the shores, low and greenly wooded, bore some resemblance to those of the Delaware, below Philadelphia. We passed several large junks, which had come through from the Bay of Hang-Chow, by a canal which leads from the old city of Chapoo to the Whang-po River. After a run of an hour and half, we moored the yacht at the mouth of a small creek, and walked to the pagoda, which was a quarter of a mile distant. It is built of pale red sandstone, and with its ten stories diminishing in beautiful proportion, each over hung by a pointed, up-turned roof, it is truly a graceful object. The pagodas are the only symmetrical things in Chinese architecture, and I think it doubtful whether the idea of them was not first borrowed from India. All of those which I saw, or which travellers generally see in China, are comparatively modern.

There was a little village scattered about the foot of the structure, and the country people were holding a market there. The supply of vegetables, sweetmeats, and cheap, coarse articles of dress was very large: the jugglers were present in strong force, and the beggars were over-zealous in their attendance, I amused myself with buying many varieties of nondescript pastry and confects, at such cheap rates, that it was difficult to pay little enough. I then distributed my purchases among the children, the larger of whom took them with avidity, while the younger and more shy held back from the foreign barbarian, until encouraged by their pleased parents. To escape from the popularity which followed, we climbed to the summit of the pagoda, whence we beheld a circular panorama, described by a radius of twenty-five miles. It was beautiful only from its extent, and its monotony of green, through which wandered a few brown veins of rivers. I soon turned to contemplate the more animated manscape at my feet. Seeing a crowd of beggars standing together in dejected attitudes, I cast a handful of cash into the air, in such wise that the coins would fall plump among them, and then dropped behind the parapet of the pagoda. There was a metallic rattle on the stones, followed by a cry of amazement, for nothing was visible, of course, and they had not seen us ascend the pagoda.

Several other miraculous showers followed, but a desire to see the beggars scramble, betrayed us at last. We were greeted with loud cries, and arms thrown greedily aloft, beckoning for more. I cast among them upwards of twenty handfuls, and by thus expending the munificent sum of forty cents, enjoyed the feelings of a monarch, who scatters golden largesse.

One day I attended a native horticultural exhibition, which was held in an old temple, within the walls. The open courts of the building were filled with rows of flowering plants, in earthen pots and vases, which were also arranged in circles around some weak fountains in the centre. There were some fine specimens of the *mau-tan*, or peony, white, pink, and crimson, and with an odor very similar to that of the rose; but the most admired flower seemed to be the *lan-whei*, a bulbous water-plant, with a blossom resembling that of the orchids in form, yet of a dirty yellowish-green hue. The great aim of the Chinese florist is to produce something as much unlike nature as possible, and thus this blossom, which, for aught I know, may be pure white, or yellow, in its native state, is changed into a sickly, mongrel color, as if it were afflicted with a vegetable jaundice, or leprosy. There was a crowd of enthusiastic admirers around each of the ugliest specimens, and I was told that one plant, which was absolutely loathsome and repulsive in its appearance, was valued at three hundred dollars. The only taste which the Chinese exhibit to any degree, is a love of the monstrous. That sentiment of harmony, which throbbed like a musical rhythm through the life of the Greeks, never looked out of their oblique eyes. Their music is a dreadful discord; their language is composed of nasals and consonants; they admire whatever is distorted or un natural, and the wider its divergence from its original beauty or symmetry, the greater is their delight.

This mental idiosyncrasy includes a moral one, of similar character. It is my deliberate opinion that the Chinese are, morally, the most debased people on the face of the earth. Forms of vice which in other countries are barely named, are in China so common, that they excite no comment among the natives. They constitute the surface-level, and below them there are deeps on deeps of depravity so shocking and horrible, that their character cannot even be hinted. There are some dark shadows in human nature, which we naturally shrink from penetrating, and I made no attempt to collect information of this kind; but there was enough in the things which I could not avoid seeing and hearing—which are brought almost daily to the notice of every foreign resident—to inspire me with a powerful aversion to the Chinese race. Their touch is pollution, and, harsh as the opinion may seem, justice to our own race demands that they should not be allowed to settle on our soil. Science may have lost something, but mankind has gained, by the exclusive policy which has governed China during the past centuries.

I soon grew tired of the jaundiced *lan-wheis*, and diverted myself with examining a labyrinthine garden in the rear of the temple. It was a piece of rock-work, of the most absurd and grotesque character. The fragments of gray, disintegrated limestone were plastered and riveted together in the form of precipices and mountain-peaks, one of which was at least twenty feet high, with a cork-screw path encirling it many times before it allowed the adventurous traveller to mount the cap-stone. In the crevices of the rocks were little basins of soil in which magnolias and *mau-tans* were growing, while, far down in the depths of the valleys you saw several green, slimy lakes, from three to five feet in length. After having sufficiently enjoyed this sublime view, I discovered a means of exit through a low, arched grotto into the street, and did not scruple to make use of it.

Continuing my walk at random, I came to a very old, dilapidated temple, in the southern part of the city. The jolly fat idols had been removed, and the place was occupied as a barrack by some of the Taou-tai's troops. Several indolent soldiers were hanging about a tank of water in the centre of the court-yard, and the thought of seeing a Chinese military drill came into my mind. I offered the least lazy and most good-humored of the party fifty *cash* to perform his exercise, and found him quite willing to comply. He soon appeared with a wooden weapon about five feet long and one foot wide, with a handle like that of a fiddle-bow, running parallel to its length, and fastened at each end. This he brandished in the air, first on one side, then on the other, sometimes swinging it like an axe, sometimes drawing it downwards with both hands like a comb, and occasionally thrusting one end of it behind him, as if he was warding off an attack in the rear. The attitudes were very amusing, and each imaginary blow was accômpanied with a howl of defiance, and an expression of face which was meant to be terrific. The performance lasted about half an hour, and I considered that the cash were well earned.

On my return home, I saw near the city gate a man suffering the punishment of the *cangue*. This is a heavy wooden wheel, which is fastened around the criminal's neck, and projects outwards so far that he cannot touch his head with his bands. He therefore runs the risk of starvation, unless he has friends or relations, who are able and willing to feed him All the inconveniences resulting from this mode of punishment soon become tortures, and when the culprit is sentenced to undergo it for two or three months, his plight would be insupportable to any but a Chinaman. The man in question had a wretched, haggard look, but I saw no one who seemed to commiserate him in the least.

On the 23d of April, the British war-steamer *Hermes* left for Nanking, with Sir George Bonham on board. As the *Hermes* drew four or five feet less water than the *Susquehanna*, it was supposed that she would be able to proceed up the Yang-tse-Kiang. Sir George's object was to communicate with the rebels, and inform them of the entire neutrality of the foreign powers. The Taou-tai of Shanghai had circulated reports throughout the interior, that all the foreign war-steamers were in league with him, and were to be dispatched to Nanking. The *Hermes* returned on the 5th of May, having been absent twelve days. She was four days in reaching Nanking, having twice grounded in the river. She passed the outposts of the rebel army near Chin-Kiang-foo, where she was fired upon, but very slightly damaged. Having reached the anchorage at Nanking, the officers succeeded in communicating with the rebel chiefs, by whom they were well received. The latter stated that they were not hostile to foreigners, and had never intended to attack Shanghai. They professed to be Christians, and declared that their leader, Tae-ping, was a younger brother of Jesus Christ. From various indications, however, it was supposed that their Christianity, such as it was, was founded on the belief that, through its supernatural influ ence, they would obtain the same divine favor to which they ascribed the success of the English in the late Chinese war.

Mr. Meadows sent to the American Embassy copies of books which were obtained from the rebels. Among them was Gutzlaff's translation of the book of Genesis. They also had the Ten Commandments, which they promulgated as a divine law, changing the seventh so as to read thus: "Thou shalt not commit adultery, nor smoke opium." The latter offence is punished with death. The chief Tae-ping (Universal Peace,) was not seen by Sir George Bonham, nor any of his suite. He professed to be divinely inspired, receiving his communications direct from the Almighty. Nanking was almost wholly deserted by its former inhabitants, and its streets presented a pitiable spectacle. The rebels went about dressed in gorgeous silks, which they had taken from the despoiled shops of the merchants; sycee silver was abundant, and the most extravagant prices were paid for umbrellas, buttons, pistols, old clothes, and other articles on board the Hermes. Many of the sailors made large sums in thus disposing of their superfluous garments. A splendid robe of the most costly furs was given in exchange for a worn-out midshipman's uniform. Hundreds of the rebels visited the Hermes, while she lay before the city, and some of her officers went ashore, and even passed a night among the people, without the least molestation

The steamer *Bombay* arrived on the 3d of May, bringing the long-delayed European and American mails, together with the intelligence that the U. S. steam-frigate *Mississippi*, the flag-ship of the Japan Expedition had left Hong Kong for Shanghai. Early on the following morning, we saw from the house-top, through a glass, her broad pennant at the mouth of the Woosung River. Although drawing more than twenty feet, she succeeded in crossing the bar without delay, and came up to the city, where she dropped anchor beside the Susquehanna. On the 9th of May, Commodore Perry transferred his pennant to the latter vessel, with the usual ceremonies of firing salutes and manning the yards—a spectacle which drew the greater part of Shanghai to the *bund*. The Commodore became a guest at the American Consulate for the remainder of his stay, and his presence and that of the Mississippi's officers, gave a fresh impetus to the social activity of the foreign population. Thenceforth there were balls, dinners, and other entertainments, in great abundance.

Among these festivities, the most notable was a Chinese dinner which Col. Marshall gave at the Consulate. The building was in a blaze of lanterns and flowers. An arched avenue of colored lights led from the gate to the door, where the visitor ascended between a double row of fragrant white and crimson *mau-tans* to the first story. Here, the quaint silk lanterns were redoubled; curious baskets and urns of grass and shells, filled with flowers, were suspended from the ceiling, and the dining-room, handsomely draped with flags, contained a veritable bower or arbor of greenery enshrining the American eagle. The dinner was prepared with great care, not only the Taou-tai's silver cups and chopsticks, but even his cook having been borrowed for the occasion. The dishes were numerous and palatable, but hardly substantial enough for a civilized taste. They were mostly soups, and some of them were distinguished by very peculiar flavors, which I found difficult to analyze. The choicest dishes were bird's-nest soup shark's fins, and a dark, stringy substance, which the Taou-ta said he had procured from Pekin, at great expense. The dinner was followed by a grand ball, and a supper in European style.

There were rumors of trouble at Ningpo, and the French steamer *Cassini* made a trip to that city. Mr. Robert Fortune, author of "Wanderings in China," and "A Journey to the Bohea Mountains," who had arrived in Shanghai a short time previous, also left for Ningpo, whence he proposed making new journeys into the interior. Mr. Fortune is a plain, unassuming man, and an enthusiastic botanist, and by his daring excursions into the tea districts, has added greatly to our knowledge of the interior of China. Mr. Forbes, who went to Ningpo in the Cassini, returned about the 10th of May in a Chinese junk, by way of Chapoo.

CHAPTER XXIX

THE U. S. EXPEDITION TO JAPAN

State of Things at Shanghai—The Sloop-of-War Plymouth—Preparations for Departure—Entering the Naval Service—Its Regulations—Procuring a Uniform—The Master's-Mates—Establishing a Mess—Departure for Japan—A Gale—Shipwrecks—Standing out to Sea—Arrival at the Great Loo-Choo Island—A Missionary—Beauty of the Harbor of Napa—The Native Authorities—Going Ashore—Jumping over a Coral Reef—Landing—The Town of Napa-Kiang—Spies—Dr. Bettelheim's Residence.

IMMEDIATELY after the transfer of Commodore Perry's broad pennant to the *Susquehanna*, active preparations were made for the departure of the squadron on its mission to Japan. Since the return of the Hermes from Nanking, there was very little apprehension of danger, either among the Chinese or the foreign residents. The former had very generally returned to their homes and opened their shops, in accordance with the Taou-tai's commands. The American commercial houses, nevertheless, addressed a letter to Col. Marshall, asking that they should not be left entirely defenceless—on account of which application, Commodore Perry detached the sloop-of-war *Plymouth* from the squadron for a few weeks longer. Col. Marshall, who had as yet not been able to find a proper Chinese official to receive his letters of credence, finally made application to the Court at Pekin. He desired to proceed to the mouth of the Pai-ho River, in the Yellow Sea, and there await his answer, but a council of sailing-masters, called together by the Commodore, reported, after a long consultation, that it would be impossible to get within sight of the shore in a vessel drawing so much water as the *Plymouth*. Tuesday, the 17th of May, was appointed for the departure of the *Susquehanna* and *Mississippi*, the sloop-of-war *Saratoga* having already sailed from Macao for an unknown rendezvous.

I had extended my travels to China with a strong hope of being able to accompany the Expedition to Japan. On the arrival of Commodore Perry, I learned that very strict orders had been issued by the Navy Department against the admission on board of any of the vessels, of any person not attached to the service and subject to its regulations. Capt. Buchanan, who had no clerk, and was justly entitled to one, very kindly proposed that I should go in that capacity; but as there were two vacancies in the rank of master's-mate, which the Commodore had power to fill, and as my willingness to enter the service temporarily, removed the only objection he had urged, I decided to take the latter chance. I therefore signed an article of allegiance, and became an officer of very moderate rank, with unlimited respect for my superiors, and the reverse for my inferiors. This enlistment, which I most gladly and readily made, rendered me subject to all the regulations of the Navy Department; especially to that order promulgated for the benefit of the officers of the Expedition, which obliged them to give up to the Department every journal, note, sketch, or observation of any kind made during the cruise. I therefore closed my old journal, and commenced a new one from the day I entered—which latter is now in possession of the Navy Department, according to agreement. Nearly all the officers, on the contrary, had ceased keeping journals from the day the order was issued. I should have had some hesitation in submitting myself to that almost absolute power, which is the life of the Naval Service, had I not already known so well the officers of the *Susquehanna.* My confidence was not misplaced, for, from the Commodore down, with but a single exception, I received nothing from them but kindness and courtesy, during my connection with the service.

I had some dfficulty in procuring the necessary uniforms There were none but Chinese tailors in Shanghai, who work entirely from ready-made patterns. By foraging among the officers I procured a sufficient number of anchor buttons, and a crest for my cap; in the shop of a French merchant I found some cloth of the proper color; I borrowed one coat for the sleeves, another for the body, and another for the arrangement of buttons; and by keeping a watchful eye upon the tailor, finally succeeded in obtaining both undress and full-dress uniforms, which came within two buttons of being correct. Having assumed the blue, and buttoned my coat up to the throat in order to display the eighteen gilded eagles and anchors which decorated its front, I walked down the bund to try its effect. I endeavored to appear careless and self-possessed, but the first man-of-war'sman who passed betrayed me. I know that I actually blushed when he lifted his tarpaulin, and I doubt to this day whether I returned his salute. A little further, a jolly, red-headed tar, with a large cargo of *samshoo* aboard, came up and shook my hand heartily, promising me an oyster-supper in New York, after our return. I felt more at home in the service after such a characteristic welcome, and was not afterwards embarrassed by my buttons.

The places of acting master's-mates (the rank of warranted master's-mates being now obsolete) had been purposely left vacant, in order that it might be filled by artists and naturalists, who would thus belong to the service and be under the control of its officers. The rank and uniform is that of a passed midshipman, but the pay—twenty-five dollars a month—is considerably less than half of what the latter receives On the East India station it just about suffices for the payment of the mess-bill. There were three master's-mates on board the *Mississippi*—Mr. Heine, the artist; Mr. Draper who had charge of the telegraph apparatus; and Mr. Brown, daguerreotypist. As they were specially subject to the Commodore's orders, they were transferred to the Susquehanna, and I joined them in forming a separate mess, to which was added Mr. Portman, the Commodore's interpreter and clerk. The vessel was so crowded, that we had some trouble in finding sufficient room for our mess-table and stores, but were finally placed upon the orlop deck, beside the main hatch, and over the powder magazine. My cot was slung in the same place at night, where it was brought by a sturdy main-topman, who had it in his particular charge. A cadaverous Chinaman, A-fok by name, was shipped as our steward, and an incorrigible black deck-hand appropriated to us as cook. We were thus provided with all the requisites of a mess, and although there was some grumbling from time to time, on account of the heat and darkness of the orlop deck, the incompetency of the steward, or the villainy of the cook, I found my situation quite as comfortable as I anticipated, and never regretted having embraced it.

At last the day of our departure, the 17th of May, arrived. It was a warm, calm, sunny day, and as the black volumes began to rise from the smoke-stacks of the two steam-frigates, the whole foreign population of Shanghai flocked down to the bund. Mr. Forbes and Mr. Cunningham came on board for a pleasure trip to the Saddle Islands, whence they intended returning in a large junk which had been sent down with a final instalment of coal. About three o'clock the cornet was hauled down, the anchor hove, and we slowly threaded our way through the shipping, the band, stationed on the hurricane deck, playing in answer to the cheers and shouts which followed us. It was an exciting moment, for we were now leaving the frontiers of commerce and national intercourse, and our next port would be in one of those strange, exclusive realms which we hoped to open to the world. The cannon and the music ceased; the shouts became faint and died away altogether; the houses of Shanghai gradually passed out of sight, and before sunset we came to anchor in the Yang-tse-Kiang, off Woosung.

The next day we proceeded down the river. There was a gale of mingled wind and rain, and we ascertained that the store-ship *Supply*, which had come from Hong Kong to join the squadron, was aground on the North Shoal. She was in imminent danger for a time, but was finally got off without damage. In the evening, the junk which had been laden with coal ran aground, and soon became a complete wreck. Her crew, consisting of twelve men, were with difficulty saved by the Mississippi's boats. The Susquehanna had a large boat in tow, belonging to Mr. Cunningham, and by some mismanagement of the native sailors, one side of it was stove in against the frigate's quarter. The wreck still held by the hawser, dragging after us, the sea breaking over the terrified Chinese, who pounded their foreheads against the piece of deck that remained, and implored to be taken off. This was done as soon as possible, and the drenched Celestials had no sooner touched our deck than they prostrated themselves, and thumped their heads vigorously at the feet of the officer.

On account of the gale, and the dangerous navigation of the Archipelago of Chusan, the squadron remained two days near the Saddle Islands. The weather then became clear, and Messrs. Forbes and Cunningham, with the shipwrecked Chinamen, having found a means of return to Shanghai, left us, and the squadron stood out to sea. Shortly after passing the islands a streak of dazzling emerald appeared on the horizon, heralding our release from the treacherous waters of the Yang-tse-Kiang. The brown, muddy tint gradually passed off the hemisphere of sea, like an eclipse from the face of the sun; the vessels fell into line, the Susquehanna in advance, and the Mississippi, with the Supply in tow, following on our port quarter, and we were at last under way for the unknown rendezvous. The ship's course soon revealed to us what we had suspected—that the squadron would first proceed to the Great Loo-Choo Island.

With calm weather, we sailed three or four days in a south-east direction, and on the morning of the 26th saw some scattered, uninhabitable islands belonging to the Loo-Choo group. The day was clouded, with frequent thunder-showers; but we succeeded in making the Great Loo-Choo early in the afternoon, and with the assistance of Capt. Beechey's chart, felt our way into the harbor of Napa-Kiang, at its south-western extremity, before dark. As the island first came in sight we descried a vessel off the weather-beam, which soon proved to be the *Saratoga* making her way up, punctual to her appointment. The first landmark we made was Abbey Point, at the southern end of the harbor, by means of which, and a curious bluff called Capstan Rock, we were enabled to find the narrow entrance leading between coral reefs to a safe anchorage within. The rain began to fall in torrents soon after our arrival, and the green, misty hills of the island were soon lost in the gloom of night.

The same evening a native boat came off, bringing Dr. Bettelheim, the sole European resident on the island. He was a missionary, who had been placed there by a society of English naval officers, who, about seven years ago, formed the design of Christianizing those parts, and selected the Dr. as their first instrument. It was eighteen months since any vessel had touched at Napa, and the missionary came on board in a state of great excitement. He was received by the Commodore, and after a stay of an hour, returned to the shore.

When the next morning dawned, bright and clear, I thought I had never seen a more lovely landscape than the island presented. The bay was clasped by an amphitheatre of gently undulating hills, in some places terraced with waving rice-fields, in others covered with the greenest turf, or dotted with picturesque groups of trees. Bowers of the feathery bamboo—next to the palm, the most graceful of trees—almost concealed the dwellings which nestled together in the little dells opening into the bay, and which, with their stone enclosures and roofs of red tiles, hinted of a much higher civilization than we had expected

The spurs of the hills which ran down to the sea terminated in abrupt bluffs, in many places so shattered and irregular as to resemble castles and abbeys in ruins. Beyond and to the right of Capstan Rock, we saw the houses of the town of Napa, with the mouth of a little estuary, wherein some Chinese and Japanese junks were anchored; while on the top of the highest hill, three or four miles inland, one of the bastions of the Regent's castle towered above the trees. The exquisite harmony in the forms of the scene, the dazzling green of the foliage, and the sweet, delicious air which came to us off the shore, charmed us like a glimpse of Paradise, after the monotonous levels and polluted atmosphere of China.

There was no intercourse with the shore until after some negotiations had taken place between the Commodore and the high native dignitaries. The latter came off in rude, flat-bottomed boats, propelled with paddles. They were exceedingly grave and dignified men, dressed in loose robes of grass cloth, and with curious yellow caps on their heads. Both their persons and their garments were scrupulously clean; their long, silky beards were carefully combed out, the particular hairs lying parallel to each other, and every thing about them gave evidence of a care and neatness which I have never seen surpassed. They were greatly astonished at the size and strength of the steamer, and when one of the field-pieces was fired three times as a salute, several of the attendants dropped upon the deck from the shock of their surprise.

On the second day after our arrival, when the Commodor had come to a good understanding with the native authorities, he gave the officers of the squadron permission to go ashore. I jumped into the first boat which put off from the Susque hanna, and which happened to be manned by a dozen Chinese, from a number who had been shipped at Shanghai, as deck hands. The wind was blowing fresh, the sea was running briskly, and the Chinamen, who had probably never had an oar in their hands before, did little but catch crabs and confuse each other. We rapidly drifted away from the vessel and away from the shore, until, finally, one of the midshipmen ordered the coolies to cease, and with the assistance of two or three others stepped the mast and set the sheet, to run in on the wind. But he did not know the harbor, and in the twinkling of an eye, the boat, which was running at the rate of seven or eight knots, dashed upon a coral reef. It was too late to wear off, so we bounced across it, the boat striking upon the tops of the growing coral trees, with every wave. Having reached deep water again, we found ourselves in a lake, or pool, completely encircled by the reef. The only means of escape was to jump back again, which we finally accomplished without staving in the boat, and after a wearisome pull, reached the steamer, where we procured a fresh crew, and were finally put ashore at the foot of Capstan Rock.

By this time several boats had landed, and groups of officers and men were strolling towards the town. Behind a hedge of the prickly *pandanus*, there was a cluster of bamboo huts, inhabited mostly by fishermen—lank, tawny, half-naked figures, who looked at us with a sort of listless curiosity. Their families were all concealed within the houses. As we advanced towards the town, I noticed that two or three individuals, in robes of salmon-colored grass-cloth, hovered near each party, and, without seeming to watch closely, took note of every movement that was made. We soon entered the main street, which was broad and well paved, and as neat as it could well be. It was enclosed by massive walls of coral and porous limestone, about ten feet high, over which hung a variety of flowering shrubs and the branches of glossy tropical trees, growing in the gardens behind them. The dwellings were within these enclosures, and if we saw, by chance, a gate unlocked, and ventured to enter, we invariably found the place vacant and deserted. The salmon-colored gentlemen did their duty well. We succeeded in getting a very accurate idea of the situation of the town, its size, the character of its architecture, and the outward appliances of its social life; but the inhabitants, except a few men and boys who lingered here and there in the streets, had totally disappeared.

On my return to the vessel, I called at the residence of Dr. Bettelheim, which was a very neat cottage furnished him by the authorities of Loo-Choo, on a slope behind Capstan Rock. His family consisted of his wife, a mild, amiable English woman, and two children. The house was plain, but comfortable, and the view from the neighboring rock enchanting, yet I could not but doubt whether any thing can atone for such a complete removal from the world of civilized men. Even the zeal of the Missionary must flag, when it is exercised in vain After seven years' labor, all the impression which Dr. Bettelheim appears to have produced upon the natives is expressed in their request, touching from its very earnestness: "take this man away from among us!"

CHAPTER XXX.

VISIT TO THE CAPITAL OF LOO CHOO.

Visit of the Regent—The Island of Loo-Choo—An Exploration of the Interior—Setting Out—Entry into the Capital—Reception—The Old Mandarin in for a Journey—His Resignation—Programme of the Exploring Trip—Espionage in Loo-Choo—Endeavors to Escape it—Taking Families by Surprise—The Landscapes of Loo-Choo—The *Cung-quds*—Watches and Counter-Watches—Commodore Perry's Visit to Shui—Disembarkation—The Order of March—Curiosity of the Natives—March to the Capital—Reception at the Gate—A Deception Prevented—The Viceroy's Castle—The Inner Courts—The Commodore's Reception—A Tableau—Salutations and Ceremonies—Visit to the Regent's House—A State Banquet in Loo-Choo—Edibles and Beverages—Extent of the Dinner—Toasts—The Interpreter, *Ichirazichi*—Departure—Riding a Loo-Choo Pony—Return to the Squadron.

Two days after our arrival at Loo-Choo, the Regent of the Island paid a formal visit to Commodore Perry, on board of the Susquehanna; and Monday, the 6th of June, was fixed upon as the day when the Commodore should return his visit at Shui, the capital, which lies some three or four miles to the north-east of Napa.

The kingdom, or vice-royalty of Loo-Choo, which is tributary to the Japanese Prince of Satsuma, though frequently visited by exploring vessels within the past fifty years, had been comparatively little known previous to our arrival. Hall, Broughton, Beechey, and the French Admiral Cecile, had sur veyed portions of the coast, but the interior of the island remained a *terra incognita*. The officers of H. B. M. steamer Sphinx, which visited Napa in February, 1852, were the first who were received in the royal castle of Shui. The heir to the vice-royalty is a boy, who was about eleven years old at the time of our visit, and the Government was therefore intrusted to the hands of a Regent, until he should have attained his majority.

As soon as communication with the shore had been established, Commodore Perry appointed four officers from the Susquehanna and Mississippi, to make an exploring tour through the island. I had the good fortune to be one of the party. We set out on Monday morning, May 30th, with a week's leave of absence, and after having explored rather more than half the island, returned on the afternoon of June 4th. We were allowed to take with us four seamen, and four Chinese coolies to carry our tents and camping utensils. The party was well armed, and furnished with ammunition and ship's rations for the necessary time. This exploration was in many respects one of the most peculiar and interesting episodes of travel I ever enjoyed. In these days of discovery, a piece of virgin earth is comparatively rare. There are few spots on the Earth's surface, so accessible as Loo-Choo, into which the European race has not yet penetrated. I regret that my application to our Government for permission to copy that portion of my journal describing it, should have been denied, and that hence I am unable to give at present a detailed account of the journey.

The island is about sixty miles in length, from north to south, with a varying breadth of from five to ten miles. The north-eastern extremity, beyond Port Melville, which we were obliged to leave unexplored, for want of time, is wild, mountainous, and but thinly inhabited. In order to avoid the cunning and deception of the authorities, no previous notice of our journey was given to them. We landed and marched directly into the interior, without so much as saying, "by your leave." We had not proceeded more than half a mile, however, before we were overtaken by a native mandarin of the fifth rank, with several subordinate officers, who had been sent in all haste to follow us and watch our movements. Their faces exhibited considerable surprise and alarm, as they beheld eight armed men, with the cool assurance natural to Americans, taking the direct road to Shui, their capital.

We carried with us, as a token of our nationality, a small boat's ensign, and on arriving at the gate of the capital, one of the sailors fastened it to a light bamboo staff, which he stuck into the barrel of his musket, and thus we bore the flag boldly through the centre of the town and around the very walls of the Viceroy's castle. But rapid as we had been in our march from Napa, scouts were in advance of us, and the capital appeared to be entirely deserted. Every house was closed, and scarcely a soul was to be seen in the streets. The few whom we met glided past us with anxious faces, and the cloud on the brows of our attendant spies grew darker as we advanced. We kept on, nevertheless, and after passing through the town, took a course by the compass, and struck across the hills towards the opposite shore of the island. From the summit of a ridge, about a mile and a half to the eastward, we had a glorious view of green valleys, sloping down to a broad bay beyond which extended the blue horizon-line of the open Pacific.

As it drew towards evening, the old mandarin who suspected that we were merely making a day's excursion into the country, intimated that it was time to return We replied by signs, that we were going much further, and would not return for several days. This was more than he had bargained for: he had been appointed to watch us and dare not leave us—and now, willing or not, he must make the tour of the whole island. His look of blank perplexity was at first very amusing, but seeing that there was no help for his case, he submitted to it with true Eastern passiveness, and laughed heartily with us at the prospect before him. I must confess that the thirst for exploration made us somewhat unfeeling. In our desire to see as much of the island as possible within the time allotted to us, we led the old mandarin such a dance as he certainly never performed before. Although he made use of his authority over the natives, and frequently obliged them to carry him in the *kago*, or sedan-chair of Japan, he would come into the encampment every evening, slapping his legs to show how fatigued they were, and amusing us, in a good-humored way, with signs of the great exhaustion he felt. Notwithstanding this, he visited us regularly every morning at daybreak, to inquire after our health, and exhibited so much patience and kindly feeling in every way, that in spite of the annoyance which his office caused us, we all felt a cordial friendship towards him.

We encamped for the night on the shore of the bay, to which the name of Matthews' Bay was given by Commodore Perry, in memory of Lieut. John Matthews, of the *Plymouth*, who first surveyed it, and who was afterwards lost at the Bonin Islands, in a typhoon. Travelling northward the next day, over the ridges of the beautiful hills, and by foot-paths through forests, we reached at sunset a village on the shore of

Barrow's Bay. On the road we discovered the ruins of an ancient castle, crowning the summit of a high peak. It was 235 paces in length by 70 in breadth, with walls from six to twelve paces in thickness. We afterwards ascertained that it had been the palace of one of the former kings of Loo-Choo, when the island was divided into three sovereignties. On the third day we proceeded around the head of Barrow's Bay, and across the northern promontory, to a village called "Ching," or "Kanafa." Thence we struck northward into the heart of the island, over a range of mountains covered with dense tropical forests, intending to make the head of Port Melville, on the opposite side, but having swerved too much to the left, came down to the shore at a village called Na-Komma. We spent the fourth night at the village of Un-na, the features of whose lovely valley I have attempted to represent in the frontispiece to this volume. The fifth day was a weary march of twenty-eight miles in a burning sun, over mountains, through tangled thickets, deep rice-swamps, and in the glaring sand of the sea-shore. We halted for the night at a place called Chando-kosa, and the next day, after travelling about twenty-five miles in a heavy rain, reached the harbor of Napa, having journeyed more than a hundred miles through a territory previously untrodden by white men.

The perfection to which the system of espionage is carried in Loo-Choo—and consequently in Japan, for the system is no doubt the same in both countries—is almost incredible. I have no doubt that before the second day of our trip was over, the fact was known throughout the whole island, and watchers were set around every village, to look out for our approach. We were surrounded with a secret power, the tokens of which were invisible, yet which we could not move a step without feeling. We tried every means to elude it, but in vain. The lovely villages with which the island is dotted were deserted at our approach, and the inhabitants so well concealed that we arely succeeded in finding them. Only the laborers who were at work in the fields were allowed to remain, and even they were obliged to keep at a distance from our path. We changed our course repeatedly, in the endeavor to mislead the spies, but they seemed to comprehend our designs by a species of instinct and wherever we went they had been before us. We scattered our forces, each one taking a separate course, but the spies were still more numerous than we. We could perceive, however, from the demeanor of the natives, that they were well disposed towards us, and felt a strong curiosity to become acquainted with us—and that it was not so much fear of ourselves, as dread of the power of their rulers, which kept them aloof. I had a great desire to learn something of their social and domestic life, and made frequent efforts to accomplish my object, by plunging into the woods from time to time, outstripping the spies, and then darting suddenly into some neighboring village. Although I entered many houses, in two or three instances only did I find the inhabitants within. On my appearance, which must have been very unexpected and startling, the women fell upon their knees, uplifting both hands in an attitude of supplication, while the men prostrated themselves and struck their foreheads upon the earth. I could only assure them by signs of my friendly disposition, and found no difficulty in allaying their apprehensions, whenever the spies gave me time enough. On one occasion, where I found two women employed in weaving the coarse cotton cloth of the country, after the first surprise was over, they quietly resumed their occupation.

In other respects, the journey was as agreeable as it was interesting. The island is one of the most beautiful in the world, and contains a greater variety of scenery than I have ever seen within the same extent of territory. The valleys and hill-sides are cultivated with a care and assiduity, which puts even Chinese agriculture to shame; the hills are crowned with picturesque groves of the Loo-Choo pine, a tree which the artist would prize much more highly than the lumberman; the villages are embowered with arching lanes of bamboo, the tops of which interlace and form avenues of perfect shade; while, from the deep indentations of both shores, the road along the spinal ridge of the island commands the most delightful prospects of bays and green headlands, on either side. In the sheltered valleys, the clusters of sago-palm and banana trees give the landscape the character of the Tropics: on the hills, the forests of pine recall the scenery of the Temperate Zone. The northern part of the island abounds with marshy thickets and hills overgrown with dense woodland, infested with wild boars, but the southern portion is one vast garden.

The villages all charmed us by the great taste and neatness displayed in their construction. In the largest of them there were buildings called *cung-quás*, erected for the accommodation of the agents of the Government, on their official journeys through the island. They were neat wooden dwellings, with tiled roofs, the floors covered with soft matting, and the walls fitted with sliding screens, so that the whole house could be thrown open or divided into rooms at pleasure. They were surrounded with gardens, enclosed by trim hedges and were always placed in situations where they commanded the view of a pleasant landscape. These buildings were appropriated to our use, and when, after a hard day's tramp, we had hoisted our flag on the roof and stretched ourselves out to rest on the oft matting, we would not have exchanged places with the old Viceroy himself. As a matter of precaution, we kept regular watches through the night, but the natives also kept a counter-watch upon us. The *cung-quà* was often surrounded with a ring of watch-fires, and as the inhabitants seized this opportunity of gratifying their curiosity, we frequently saw hundreds of dusky heads peering at us through the gloom until the appearance of one of the Government spies scattered them as effectually as if a bomb-shell had exploded among them.

On our return to the squadron, I was gratified to find myself among the number chosen to accompany the Commodore on his visit to the Regent, at Shui, on the Monday morning following. The hour of departure was fixed at nine o'clock, and the boats pushed off from the different vessels at the same time. The Susquehanna's launches and cutters, conveying the field-piece, seamen, bandsmen and marines, presented a very lively and animating show, as they rocked over the swell ing waves. The morning was cloudy, with a brisk wind; but though a passing shower threw its veil over the hills while on our way to the landing-place, the sky soon came out bright and blue, and the day was as fresh and pleasant as could have been wished.

The point of disembarcation was the little village of Tu maï, lying north of the sandy flats (covered at high tides), which separate the promontory of Napa from the hills of the island. From this place it is not more than two miles to Shui

On entering the creek which runs up to Tumai we found most of the boats already arrived, and the marines drawn up in line along the road under a grove of trees. Groups of officers, in undress uniform, were gathered in the shade; the boats' crews, in high spirits, were watching the preparations, and some hundreds of natives, among whom were many of the more respectable class, looked on with evident interest. The Commodore's barge having arrived, he, with Commander Adams, Captain of the fleet, Lieut. Contee, Flag Lieutenant, and Commanders Buchanan, Lee and Walker, passed in review the files of marines and artillerymen.

The procession then formed in regular order. First went the two field-pieces, each with the American ensign displayed, under the command of Lieut. Bent, of the Mississippi; the interpreters, Mr. Wells Williams and Dr. Bettelheim, walked in advance, followed by Mr. Bennet, Master of the Susquehanna, who commanded the first field-piece. After the artillery followed the Susquehanna's band, and a company of marines, under Major Zeilin. The Commodore came next, in a sedan-chair, which our carpenter had made for the occasion. It was carried by four Chinese coolies, with a relay of four more. A marine walked on each side as body-guard, with two of the Commodore's personal attendants. Behind the chair were the Captain of the Fleet, the Flag Lieutenant, and the Commodore's Secretary. Six coolies followed, bearing the presents intended for the Prince and Queen Dowager, guarded by a file of marines. Among them I noticed arms of different kinds, and specimens of American manufactured goods. The officers accompanying the Commodore followed in a body, headed by Commanders Buchanan, Lee and Walker. Their servants, the

Mississippi's band, and a second company of marines, under Capt. Slack, of the Mississippi, closed the procession. The entire number of persons composing it, was about 215, of whom 32 were officers, 122 seamen and marines, and 30 musicians.

It was one of the most picturesque processions of its size that I have ever seen. The beauty of the day, the brilliant green of the wooded hills through which our road lay, and the cheerful strains of the bands, gave the occasion a most inspiring character. Numbers of the natives gathered on both sides of the road to see us pass, and a large crowd followed in our rear. There did not appear to be the least alarm on their part, but a pleased excitement, for the procession, notwithstanding its martial character, had a festive and friendly air. In the narrow lanes branching into the road, the foremost ranks of the crowd knelt, the next stooped, and those in the rear stood upright, in order to allow as many as possible to see the display Very soon, however, we emerged from the village, passed a large temple at the foot of the hill behind it, and came out upon the open, undulating country south of Shui. The rice-fields rolled in heavy waves before the wind, and the dark green foliage of the groves in which Shui is embowered, glittered in the sun. The natives were grouped here and there, in the shade of clumps of the Loo-Choo pine, and numbers of them were seen running along the ridges between the rice-fields in order to get ahead of us and obtain another view.

The march occupied nearly an hour, the bands playing alternately during the whole time. The road was familiar to me, as we had passed through Shui on our tour of exploration, but the other officers were charmed with the scenery, especially as we climbed the hill on which the capital is built, and saw the rich cultivated landscape spreading away southward and westward. The Loo-Choo official, appointed to meet us at the landing-place, and accompany us to Shui, proved to be Chang-yuen, the same old Pe-ching, or mandarin of the fifth class, who had been our guide and companion during the expedition. At the gate of Shui, we were met by a crowd of native dignitaries, with their attendants, all in brilliantly clean robes of grass-cloth, and red and yellow hatchee-matchees, as the peculiar cap worn in Loo-Choo is called, upon their heads. The old Regent, and his three venerable coadjutors, the Treasurers of the Kingdom, here made their appearance, and after saluting the Commodore, turned about and accompanied the procession, which passed in through the central arch, without halt, and marched up the great street of the city. There was a large train of native servants, in attendance upon the Regent and Chiefs, bearing umbrellas, "chow-chow" or refreshment boxes, cases for caps, and other articles. The inscription over the gate is "The Central Hill," signifying, according to Mr. Williams, "the place of authority." The lower orders of the natives are not permitted to pass through the central arch.

The main street is lined with high walls, with but few alleys branching out of it. It was kept clear of spectators by the native officers who preceded us, except in a street on the left, leading to the house of the Regent, which was filled with a concourse of persons. On reaching this point, the Regent, who was in advance, requested, through his interpreter, that the procession should proceed at once to his house. As this was evidently a scheme to prevent our entering the castle, a determination on the Commodore's part which seemed to give them much anxiety, Mr. Williams paid no attention to the request, but marched on toward the castle gate. The reception of the officers of the Sphinx within its walls, left the Commodore no alternative but to exact equal respect.

The Regent did not seem to have anticipated that we should carry the point, for the gate of the castle was closed. A messenger was sent forward at full speed to open it, and make preparations for the Commodore's reception. On reaching the entrance, the artillery and marines were drawn up in line, and the Commodore, followed by his staff and suite of officers, walked past into the castle, while the troops presented arms and lowered the ensigns, and the band struck up "Hail Columbia."

Entering the first gateway, we found a second wall and portal above us, still further strengthened by a natural cliff, upon which part of it was built. Along the foot of this wall and the parapet of the one below, grew clusters of the beautiful sago palm, many of which were in flower. A small stream of water, trickling from an aperture above, fell into a subterranean drain. On either side of it were planted two tall stone tablets, with sculptured inscriptions upon them. Two rudely sculptured lions, nearly the size of life, were placed at the second entrance, which ushered us into an outer court of the palace, on the summit of the height. It was irregular in shape, and surrounded by houses which appeared to be designed for servants and others attached to the royal household. On the eastern side was another gateway, resembling the Chinese portals of honor. It consisted of two arches, and the Commodore and his suite were conducted through the right-hand one. This brought us into what appeared to be the central court of the palace. It was not more than eighty feet square, surrounded with one-story wooden edifices, remarkable neither for style nor decoration. The court was paved with gravel and large tiles, arranged in alternate lozenges. The hall of reception was on the northern side, the other buildings, or portions of the main edifice, being closed by screens against all view from without. Into this hall, which, like all Loo-Choo houses, had an outer verandah, the Commodore was conducted, and placed at its head on the right hand, followed by the other officers, according to their rank. Chairs of dark wood, varnished, and made exactly upon the principle of our camp-stools, were brought, and all the guests were soon ranged in a single row along the right hand, and a double one across the bottom of the room, while the Regent and Treasurers sat upon the left side, with a double rank of attendants behind them. The Interpreters occupied a position at the head of the room, between the Commodore and Regent. On the wall above them was a large red tablet, with an inscription in gilded characters, which Mr. Williams translated as signifying: "The Elevated Enclosure of Fragrant Festivities."

Neither the Queen Dowager nor the young Prince made their appearance. Among the reasons urged by the Regent why the Commodore should defer his visit to Shui, was the alleged illness of the Queen, caused by the visit of the officers of the Sphinx. The royal lady's nerves, it was said had been so agitated by that event, that she had been under medical treatment ever since, and another occurrence of the kind might prove dangerous to her. The Commodore politely offered to send one of his surgeons to prescribe for her, but this was declined. It was probably not considered politic to produce the Prince, on account of his youth. After the first salutations had been made, tables were brought, and cups of very weak tea presented to the guests. Smoking boxes were distributed around the room, and dishes of leathery twists of gingerbread placed upon the tables. But it was evident that our coming had not been expected, and no preparations made to receive us. The sides of the room were separated from the other parts of the building by paper screens, and I fancied that there were listeners and observers (possibly the old Queen herself) behind them. The whole scene, in fact, could hardly have been less interesting to the native spectators than to ourselves. The strong contrast between the American uniforms of blue and gold, and the simple gray and fawn-colored robes of the four dignitaries who confronted them, as well as between the keen eyes and active, energetic faces of the one race, and the venerable gray beards and impassive features of the other, gave it somewhat of a dramatic air, which rather added to, than diminished the impression it made. Those four personages had all the gravity and dignity which might have belonged to Roman Senators, or rather, to members of the Venetian Council of Ten.

After the usual salutations on both sides, the Commodore invited the Regent and his three associates to visit him on board the Susquehanna. He stated that he intended leaving Napa in a day or two, but that he should return again after ten days, and would receive them at any time they appointed, either before or after his absence. To this they replied that they would leave the time of the visit to be fixed by the Commodore himself, whereupon he stated that he preferred it should be postponed until after his return. They acceded to this with apparent gratification. Several large red cards, similar to those used on state occasions in China, were then produced. The Regent taking them in his hand, all four rose came forward a few steps, and bowed profoundly. The Commodore and all the others rose and returned the salutation The Commodore then stated, that if there were any articles on board any of the vessels which the Regent might need, or desire to possess, he would gladly supply him with them. They again rose, advanced, and bowed as before. The dignitaries did not seem quite at ease, probably on account of our having stolen a march upon them, in entering the castle.

The interview had lasted nearly an hour, when the Regent rose and proposed that the Commodore should pay him a visit at his official residence. The procession was thereupon formed in the same order, and returned to the street, where we had been invited to enter, on our arrival. The Regent's house was in this street, a short distance from the main avenue. The seamen, marines and musicians remained behind, in charge of a few officers. The Commodore and his suite were conducted into the house, which was rather larger than usual, but not distinguished by any appearance of wealth, or insignia of office. It consisted of a central hall with wings, open toward the court-yard, from which it was only separated by a narrow verandah, approached by a flight of stone steps. The building was of wood, and the pillars supporting it, with the beams of the ceilings, were painted of a dark-red color. The floor was covered with thick, fine matting, each mat being rigorously made according to the legal dimensions.

Four tables were set in the central apartment, and three in each of the wings, and already covered with a profuse collation. Immediately on entering we were requested to seat ourselves. The Commodore, with Commanders Buchanan and

Adams, took the highest table on the right hand, and the Regent and his associates the one opposite on the left. At each corner of the tables lay a pair of chop-sticks. In the centre stood an earthen pot filled with sackee, surrounded with four acorn-cups, four large cups of coarse china, with clumsy spoons of the same material, and four tea-cups. From this centre radiated a collection of dishes of very different shapes and sizes, and still more different contents. There were nineteen on the table at which I sat, but I can only enumerate a few of them: Eggs, dyed crimson and sliced; fish made into rolls and boiled in fat; cold pieces of baked fish; slices of hog's liver; sugar candy; cucumbers; mustard; salted radish tops; curds made of bean flour; fragments of fried lean pork, and several nondescripts, the composition of which it was impossible to tell.

The repast began with cups of tea, which were handed around, followed by tiny cups of sackee, which was of much superior quality to any we had yet tasted on the island. It was old and mellow, with a sharp, sweet, unctuous flavor, somewhat like French *liqueur*. Small bamboo sticks, sharpened at one end, were then presented to us. We at first imagined them to be tooth-picks, but soon found that they were designed to stick in the balls of meat and dough, which floated in the cups of soup, constituting the first course. Six or eight cups of different kinds of soup followed, and the attendants, meanwhile, assiduously filled up the little cups of sackee. We had a handsome, bright-eyed youth as our Ganymede, and the smile with which he pressed us to eat and drink, was irresistible. The abundance of soup reminded me of a Chinese repast. Of the twelve courses —the number appropriated to a royal dinner—which were served to us, eight were soups, and many of them so similar in

17

composition as not to be distinguished by a palate unpractised in Loo-Choo delicacies. The other four were—gingerbread; a salad made of bean-sprouts and tender onion-tops; a basket of what appeared to be a dark-red fruit, about the size of a peach, but proved to be balls, composed of a thin rind of unbaked dough, covering a sugary pulp; and a delicious mixture of beaten eggs, and the aromatic, fibrous roots of the ginger-plant. The gingerbread had a true home flavor, and was not to be despised. The officers did their best to do honor to the repast, but owing to the number of dishes could do little more than taste the courses as they were served up. Although we left at the end of the twelfth course, we were told that twelve more were in readiness to follow.

After the eighth or ninth course, the Commodore rose and proposed as a toast, the health of the Queen Mother and the young Viceroy, adding: "Prosperity to the Loo-Chooans, and may they and the Americans always be friends!" This toast, having been translated to the Regent, appeared to gratify him highly, and it was drunk standing, with Loo-Choo honors, which consists in draining the tea-spoonful of sackee at one gulp, and turning the cup bottom upwards. The Commodore afterwards proposed the health of the Regent and his associates, which the latter returned by giving that of the Commodore and the officers of the Squadron. By this time the anxiety and embarrassment of the Chiefs had entirely worn off, and the entertainment wound up with the best possible feeling. How much of the anxiety was assumed, or what was its cause, we had no means of ascertaining; but from what little I have seen of the Loo-Chooans, I am satisfied that there is a strong basis of cunning in their character. The interpreter on the part of the

Regent was a very intelligent young native, name *Ichirazichi*, who had been educated at Pekin, where he remained three years. He spoke a little English, and had some knowledge, both of the geographical position of the United States, and their history. He spoke of Washington as a very great Mandarin. He had a more swarthy complexion than is usually found among the educated Loo-Chooans, a keen black eye, and a shrewd, cunning expression of countenance.

The Commodore left the Regent's house about one o'clock, when the procession formed in the same order as before. The subordinate officials accompanied us to the gate, and the old Pe-ching again took his station in advance. On starting down the hill, the four ponies, which had gone up with us without finding riders, were again led to the rear. Several of us profited by this neglect, to mount for a ride down, and try the temper of the Loo-Choo horses. The ponies were very small animals, of a bay color, but rather active and spirited. They were accoutred like the Chinese horses, with saddles of Turkish fashion, and enormous iron stirrups, curved backwards, so as to admit not only the foot but part of the leg. They were led by grooms, and we could not succeed in bringing them into line behind the rear company of marines, on account of their jealousy of each other. The little chargers kicked and plunged several times with great vivacity.

The sun, shining full in the face of the hill, made our descent a sultry one, but as we came upon the wooded slopes a sea-breeze met us, and groups of the boats' crews who had come off to convey us back to the vessels, were seen under the trees, watching our approach Several hundreds of the natives followed us, and as we drew near the shore, they were seen scampering over the rice-fields in every direction, to get a final view of our array. Fifteen boats, each flying the American colors, lay in the mouth of the creek. The Commodore and suite immediately embarked, and the wind being fair, the cutters hoisted sail, and dashed away over the bright blue waves, passing the slow white launches, with their loads of marines and artillerymen. All were on board by half-past two, without any untoward incident having occurred to mar the successful issue of the trip.

CHAPTER XXXI.

VOYAGE TO THE BONIN ISLANDS.

Departure—The Bonin, or Arzobispo Isles—Death of a Chinese Opium Smoker—A Peruvian Bark—Approach to the Bonin Islands—Pilots—Entering Port Lloyd—Going Ashore—A Settler's Hut—Society on the Island—Mode of Life—An Old Inhabitant and his Mate—Productions of the Island—A Coaling Station for Steamers—Buckland Island—A Basaltic Cavern—English Claims to the Islands.

On the 9th of June, Commodore Perry left the harbor of Napa in the Susquehanna, for a visit to the Bonin or Arzobispo Isles, which lie in Lat. 27° N., Long. 140° 30′ E., or between eight and nine hundred miles from Loo-Choo. We took the sloop-of-war Saratoga in tow, leaving the Mississippi behind, as we did not expect to be absent more than two weeks.

The Bonin Islands have scarcely been heard of in the United States, except through an occasional whaling vessel, some of which are in the habit of touching there, in order to procure fresh provisions. They are about 500 miles in a southerly direction from the Bay of Yedo, and are called by the Japanese *Mo* or *Mou nin sima*, signifying "uninhabited islands," whence the English term, *Bonin*. In Kömpfer's work on Japan, there is an account of their discovery by the Japanese, two and a half centuries ago, and the same, with a more minute description of their appearance and productions, is to be found in Klaproth's translation of a Japanese work on the three tributary Kingdoms of Corea, Loo-Choo, and Jeso. They were also discovered by a Spanish Admiral, and named the "Islas del Arzobispo," long prior to Capt. Beechey's visit and survey in 1827. To the latter navigator, however, we are indebted for the first accurate account of their location and extent.

We were favored by the south-west monsoon, and had a delightful run of five days, with nothing to interrupt the uniformity of sea life, except frequent calls to "general quarters," and the death of Mr. Williams' Chinese Secretary The latter fell a victim to the practice of smoking opium. He attempted to give it up, and this, with a spell of sea-sickness on board the Saratoga, so enfeebled him that no medicines produced any effect, and he sank into a state of nervelessness and emaciation shocking to witness. His body was reduced to a skeleton, and all his nervous energy so completely destroyed, that for a week before his death every fibre in his frame was in a state of constant agitation. His face was a ghastly yellow, the cheeks sunken upon the bones, and the eyes wild and glassy with a semi-madness which fell upon him. His whole aspect reminded me of one of those frightful heads in wax, in the museum of Florence, representing the effects of the plague. He was a complete wreck, both in mind and body, and nothing that I ever saw of the results of intoxication from spirituous liquors has impressed me with half the horror.

On the morning of the 12th we passed a Peruvian bark, with a cargo of coolies, bound for the guano islands. She was steering nearly the same course as ourselves, under a cloud of canvas, with studding-sails and royals set, but we did not pass within hail. The sight of a leviathan steamer—the first that ever ploughed those seas—towing a large vessel after her, must have greatly astonished the Peruvians.

At sunrise on the 14th, we saw the Bonin Islands before us, with the Bailly Islands about fifteen miles distant, in a south-easterly direction, and Parry's Group barely visible in the north-east. The three islands of the Bonin Group, Peel, Buckland, and Stapleton, lie close together, within an extent, collectively, of ten miles from north to south. We made for the harbor of Port Lloyd, on the western side of Peel Island, where the only inhabitants—a small community of Kanakas, with some runaway English and American sailors—have taken up their abode. On approaching the entrance to the harbor a gun was fired for a pilot, which, it appeared, was the first intimation the residents had of our arrival. In a short time two canoes appeared, and we were boarded by two natives, who attracted considerable attention, as being the vagabond inhabitants of that remote corner of the world. One of them appeared to be a cross between Portuguese and Kanaka. He wore a tattered straw hat, blue cotton jacket and pantaloons, and was bare-footed. The other was a youth about twenty years old, lithe and graceful in his form, and with a quick, bright eye and rather intelligent face. He was the only native of the island, and the son of a Portuguese named John Bravo.

Their sailing directions were of little use, but the entrance to the port was broad and deep, and we moved on slowly and securely to an anchorage in twenty-one fathoms, abreast a dense grove of trees, bordering a beach on the northern shore Nearly east of us rose the high twin peaks, named "The Paps" by Capt. Beechey; a little further to the south, beyond a rocky islet named "Castle Rock," was a narrow beach, at the foot of a ravine, down which flowed a stream, the usual watering-place of the whalers. With the exception of three or four similar beaches, the shores were bold and precipitous, and the mountains behind, rising in steep, picturesque outlines, were covered to their very summits with the richest tropical vegetation.

Towards evening I went ashore in the gig. Near the northern beach there is a bank of coral, dropping suddenly into a track of deep water, which forms what is called "Ten Fathom Hole." This extends so far up the bay, that vessels of the largest size may lie within a hundred feet of the shore, in a position completely landlocked, and sheltered from every wind. The trees which lined the beach were entirely new to me. They had heavy, crooked trunks and boughs, and large ovate leaves of a bright-green color. The settlers called them *tamanas.* Two immense turtles, which had been caught the night before, lay sprawling upon their backs in the shade, and a white man, who described himself as an Englishman named Webb, with two Kanakas, were sitting lazily upon an inverted canoe, made of the hollowed trunk of a tree. The shells of other turtles were lying on the sand, and exhaled not the freshest of odors. An opening through the trees showed us a neat cabin behind, surrounded with a low paling.

The Englishman, who was civil and respectful, though silent, rarely speaking unless in answer to our questions, led the way and opened the door. The interior was small, but exceedingly neat and tasteful. The frame of the hut, and the ridge-poles and rafters were all of equal size, and painted a light blue color. The thatch was of leaves of the fan-palm, and impervious to rain. There was an outer room, with a table and a few chairs, and two sleeping apartments in the rear, which were kept carefully closed during the day, on account of the abundance of mosquitos. The walls were covered with Chinese matting, and a row of gaudily-colored French lithographs of female figures hung across the partition. Within the paled enclosure were two other low, rude structures of palm leaves, one of which served as a kitchen, while the other was appropriated to the Kanakas, a well, and three flourishing papaya trees. Behind the house was a narrow and beautiful plain, covered with sweet potatoes, melons, and sugar cane, with the palm forests of the mountains in the background. The line of trees along the beach was narrow, and merely left to protect the garden-land in the rear from the violence of sudden squalls, which sometimes prevail in the summer.

The Englishman stated that he had been seven years on the island. There was a kind of hesitation in his manner of speaking, which I fancied arose from an absence of intercourse with civilized society, as he seemed to be a man of average intelligence. There was, apparently, little association among the settlers. So far as I could learn, there are no rules of government accepted by them; each lives upon his own soil, by virtue of the right of pre-emption, and interferes as little as possible in the affairs of his neighbors. The oldest inhabitant, who probably exercises a sort of authority in cases of dispute, is a native of Massachusetts, named Savory, who has been on the island since 1831, and is considered the richest of the settlers. His money has been principally made by selling sweet potatoes to whaling ships, at the rate of two dollars a barrel; in addition to which he has a still, and manufactures rum from sugar-cane. At the time of our visit he had two hogsheads of it, which was said to be of excellent quality. The population is continually floating, with the exception of four or five persons who were among the original settlers of the island. Sailors from the whaling vessels frequently desert, and remain a year or two, after which they embark again. The whalers are mostly American, and, according to the settlers, generally conduct themselves peaceably. There was a flagrant exception, however, in the case of one vessel, the crew of which robbed Savory of $2,000 and carried off the daughter of Bravo, together with a Kanaka woman. The persons implicated were afterwards arrested at Honolulu for the abduction, but by that time the women were satisfied with their captivity, and declared that they left the island of their own accord.

Further up the beach, we found another hut, inhabited by an old Englishman, who had been there for more than twenty years. He was upwards of fifty years old, of small stature, but hale and active, and the sun, which had bleached his brown hair into a tow color, had burned his face, neck, breast and arms of a deep red. He seemed to have wholly forgotten the world from which he came, and declared his intention never to leave the island, but to die, as he had lived, in that Pacific solitude. He had a Kanaka woman, named Bet, a frightfully fat and ugly creature, but very good humored. On our asking for water-melons, he sent her with a bag into the field, and when she had returned with three or four of the ripest, the good woman sat down to take breath, and never ceased chuckling with delight at the rapacity with which we sliced and ate them. We saw a number of banana trees, but it was too soon in the season for the fruit to be ripe. The sweet potatoes were a round, mealy variety, and superior in every way to the Chinese. The old man had a rough apparatus for crushing sugar-cane, and a boiler in which he made molasses from the juice. There were a number of fowls and ducks in the vicinity of all the cabins, but so wild, the people informed me, that it was impossible to take them alive. In fact, the settlers seemed to lack nothing which the simple wants of nature required, and probably preferred the easy, quiet life of the island, and its genial climate, to the society of their homes and the ruder toils which would await them there. There have been moments when I have coveted such a lot; but now, nothing could have been more terrible than the prospect of being left among them. While I inhabit the world, let me be borne on its most crowded stream, and feel the pulses of its deepest and most earnest life!

Commodore Perry saw at once the advantages of Port Lloyd as a station for steamers, whenever a line shall be established between China and California. It is not only the most eligible, but perhaps the only spot in the Pacific, west of the Sandwich Islands, which promises to be of real advantage for such a purpose. It is about 3,300 miles from the latter place, and 1,100 from Shanghai, and almost on the direct line between the two points. If the Sandwich Islands are to be included in the proposed route (as is most probable), Peel Island is even preferable to a port in Japan, which, on the other hand, would be most convenient for a direct northern line from Oregon. The Commodore, on the day after our arrival, obtained from Mr

Savory the title to a tract of land, on the northern side of the bay, near its head. It has a front of 1,000 yards on the water, and extends across the island to a small bight on the northern side, which he named Pleasant Bay. The location is admirably adapted for a coaling station for steamers, since a pier fifty feet long would strike water deep enough to float the largest vessel The soil of Peel Island is the richest vegetable mould, and might be made to produce abundant supplies, while its mountain streams furnish a never-failing source of excellent water.

The Commodore also paid a visit to Buckland Island, accompanied by Commanders Buchanan, Adams and Walker, and a number of officers. The cattle which we had brought from Shanghai were put ashore on the eastern side of Peel Island, at a point where there was good water, and, as Savory stated, a tolerably large tract of table-land. The sheep were left on Stapleton Island, where there were already about six thousand wild goats.

On the day before leaving Port Lloyd, I went in a boat to examine a fine marine cave in a bold island rock, at the southern entrance of the Bay, to which Beechey gave the name of "Southern Head." The trap rock, which here takes a basaltic form, exhibits several large apertures, one of which extends through the Head, to the beach on the opposite side. The entrance is about fifteen feet wide and thirty high, with from one to two fathoms of water. Soon, however, the roof expands to a height of forty or fifty feet, in the form of a Gothic arch, with a longitudinal beam, or keystone, inserted in the centre After rowing along for twenty-five yards, we came to a beach of smooth pebbles, upon which a light shone through from the other side, and passing a low arch, and climbing a mound of earth and stones, we stood upon the opposite shore. In a large rocky headland, lying opposite to us, there was a cave a hundred yards long, passing entirely through, and traversed by the canoes of the natives. After taking a bath in the clear, shaded waters, where we had moored our boat, we pulled out again through another branch of the cave, with a narrower entrance. Not far from this there was still another cave, wth two entrances, separated by a huge pillar of rock. The water was so clear that we distinctly saw bottom at four fathoms. The bed of the cavern was varied with groves of blue and purple corals, and the rocks beneath the water line were studded with patches of the purest emerald green, caused, apparently, by the combination of some of their component parts with the salts of the sea. Through the dark, rugged arch of the entrance, the bright blue surface of the bay, and the sides of the palmy hills beyond, shone with indescribable lustre, like a picture burnt in enamel.

Capt. Beechey took possession of the Bonin Islands in the name of Great Britain, though with what justice I cannot see, since he could not claim the right of discovery. There was some attempt at one time, I believe, to found a colony, but it has long since been relinquished. The only show of English sovereignty at the time of our visit was a ragged flag, left in the charge of a Kanaka, who hoisted it the day after our arrival. Mellichamp, who was sent to Port Lloyd by the English Consul at Honolulu, had left nearly two years previous, fo Guam, where he was then remaining, unable, it was said, to leave the place.

CHAPTER XXXII.

AN EXPLORING TRIP THROUGH PEEL ISLAND.

Exploring Parties Appointed—My Part—Setting Out—Climbing the Hills—The Soil and Productions—Land-Crabs—Crossing a Ridge—A Tropical Ravine—Signs of Habitation—A Marquesan and his Household—South-Sea Pilots—The Valley—The Forest Again—Trees—Shooting a Wild Boar—The Southern Coast—A Precipice—Dangerous Climbing—A Frightful Ravine—Descending the Precipices—South East Bay—The Nom-Camp—Ascent of the Ravine—The Party beginning to Fag—The Valley Again—A Slippery Ascent—A Man Lost—Firing Signals—Return to the Vessel.

On the day of our arrival at Port Lloyd, Commodore Perry announced his determination to send two exploring parties into the interior of the island on the following day. Dr. Fahs, Assistant Surgeon, was appointed to the command of one, and myself of the other. A number of volunteers at once offered themselves, and we made our selections and arranged our plans without delay. We were supplied with carbines, ammunition and haversacks, with a day's rations. The island is not more than six miles in length, in a straight line, so that it was thought that two parties might readily explore the whole of it in the course of a day. Dr. Fahs and I accordingly divided it between us, he taking the northern portion, or that lying immediately around Port Lloyd, while I decided to strike across the central part of the island to its southern extremity touching by the way, if possible, on Fitton Bay, a harbor on the eastern coast.

My party consisted of Mr. Heine, artist; Mr. Boardman, Midshipman; Mr. Lawrence, Assistant Engineer; Mr. Hampton, Purser's Steward; Dennis Terry, a seaman; Smith, a marine, and a Chinese coolie. We left the ship's side before sunrise, and were put ashore at the watering-place at the head of the bay. I divided the rations and ammunition, allotting to each man his share, so that we all carried light loads. There was no one at the watering-place except a Kanaka, whom we could not obtain for a guide. He pointed out, however, a small foot-path, which he said went over the hills to a Kanaka settlement, about three miles distant. We struck into it at once, plunging into a wilderness of dense vegetation, which furnished a faint type of our experience for the rest of the day.

The path was steep and slippery; the plants were wet with a heavy dew, and the wild parasitic vines which hung from tree to tree, continually caught us in their toils. The trees were principally palm, among which I noticed the true sago palm, from which the sago of commerce is made. The soil was a rich, dark red loam, composed of disintegrated trap rock and vegetable mould. The same soil prevails all over the island, so far as my observations extended, except on the northern shore of Port Lloyd, where it is mixed with a grayish sand and pebbles. Trap rock, of a coarse texture, appeared frequently on the steeper declivities of the ridge, and I noticed growing in the crevices a variety of the *hibiscus*, with a large flower of a dull orange color The ground was in many places covered with a shower of white blossoms, which I afterwards found had dropped from a tree about thirty feet high, with a small glossy leaf, thick foliage, and a stout trunk of a whitish color.

The forest became more dense as we reached the summit of the ridge. The thick, luxuriant crowns of the palms, above our heads, kept out the rays of the sun, and the trunks and creepers combined made such an impervious shade that it was impossible to see more than fifteen or twenty yards in any direction. The path was but little used, and rather difficult to be traced. As we came into the beds of water-courses leading down the opposite side, the multitudes of large brown land-crabs that scampered out of our path was truly amazing. The ground was alive with them in the cool, moist corners of the ravines, and some of them were fully six inches in breadth. The top of the ridge, an undulating region, furrowed with deep gulleys, was about a mile and a half in breadth, after which we came upon a descent at so sharp an angle that we were obliged to swing ourselves down from tree to tree, to prevent tumbling into the bottom of the ravine. An opening through the woods showed us a wild dell, completely shut in by precipitous mountains, every foot of whose sides, except the walls of naked rock on either hand, was covered with the richest foliage. A stream of good water lapsed over the rocky bottom, fringed by rank thickets of palm and other trees, while the bristling *pandanus* thrust its serried, spiky leaves over the tops of the cliffs, and the long, loose tresses of flowering creepers, shaken from some overhanging bough, swung in the air. The scenery was tropical in every feature, and as wild and rugged as nature could make it.

The ravine opened to the southward into a narrow valley

which showed signs of being inhabited. Crossing the stream we came upon a patch of the *taro* plant, the stalks of which were the highest and most luxuriant I ever saw. We here lost the path, and struck directly through the taro. It was fully six feet high, and so drenched with the night's dew that we were speedily wet to the skin. Finding the forest beyond impracticable, on account of its steepness and density, we returned to the bed of the stream. The little valley into which it ushered us was covered with patches of sweet potato, taro, pumpkins, tobacco, sugar-cane, and the *sida*, or Indian goose berry, growing with a prodigal strength and luxuriance. Two huts thatched with palm-leaves, stood in the centre of the valley. Finding them both deserted, though exhibiting evi dences of having been occupied that morning, we fired our guns, the report of which was answered by a hail. Presently a South-Sea Islander, in a coarse cotton shirt and pantaloons, and with one half of his face tattooed a light blue, made his appearance. He said he was a native of Nukaheva, in the Marquesas, and his name was "Judge." He conducted us around the corner of the mountain, where the valley opened westward to the sea. The stream became a creek deep enough for canoes, in one of which the Judge had just arrived, bringing a large turtle with him He was already half through with the operation of cutting up the flesh, while four dogs looked on wistfully, waiting to pick the shell when he should have finished. The Judge was apparently in good circumstances, having in addition to his hut, his plantation, his turtles and dogs, a pen of black hogs. I asked him to accompany us to the southern extremity of the island, which he said was about three or four miles distant. There was no path, and he did not seem inclined to go, but he sent his boy after a companion, who, he said, could pilot us over the hills. The latter was a tawny native of Otaheite, and spoke very little English. He confessed that he knew the way, as well as the wild-boar haunts in the woods, but refused to go without the Judge. As it was next to impossible to find our way without a guide, I settled the mattei by taking both.

The valley was bounded on the south by high mountains, which appeared to us impassable, on account of the lines of mural rock, rising one above another to their very summits. The main branch, however, was not that into which we had at first descended, but ran away to the eastward, whence the stream came down a long ravine, between two peaks. The natives informed me that the sea was about half a mile distant, from which I should judge the entire length of the valley to be near a mile and a half, with an average breadth of a quarter of a mile. Its bed is the richest loam, and all the vegetables planted by the settlers were unequalled of their kind. The stream of water is sweet and pure, and the supply is constant in all seasons. I saw several lemons in the Judge's hut, which had been raised in the valley. The tobacco was five feet in height, and had the same pale green, velvety leaves, which characterize the famous tobacco of Latakieh.

We proceeded in a south-castern direction into the ravine, which we ascended, following the water course. Large rounded masses of trap rock lay in its bed, and still further we came upon large perpendicular crags of greenstone, from ten to forty feet in height. In some places beds of a coarse conglomcrate, which had frequently an appearance of sandstone, rested upon the trap. The forest was very dense, and from the moist, unctuous nature of the soil, our progress was exceedingly toil some. The further we ascended, the darker and deeper became the wood, and as the Otaheitan informed us we were now in the neighborhood of wild boars, we crept forward silently and cautiously. While we were resting on the top of a cliff, two of the party, who were in the rear, started a boar and shot at him, but unsuccessfully. After leaving the water course we climbed the side of the ravine by clinging to the roots of trees and the tough cordage of parasitic vines. The party became scattered, owing to the absence of any path, and the impossibility of seeing more than ten yards in any direction. Among the palms I noticed a variety with broad fan-leaves, and leaf-stems six to eight feet in length, the jagged edges of which wounded our hands. There was also a variety of the *pandanus*, with a single straight trunk, from near the base of which projected a number of shoots or props, which became roots after they reached the soil. There were frequently twenty or thirty of them, forming a pyramidal basis to the slender column, which rose about fifteen feet, crowned with its leafy capital.

While halting on the top of the ridge for the rest of the party to come up, the dogs commenced barking in a ravine on the other side. Two of the officers started off at once, and in a short time we heard shots at a distance. We made for the sound, and after plunging through a frightful thicket of the horny-leaved *pandanus*, in the midst of which I found a wild boar's lair, reached the bed of a brook, where the hunters were gathered about a young boar. He was about a year old, and of a dark brownish-gray color, with a long snout, resembling the Chinese hog. We took out the liver and kidneys, and suspended the body to a tree, to be left until our return In another half hour we had crossed the dividing ridge of the island, and began to descend the southern side. Through an opening in the foliage I caught a glimpse of the sea, and climbed a tree to obtain a look-out. I found that we were on the brow of a very steep ridge, about 1,500 feet in height, looking down upon a small bay, opening to the south-east. Beyond its southern promontory the sea was again visible, with the group of Bailly's Islands in the distance. The mountains descended in precipices to the water, so that access was impossible, except near the head of the bay, where two abrupt ravines, or rather chasms, showed a speck of sandy beach at their meeting.

The Otaheitan professed to know the way, and set out, creeping slowly down the steep, we following, forcing our way on our hands and knees through almost impervious thickets, until a sudden light broke through the wilderness, and we found ourselves on the brink of a precipice, the height of which we could not then estimate, though I afterwards saw that it must be near two hundred feet. From its base the mountain sloped away so steeply to the brink of other precipices below that we seemed to swing in the air, suspended over the great depth which intervened between us and the sea. My head reeled for a moment, as I found myself perched on such a giddy height, and either retreat or descent seemed impossible. The guide, it was evident, had taken us too far to the left, and it was necessary partly to retrace our steps, in order to regain a position which would enable us to avoid the precipice. We clung cautiously to the strong grass which grew on the brink, and thus crept along for about two hundred yards, over a place where the least impetus would have sent us headlong hundreds of feet below. On this part of the mountain I found a shrub with a dark, glossy leaf, which diffused a powerful balsamic odor. Finally, attaining a point where the precipice ceased, we commenced going downward at the angle of about 60°. The soil was so slippery, and the vines and horny leaves of the palms hung so low, that the best way of descending was to lie flat on one's back, and slide down until brought up by a thicket too dense to get through.

With an infinite deal of labor, and at the risk of our necks, we at last reached the ravine, or chasm, and hoped that the worst of our toils were over. But the worst was yet to come. I can place implicit faith in Herman Melville's account of the precipices of Typee, after our own experience, which, in fact, bore a striking resemblance to his. The ravine descended by a succession of rocky steps from ten to forty and fifty feet in perpendicular height, down which we clambered with hands and feet, often trusting the soundness of our bones, if not our very lives, to the frail branch of a tree, or to the hold of a root dangling from the brink. As from the top of a tower, we looked on the beach, lying at our very feet, and seemingly to be reached by a single leap, though still far below. Down, down we went into the black depths of the chasm, in constant fear of reaching a wall which we could not pass, until at the junction of another ravine, we came upon the hewn stump of a tree, a sign that others before us had penetrated the wilderness, and heard the roar of the surf near at hand. The seaman, Terry, who had accompanied me on the exploring trip through Loo-Choo, and myself, were considerably in advance of the rest of the party. Terry was a man after my own heart, for such an expedition. Nothing could daunt him, and no hard ships could tire him out. We sat down on the beach, under an overhanging rock, and looked back on the steep down which we had clomb. When I saw it from below, and discerned the last of the party standing on the brink of one of the crags, showing us what our own position had been, I could scarcely believe our descent possible.

The guides called the place "South-East Bay." They stated that it was frequently visited by whalers, for wood and water; which accounts for the stump of the tree, and the presence of a patch of tomatoes, which we found growing in a wild state, along the banks of the stream. The fruit was about the size of a cherry, and very fresh and palatable. When all had arrived, we built a fire under the eaves of the rocks, and while the dry drift-wood was burning to embers, took a bath in the sea. The water was deliciously cool, and the long, heavy swells rolled directly in from the Pacific and broke over our heads. We broiled the boar's liver on pieces of coral, and this, with a ship's ration of salt pork and biscuit, and a few handfuls of raw tomatoes, made us a most palatable repast. By the time we had sufficiently rested, and Mr. Heine had made a sketch of the bay, it was two o'clock, and I therefore broke up the camp and started homeward.

The natives said that there was no other way of returning except the road by which we came. We all shrank from the idea of climbing that terrible path, but there was no help for it. Up we must go, and up we went, clinging for life to the roots of trees, or the sharp little corners of the rocks with one hand, while we clutched our carbines with the other. There was not a breath of air: the thermometer must have shown at least 90°, and the toil was so severe that one of the party became ill, and lagged behind. We were obliged to halt every five minutes, for two others also began to show signs of exhaustion, and were more than once on the point of giving out. But all things must have an end, and at length we reached the summit ridge, whence the descent to the ravine where we had left the wild boar was comparatively easy, after what we had already gone through. The Otaheitan shouldered the boar, and we returned, with but one or two halts to rest the exhausted members of the party, to the native huts in the valley, where we arrived a little before six o'clock. One of the gentlemen was by this time so much spent that he hired the Otaheitan to carry him in a canoe round to the Kanaka settlement at the southern end of Port Lloyd, the rest of us taking a path which led thither by land.

The evening was cloudy and rain began to fall, which hastened our departure. Ascending the same ravine by which we had reached the valley, as far as the taro patch, the Judge turned suddenly to the left and began climbing the slippery side of the mountain at an angle of about 50°. He declared that this was the usual road, but my eyes, although somewhat exercised in wood-craft, could not detect the least trace of a path. Under the thick clusters of sago palms was a dense undergrowth of fern, in which we could gain no foothold, and were continually falling flat on our faces. The Judge himself began to be fagged by this time, and frequently proposed that we should rest. The others were in no wise averse to this, but I felt little fatigue from the labors of the day, and was so anxious to reach the Kanaka settlement before dark that I hurried them onward. After gaining the summit, the way was easier, and we met with occasional faint traces of a path Passing over an undulating tract for a mile or more, we came upon the western slope of the island, overlooking Southern Head, and the entrance to Port Lloyd. I now saw that a deep, picturesque bight made in below the Head to the mouth of the valley we had left, and that the shortest and most usual route of the natives between the two settlements, was by sea. The sides of the hills we traversed were covered with a deep, coarse grass, waist-high, and so thick that we fairly waded through it. It was a fortunate circumstance for us that there are no venomous reptiles on the island.

I was in advance, the others being scattered along the side of the hill, when I happened to notice that one of the party was missing. I sent back the coolie, and then the Judge, and finally ordered a halt, while I returned to look for him. After calling and searching for some time without effect, he was at last found lying in the bottom of a glen, asleep, as he stated. He stumbled along with us for a short time, when he tumbled into the grass, declaring that he was utterly exhausted, and would remain there all night. Finding that we could not get him to go forward, we picked him up by main force, and carried him to the summit of the hill, where I left a man in charge of him while we hastened down, in order to gain the flag-staff above the Kanaka settlement, and fire a volley to bring a boat off for us. We plunged through the cane-fields, stumbled up the hill, and found ourselves on a high cliff, overlooking the bay. The big hull of the Susquehanna was barely visible in the darkness. We fired half a dozen volleys, when we heard the report of musketry from the base of the Paps, at the head of the bay. It was, as we conjectured, the party of Dr. Fahs, signalizing like ourselves for a boat. At length, fearful lest our signal should not have been heard, I sent the marine in a canoe to bring a boat. He met the first cutter half way, but the tide being out, she was obliged to anchor off the reef in front of the settlement, and send the canoe to take us in small companies.

We waited half an hour for our missing comrade, and finally reached the ship's side about 10 o'clock weary and famished. Though I suffered less, I believe, than most of the others it was certainly the hardest day's work of my life.

CHAPTER XXXIII.

VOYAGE TO JAPAN AND RECEPTION THERE.

Return to Loo-Choo—Mails—Departure for Japan—The Island of Ohosima—The Japanese Coast—The Headland of Idzu—Precautionary Measures—Cape Sagami—The Bay of Yedo—Approach to Uraga—A Hint—The Squadron Halts—Japanese Boats—A Talk at the Gangway—The Vice Governor of Uraga—His Reception—The Boats Repulsed—Japanese Boatmen—Watch-fires—Yezaimon, Governor of Uraga—Consultations—An Express to Yedo—The Emperor appoints a Commissioner—Permission to Land—Skilful Negotiations—Scenery of the Bay—The Fortifications—The Peak of Fusi-Yamma—Canvas Defences—A Surveying Party—Sounding along Shore—Forts and Soldiers—Threatened Collision—A Second Survey—A Mirage—Warlike Appearances—Lieut. Bent's Encounter with Forty-five Japanese Boats—Result of the Survey.

On our return to Loo-Choo, where we arrived on the 24th of June, we found the Plymouth in the harbor. She had left Shanghai in comparative quiet, and with no present apprehension of an attack. She was most welcome, on account of having brought the mails for the squadron. After having been seven months without news from home, the delight with which I received a large package of letters can only be comprehended by those who have had similar experiences. As all the vessels composing the squadron at that time were now at the rendezvous, immediate preparations were made for our departure for Japan. Owing to the foresight with which the vessels had been supplied, little was needed except a stock of fresh provi sions, which the Loo-Choo authorities, after some delay and equivocation, furnished us at double the ordinary price.

The squadron, consisting of the Susquehanna (flag-ship), Mississippi, Plymouth and Saratoga—the two sloops of war being taken in tow by the two steamers—sailed from the harbor of Napa-Kiang, on the 2d of July. On the night of the 3d and morning of the 4th, we passed the large island of Oho-sima, part of the Kingdom of Loo-Choo. This island, which has been known to the Dutch, through the Japanese charts, and was seen by the French Admiral Cécille in 1846, is not found on English charts. The U S. ship Preble, in 1849, supposed she had made the first discovery of it, and gave it the name of "Preble Island." It has never been visited by a foreign vessel. It is thirty or forty miles long, mountainous, and thickly inhabited. After passing it we had very sultry weather, until we reached Japan—the thermometer standing at 84° at night, and 88° to 90° at noon, in the coolest place on board.

At daybreak, on the morning of July 8, we first made land, which proved to be Cape Idzu, a lofty headland on the coast of Niphon, not far south of the entrance of the great Bay of Yedo. The Brocken and Vulcan Islands were in sight on our right. After passing Rock Island, we stood in nearer to the shore, which loomed up grandly through the hazy atmosphere. The promontory of Idzu is a group of mountains, rising to the height of five or six thousand feet, their summits scarred with slides, and their sides mostly covered with forests, though here and there we could discern patches of cultivated land. There were a number of fishing junks off the coast, some of which put back again as we approached. The wind was ahead, we had all sails furled and the yards squared, and the sight of our two immense steamers—the first that ever entered Japanese waters—dashing along at the rate of nine knots an hour, must have struck the natives with the utmost astonishment.

Leaving the mountains of Idzu behind us, we stood across the mouth of the Bay of Kowadzu (as the southern half of the bifurcate Bay of Yedo is called), toward Cape Sagami at the extremity of the promontory which divides the two. The noon observation gave lat. 34° 57′ N. and soon afterwards Cape Sagami came in sight. We lay to while the Captains of the Mississippi, Plymouth and Saratoga came on board, to receive instructions, and then resumed our course. The decks were cleared for action, the guns shotted, the small arms put in complete order, and every precaution taken, in case we should meet with a hostile reception. Near Cape Sagami we descried a large town, and as we came within two miles of the shore, a number of junks, amounting to twelve or fifteen, put off, with the evident intention of visiting us. Each one bore a large banner, upon which characters were inscribed. The rapidity of our progress, against the wind, soon left them behind, no doubt completely nonplussed as to the invisible power which bore us away from them. The Bay now began to be thickly studded with fishing smacks, with here and there a large junk.

The shores of Sagami are exceedingly picturesque and beautiful. They rise in abrupt bluffs, two hundred feet in height, gashed with narrow dells of the brightest verdure, which slope steeply down to the water, while the country behind rises in undulating hills, displaying a charming alternation of groves and cultivated fields. In the distance rose mountain ranges, receding behind each other until the vapor hid their farthest summits. The eastern coast, belonging to the province of Awa, now came in sight ahead of us, for we were entering the narrowest part of the Bay, leading to the upper Bay of Yedo. The distance from shore to shore here varies from five to eight miles, but afterwards expands to twelve or fifteen.

We kept directly up the Bay, and in half an hour after doubling Cape Sagami saw before us a bold promontory making out from the western coast, at the entrance of the Upper Bay. Within it was the Bight of Urága, and we could plainly see the town of the same name at the head of it. The Plymouth and Saratoga were cast off, and we advanced slowly, sounding as we went, until we had advanced more than a mile beyond the point reached by the Columbus and the Morrison. We were about a mile and a half from the promontory, when two discharges of cannon were heard from a battery at its extremity, and immediately afterwards a light ball of smoke in the air showed that a shell had been thrown up. An order was immediately given to let go the anchor, but as the lead still showed 25 fathoms, the steamer's head was put in toward the shore, and in a few minutes the anchor was dropped.

Another shell was fired after we came to anchor, and four or five boats filled with Japanese approached us. The rowers, who were all tall, athletic men, naked save a cloth around the loins, shouted lustily as they sculled with all their strength toward us. The boats were of unpainted wood, very sharp in the bows, carrying their greatest breadth of beam well aft, and were propelled with great rapidity. The resemblance of their model to that of the yacht America, struck every body on board. In the stern of each was a small flag, with three horizontal stripes, the central one black and the other white. In each were several persons, who, by their dress and the two swords stuck in their belts, appeared to be men of authority.

The first boat came alongside, and one of the two-sworded individuals made signs for the gangway to be let down. This was refused, but Mr. Wells Williams, the Interpreter, and Mr. Portman, the Commodore's clerk (who was a native of Holland), went to the ship's side to state that nobody would be received on board, except the first in rank at Urága. The conversation was carried on principally in Dutch, which the interpreter spoke very well. He asked at once if we were not Americans, and by his manner of asking showed that our coming had been anticipated. He was told that the Commander of the squadron was an officer of very high rank in the United States, and could only communicate with the first in rank on shore. After a long parley, the Vice-Governor of Urága, who was in the boat, was allowed to come on board with the Interpreter and confer with Lieut. Contee, the Flag Lieutenant. The Japanese official, a fiery little fellow, was much exasperated at being kept in waiting, but soon moderated his tone. He was told that we came as friends, upon a peaceable mission; that we should not go to Nangasaki, as he proposed, and that it was insulting to our President and his special minister to propose it. He was told, moreover, that the Japanese must not communicate with any other vessel than the flag-ship, and that no boats must approach us during the night. An attempt to surround us with a cordon of boats, as in the case of the Columbus and Vincennes, would lead to very serious consequences. They had with them an official notice, written in French, Dutch and English, and intended as a general warning to all foreign vessels, directing them to go no further, to remain out at sea, and send word ashore, why they came and what they wanted. This Lieut. Contee declined to see or ackowledge in any way. The same notice was taken to the Plymouth by another boat, which was at once ordered off.

Commodore Perry had evidently made up his mind from the first not to submit to the surveillance of boats. The dignified and decided stand he took produced an immediate impression upon the Japanese. They were convinced that he was in earnest, and that all the tricks and delays with which they are in the habit of wheedling foreign visitors would be used in vain. Several boats having followed the first one, and begun to collect round us, the Vice-Governor was told that if they did not return at once, they would be fired into. One of them went to the Mississippi; and after being repulsed from the gangway, pulled forward to the bows, where some of the crew tried to climb on board. A company of boarders was immediately called away, and the bristling array of pikes and cutlasses over the vessel's side caused the Japanese to retreat in great haste. Thenceforth, all the Japanese boats gave us a wide berth, and during the whole of our stay, none approached us except those containing the officials who were concerned in the negotiations. I may here remark that our presence did not seem to disturb, in the least, the coasting trade which finds its focus in Yedo. Without counting the hundreds of small boats and fishing smacks, between sixty and seventy large junks daily passed up and down the bay, on their way to and from Yedo. The Japanese boatmen were tall, handsomely formed men, with vigorous and symmetrical bodies, and a hardy, manly expression of countenance. As the air grew fresher towards evening, they put on a sort of loose gown, with wide, hanging sleeves. As the crew of each boat were all attired alike, the dress appeared to be a uniform, denoting that they were in Government service. The most of them had blue gowns, with white stripes on the sleeves, meeting on the shoulder, so as to form a triangular junction, and a crest, or coat-of-arms, upon the back. Others had gowns of red and white stripes, with a black lozenge upon the back. Some wore upon their heads a cap made of bamboo splints, resembling a broad, shallow basin inverted, but the greater part had their heads bare, the top and crown shaved, and the hair from the back and sides brought up and fastened in a small knot, through which a short metal pin was thrust. The officers wore light and beautifully lacquered hats to protect them from the sun, with a gilded coat-of-arms upon the front part. In most of the boats I noticed a tall spear, with a lacquered sheath for the head, resembling a number or character, and apparently referring to the rank of the officer on board.

After dark, watch-fires began to blaze along the shore, both from the beach and from the summits of the hills, chiefly on the western side of the bay. At the same time we heard, at regular intervals, the sound of a deep-toned bell. It had a very sweet, rich tone, and from the distinctness with which its long reverberations reached us, must have been of large size. A double night-watch was established during our stay, and no officers except the Purser and Surgeons were exempt from serving. But the nights were quiet and peaceful, and it never fell to my lot to report a suspicious appearance of any kind.

The next morning, Yezaimon, the Governor of Urága, and the highest authority on shore, came off, attended by two interpreters, who gave their names as Tatsonoske and Tokoshiuro. He was received by Commanders Buchanan and Adams, and Lieut. Contee. He was a noble of the second rank; his robe was of the richest silken tissue, embroidered with gold and silver in a pattern resembling peacock feathers. The object of his coming, I believe, was to declare his inability to act, not having the requisite authority without instructions from Yedo. At any rate, it was understood that an express would be sent to the Capital immediately, and the Commodore gave him until Tuesday noon to have the answer ready. Sunday passed over without any visit, but on Monday there was an informal one.

From Tuesday until Wednesday noon, Yezaimon came off three times, remaining from two to three hours each time. The result of all these conferences was, that the Emperor had specially appointed one of the Chief Counsellors of the Empire to proceed to Urága, and receive from Commodore Perry the letter of the President of the United States, which the Commodore was allowed to land and deliver on shore. This prompt and unlooked-for concession astonished us all, and I am convinced it was owing entirely to the decided stand the Commodore took during the early negotiations. We had obtained in four days, without subjecting ourselves to a single observance of Japanese law, what the Russian embassy under Resanoff failed to accomplish in six months, after a degrading subservience to ridiculous demands. From what I know of the negotiations, I must say that they were admirably conducted. The Japanese officials were treated in such a polite and friendly manner as to win their good will, while not a single point to which we attached any importance, was yielded. There was a mixture of firmness, dignity and fearlessness on our side, against which their artful and dissimulating policy was powerless. To this, and to our material strength, I attribute the fact of our reception having been so different from that of other embassies, as almost to make us doubt the truth of the accounts we had read.

From our anchorage off Urága, we enjoyed a charming panorama of the bay. It far surpassed my preconceived ideas of Japanese scenery. The western shore is bold and steep, running here and there into lofty bluffs of light-gray rock, but the greater part of it is covered with turf, copsewood and scattered groves of trees, all of the brightest and freshest green. From Urága to another and shallower bight, which makes in nearly two miles below, the shore is less abrupt, and shows more signs of cultivation. The hills behind, though not above 500 feet in height, are beautifully undulating in their outlines, and dotted with groves of pine and other trees. From Urága to the end of the promontory—a distance of a mile and a quarter—there is an almost unbroken line of villages. The houses are of wood, with sharp roofs, some pointed in the Chinese style, some square and pyramidal. A few were painted white, but the greater number were unpainted and weather-beaten. At least a hundred small craft, with a number of junks, lay in the harbor of Urága, and thence to the headland there were two hundred boats, lying close in-shore.

I examined the fortifications frequently and carefully, through a glass, and found that their strength had been greatly exaggerated. Two of them appeared to have been recently made, and on a bluff, half enclosing the little harbor of Urága on the east, there was another, still in the course of construction. Between this and the headland there were three batteries, and at the extremity one, making five in all. The embrasures were so large, that from our position a good marksman might in a short time have dislodged every one of their guns. The chief post was the central battery, near which was a village, and several buildings of large size, apparently arsenals or barracks.

Every morning and evening, when the air was clear, we had a distinct view of the famous volcanic peak of Fusi-Yamma, rising in the western heaven, high above the hills, and sixty miles away. In the evenings its solitary cone, of a pale violet hue, was defined with great distinctness against the rosy flush of sunset, but in the morning, when the light fell full upon it, we could see the scars of old eruptions, and the cold ravines of snow on its northern side. It is the highest mountain in Japan, and estimated to be twelve or thirteen thousand feet above the sea-level.

On the morning after our arrival, the Japanese put up a false battery of black canvas, about a hundred yards in length, on the shore south of Urága. There was no appearance of guns, but with a glass I saw two or three companies of soldiers in scarlet uniform, riding through the groves in the rear. In most of the batteries they also erected canvas screens behind the embrasures—with what object it was difficult to conceive. These diversions they repeated so often during our stay, that at last we ceased to regard them; but it was amusing to hear some of our old quarter-masters now and then gravely report to Captain Buchanan: "Another dungaree fort thrown up, sir!"

On Saturday morning a surveying expedition, consisting of one boat from each ship, under the charge of Lieut. Bent, of the Missisippi, was sent for the purpose of sounding up the bay. The other officers were Lieut. Guest, of the Susquehanna, Lieut. Balch, of the Plymouth, and Mr. Madigan, Master of the Saratoga. The boats carried, in addition to the usual ensign, a white flag at the bow, and were fully manned with armed seamen. They ran up the bay to a distance of about four miles, and found every where from thirty to forty-three fathoms of water. The recall was then hoisted, and a signal gun fired, to bring them back. In the afternoon they sounded around the bight of Urága, keeping about a cable's length from the shore. They found five fathoms of water at this distance, though nearer to the beach there were occasional reefs. Mr. Heine, the artist, obtained a panoramic sketch of the shore, with the batteries, villages, and other objects in detail. On approaching the forts, the soldiers at first came out, armed with matchlocks, but as the boats advanced nearer, they retired within the walls. The forts were all of very rude and imperfect construction, and all together only mounted fourteen guns, none of which were larger than nine-pounders. The whole number of soldiers seen was about four hundred, a considerable portion of whom were armed with spears. Their caps and shields were lacquered, and glittered in the sun like polished armor. The carriages of the guns were also lacquered. The embrasures were so wide that the guns were wholly unprotected, while they were so stationed that the forts could be stormed from either side, with very little risk to the assaulting party. The parapets were of earth, and about twelve feet in thickness, and the barracks in the rear were of wood. Indeed, the whole amount of the Japanese defences appeared laughable, after all the extravagant stories we had heard

Mr Madigan approached, at one place, to within a hundred yards of the shore. Three official personages were standing upon a bank of earth, when some one in the boat raised a spy-glass to get a nearer view of them. No sooner did they behold the glittering tube pointed at them than they scrambled down as quickly as possible, and concealed themselves. There were three boat-loads of soldiers near the shore, who made signs to him to keep off, but he answered them by pointing out the way he intended to go. Thereupon they put off, and bore down upon him so rapidly, that he at first thought they intended to run into him, and ordered his men to trail their oars and put caps on their carbines. The boats stopped at once, and made no attempt to interfere with the cutter's course.

On Monday morning the same surveying party was again dispatched up the bay, followed by the Mississippi, which was designed to protect them, and tow them back in the evening. Lieut. Bent's boat was in advance, and as he passed the promontory of Urága, three Japanese boats put out to meet him. The officers in them made signs to return, but he kept steadily on his way. We watched the progress of our boats with glasses, but at the distance of four miles, they, with the Mississippi, passed out of sight behind the point.

Several Government boats, fully manned, were seen from time to time, pulling across the bay, in the direction of the surveying fleet, but no prominent movement occurred until noon. At this time the distant shores were so lifted by the effect of a mirage, that we saw land extending entirely around the head of the bay, where previously none had been visible. The eastern shore was remarkably distinct, and for the first time we observed a low, sandy promontory stretching out into the bay, five or six miles to the north of us. Near the middle of it rose a low mound, on which, by the aid of a glass, we could discern a number of soldiers, clustered around some white objects, which I took to be tents. In a short time several hundred men were marched down to the beach, where they formed a line nearly half a mile in length. At least fifty banners, of various colors and devices, were planted along the line. A number of Government boats, similar to those which had visited us, were drawn up on the beach. The greater part of the soldiers embarked in the boats, which put off, one after another, and made directly across the bay. We saw nothing more until 4 o'clock in the afternoon, when the Mississippi made her appearance, at a distance of ten miles. The headland of Urága was crowded with soldiers, who came out to see her pass.

From some of the officers who were of the party, I learned the following particulars: In ascending the bay, they were constantly met by Government boats, the officers in which urged them, by signs, to return. They kept on their course, however, until Mr. Bent endeavored to proceed to the head of a deep bay on the western coast. Here he was met by forty-five Japanese boats, which placed themselves in front of him, to intercept his progress. He ordered his men to lay on their oars and fix bayonets to their muskets, but this produced no impression. As the Mississippi was more than two miles astern, he dispatched one of the boats to summon her, and then, ordering half his men to pull directly towards the Japanese boats, while the other half held their arms in readiness, he steadily approached their line. They made signs and threatening gestures, to which he paid no heed, and as this cutter al most touched their oars, they gave way, overawed by what must have seemed to them an insane determination. The approach of the Mississippi soon dispersed the whole of them.

The boats every where obtained deep soundings, with a bottom of soft mud. The furthest point reached was ten or twelve miles from our anchorage. The shores were bold and steep, with mountains in the background, and the bay (to which Lieut. Bent gave the name of Perry's Bay) offered a secure and commodious anchorage. On her return, the Mississippi came down the centre of the bay, finding every where abundance of water.

CHAPTER XXXIV.

THE FIRST LANDING IN JAPAN.

The Day of Landing—Preparations on Shore—The Bight of Gori-hama—Japanese Military Display—Arrival of the Governors—Their Official Dresses—Precautions on Board—The Procession of Boats—An Inspiring Scene—The Landing—Numbers of the Escort—The Japanese Troops—The Commodore's Landing—March to the House of Reception—Japanese Body-Guard—The Hall of Audience—Two Japanese Princes—Delivery of the President's Letter—An Official Conversation—Return to the Squadron.

It was finally arranged with the Japanese officials, that the President's letter should be delivered on Thursday morning, July 14, at the town of Gori-hama, two miles south of Urága.

The morning was heavy and dark before sunrise, but soon afterwards cleared off brilliantly. As soon as the shore could be distinguished, it was seen that the principal battery on the promontory of Urága had been greaty amplified and adorned by screens of cotton canvas, in honor of the occasion. On the hill above, among the trees, there were two small forts, or rather pavilions, of the same material. The canvas was stretched along a row of stakes so as to form a species of panelling, on which the Imperial coat-of-arms was painted, alternating with other devices. Behind the canvas we could see that numerous companies of soldiers were drawn up in different costume from that which they usually wore. Their arms were bare, and the body covered with a short tunic of a dark-brown, blue or purple color, bound with a girdle at the waist.

About eight o'clock the anchors were lifted, and the Susquehanna and Mississippi moved slowly down the Bay, leaving the Plymouth and Saratoga. We soon saw two boats bearing the Government flag pulling abreast of us, but further in shore, and accompanied by four other boats with red banners, probably containing a military escort. As the bight opened behind the promontory, we saw a long line of canvas walls, covered with the Imperial crest, stretching quite around the head of the bight. In front were files of soldiers, standing motionless on the sandy beach. A multitude of banners of various brilliant colors gleamed in the sun. Near the centre of the crescent formed by the troops, were planted nine tall standards—four on one side and five on the other—from which broad scarlet pennons hung to the ground. In the rear of these three new pyramidal roofs showed that a house had been prepared expressly for the Commodore's reception. On the right, upwards of fifty or sixty boats were drawn up in a line parallel to the beach, each having a red flag at its stern. From the head of the bight a narrow valley extended inland between luxuriantly wooded hills. On the left side was a picturesque little town, the name of which the Japanese informed us, was Gori-hama. The place was undoubtedly chosen, both on account of its remoteness from Urága, which is a port of customs, and the facility which it afforded to the Japanese for the exhibition of a large military force—a measure dictated alike by their native caution, and the love of display for which they are noted.

The anchor was no sooner down, than the two Government boats sculled alongside, and Yezaimon, with the Interpreters, Tatsonoske and Tokoshiuro, came on board. The second boat contained the Deputy Governor, Saboroske, and an attendant officer. They were accommodated with seats on the quarter-deck until all our preparations for landing were completed. They were dressed, as they had hinted the day previous, in official garments of rich silk brocade, bordered with velvet. The gowns differed little in form from those they ordinarily wore, but were elaborately embroidered, and displayed a greater variety of gay colors than taste in their disposal. Saboroske had a pair of short and very wide pantaloons, resembling a petticoat with a seam up the middle, below which appeared his bare legs, and black woollen socks, with an effect rather comical than otherwise. His shoulders contained lines of ornament in gold thread. All the officers wore their crest, or coat-of-arms, embroidered upon the back, sleeves and breasts of their garments.

The boats of the Mississippi, Plymouth and Saratoga, were alongside in less than half an hour after our anchor dropped, and preparations were made for leaving at once. Both steamers lay with their broadsides to the shore, and the decks were cleared, the guns primed and pointed, ready for action, in case of treachery. Commanders Kelly and Lee remained on board their respective ships, in order to act in case of necessity. The morning was very bright and clear, and the fifteen launches and cutters, containing the officers, seamen, marines, and bandsmen, presented a brilliant appearance, as they clustered around our starboard gangway. Commander Buchanan took the lead, in his barge, with one of the Japanese Government boats on each side. Merrily as the oars of our men dipped the waves, it required their utmost to keep pace with the athletic scullers of Japan. The other American boats followed nearly in line, and the van of the procession was more than half-way to the shore when the guns of the Susquehanna announced the Commodore's departure. The gleam of arms, the picturesque mingling of blue and white, in the uniforms, and the sparkling of the waves under the steady strokes of the oarsmen, combined to form a splendid picture, set off as it was by the background of rich green hills, and the long line of soldiery and banners on the beach. All were excited by the occasion, and the men seemed to be as much elated in spirits as those who had a more prominent part in the proceedings. We all felt, that as being the first instance since the expulsion of the Portuguese from Japan, when a foreign Ambassador had been officially received on Japanese soil, it was a memorable event in the history of both countries, and that, if not an augury of the future and complete success of the Expedition, it was at least a commencement more auspicious than we had ventured to anticipate.

An impromptu jetty composed of bags of sand, had been thrown up for the occasion near the centre of the crescent-shaped beach at the head of the bight. Capt. Buchanan, who had command of the party, was the first to leap ashore. The remaining boats crowded rapidly in beside the jetty, landed as many of their crews as had been detailed for the escort on shore, and then pulled off about fifty yards. The seamen and marines were formed into a line as soon as they were landed, and presented a compact and imposing file along the beach. The officers commanding detachments were Commanders Bu chanan and Walker, and Lieuts. Gillis and Taylor. The bodies of seamen were in immediate charge of Lieut. Duer, of the Susquehanna; Lieut. Morris, of the Mississippi; Lieut. Matthews of the Plymouth, and Passed Midshipman Scott, of the Saratoga. Including the other officers, there were upwards of 320 persons landed, while the Japanese troops amounted, as they themselves informed us, to five thousand. We had 112 marines, about 120 seamen, 50 officers, and 30 or 40 musicians. About a hundred yards from the beach stood the foremost files of the Japanese, in somewhat loose and straggling order. Their front occupied the whole beach, their right flank resting on the village of Gori-hama, and their left against a steep hill which bounded the bight on the northern side. The greater part were stationed behind the canvas screens, and from the numbers, crowded together in the rear, some of the officers estimated their force at nearer ten than five thousand men. Those in the front rank were armed with swords, spears and matchlocks, and their uniform differed little from the usual Japanese costume. There were a number of horses, of a breed larger and much superior to the Chinese, and in the background we saw a body of cavalry. On the slope of the hill near the village, a great number of natives, many of whom were women, had collected, out of curiosity to witness the event.

A salute was fired from the Susquehanna, as the Commodore left, accompanied by his staff, Commander Adams, and Lieut. Contee, and the men had scarcely been formed into line before his barge approached the shore. The officers composing the Commodore's escort formed a double line from the jetty, and as he passed between them fell into proper order behind him. He was received with the customary honours, and the procession immediately started for the place of reception. A stalwart boatswain's mate was selected to bear the broad pennant of the Commodore, supported by two very tall and powerful negro seamen, completely armed. Behind these followed two sailor boys, bearing the letter of the President and the Commodore's letter of credence, in their sumptuous boxes, wrapped in scarlet cloth. Then came the Commodore himself, with his staff and escort of officers. The marine force, a fine, athletic body of men, commanded by Maj. Zeilin, with a detachment from the Mississippi, under Capt. Slack, led the way, and the corps of seamen from all the ships brought up the rear.

The house of reception was directly in front of the landing, but an intervening screen rendered a slight detour necessary in order to reach the entrance; and Maj. Zeilin made the most of this circumstance, in order to display our forces to the Japanese. There certainly was a marked contrast between the regular, compact files of our men, and their vigorous, muscular figures, and the straggling ranks of the mild, effeminate-featured Japanese. In front of the house were two old brass four-pounders, apparently of Spanish manufacture, and on each side stood a company of soldiers, who belonged either to the Imperial forces, or to the body-guard of the Prince. Those on the left wore a uniform somewhat resembling the modern Egyptian dress. It was of a dark gray color, having full trowsers, gathered below the knees, a broad sash around the waist, and a white cloth, similar to a turban, bound upon the head. They were armed with the old Tower muskets, which are to be found in every part of the world, with flint locks and bayonets. Those on the right wore a different uniform, exhibiting a mixture of dull brown and yellow in its colors, and carried matchlocks of an antique fashion.

Yezaimon and the Interpreters preceded us, in order to show the way. The distance from the jetty to the door of the building was so short, that little opportunity was given me for noticing minutely the appearance of the Japanese, or the order of their array. The building into which the Commodore and suite were ushered was small, and appeared to have been erected in haste. The timbers were of pine wood, and numbered, as if they had been brought from some other place. The first apartment, which was about forty feet square, was of canvas with an awning of the same, of a white ground, with the Imperial arms emblazoned on it in places. The floor was covered with white cotton cloth, with a pathway of red felt, or some similar substance, leading across the room to a raised inner apartment, which was wholly carpeted with it. This apartment, the front of which was entirely open, so that it corresponded precisely to the *diwan* in Turkish houses, was hung with fine cloth, containing the Imperial arms, in white, on a ground of violet. On the right hand was a row of arm-chairs, sufficient in number for the Commodore and his staff, while on the opposite side sat the Prince who had been appointed to receive the President's letter, with another official of similar rank. Their names were given by the Interpreter as "TODA IDZU-NO-KAMI," Toda, Prince of Idzu, and "IDO IWAMI-NO-KAMI," Ido, Prince of Iwami. The Prince of Idzu was a man of about fifty with mild, regular features, an ample brow, and an intelligent, reflective expression. He was dressed with great richness, in heavy robes of silken tissue, wrought into elaborate ornaments with gold and silver thread. The Prince of Iwami was at least fifteen years older, and dressed with nearly equal splendor. His face was wrinkled with age, and exhibited neither the intelligence nor the benignity of his associate. They both rose and bowed gravely as the Commodore entered, but immediately resumed their seats, and remained as silent and passive as statues during the interview.

At the head of the room was a large scarlet-lacquered box, with brazen feet, beside which Yezaimon and the Interpreter, Tatsonoske, knelt. The latter then asked whether the letters were ready to be delivered, stating that the Prince was ready to receive them. The boxes were brought in, opened, so that the writing and the heavy golden seals were displayed, and placed upon the scarlet chest. The Prince of Iwami then handed to the Interpreter, who gave it to the Commodore, an official receipt, in Japanese, and at the same time the Interpreter added a Dutch translation. The Commodore remarked that he would sail in a few days for Loo-Choo and Canton, and if the Japanese Government wished to send any dispatches to those places he would be happy to take them. Without making any direct reply, the Interpreter asked: "When will you come again?" The Commodore answered, "As I suppose it will take some time to deliberate upon the letter of the President, I shall not wait now, but will return in a few months to receive the answer." He also spoke of the revolution in China, and the Interpreter asked the cause of it, without translating the communication to the Prince. He then inquired when the ships would return again, to which the Commodore replied that they would probably be there in April or May. "All four of them?" he asked. "All of them," answered the Commodore, "and probably more. This is but a portion of the squadron." No further conversation took place. The letters having been formally delivered and received, the Commodore took his leave, while the two Princes, who had fulfilled to the letter their instructions not to speak, rose and remained standing until he had retired from their presence.

The return to the boats was made in the same order, the bands playing "Hail Columbia" and "Yankee Doodle," with more spirit than ever before, and few of those present, I venture to say, ever heard our national airs with more pride and pleasure. Yezaimon, Saboroske, and the two Interpreters attended the Commodore to the boat, and as the embarkation of the different boats' crews occupied some time, on account of the smallness of the jetty, several of the Japanese soldiers profited by the delay to come down and examine us more closely. Many of our men strayed along the beach, picking up shells and pebbles as mementoes of the visit. In less than twenty minutes, however, all were embarked, and we returned to the ships, accompanied by the two Japanese boats which had piloted us to the shore. Before twelve o'clock the anchors were lifted, and both vessels were under way on a cruise up the bay.

CHAPTER XXXV.

THE UPPER BAY OF YEDO.

The Japanese Officers on Board—Their Manners—Their Dislike to the Chinese—Their Swords—Their Curiosity—Passing up the Bay—Beauty of the Scenery—"Perry's Bay"—Junks bound for Yedo—Another Visit—Further Surveys—The Natives—An Excursion towards Yedo—Extent and Capacity of the Upper Bay—Change of Anchorage—The Surveys Proceed—Interchange of Presents—A Dilemma—Final Satisfaction — Farewell of the Japanese Officials—Commodore Perry's Diplomacy—Departure from Japan—A Multitude of Boats—Oosima—The Islands off the Bay—Discoveries—Formation of the Group—We Sail for Ohosima—A Typhoon—Return to Loo-Choo—The Second Visit to Japan.

YEZAIMON, Saboroske, and the Interpreters accepted an invitation to remain on board until we reached Uraga, and have their boats towed at our stern. This gave them a chance of seeing the steam-engine in operation, for which they had expressed a great desire. They were conducted over the ship, and saw the engine from all points of view, betraying a great deal of curiosity in regard to its operation, but no fear. They even obtained a glimmering idea of the manner in which the steam acted, to set the enormous mass in motion. Tatsonoske asked if it was not the same machine in a smaller com pass which we used on railroads. During their inspection of the ship they saw many things which must have been new and strange to them, but their composure and self-possession were not in the least disturbed. Notwithstanding the decks were crowded with officers and men, whose curiosity to see them was very great, they were to all appearance unconscious of it, and conducted themselves with as much ease and propriety as I ever saw among the most refined people. The complexion of these officers was a dark olive, but not too dark to allow a ruddy tinge on the lips and cheeks. Their eyes were somewhat larger, and not so obliquely set as those of the Chinese, their foreheads broader and more open, with a greater facial angle, and the expression of their faces denoted a lively and active mind. Notwithstanding that spirit of cunning and secrecy which, through the continual teachings of their government has become almost a second nature to them, their faces were agreeable and expressive. Their motions and gestures were characterized by an unstudied grace, and it was the unanimous opinion of all our officers that they were as perfect gentlemen as could be found in any part of the world. A curious illustration of their dislike to the Chinese, who are greatly inferior to them in propriety, and elegance of manner, occurred while they were on board. One of their Interpreters, noticing some of the Chinese deck-hands, who had been shipped at Shanghai, asked. with a face expressive of great contempt and disgust' "Is it possible that you have Chinese among your men?" Mr Portman with much readiness, but not entire candor, replied "These men are *the servants of our sailors*," and thereby reinstated us in the good opinion of the Japanese.

While going their rounds their swords were left in the

cabin, and most of the officers made use of the opportunity to examine them. The steel was of admirable quality, and kept in good condition, although the shape of the blade was rather unwieldy, and the handle was without a guard. The scabbards were made of shark-skin very handsomely polished. While in the cabin, a globe was brought, and the position of the United States shown to the Japanese. Tatsonoske immediately pointed out Washington and New York, and seemed tolerably familiar with the geography of our country, as well as that of Europe. He asked whether in America many of the roads were not cut through the mountains—evidently referring to railroads. Yezaimon expressed his desire to examine a revolver, several of which the Japanese had noticed in the officers' belts. Commander Buchanan therefore fired off all the chambers of a genuine "Colt," from the quarter-deck, to his great astonishment. Before we had half gratified their curiosity, (which the steam-whistle raised to the highest pitch,) we were off Urága, and they were obliged to leave.

As we moved out past the promontory of Urága, the western shore opened on the left, showing a broad deep bay, embosomed by hills covered with the greenest and most luxuriant foliage, and with several large villages at their base. We approached within three miles of the eastern shore, which is loftier and wilder than the western, rising into a range of rugged mountains, which showed no signs of habitation or cultivation. But the lower slopes, which undulated gently to the water, charmed me by the rich beauty of their scattered groves, and the green terraces and lawns into which centuries of patient culti vation has formed them. Outside of England there is nothing so green, so garden-like, so full of tranquil beauty. To the north the hills gradually sank away, and a sandy spur three or four miles in length, stretched into the bay. This proved to be the ground whereon we had seen the parade of Japanese soldiers, when the surveying boats ascended the bay. The two mounds which I had noticed through a glass, were surmounted with batteries of about five guns each.

Changing our course we made over toward the other side, steering for a bold projecting headland, about twelve miles beyond that of Urága. In the intervening bight, to which Lieut. Bent, as the first surveyor, gave the name of "Perry's Bay," there are two lovely, green islands. The shores of the bay are as thickly settled and as assiduously cultivated, as about and below Urága. During the voyage up, we had at no time less than seven fathoms, and generally from thirty to forty. After going a short distance, beyond the point reached by the Mississippi, and upwards of ten miles beyond our former anchorage, we dropped anchor a mile and half from the shore, in thirteen fathoms. The inward-bound junks, I noticed, made for a point a little east of north from our position. According to the Japanese charts, and the best descriptions of Yedo, this must have been the direction of the capital. A long, low headland was visible with the glass, with (apparently) another bight beyond it; but to the north-east, for a segment of about 30°, no land could be seen. This also corresponded to the form of the bay, as given in Japanese charts.

Toward evening we had another visit from Yezaimon, who had followed us from Urága, with the intention of finding out what our motives were in proceeding so far up the bay. Whatever objections he may have made, they did not appear to be effectual, for as long as we remained, the survey was prosecuted with great spirit and activity. On the following day (Friday), Lieuts. Cooper, of the Susquehanna, Clitz, of the Mississippi, Goldsborough, of the Saratoga, and Mathews, of the Plymouth, sounded around the islands and up the head of the bight, where they found a deep inlet, into which flowed a beautiful river. The banks were studded with villages, groves, and gardens, and the officers were enraptured with the beauty of the scenery. The natives of both sexes, old and young, came down the banks and saluted them in a friendly manner, bringing them cool spring-water to drink, and ripe peaches from their gardens.

On Friday afternoon, the Commodore went on board the Mississippi, transferring his broad pennant to that ship for a few hours, while he made an exploring trip still further up the bay. After going ten miles in the direction of Yedo, the Mississippi put about in twenty fathoms water, and returned to her former anchorage, having reached, as was supposed, a point within eight miles of the capital. On the western shore the large towns of Kanagawa and Kowazacki were seen; while on the extremity of a cape in front, not more than four miles distant, stood a tall white tower, resembling a lighthouse. Three or four miles beyond and within this point was a crowd of shipping, which was without doubt the anchorage of Sinagawa, the southern suburb of Yedo. There was every probability that the Mississippi could have advanced to a point within cannon-shot of the city. The head of the bay rounded to the eastward, and in that direction the shores became low and flat, and finally disappeared below the horizon The squadron had, therefore, advanced twenty miles farther up the Bay of Yedo than any previous vessel, and shown con clusively that, instead of being shallow and unnavigable, as had formerly been supposed, it contains abundance of water and excellent harbors. It is, in fact, one of the largest and finest bays in the world, and second to none in the varied and delightful scenery of its shores.

Early on Saturday morning we moved from our first anchorage to another, five or six miles further down the bay, and much nearer to the shore. There was abundance of water every where, and all around the beautiful little island, a line dropped close to the shore gave five fathoms. The western coast, which was less than a mile distant, appeared wonderfully green and beautiful. It curved inward so as to form a charming sheltered bay, near the head of which the two villages of Otsu and Torigasaki lay embosomed in foliage. There was a small battery, almost masked by trees, on the summit of the island, and another on the point of the cape below us. This part of the bay is completely land-locked, the promontory of Urága projecting so far as to cover one third of the eastern shore. The surveying boats were occupied during the whole of the day, without any interference on the part of the Japanese, who seemed to have made up their minds to submit to these unusual proceedings. Too much credit, however, cannot be awarded to the different officers, and especially to Lieut. Bent, for the coolness and courage with which they prosecuted their work. When we consider that this, one of the greatest bays in the world, had hitherto never been surveyed, the interest and value of their labors will be better understood.

Yezaimon came again on Saturday morning, accompanied by both the Interpreters. This time they brought a number of presents, as souvenirs of our visit—consisting of lacquered cups, very light and elegant in form, brocade silks, richly wrought with gold and silver thread, tobacco pipes and pouches, and fans covered with hideously distorted and lackadaisical pictures of Japanese ladies. The Commodore was willing to receive them, but insisted on giving something in return. A selection of American manufactures was made, which, with some maps, engravings, arms and other articles, formed a return more than equal in value. They refused to take any thing, affirming that it was forbidden by their laws, and would subject them to the danger of losing their lives: besides, they declared, the presents offered them were too valuable to be accepted. They were each willing to receive some small articles, which could be readily concealed about their persons, but were positively informed that we could accept of nothing unless they took our gifts, with the exception of the arms, which were removed, as they stated that they could in no case give or receive arms. When Yezaimon saw his presents about to be tumbled back into his boat, he yielded at once, choosing what he probably considered the least dangerous horn of the dilemma.

In the afternoon they returned in the best possible humor, their course having apparently been sanctioned by some higher authority on shore. They brought off a quantity of fowls in light wicker coops, and three or four thousand eggs in boxes, taking away in return a large case of American garden-seeds. The interview lasted a considerable time, as they were socially disposed and partook of refreshments, both solid and liquid. Tatsonoske stated, in a half-confidential way, that the letter of the President had been received in Yedo, and that if the translation which they had already obtained through the Dutch correspond ed with the original, the Government would be disposed to re gard it very favorably. He also hinted that Yezaimon would shortly be promoted to a much higher rank. The latter was exceedingly jovial, and stated, by an expressive pantomime, that he would shed tears on the departure of the squadron. It was dusk when the boat pulled off, and the shadows of the wooded hills, lengthening over the water, soon hid from sight the last glimpse of our Japanese friends.

On Sunday morning, the 17th we hove anchor and started for Loo-Choo, having in the space of ten days accomplished more than any other nation had been able to effect for the last two centuries. The universal feeling on board was one of honest pride and exultation. Knowing the cunning and duplicity of the people with whom we had to deal, it was a satisfaction to find all their arts of diplomacy completely shattered by the simple, straightforward, resolute course adopted by Commodore Perry. Nothing could have been better managed, from first to last; and I have reason to know that the final success of the Expedition was owing to no fortunate combination of circumstances, but wholly to the prudent and sagacious plan pre-arranged by its Commander.

The day of our departure was clear and warm, and the morning light fell softly on the verdurous shores, as we passed the promontory of Urága. The soldiers were all gathered on the terraces, in front of the batteries to see us pass. The Mississippi kept such a station on our port quarter, that from the shore she would appear as far behind the Saratoga, as that vessel from the Susquehanna; and the sight of four great war-ships, with all sails furled and yards squared, keeping equi-distant from each other to a hair's breadth, yet moving through the water at the rate of eight or nine knots, must have struck the Japanese as something miraculous. The day was so clear that the inhabitants of both shores had an excellent opportunity of seeing the performance of the vessels, and we soon found that the news of our departure had preceded us. As we drew abreast of Cape Sagami, and made down the centre of the bay, keeping much nearer the eastern shore than on our entrance, we found the water covered with boats, which had brought out loads of the Japanese to get a nearer view. The bay was sprinkled with them, far and near, and at a moderate calculation, I should say that there were at least five hundred. Some of them were so curious as to approach within four or five hundred yards, when the men lay on their oars, and remained standing motionless until long after we had passed. I caught a parting glimpse of the cone of Fusi-Yamma through the rifts of a pile of fleecy clouds, high over the head of the Bay of Kowadzu.

We steered for the northern or main entrance of the bay, keeping between three and four miles from the northern shore, which belongs to the province of Awa. Vries Island, or Oosima, lay to the south of us. It has a bold, convex outline, and its summit was lost in the clouds. It is an admirable landmark for mariners, and in connection with Cape Idzu and Rock Island, forms a sure guide for vessels entering the Bay of Yedo from the east or south. Our course was nearly due south for the remainder of the day, and the chain of islands which extends from the mouth of the bay to the penal colony of Fatsisio, gradually rose to view. They seem to have been very imperfectly explored, for on none of our charts were they laid down correctly. Vulcan Island is conspicuous for its lofty, conical summit, the sides of which are streaked with deposits of lava. It was covered, from the brink of its sea-worn crags, with the most luxuriant vegetation. To the east of it was another island, not given in any chart, and the Commodore accordingly took the explorer's right, and named it "Mississippi Island." A cluster of very peculiar pointed rocks, rising like broken obelisks to the height of a hundred feet, received the Susquehanna's name. The Plymouth and Saratoga were also honored—the first with a large isolated rock, the second with an island—both of which we claim the merit of discovering.

The features of this group are grand and imposing. The shores of these islands are mostly precipitous, presenting few accessible points, and being nearly circular in form, enhance the effect of the lofty summits into which they rise. I counted eight around us at one time; some bold and strongly defined, from their vicinity; others distant, blue, and floating in a vapory atmosphere, like the phantoms of islands. We could not discern any dwellings upon them, but it is probable that they are partly inhabited. We passed through them all before sunset, and still steering southward, hoped to have caught a glimpse of Fatsisio, which could not have been more than twenty-five miles distant; but night set in, and the vessels were put upon their course for Loo-Choo.

For the next two days, we ran in a south-westerly direction, aided by a strong east wind. The Saratoga was cast off in Lat. 30° N., and left to make her way to Shanghai, where she was ordered to winter. The Mississippi also cast off the Plymouth, which was directed to sound and survey along the western side of Ohosima (the island supposed to have been discovered by the Preble), while the Susquehanna would cruise along the eastern side. Commodore Perry's intention was to spend two or three days in fixing the position and dimensions of the island, and in communicating, if the nature of the coast would allow, with the inhabitants. We looked forward to the visit with interest, as there is no account of any vessel having ever touched there. It is not often that the traveller meets with a large community of semi-civilized people, to whom the European race is unknown.

On Wednesday, July 20th, however, a typhoon came on from the east. Our topmasts and topgallant-masts were sent down, and we scudded along with only the trysails set. The Susquehanna rolled in a most extraordinary manner, and the great pivot-gun on her poop, was so secured with lashings, and bindings of every description, that it resembled an immense cast-iron babe in swaddling-bands. For two days the storm continued to rage with much violence. Both our fore and main trysail-gaffs were carried away, and the Mississippi lost two of her boats. We stood off and on for two days, but the sea continued so rough that the idea of proceeding to Ohosima was finally abandoned, and we made for the harbor of Napa, in Loo-Choo, where we arrived on the 25th. Thus ended the first campaign of the United States Expedition to Japan—concerning which, it will ever be to me a source of pride and satisfaction, to say: *Pars parva fui.*

NOTE.—The result of the Expedition to Japan is now known all over the world. Commodore Perry returned to the Bay of Yedo in February, 1854, his squadron augmented by the steam-frigate *Powhatan*, the sloops-of-war *Macedonian* and *Vandalia*, and the store-ships *Lex ington* and *Southampton*. He anchored before Kanagawa, a remote suburb of Yedo, and after various interviews with a Council of five Princes of the Empire, appointed to confer with him, concluded a treaty of amity and commerce between the United States and Japan, at the village of Yoko-hama, near Kanagawa, in the beginning of April. By this treaty the ports of Simoda, in Niphon (about 120 miles from Yedo), Hakodadi in the island of Jesso, and Napa-Kiang in Loo-Choo, are opened to American vessels for the purposes of trade. The squadron visited both the former ports, and the officers of the Expedition were allowed perfect liberty to go on shore, mingle freely with the inhabitants, and make excursions inland to the distance of twenty miles. The success of the negotiations was as complete, in fact, as the most sanguine friend of the undertaking could have desired, and reflects great honor on the skill and prudence which marked the course of Commodore Perry. As my connection with the Expedition ceased after our return to China, I shall not attempt a history of its second and far more interesting campaign—a complete account of which the public will soon possess in the national work now being published under the supervision of Commodore Perry.

CHAPTER XXXVI.

NEGOTIATIONS IN LOO-CHOO.

Negotiations with the New Regent—Capt. Hall's Account of Loo-Choo—Napoleon's Incredulity—Its Correctness—Verification of the Japanese Chronicle—The Three Castles—The Government of Loo-Choo—Provisions for the Squadron—Duplicity of the Officials—The Markets deserted—The Spies—The Telegraph and Daguerreotype in Loo-Choo—Demands of Commodore Perry—The Regent's Reply—The Commodore successful—A Scene in the Market-place—Chase and Capture of a Spy—The Coal Depot—Exhibition of Loo-Choo Industry—National Contrasts—Steamship Line across the Pacific.

DURING our second visit to Napa-Kiang, on our return from Japan, Commodore Perry opened negotiations with the new Regent (the old one having been deposed during our absence), for the purpose of procuring privileges, which would enable him to make the island a permanent rendezvous for the squadron during its stay in the East. In order to grant his requests, it was necessary to depart in some degree from the exclusive principle, which the Loo-Chooans have either borrowed from, or had forced upon them by Japan; and consequently, while—knowing our strength and their weakness—they avoided a candid opposition, they know how to assume an attitude of passive resistance, which was far more perplexing. The apparent insincerity of their declarations, the shifts to which they resorted, and the deception they attempted to practise upon us taught the Commodore, finally, the only effective method of dealing with them, and gave us a better insight into their real character than has fallen to the lot of any explorers who visited the island before us.

I cannot here avoid allusion to the well-known work of Capt. Basil Hall, who has given the most full and detailed account of Loo-Choo which we possess. He was commander of the *Lyra*, which, with the frigate *Alceste*, visited the island thirty-five years ago, and remained about six weeks at Napa-Kiang. He had considerable intercourse with the natives, whom he paints in the most glowing colors, as models of primitive simplicity, innocence and goodness, such as are to be found in no other part of the globe. He announces as facts that they were ignorant of the use of money, that they had no arms, and that wars were unknown in their history. When Capt. Hall afterward mentioned these things to Napoleon, at St. Helena, the Emperor shook his head incredulously, and exclaimed: "*Point d' armes! point de guerres!—impossible!*" He was right; and the Captain, on these and many other points, was thoroughly cajoled by the Loo-Chooans. When we first arrived they told us the same things, yet we soon found that they were familiar with money and arms—especially the former—and Klaproth's translation of the "*Ran To Sets,*" a Japanese chronicle, gives an account of their wars Their wonderful innocence and simplicity prove to be the disguises assumed by a marvellous cunning, and their alleged goodness of heart is illustrated by a Government which makes luxurious drones of a small class, and abject slaves of all others.

During our exploration of the island, we found an interesting verification of its former history, as given in the Japanese chronicle. It is there stated, that there were originally three kingdoms, called the Northern, Central and Southern, the first nd last named of which were in the course of time, and after lingering civil wars, absorbed by the third. On our expedition into the interior, in the beginning of June, we discovered, as I have already stated, the ruins of the fortress-palace of the Northern King—a massive edifice, 600 feet in length, on the summit of a mountain. The present Viceroy, descended from the rulers of the Central Kingdom, still inhabits their castle the inscription over the gate of Shui, the capital, is: "The Central Hill," and it was therefore to be expected that the castle of the third King might be found in the southern part of the island. Accordingly, on our return from Japan, Commodore Perry directed several officers, of whom I was one, to make explorations in that quarter, and we finally discovered the ruins of the castle, about four miles south-east of Napa, on the summit of a precipitous cliff, which commanded a view of an extensive and beautiful landscape. The place is called by the natives "Timagusku," and has been so despoiled that only two gateways remain entire. The outer walls inclose an area of nearly eight acres.

It was not so easy to obtain correct particulars concerning the structure of the Government, although its character was exhibited in its effects upon the population. The present Viceroy is a minor, and the chief authority is exercised by a Regent, the three Treasurers of the kingdom, and perhaps some additional officers, forming a Council which he consults, and in which, apparently, is vested the right to appoint or de pose him. There are also various grades of civil rank, as in China and Japan. The soil is considered the property of the State, and all that it yields is divided into ten parts, six of which are appropriated by the Government. There is every evidence that a system of espionage, similar to that of Japan, is practised. The deep-rooted fear and mistrust of the people toward the officers of the Government, can only be accounted for by the existence of such a system. Wherever we went we found ourselves preceded and followed by spies, who drove the populace from our path, forced them in some instances to quit their dwellings or abandon their villages, and prevented them from holding any communication with us. Although, owing to the remonstrances made by Commodore Perry, this annoying surveillance was relaxed toward the close of our stay, it was never wholly abandoned.

After our arrival at Napa-Kiang, in May, the squadron was in want of fresh provisions, and the Commodore requested that supplies might be furnished, promising that full value should be paid for every article. The Loo-Choo authorities at first objected, stating that their island was poor, and that money was of no use to them, but that they would furnish gratuitously what little they could spare from their own needs; yet after some negotiations, they agreed to the demand, and fixed a scale of prices, which, on comparison with those of China, we found to be sufficiently high. The well-stocked markets of Napa, and the rich gardens and harvest-fields which covered the island, contradicted their complaints of poverty. When the day of settlement came, they were always in readiness to receive the money, and took the Spanish dollars and American eagles with great satisfaction. Thus the way was broken for a closer intercourse with the people.

The next step was to obtain our supplies direct from the markets of Napa. The persons appointed to fill up the lists sent from the different vessels fulfilled their office in a very satisfactory manner. In few instances was more than half the amount supplied, which had been called for, and at last, when a mess needed a dozen fowls and a hundred eggs, it was necessary to demand 50 of the one, and 500 of the other. The object of this was to keep up the appearance of poverty, though at the same time the public markets, open to the natives, abounded in every thing which we stood in need of. Many persons—both officers and men—went ashore repeatedly, and endeavored to make purchases, but they were successful in very few instances. They were dogged by spies, whose appearance sufficed to clear the market in a few minutes. The natives fled precipitately in all directions, leaving their stands of fruit, vegetables, pottery and other articles of sale or barter, entirely unprotected, and the market-square which, when we first caught sight of it, was crowded with hundreds of busy buyers and sellers, was left vacant and desolate. The same course was followed in all parts of the town. Shops were closed, streets deserted, and though we sometimes endeavored to steal a march upon the inhabitants by darting suddenly into a private dwelling, we rarely succeeded in finding any one within. Yet, whenever, by chance, we met with them when no spies were visible, they showed an evident good-will towards us, and a desire to cultivate a familiar intercourse. At such times they thankfully accepted money or presents, which they steadfastly refused, when any agent of the Government was near. On our tours of exploration, we generally carried with us a quantity of ship's biscuit, which the inhabitants of the villages took very eagerly, seeming to consider it a great delicacy.

During our first visit, the Commodore applied to the authorities to lease him a house on shore for a short time, that the daguerreotype and telegraphic apparatus might be put up and tested. They designated the little temple near the village of Tumai, two miles north of Napa, which had been given to Capts. Maxwell and Hall, as a hospital for their seamen. There is a correct sketch of it in Hall's work. Messrs. Brown and Draper, the artists, went ashore with their assistants, and remained there three weeks. They were daily visited by numbers of the better class of natives, who watched their operations with the greatest curiosity. They at once comprehended the properties of the daguerreotype, and willingly sat for their portraits. They understood the necessity of remaining perfectly quiet, and were as rigid as statues, not venturing to move an eyelid. When the impression was good, nothing could exceed their wonder and delight. The excessive moisture in the air of Loo-Choo, and the absence of any fitting location for the instruments, operated unfavorably upon the plates, and not more than twenty good pictures were procured. These, however, are of much value, as giving perfect representations of the features and costumes of the Loo-Chooans. The telegraphic apparatus worked admirably, and though the natives could only partially comprehend its character, they regarded it with a kind of superstitious awe.

Considering the advantages which the island of Loo-Choo offered as a temporary naval station, and rendezvous for the squadron—its proximity to Japan; its temperate and healthy climate; its secure harbor, and its remoteness from the jealous watchfulness of rival nations—Commodore Perry made the following demands of the Regent: 1st, that the Government should lease him a building suitable for a coal depot; 2d, that the markets of Napa should be thrown open to us, and the natives be allowed to deal directly with us, without the tedious and unsatisfactory agency of the official purveyors; 3d, that the system of espionage to which we had been subjected, should be relinquished in future; and 4th, that the Government should make a collection of the articles manufactured in the island, in order that we might have an opportunity of purchasing specimens. It was represented, in support of these demands, that two months of intercourse, during which they had no single cause of complaint against any person belonging to the squadron, should be sufficient to convince them of our friendly disposition toward them; that in allowing us to purchase the commodities which their people offered for sale, we conferred a direct benefit upon them; that we had explored their island, seen its abundant resources, and knew that they would be enriched, not impoverished, by the supplies which they furnished us; and lastly, that both as friends to the Loo-Chooans, and as the representatives of a great nation, the employment of spies to watch our motions was an indignity to which we could no longer submit.

The reply of the Regent was a good illustration of the insincere, evasive diplomacy of Eastern nations. It granted nothing and denied nothing. With regard to the coal depot, it was suggested that the people would steal the coal in case it was deposited there; that typhoons might blow down the building; that there was no part of the harbor where coal could be landed, &c. As for the markets, they had never prevented us from going there to purchase, but the people feared and they fled away because they were afraid. The persons who followed us were not spies, but officers appointed to watch over, protect and assist us. If we did not desire them they would be released from their service. The reply wound up as usual, by a declaration of the smallness and poverty of the island. The Commodore however took a blunt, straight forward course which obliged them to give a decisive answer, and as in the case of the Japanese, he gained his point. His diplomacy, no doubt, seemed somewhat arbitrary in both cases, but where dissimulation and evasion form the web of a policy, as with these nations, there is no course so effective as plain common sense, backed up by a good reserve of physical force.

A number of us went ashore the day after the concessions were made, in order to test their good faith. We entered Napa, and set out for the market-place, keeping a good watch to see whether any spies were lurking about. Most of the shops were shut as usual, but we found the market crowded, and a brisk trade going on in vegetables, cheese, pork, earthenware, paper, plain cotton goods, and the other articles in common use among the natives. At first, our appearance created no disturbance, but we had scarcely reached the middle of the square, when the crowd began to scatter as if a bomb-shell had fallen among them. The superannuated old women who could not get out of the way, crouched behind their umbrellas, and if we approached them, turned their heads aside or stuck them under their arms, that they might not see us. Except by them, and a few men of the lowest class, the place was soon deserted

We looked in all directions for the source of this dispersion, and at last caught a glimpse of the head of a spy, peeping cautiously around a corner. We instantly gave chase, but he escaped us. Wherever we went, we saw them dodging us in the distance, and if we turned on our steps and followed them, they took to their heels. But there was one—an ill-favored, one-eyed gentleman in a robe of yellow grass-cloth—who persisted in keeping close to us. At last a spirited midshipman started in chase of him. Away they raced through the pork market, the people scattering on both sides before them, yet looking on with evident amusement. The one-eyed gentleman spread his robes on the wind, but the midshipman gained on him, and finally grasping him by the back of the neck, gave him a shaking that made his remaining eye quiver in its socket. He did not return, and we had the satisfaction of purchasing some cucumbers in the market—which was at least a beginning of trade.

The site for a coal depot was at once selected, the dimensions given, and before we left, a company of Loo-Choo carpenters were on the ground, hewing the timbers which were to form the frame of the building. It was located in the creek of Tumai, the most convenient place for landing, and near the little temple, which was at that time occupied by an officer and two or three men from the storeship *Supply*. The sloop-of-war *Plymouth* was ordered to remain at Napa, until relieved by the *Vandalia*, so that the entering wedge we drove into Loo-Choo exclusiveness, which had remained intact up to the time of our arrival, will continue to widen the breach, and effect a permanent opening for intercourse with the rest of mankind.

The "Great Exhibition" of Loo-Choo Industry came off on the morning we left Napa for Hong Kong. It took place in the *cung-qua*, a government building of the town, under the auspices of the Mayor and a number of civil officers. As it was probably the first attempt at such a display ever made in the Island, it was got up in creditable style. The articles consisted of Loo-Choo cotton and grass-cloths, in pieces and made into garments; Japanese silks; brass hair-pins; straw sandals; fans; tobacco pipes and pouches, of various kinds; chow chow, or refreshment boxes; paper, of different colors; earthen pots, pans and vases, some of them neatly glazed, and a great variety of black and scarlet lacquered ware. The fair was attended by all of the officers who could be spared from the vessels, and as they were all anxious to procure some souvenir of the Island, the sales were brisk and rapid, and most of the articles went off at a premium. We computed that there were at least a hundred dollars spent on the occasion. The steamers were under sailing orders, and the activity that prevailed on our part seemed to puzzle and bewilder the deliberate and impassive Loo-Chooans. Such avidity to purchase, such apparent recklessness of expenditure, were quite beyond their comprehension. They lost "the run" of us, and looked on in helpless amazement, trusting to Fate for the final balance to show a preponderance in their favor.

Thus, in addition to the establishment of friendly intercourse with Japan, Commodore Perry has opened Loo-Choo, its most important dependency. At the same time, by his purchase of the tract of land best adapted for a coal depot, on Port Lloyd, in the Bonin Islands, he has secured to the United States the most available station in the Western Pacific for a line of steamers between China and California. Honolulu and Port Lloyd are the natural stopping-places on the route between San Francisco and Shanghai. For the first, coal may be transported from Oregon and Vancouver's Island; for the second, from the Japanese island of Kiusiu, less than five hundred miles distant. Loo-Choo lies too far south for the route to Shanghai, but that to Hong Kong passes near it. Its commerce is too trifling to be an object of consideration; but as a naval station or a port for supplies, it has many things to recommend it, and the step which has been made toward bringing it into the list of lands which are open to intercourse with the civilized world, deserves to be recorded

CHAPTER XXXVII.

NAVAL LIFE.

Return to Hong Kong—End of the Cruise—Experience of Naval Life—My Duties on Board—"General Quarters"—Our Crew—Decline of Naval Discipline—False System of Promotion—Delays—What is Needed—Harmony of Government at Sea—The Abolition of Corporeal Punishment—Want of an Efficient Substitute—Government on Sea and Land—Mr. Kennedy's Proposal for Registered Seamen—Effect of Long Cruises—Need of Small Vessels in Chinese Waters.

We sailed from Loo-Choo on the 1st of August, but were delayed by strong head-winds, until we had doubled the southern end of the island of Formosa, and entered the China Sea. On the second day out from Napa we saw some of the Madjicosima Islands, which lie between Formosa and the Loo-Choo group, and at dusk the same evening met the sloop-of-war *Vandalia*, on her way to join the squadron. Salutes were exchanged, Capt. Pope reported himself to the Commodore, received his orders, and the vessels lost each other again in the darkness. The rest of the voyage was without incident. B taking a more southern course than usual across the China Sea, we missed encountering the steam-frigate *Powhatan*, which sailed from Hong Kong on the 6th, the day previous to our arrival there. At sunset on the 7th, I saw again the bleak hills and the long semi-European town which I had left in March previous, and when the anchor dropped in the harbor, my last cruise on a Government vessel was at an end.

I shall always look back upon my short experience of naval life as one of the most agreeable and interesting episodes of my travels. Apart from the rare opportunity which it afforded me of visiting and exploring remote and unfrequented portions of the earth, it has enabled me to gain some insight into the nature and operations of a service, which, to a commercial nation, like our own, must ever be the most important arm of protection and defence. I cannot avoid making a few remarks upon our naval system before taking a final leave of it—and such observations as I make, may not be inappropriately offered at present, when our Government, after a long and culpable neglect of the Navy, seems to be at last slowly awaking to the necessity of reorganizing it.

Although my rank of acting Master's Mate rendered me liable to be called upon at any time to discharge the duties usually assigned it, it imposed upon me no higher obligation in reality, than that of conforming in all respects to the etiquette of the service. I was attached to the corps of artists, who held the same rank, and were especially subject to the Commodore's orders; and when not employed on explorations—a branch of duty of which I was never weary—occupied myself with making sketches of birds, flowers, fish and landscapes, and with keeping a faithful record of our experiences. The fact that I messed on the orlop deck, went up and down the port ladders, and smoked forward of the main shaft, did not exclude me from the hospitalities of the ward-room and the commanders cabins. By Commodore Perry and Capt. Buchanan, especially I was treated with unvarying kindness.

The only ship's duty I was called upon to perform, besides taking charge of a boat now and then, and keeping a two-hour watch in Japan, was to appear in my station at "general quarters," which were beaten quite frequently previous to our arrival in the Bay of Yedo. "General quarters," I should state for the information of the landsman, is a combination of a review and a sham fight. Every one of the ship's company has his place assigned to him, and at the well-known *rappel*, and fife-call, officers, seamen, mariners and boys fall into their proper places, the rolls are called, and the formalities of a naval engagement are practised. The guns are run in, loaded, and run out and fired; the seamen, armed with cutlasses and boarding pikes, trot fore and aft, crowding the rail on alternate bows and quarters, to repel imaginary boarders; the marines, behind them, load and discharge noiseless volleys in rapid succession; the bell gives the signal of fire, for the ship has been ignited by an intangible hot shot; the pumps are rigged, and by great exertions the invisible flames are extinguished—and, last of all, the hostile flag strikes, and the band plays "Yankee Doodle" in token of victory. My station was at first on the orlop deck, over the magazine, to superintend the passing up of immaterial powder-cans, but I was afterwards transferred to the quarter-deck, where I spent the hour in watching the performance of our great pivot-gun. There was also target practice, in which the officers usually joined, and I was struck with the large proportion of good shots among the ship's company.

Although I was not often brought into direct contact with the crew, I soon made acquaintance with them, and learned to understand and appreciate the blunt, hearty, generous sailor character. There is a great variety of elements in every crew, but the good and bad are more readily known than in any society on shore. Dissimulation is soon detected on shipboard; as on the battle-field, no man can purchase a substitute or shift his duty upon other shoulders than his own. Whatever may be the faults of seamen, they are, as a class, honest, open-hearted and courageous—full of firm masculine fibre and a healthy cheerfulness—and I confess to a warm attachment for them.

It is a serious fact, felt even more keenly by those in the service than by the public at large, that the efficiency of our Navy has been of late years greatly impaired, and that it is no longer animated by the same prompt, active, energetic spirit, which drew into its ranks some of the boldest and bravest characters which adorn our history. The nature of the service is such as to stimulate and keep alive the ambition of those enlisted in it; and we must therefore look to the legislation which controls it, for the cause of this change. The two prominent evils under which the Navy now labors are, a relaxation of discipline among the men, and a system which, among the officers, makes promotion dependent entirely upon seniority, and, by rendering null any amount of brilliant service, discourages all manly emulation.

As there has hitherto been no retired list, the officers who are incapacitated by age or disease, or any other cause, from active service, hang as a dead weight upon the chances of all those whose term of service is less than theirs. In time of peace, their ranks are continually accumulating, so that the number allotted to each grade having once been filled up, promotions after that can only take place to fill the vacancies caused by death. The younger officer, therefore, grows old in an inferior rank, and by the time he is invested with a command, having passed the best years of his life in a subordinate position, is naturally timid and distrustful of himself under responsibilities which he would have borne lightly, if bestowed before his youthful energy and ambition were wholly deadened. This very energy and ambition of youth constitutes the stamina of naval and military life, and that service will inevitably decay, which does not extend to it at least a partial encouragement.

Under the system at present pursued by the Government, our Navy is gradually filling up with Passed Midshipmen of thirty, and Lieutenants of forty-five, while an officer whose hair is not entirely gray (if indeed he has any left to show), before attaining the rank of Post Captain, may consider himself especially fortunate. There is a weight of invalided, indolent, or superannuated material above him, which nothing but the slow process of death can remove. No deed of daring, no bold achievement, no amount of hazardous and arduous duty, involving years of absence from all the amenities of civilized life, will advance him one step nearer the post, which terminates the vista of his ambition. No one complained of the efficiency of the Navy when Perry, Decatur and Lawrence were Captains, at an age when no Passed Midshipman is now rash enough to dream of a Lieutenant's commission. Heroes are made early; and the English and French Governments acknowledge the fact by promoting for meritorious conduct, as well as for length of days. In the French Navy, I believe, one third of the promotions are based on this ground.

A retired list, such as has recently been provided for by an act of Congress, will partly remedy the evil, but it is not sufficient. A man who has rendered special and signal service to his country deserves to be rewarded. This claim, which is partially recognized in our Army, ought to have equal weight in the Navy. Not that I believe that in cases where the honor of the country is at stake, our naval officers would be found wanting in courage and spirit, but the prospect of reward would keep alive an active pride and emulation, which would manifest itself at all times, and on all occasions. Our most promising officers would not then be driven to resign as they are now by the disheartening prospect of twenty or thirty years of subordinate rank, which no exertion of theirs can render more brief.

It is impossible that such a state of things should not tell upon the discipline of the ship, even where there are no more direct influences at work. The relations in which all, officers and men, stand to each other, on board of a man-of-war, are so intricate and so nicely adjusted, that a derangement in any quarter is felt throughout the whole machine. When it operates in perfect harmony, no pyramid could be more symmetrical. But if the Captain, or cap-stone press uncomfortably hard on the layer beneath him, the pressure makes itself felt through all the courses that follow, down to the seamen—the broad base on which all rest. A well-appointed frigate, where discipline is encouraged by duty, and authority tempered by justice, is to me the crowning miracle of social government.

There is at present no effective system of punishment for minor offences on board our men-of-war. Congress, by taking away the only recognized penalty, that of corporeal punishment without fixing any legal substitute has thrown upon the officers the responsibility of inventing new forms of punishment, which shall correct the faults of the offender without withdrawing him from active duty, or rendering the officer himself liable to censure, on the ground of inhuman or extraordinary measures. No such punishment has yet been discovered. That which was recommended at the time flogging was abolished—solitary confinement, on bread and water—is no punishment at all to the vicious or refractory seaman, who sees in it an excellent opportunity of skulking from work; while the other plans in force—such as carrying a sixty-eight pound shot, standing lashed fast in one position for a certain number of hours, &c., are looked upon as a kind of slow torture, and in many cases tend to exasperate still further a nature already vicious. Either of these methods punishes the good as well as the bad, by removing the offender from his work, which thus falls upon the honest and faithful seamen. The good men who are never punished, are rewarded for their fidelity by being obliged to perform more than their share of the labor, and are gradually being driven out of the service. I have heard it proposed that the idle and insubordinate shall be mulcted in their wages, and the sums thus deducted divided among the others. I am correct in my estimate of the sailor character, when I say that very few of them would accept such a reward. In fact, where a man really guilty has been punished by the loss of his wages for a number of months the entire crew has united to repay him the loss. Few sailors are destitute of a sense of honor, which would lead them to spurn the taking of a shipmate's wages, no matter how culpable that shipmate might be.

No deductions can be drawn from the experience of society on shore which would be of much advantage in the government of a ship on the open ocean, cut off from the world, and a world in itself, but in many respects of a very different order from that with which landsmen are acquainted. Every member of this world has his appointed station and his regular daily duties. He is subject to inexorable laws, and obedience to those laws must be enforced at every hazard Without entire and absolute subordination a navy cannot exist. Its character is necessarily despotic, in fact, all sea life is so, and must always be so. Its government demands the exercise of the strictest justice, and of *justice to all.* In its forms of punishment, therefore, that which most effectually preserves discipline, which corrects the guilty without throwing an additional burden on the good, is the most expedient.

Among the seamen who compose the crews of our national vessels, there is every variety of character. Men as brave, manly and generous as any class can afford, there are; in most cases, no doubt, the major part of the crew are reputable in their conduct; but there is always—at least, under the present system—a leaven of depravity and sullen, dogged wickedness, which will bend to nothing but material force. I have seen so frequently the inefficiency of the other methods of punishment employed, and have heard, from the men themselves, such honest desire for the restoration of the old *régime*, that I cannot avoid the conclusion that the entire abolition of corporeal punishment in the Navy, without authorizing some effective substitute, was one of those mistaken acts of philanthropy which are founded on abstract ideas of humanity rather than a practical knowledge of human nature. It has more than once happened, on board our vessels, that the seamen, in defiance of authority, have seized below decks and soundly flogged the idle and vicious, whom all other punishments had failed to intimidate.

Mr. Kennedy, Ex-Secretary of the Navy, in one of his Annual Reports, recommends a course which will partly remedy the evil by drawing into the service a better class of men, and thereby rendering punishments of all kinds less frequent. I allude to his proposal for creating a class of "registered seamen," who shall be permanently attached to the Navy, and receive an increased rate of pay with every five years of their service. The high wages now paid to sailors in the merchant service will soon render the adoption of some such plan necessary, in order to procure seamen at all—notwithstanding the superior comforts which a man-of-war affords, and that representative national character which is so gratifying to the pride of an American tar. There are many noble fellows among our seamen, and the adoption of a measure like Mr. Kennedy's, which would retain them in the service and identify them with its achievements, would go far toward restoring that energy and *morale* which once made our crews the finest in the world. I am too proud to admit that they are not so still; but every year makes the difference between the slackening discipline of our vessels, and the perfect and thorough subordination witnessed in the English Navy, more painfully perceptible.

While upon this theme I must allude to another circumstance which has an injurious operation—at least upon the vessels attached to the East India station, and I have no doubt the Pacific and African stations as well. I allude to the length of the cruise. Three years in those climates, hot and unhealthy as they are, is trying to any constitution, while from the absence of all that can excite or amuse, the men gradually become spiritless and depressed. So far removed from home, exposed to gross sensual temptations, where every indulgence is followed by a terrific penalty, the length of the cruise tends inevitably to demoralize the crew. An *active* cruise of two years would accomplish far more than an idle one of three.

What is needed for the East India station is not a leviathan war-steamer like the Susquehanna, which cannot go within thirty miles of Ning-po and Foo-chow-foo, and can barely manage to reach Shanghai, but two small steamers, drawing not more than twelve or fourteen feet of water. When Canton was menaced, we could with difficulty get a store-ship within reach of the factories, to watch over the interests of our citizens. If a fleet of piratical junks was hovering about the Ladrone Islands, and one of our big vessels attempted to follow, they were off at once into water too shallow for us. The small English steamers Hermes and Styx did more in this way for the security of commerce, than all other men-of-war on the coast collectively.

CHAPTER XXXVIII.

HONG-KONG—SOCIETY IN CHINA.

Impressions of Hong-Kong—A Man Drowned at Midnight—Hong-Kong from the Water—The town of Victoria—The Island of Hong-Kong—The Hong-Kong Fever—Hospitality of Foreign Residents in China—Their Princely Style of Living—Rigid Social Etiquette—Balls—Tropical Privileges—The Anglo-Saxon Abroad.

My first impressions of Hong-Kong were not very favorable, but I attributed them partly to the gloomy March weather which prevailed during my stay. After the genial quiet of Macao, and the mellow historic light which plays about its decaying palaces, the thoroughly modern air and desolate surroundings of the place became still more distasteful to me, and an unfortunate association which I shall never be able wholly to banish from memory, increased the feeling into absolute dislike.

On the second evening after our arrival I went ashore with some friends, and did not return until ten o'clock. My cot was not yet slung, for my hammock-boy was one of the crew of the Captain's boat which had also gone ashore. He was a strong, dark-eyed, lusty fellow named John Williams—one of the maintopmen, who are generally the picked men of the ship. About eleven o'clock Williams made his appearance, with my cot, which he slung in its accustomed place; but instead of silently going forward again, as was his wont, he turned suddenly and asked me whether I thought it possible that he could get a release from the service. His mother, he said, had died, and some property had fallen to him which he wished to secure. I advised him to consult with some of the officers, who were better acquainted with the customs of the service. He seemed to labor under a singular depression of spirit, and after lingering for some time in silence, as if reluctant to turn away, he finally said: "Well, sir, it is the last cruise I shall ever make,"—and left me.

My cot was slung in a temporary poop-cabin on deck, which Commodore Perry had ordered to be erected for the use of the artists. I had not slept more than two hours, when my sleep was suddenly broken by a cry—a wild, gurgling, despairing cry which still rings in my ears whenever I think of that night. I sprang from my cot and listened. There was a trampling of feet on the deck outside, a hurried order, "cut the painter!" and again a bubbling cry, but feebler, under the stern. I sprang to one of the windows, looked out, and saw a hand beating the water blindly and convulsively in the eddy of the rudder. I was about to spring out when a coil of rope fell in the water and the hand grasped it. A horrible phosphorescent light shone around the body, struggling beneath the surface. Three men were in the little dingey which lay under the stern, but before they could cut the painter, the hand let go its weak hold, the rope slackened, and the body sank. The men had no oars, but half drifting with the tide, half paddling with their hands, they floated over it. Just beyond—just out of their reach—a head rose an instant to the surface once more, making a ring of ghastly light. There was one bubble, and it sank forever, the phosphorescent gleam sinking slowly with it, until nothing more was seen.

The drowned man was no other than John Williams. He had the mid-watch, and his station was on the forward guard of the star-board paddle-box. It was conjectured that he had sat down upon a bucket to rest, near the edge of the guard, and had either fallen asleep and reeled over, or lost his balance by the tilting of the bucket. One of the cutters was moored beside the paddle-box, and he probably struck upon it and disabled himself, as he was known to be an excellent swimmer. Some of the men asserted that they had seen a large fish dart past just before he let go his hold of the rope, and supposed that he had been carried under by a shark. His body was found however two or three weeks afterwards unmutilated, and was placed in the cemetery at Hong-Kong, where a tomb-stone was erected over it by his messmates. I have seen death in many shapes, but there was an awful fatality about this which shocked me profoundly. Night and day I heard the terrible drowning cry, until I feared that my ear would never lose the consciousness of it. Nearly a month afterwards, I again visited Hong-Kong, and having been rowed ashore from the steamer, in the dusk of evening, the oars struck a phosphorescent lustre from the water; I grew deathly sick at the image which those gleams recalled.

It is, therefore, if not my fault, at least my misfortune, that I cannot endorse the praises of Hong-Kong, which its residents are accustomed to bestow upon it. Seen from the water, the town, stretching for a mile along the shore, at the foot of Victoria Peak, whose granite cliff towers eighteen hundred feet above, bears considerable resemblance to Gibraltar. The Governor's mansion, the Bishop's Palace, the Church and Barracks occupy conspicuous positions, and the houses of merchants and government officials, scattered along the steep sides of the hill, give the place an opulent and flourishing air. So far from being disappointed in this respect, one is surprised to find that ten years of English occupation have sufficed to civilize so completely a barren Chinese island.

The town is almost entirely made up of the long street called Victoria Road, which runs parallel to the shore. It is broad, well built and well paved, and being the great thoroughfare of the place, lengthening into a military road which makes the circuit of the island, has at all times a busy and animated air. The streets which cross it strike directly up the hill. and are in many places so steep that it has been found necessary to turn them into flights of steps. The gray granite of which the island is composed furnishes excellent material for building purposes, and is extensively employed in the houses, streets and piers. Large quantities of it, dressed in the quarries by Chinese laborers, are shipped to San Francisco where it is in great demand. Several entire buildings have been sent over and erected in that city. The English Church is a large Gothic building, without any pretensions to architectural beauty. On a natural platform above it, stands the palace of Bishop Smith—a long mansion in the Elizabethan style. The Governor's new residence was in the course of construction, and not sufficiently advanced to hint at its char acter.

The island of Hong-Kong is about thirty miles in circumference, and consists of a desolate cluster of mountains, which offer no opportunity of cultivation. Nearly all the fruit and vegetables consumed in the town come from Macao. There is a small village, inhabited by Chinese fishermen, on the southern side, and a Military Hospital on the east, looking upon the Lymoon Passage, which opens into the China Sea; but the English colony is concentrated in and about the town of Victoria, which is built on the northern side, facing the mainland. The harbor is spacious, with a good anchorage, and well sheltered, except in case of an unusually violent typhoon. From the position of the town, it is cut off from the south-west monsoon in summer, while the vapors collected by the mountain contribute to produce an intense moist heat, which occasions violent fever. The "Hong-Kong fever," as it is called, has been described by some facetious traveller as combining the worst symptoms of cholera, yellow and typhus fevers, with other and worse features of its own. The mortality among the troops stationed here was formerly very great, but it has been lessened of late years by the adoption of stringent sanitary measures.

For amusements, besides riding, boating, yacht regattas, &c., there is a club, with a library, reading and billiard rooms, and a bowling-alley, much frequented by Americans. The society is not extensive, but intelligent and agreeable, and the same lordly hospitality, with which I first became acquainted in India, prevails not only here but throughout all the foreign communities in China. This custom originated long ago, in the isolation to which the foreign merchant was condemned, and the infrequency of visitors from the distant world, which he had temporarily renounced. Then all houses were open to the guest, and the luxury which had been created to soften the gilded exile, was placed at his command. The establishment of steamship lines, the building of hotels and other progressive agencies, have somewhat moderated this liberality, and may in time reduce it to the cautious and guarded hospitality of home; but there is still enough of the old genial spirit left to make a stranger feel satisfied with the welcome he receives.

I doubt if there be another class of men, who live in more luxurious state than the foreign residents in China. Their households are conducted on a princely scale, and whatever can be had in the way of furniture, upholstery or domestic appliances of any sort, to promote ease and comfort, is sure to be found in their dwellings. Their tables are supplied with the choicest which the country can afford, and a retinue of well-drilled servants, whose only business it is to study their habits, anticipate all their wants. All the management of the household is in the hands of native servants. The "comprador" furnishes the necessary supplies—for which he generally obtains a fat commission—the butler regulates the internal economy; and every inmate has one or more personal servants, who have charge of his own private wants. The expense of keeping up such an establishment is of course very large; but so also are the profits of a flourishing commercial house, and this easeful and luxurious mode of life, while it tends to preserve health in a climate hostile to the Northern race, furnishes a solace, sensuous though it be, for the want of those more enlightened recreations which a civilized land affords.

These little communities, nevertheless, are subject to iron laws of etiquette, any infraction whereof, either purposely or through ignorance, makes society tremble to its foundations. A custom which refers particularly to strangers, has been transplanted thither from India, and is now in full force. The newly arrived, unless he wishes to avoid all society, must go the rounds of the resident families, and make his calls. The calls are returned, an invitation to dinner follows in due course of time, and every thing is *en train* for a footing of familiar intercourse. This custom seems to me to reverse the natural course of social ethics. It obliges the stranger to seek his welcome, instead of having it spontaneously tendered to him. The residents defend the practice, on the ground that it allows a man to choose his own society—an obvious bull, since he cannot know who are congenial to him until he has met them; and on the other hand, the opposite course would allow *them* to choose *his* society or not, as they preferred. In India, among the Company's servants, the rule is rigidly enforced, and nothing creates greater scandal than a violation of it.

There are private balls occasionally—public, rarely, if ever—where quadrilles, and waltzes, and polkas, are danced with as much spirit as at any outside the Tropics; but there is a considerate departure from the etiquette of the North, in allowing the gentlemen to appear, on such occasions, in a white linen jacket, and with a simple ribbon in place of a cravat. Nay, if so minded, he may even throw wide his collar, and enjoy a cool throat. This barbarism—as every young lady of proper taste must consider it—I find highly commendable But it requires a great struggle in John Bull to throw down those starched barricades which flank his closely-rasped chin and protect his mutton-chop whiskers. In Calcutta, even in the dog-days, nothing less than a collar rigid as plank, and a black cloth dress-coat, is tolerated. Verily, the Saxon clings to his idols with a pertinacity which we cannot sufficiently admire. Make a certain costume the type of respectability with him, and he carries the idea all over the world. If bear-skins and woollen blankets were the evening costume of the West-End or Fifth-Avenue, you would soon find him complacently sporting them on the Equator. In the incessant heat of the Tropics he drinks his heavy sherry, and indulges in his brandy-and-water, with as much freedom as in the airs of England, and if not cut short in his career by fever, finally goes home with a damaged liver and no digestion at all. On the shores of Cathay, he keeps up the hours and habits of the London season; in the cinnamon groves of Ceylon, he breathes the atmosphere of Pall-Mall.

CHAPTER XXXIX.

A PICTURE OF MACAO.

Movements of the Squadron—Cumsingmoon—The Naval Hospital at Macao—Quiet Life—A Chinese Beggar—The Band—The Memories of Macao—Situation of the Town—Its Appearance—Desertion of the Place—Its Tropical Gardens—The Campo—The Temple of Wang Hyà—Anecdote of Cushing—Society in Macao—Chinese All-Souls' Day—Discordant Noises—The Grotto of Camoëns—The Casa Gardens—The Grotto at Daybreak—French Irreverence—Preparations to Return Home—Leaving the Naval Service—Trips to Hong-Kong and Cumsingmoon.

We remained but two or three days at Hong-Kong: the season of typhoons was at hand, and it was considered advisable to place the squadron in some more sheltered anchorage. The Mississippi proceeded to Blenheim Reach, near Whampoa, where part of the British East India Squadron was already anchored; the Susquehanna, after touching at Macao, to land Commodore Perry, was ordered to Cumsingmoon, about fifteen miles further to the north. This is merely a small Chinese village, on an island of the same name, with the advantages of a sheltered anchorage in front of it, a healthy air and good water. The hills are bare and bleak in aspect, and no place could well be more forlorn, as a sojourn. After four days, however, the artists corps received notice that rooms had been appropriated to them in a building in Macao, which had been leased as a Naval Hospital. A Portuguese *lorcha* was dispatched to carry us and our baggage to the city, and we took leave of the good old Susquehanna. We had a slow but agreeable run down the coast, anchored in the inner harbor of Macao, and before night were fully installed in our new quarters.

The Naval Hospital stood upon the central ridge of the island, and was consequently in the highest part of the city, overlooking the broad Canton Gulf on one side, and on the other the tiled roofs of the Portuguese houses below, the inner harbor, with its scanty fleet of junks, lorches and *tauka* boats, and the bare, stony hills of the island beyond. In front rose a hill, with a deserted convent on its summit glowing in the broad white glare of the breathless August noons. The lower story of the Hospital was appropriated to the invalids, of whom there were about twenty, and the Commodore's band; the surgeons and artists occupied the rooms above. With A-fok as steward, and the market of Macao at hand, rich in fruit and vegetables, we fared rather better than on ship's rations and tough Japanese fowls, while the enclosed verandah, on account of its airiness, furnished admirable sleeping accommodations during the dog-days. The time passed on quietly and without particular incident, and I found the repose of our life very grateful, after the active experiences and vicissitudes of the past year. There was no serious duty to interfere with the indulgence of that tropical indolence, which is such a luxury after the fatigue of travel.

Our principal annoyance was an old Chinese beggar-woman who sometimes drove us to desperation with her piercing, monotonous wail, from her station in the shade of the house oppo site, and no amount of "cash" (the cheapest alms in the world; would drive her away. She would then only howl the more pertinaciously for more. Nothing could have been more trying to the nerves than her eternal: "*Chin-chin—a—a—a! poor man—a—a! how kin do—a—a—a!*" But twice a day our fine brass band of twenty instruments rehearsed in the long hall below, usually commencing with the ringing chant of the Portuguese National Hymn. The old beggar then retired from the field in confusion. A few tawny Portuguese, with close-cropped, blue-black hair, would sometimes pause to listen as they passed through the almost deserted streets. The music awoke no chord of patriotism or pride in their breasts; Macao has out-lived even that. The strain ceased, and then the rich, lyrical throb of "Hail Columbia" would rise exultingly into the still blue air, while the stars and stripes hung motionless from the peak of the flag-staff, at the American Consulate below us. Though I heard our country's anthem every day, my heart beat more quick and warm under all that summer languor, and my thoughts would turn for a moment to the dear land on the other side of the world.

I prefer Macao to any other place in China, partly on account of the picturesque beauty of its position, and partly because it is less Chinese. It has a history which attaches it to the history of *our* race; it has human associations with which we can sympathize. The annals of the Ming and the Hang dynasties are no more to me (with the exception of the reign of that splendid invader, Kublai Khan,) than those of the Man in the Moon; but the memories of Camoëns, the Poet, and St. Francis Xavier, the Apostle, embalm Macao for ever in the eyes of the European race. It was the first beacon whence the light of Christianity and the liberalizing influences of commerce went forth into the dark places of the East. And now useless and worn out as it seems, with its commerce destroyed, its palaces vacant, its grandees beggared, and its importance as a foothold of civilization totally gone, there is a mournful charm in the silence of its grass-grown streets, and the memory of its former power and opulence still clothes it with a shadowy dignity. Here, at least, there are traces of Art and Taste, and all those monstrosities of Chinese *Un*-taste, which would make China a living purgatory to any one with a keen appreciation of the Beautiful, are thrust into the background, and do not spoil the harmony of the picture.

The Portuguese settlement of Macao comprises a ridgy peninsula about four miles long, attached to the southern end of a large Chinese island, by a narrow, sandy neck, across which a wall was thrown in the early days of the colony. The city is built in a dip of the hills, near the extremity of the peninsula, and to the east faces the Roads, the usual anchorage of foreign shipping. It has another face on the west, looking upon the Inner Harbor, a narrow strait shut in by lofty islands. Another channel, called the Typa, between two barren islands, about a mile and a half to the southward, is the usual anchorage of vessels during the typhoon season, on account of its sheltered situation. The view of the city from the Roads is very imposing, and with the island-mountains in the background, has been compared by many persons to that of Naples from the bay, but I could see scarcely a single point of resemblance. A crescent-shaped bay, nearly a mile in length, fronts the water, and behind the massive stone pier, or Praya, rises a row of stately buildings of a pale yellow or pink color. The foliage of tropical gardens peeps out behind them, and the ridge is crowned with the square-towered Cathedral and several churches. At the northern point is an Alameda, or public square, planted with trees, above which rises a fortress. Further to the north, on the top of a lofty hill, is the Fort of Guia or Del Monte, and a larger but somewhat dismantled fortification looms behind, on the middle ridge of the peninsula.

Even before landing, one notes the deserted aspect of the place. There are no crowds on the Praya; the houses have a decaying, mouldy appearance, and you listen in vain for that hum of life which floats about the centres of trade or industry. The solitary sentry at the foot of the Portuguese flag-staff seems to be dozing at his post. Now and then some Chinese porters pass, or four servants carrying a sedan chair with all the blinds down. During the summer, when most of the foreign merchants in Canton send their families there, on account of the temperate sea air, many of the spacious old mansions are inhabited, and servants with impudent faces lounge about the open gateways. Were it not for the scanty revenue which they derive from the lease of their ancestral palaces, many of the old Portuguese families would be entirely destitute. Indeed, it is already a mystery how some of them contrive to exist. Piece by piece the old plate, and diamond by diamond the old jewels are sold, while the parsimony of the household belies the appearance of wealth which still lingers about the massive buildings and the luxuriant gardens.

These fine old gardens are the greatest ornament of the city, hiding its dilapidation, and recalling, in the care and taste which they have not wholly outgrown, those which adorn the cities of Southern Spain. Although the winters are wet and cold, all the hardier varieties of tropical fruits thrive well, and even the mango, the papaya and the guava are found in the markets. On the garden-terraces, in the upper part of the city, whence you have a charming panorama of the island-studded gulf, the spiry cypress and the orange of Portugal mingle their foliage with the palm, the bamboo and the Indian banyan In August, the high walls which enclose them are festooned with enormous masses of the night-blooming cereus, whose milky blossoms, a foot in diameter, diffuse a sweet and powerful odor. Around the fountains the sacred lotus opens its sunny cup, tipped with as pure a rose as summer daybreak can show The *lagistræmia*, with its soft, crape-like racemes of white or crimson, and the burning scarlet of the pomegranate flower, star the deep green masses of foliage. Nature is always luxurious within the Tropics.

Two gates in the northern wall of the city lead to what is called the Campo—an open, cultivated tract of country separated by a bleak ridge from the sandy flat which divides the Portuguese territories from the Chinese. The Campo is traversed by an excellent road, uniting with a new one which has been cut along the face of the bluffs on the eastern side of the island. The two combined form an agreeable drive, and every evening towards sunset, all who possess or are rich enough to hire a horse or equipage, may be seen taking their way along the Praya to the Alameda, and thence striking out on the course of the Campo. This drive of three or four miles, with a gallop over the sands to the Chinese barrier, is a grateful release to the Canton merchant, and in comparison with the confinement of his hongs, the Campo appears as boundless and as free as an Illinois prairie. The fort of Guia, with a steep zigzag path leading up to its battlements, towers high over it, on the east on the opposite side the Chinese village of Wang-Hyà, lies embedded in bamboo and Indian fig-trees; over a level covered with rice-fields and vegetable gardens, stretches a wide blue arm of the bay, and the mountains of the western island lean away to the south, disclosing other channels and other islands beyond.

I paid a visit to Wang-Hyà (or in the Macao dialect, Mong-ha), which gives its name to the treaty concluded between the United States and China, under the auspices of our great mandarin Cushing (Coo-Shing, a genuine Chinese name), and the Commissioner Keying. The signing of this treaty and the festivities consequent thereupon, took place in the great temple of Wang-Hyà—a large building of gray granite, rather more simple and tasteful in its architecture than Chinese temples usually are. In fact, but for the enormous misshapen gods, glaring all over with vermillion and gilding, those massive courts and heavy, overhanging roofs, shaded by the broad arms of several giant Indian fig-trees, would afford a very pleasing picture. There is a Macao legend to the effect that, when Cushing went out in state to meet Keying, he was attended by the Portuguese band belonging to the Governor, and that the drum-major of the band made such an impression upon the Chinese authorities by his portly size, and the glitter of his full-dress uniform, that they imagined him to be the American mandarin, and wasted several profound salutations upon him before the mistake was discovered.

As for amusements in Macao, there were none except the daily stroll on the Praya and ride in the Campo, with an occasional dinner or dance. The Governor, Senhor Guimaraes, was an urbane and polished gentleman, and entertained frequently, and there were a few Portuguese families who still kept up something of the old state. The theatre, a reminiscence of the palmy days of Macao, had long been closed, but was again opened for a concert given by our band, who made Macao ring with such music as had not been heard for years. The bugle-players belonging to the Portuguese garrison are very fine, but the Governor's band would scarcely be tolerated any where else. By the Commodore's permission, our band performed on the Alameda every Thursday evening, and all Macao went there in the moonlight to look upon the sparkling bay, and drink, with thirsty ears, the sweet strains.

During my stay, the Chinese residents celebrated their great religious festival—a sort of All Soul's Day, or worship paid collectively to all the gods and saints in their mythology, their own ancestors included. It is a convenient way of lumping together a number of minor worships, and wiping out with one grand stroke the delinquencies of the year; and the essence of the Chinese religion not being love of God, but fear of the devil, they manage to propitiate their neglected Satans by a terrific thumping of tom-toms, and a fizzle and splutter of fireworks, which lasts three days. On the occasion, they constructed a large framework on the Praya, which was covered with muslins, silks, and spangled paper, so as to represent the shrine of a temple. It was about 15 feet high, by 30 in length, and hung with lamps of every quality and fashion, from Bohemian crystal to horn and mica. A variety of hideous divinities, with black or copper-colored faces, squatted on shrines or stood stiffly erect in niches; and in a recess at one end, three or four *noisi cians* made an infernal din with gongs, tom-toms and long hol low bamboos which emitted shrieks that made your nerves quiver. I doubt if the word "harmony" is to be found in the Chinese language. Not even the sense of a rhythm could be extracted from the dreadful discord, but each instrument of torture raved in its own way, regardless of the others. What must be the nature of those who take delight in such sounds?

The loveliest spot in Macao is the garden and grotto of Camoëns, and thither the stranger first turns his steps. During my first visit there, in March, it was the only thing I saw. The Susquehanna was to leave for Shanghai early in the morning, and as there was a chance that I might not return, I succeeded, with much difficulty, in making the swarthy landlord of the "National Hotel" comprehend what it was that I wanted to see. He called me before daybreak, and gave me an old Chinaman as guide to the place. We threaded a number of crooked streets in the dusk, passed the façade of an eminent Jesuit church, which was destroyed by fire, and at length reached a little grassy square on the hill, in the north-western corner of the city. By dint of knocking and calling, my guide aroused a sleepy servant, who opened a gate and admitted me into a trim parterre, redolent of rose and jessamine, and opening into a deep garden, wherein the shadows still lingered thick and dark under the trees. A large and stately mansion now occupies the site of the Franciscan Convent in which Camoëns lived. The property belongs to Count Salvi, who has offered it for sale, for the sum of $5,000, without finding a purchaser.

I took my way at random through the garden, seeking, in the gray morning twilight, for the grotto whose shelter gave birth to the "Lusiad." It was a wilderness of large trees made still more intricate in some places by a thick undergrowth, and the rank parasitic vines which clung from bough to bough. It followed the slope of the hill, terraced here and there, while the highest part was overhung by immense granite boulders, heaped one upon the other, till the topmost masses towered above the trees. I found an aviary with a dead tree in it, showing that birds had once been there; a fountain, dry and cracking to pieces; and finally, noticing a small chapel reared upon a rock in the thickest part of the wood, was led to the object of my search. The grotto is simply a natural portal formed by three great boulders of grey granite, within whose arch the poet found shade and coolness and privacy. It is not a cavern of Jeremiah, to feed austere thoughts and gloomy prophecies, but a grotto just too stern not to be Arcadian and idyllic. The portal is now closed at each end by an iron grating, and within it stands a bronze bust of the poet, elevated on a lofty pedestal, containing three stanzas from the Lusiad, in bronze letters. The dawn gradually brightened, as I stood beside the grating; the darkness under the trees faded into twilight, but the features of the poet were not discernible in the gloom which filled the recess. Fit monument to him, who turned into glory the shame of banishment and the sorrow of exile—who made the power and the injustice of the land that gave him birth alike immortal!

I frequently went there afterwards by daylight, but the *genus loci* was less distinct and impressive than in that silent morning hour. The Chevalier di Rienzi, a Frenchman who styles himself, "poete exilé," has had a tablet cut upon the rock beside the grotto, and a poem of his own in praise of Camoēns inscribed upon it. The poem is good, considering that it is French, and if the Chevalier di Rienzi had a name in literature, we might pardon, and even approve, his desire to couple it with the illustrious Camoëns. To me, who never heard of him before, the deed is presumptuous and profane; though a housand times less so than some French doggerel upon Camoëns written in the visitor's book. From the terrace on the western side of the garden there are lovely views of the inner harbor, especially towards sunset; and the "Casa Gardens," as they are called, are a frequent resort of the foreign residents at that hour.

My days passed away quietly and indolently enough, through the remainder of August. The thermometer ranged from 80° to 93° in the shade, and the sun, hanging directly in the zenith at noon, poured down a flood of white heat. Macao seemed wholly deserted at such times, notwithstanding its society was larger and more animated than usual. I began to make preparations for returning home, a course which was rendered necessary by my long absence. The fact of my having entered the service bound me for the entire cruise, but Commodore Perry, with his usual kindness, on learning that a prolonged absence would be a serious disadvantage to me, gave me leave to resign. I desired to return by way of San Francisco, but as no vessel was then up for that port, I changed my plans and took passage for New York in the clipper ship *Sea Serpent*, Captain Howland, which was announced to sail from Whampoa on the 9th of September.

I made a trip to Hong-Kong to draw some funds from the Oriental Bank, and had the satisfaction of receiving $347 for a letter of credit on London for $500. In returning I took a *sampan*, as the Chinese boats are called, and made the run to

Macao in five hours and a half, at the risk of falling into the hands of the pirates who infest the Lemma and Lin-tin Islands I also went up to Cumsingmoon, in the fast boat of old Eyòk, who supplied the squadron with fresh provisions, and passed another night on board the dear old Susquehanna. I began to ove the very timbers of the staunch frigate that had been my home, more or less, for six months, and I felt a keen pang on moving away from her huge black hull and the gallant souls within it. May prosperous breezes attend her and them, wherever they sail!

CHAPTER XL.

SCENES IN AND AROUND CANTON.

Increase of the Squadron—Disposition of the Vessels—Passage to Canton—First Visit of the City—The Foreign Factories—Old and New China Streets—Talking "Pigeon English"—The Great Temple of Honan—Ceremonies of the Priests—Sacred Books and Pigs—The Lotus Blossom—Dwellings of the Priests—A Retired Abbot—Opium Smoking in China—The Opium-Pipe—Flavor and Fascination of the Drug—Its Effects—A Walk around Canton—The Walls—Entering the City—Foreign Devils—A Tea-House—Beyond the Suburbs—A Chinese Panorama—The Feast of Lanterns—Dr. Parker's Hospital—The Eve of Departure.

By the end of August, all the vessels of the squadron had arrived in China, with the exception of the store-ship *Lexington.* The *Macedonian*, *Vandalia* and *Southampton* were sent to the anchorage at Cumsingmoon, whither the *Powhatan*, which returned to Hong-Kong on the 25th, also proceeded. She was detained eight days at Loo-Choo, in order to remedy a slight defect in one of her engines. The store-ship *Supply*, arrived at Hong-Kong on the 27th, having touched at Amoy on her way from Loo-Choo. Canton was in a very unsettled state, and the foreign merchants anticipated trouble, on account of the spread of the rebellion. All the American firms addressed a letter to Commodore Perry, begging that a national vessel might be sent up to the Macao Passage, within a mile and a half of the factories. The Supply was therefore ordered up the river, as all the other vessels of the squadron drew too much water to pass the bar. Our great steam frigates certainly contributed to our success in Japan, but they are nearly useless for service in the Chinese waters.

I took the anchor from my cap on the 5th of September after four months' service, and in the evening of the same day bade adieu to my messmates and embarked on board the steamer for Canton. Mr. Contee, the Flag-Lieutenant of the Squadron, who had procured leave of absence on account of ill-health and had also taken passage on the Sea Serpent, accompanied me It was after sunset when we left, and my last glimpse of Macao was the dark silhouette of its hills against the fading sky. We had an indistinct night-view of the Bogue Forts, at the Bocca Tigris, or mouth of the Whampoa River, after which I sought a couch on one of the hard benches in the cabin, but failed to extract much repose from it.

The steamer did not reach her destination until daybreak the next morning. Consequently, whatever there may be of the picturesque or striking in the approach to Canton, was lost to me. As the rapid dawn of the South brightened into sunrise, I found that we were anchored in the middle of the stream between the foreign Factories and the famous temple of Honan. The Pearl River, at this place, is not more than a quarter of a mile wide, and thickly studded with junks, flower-boats and those crowded hulks which contain the "floating population"—an important item in the census of the city. What little can be seen of the native part of Canton from this point, is low and mean, unrelieved by a single pagoda. The foreign Factories on the contrary, inclosing a parallelogram of three or four acres, which extends down to the river, are substantial blocks of buildings, four stories in height. The open space has been turned into a Botanical Garden, which is kept in excellent order, as it affords the residents their only chance for agreeable exercise, except that of boating on the river. In this garden four lofty flag-staffs, planted at regular intervals, display the colors of America, France, England and Denmark, and in the centre a neat Gothic Chapel stands on the site of the old Hog-Lane, renowned during the troubles of 1841. The factories are divided into different "hongs"—English, American, Danish, &c.—but the foreign community is crowded into narrow bounds, hemmed in on all sides by the jealousy of the native authorities, and a five minutes' walk will embrace its utmost limits.

Adjacent to the factories are the streets occupied by the Chinese "hong merchants," whose dealings are almost wholly with foreigners, and the markets and shops of mechanics, which depend on foreign custom. The most noted thoroughfares are Old and New China-streets, and Looking-Glass and Spectacle-streets, which in their quaint forms and brilliant coloring, their gay, bustling and lively aspect, resemble the bazaars of Oriental cities. They are narrow, the houses two stories in height, with projecting roofs, the fronts of a dark blue or green color, with a mixture of bright red, and still further relieved by the gilded hieroglyphics which cover the vertical swinging signs. In Old and New China-streets there are also English signs which inform you that A-Kow or Hu-ping deals in silks, or porcelain, or lacquered ware, or ivory, or mother-of-pearl, or sandal-wood, or silver. The predominant talent of the Chinese is their faculty of imitation, and since their intercourse with foreigners has become less restricted, they have been obliged to abandon many of their former grotesque models and accept others more consonant with a civilized taste. This is shown in the patterns of their silks, the form and style of their articles in silver and ivory, and their furniture. The display in their shops is tempting to a stranger, but purchases were ruinous at a crisis, when money commanded fifty per cent. premium at Canton, and seventy-five per cent. at Shanghai.

Whoever first invented the "pigeon English," as it is called —the jargon used by foreigners in their intercourse with Chinese—deserves an immortality of ridicule. The jargon has now become so fixed, that it will take several generations to eradicate it. The Chinaman requires as much practice to learn it as he would to learn correct English, while the Englishman, in his turn, must pick it up as he would a new language. Fancy, for instance, a man going into one of the silverware shops in New China-street, and saying, "My wantye two piece snuff-box: can secure?" when his meaning is simply—"I want two snuff-boxes: can you get them?" To which A-Wing gravely answers: "Can secure." Or, another declaring: "My no savey that pigeon"—which signifies in English: "I don't understand the business." If you make inquiries at a hotel, you must ask: "What man have got top-side?" (who are up stairs?) and the Chinese servant will make answer: "Two piece captain, one piece joss-man, have got." (There are two captains and a clergyman.) It was some time before I could bring myself to make use of this absurd and barbarous lingo, and it was always very unpleasant to hear it spoken by a lady.

As far as sight-seeing is concerned, Canton has very little to offer the traveller, and I was so thoroughly surfeited with China that I made no effort to see more than the most prominent objects. Mr. Wells Williams and the Rev. Mr. Bonney were kind enough to accompany me through the Temple of Honan, on the opposite side of the river. This is a place of great sanctity, embracing within its bounds a well-endowed college of Boodhist priests. There are a number of temples, or rather shrines of the gods, standing within enclosed courts, which are shaded by large and venerable trees. We first passed through a portal, placed in advance, like the pylon of an Egyptian temple, with a colossal figure on each side, of the watchers or guardians of the edifice. With their distended abdomens, copper faces and fierce black eyeballs, they might very well have passed for Gog and Magog. The temples were massive square structures, with peaked roofs, containing colossal gilded statues of various divinities, most of whom were seated cross-legged, with their hands on their stomachs and a grin of ineffable good-humor on their faces. They were no doubt represented as having dined well, and therefore the more easily to be propitiated. We reached the main temple in time to witness the rites of the Boodhist priests. Numerous candles and "joss-sticks" of sandal-wood were burning at the feet of the vast statues, and the shaven-headed priests, thirty or forty in number, walked solemnly in a circle around the open space before them, chanting their hymns. The character of the chants was very similar to some of those used in the Roman Catholic service, and there were other features in the ceremonies of the priests which showed the same resemblance. I believe this fact has been noticed by other travellers.

After the chanting was concluded, the priests came out in single file and passed into the large building which they inhabited in common. Some of them paused to speak with Mr

Bonney, who was known to them, and whom they seemed to regard without the least animosity, notwithstanding his missionary character. We then entered a labyrinth of smaller buildings, in one of which was a printing establishment, where the legends of Boodhism were multiplied in great quantities. Many of the books were illustrated with curious wood-cuts. A little further, we came upon the stable of the sacred hogs, and were allowed a look at the venerated animals. Alas! like many humans, their swinish nature was only increased and intensified by their exalted station. Very slothful and greedy were they.

The temple, without its various attendant edifices, courts and gardens, covers an area of forty-two acres. The garden, however, is a mere vegetable patch, with a pond of the sacred lotus in the midst. Several of these superb plants were in bloom, and we bribed a laborer to wade out into the slimy pool and procure us a few blossoms. The slender stem, five feet in length, upholds a broad cup, as elegant in form as the Warwick Vase, and about eight inches in diameter, when fully expanded. The leaves have the velvety whiteness of alabaster, veined with delicate pencillings of the purest rose-color, and in the centre lies the fruit, an inverted cone of pale green, surrounded with a fringe of golden anthers. The perfume has that fresh and healthy sweetness which never cloys the sense. The Rose may be a queen among flowers, but the Lotus, sublime in its purity, grace and exquisite beauty, is a goddess. How gorgeous a show must its blossoms make, on the White Nile, where, at the first ray of sunrise, tens of thousands flash open all at once, along leagues of shore!

Beyond the pool was a little copse, in which stood a small

building, used in the incremation of the dead priests. It was a simple chamber, with a small entrance, and vents for the escape of the smoke. The body is placed on a funeral pile, which is replenished until the flesh is roasted into cinders and the bones calcined into dust. On our way back to the river, we passed through the habitation of the priests, taking a look at their kitchens and refectories. A number of the younger brethren gathered around us, lusting strongly after the carnal gratification of cigars, and my whole stock was soon divided among them. Mr. Bonney took me to visit a former abbot, a man of much learning, who was then living in a quiet way, on a pension. He received us with much cordiality, and showed us his bachelor establishment of three rooms and a little garden, which were kept in great neatness and order. He was about sixty years of age, and his pale face, calm eye and high, retreating brow, spoke of a serene and studious life. In an inner chamber, however, I noticed one of those couches which are used by the opium-smokers, and the faint, subtle odor of the drug still hung about the furniture and the walls.

In spite of the penalties attached to it by Chinese law, the smoking of opium is scarcely a concealed practice at present. I have seen it carried on in open shops in Shanghai, where there are some streets which are never free from the sickening smell. It had always been my intention to make a trial of the practice, in order to learn its effects by personal experience, and being now on the eve of leaving China, I applied to a gentleman residing in Canton, to put me in the way of enjoying a pipe or two. He was well acquainted with a Chinaman who was addicted to the practice, and by an agreement with him, took me to his house one evening. We were ushered into a long room, with a divan, or platform about three feet high, at the further end. Several Chinamen were in the room, and one, stretched out on the platform, was preparing his pipe at a lamp. The host invited me to stretch myself opposite to him, and place my head upon one of those cane head-stools which serve the Chinese in lieu of pillows.

The opium-pipe is a bamboo stick, about two feet long, having a small drum inserted near the end, with an aperture in its centre. A piece of opium, about twice the size of a pin's head, is taken up on a slender wire and held in the flame of the lamp until it boils or bubbles up, when it is rolled into a cylindrical shape on the drum, by the aid of the wire. It loses its dark color by the heating and becomes pale and soft. Having been sufficiently rolled, it is placed over the aperture, and the wire, after being thrust through its centre, to allow the air to pass into the pipe, is withdrawn. The pipe is then held to the flame, and as the opium burns, its fumes are drawn into the lungs by a strong and long-continued inspiration. In about half a minute the portion is exhausted, and the smoker is ready for a second pipe.

To my surprise I found the taste of the drug as delicious as its smell is disagreeable. It leaves a sweet, rich flavor, like the finest liquorice, upon the palate, and the gentle stimulus it communicates to the blood in the lungs, fills the whole body with a sensation of warmth and strength. The fumes of the opium are no more irritating to the windpipe or bronchial tubes, than common air, while they seem imbued with a rich ness of vitality far beyond our diluted oxygen. I had supposed that opium was smoked entirely for the purpose of mental exhilaration, and that to the smokers, as to many who intoxicate themselves with ardent spirits, there was no sensual gratification in the mere taste of the article. The reverse is undoubtedly the truth, and the practice, therefore, is doubly dangerous. Its victim becomes hopelessly involved in its fascinating illusions, and an awful death, such as I had witnessed not long before, is sure, sooner or later, to overtake him who indulges to excess. I have a pretty strong confidence in my own powers of resistance, but do not desire to make the experiment a second time.

Beyond the feeling of warmth, vigor and increased vitality, softened by a happy consciousness of repose, there was no effect, until after finishing the sixth pipe. My spirits then became joyously excited, with a constant disposition to laugh; brilliant colors floated before my eyes, but in a confused and cloudy way, sometimes converging into spots like the eyes in a peacock's tail, but oftenest melting into and through each other, like the hues of changeable silk. Had the physical excitement been greater, they would have taken form and substance, but after smoking *nine* pipes I desisted, through fear of subjecting myself to some unpleasant after-effect. Our Chinese host informed me that he was obliged to take twenty pipes, in order to elevate his mind to the pitch of perfect happiness. I went home feeling rather giddy, and became so drowsy, with slight qualms at the stomach, that I went to bed at an early hour. I had made an arrangement to walk around the walls of Canton the next morning, with Mr. Bonney, and felt some doubt as to whether I should be able to undertake it; but, after a deep and refreshing sleep, I arose at sunrise, feeling stronger and brighter than I had done for weeks past.

The walls of Canton are about eight miles in circuit

This is but a limited extent for a city, which contains upwards of a million of inhabitants, and more than half the population probably live without the walls, on the side next the river In those dark, narrow, and crooked streets which lie behind he factories, the swarm of human beings is uninterrupted from the earliest dawn until late in the night. We set out at an hour when few of the Europeans were stirring, and the streets were already so crowded that it was difficult to avoid contact with the porters and water-carriers—a contact to be shunned at all hazards. Though there was less noisome filth than in the streets of Shanghai, more senses than one were offended, and I felt much relieved when, after a walk of more than two miles, we came into a less thickly settled quarter. A Chinese city is the greatest of all abominations, and one ceases to wonder at the physical deformity, or the monstrous forms of licentiousness, which are to be found among the lower classes of the natives, when he has seen the manner in which they live.

Our road in many places skirted the wall, which is of brick, about twenty-five feet high, and with a machicolated parapet. At the angles there is sometimes a rude square bastion, surmounted by an ornamental edifice—probably a pleasure-house belonging to gardens within. We passed several gates, into all of which I looked, but could not see that the streets within differed in the least from those without. Near the south-eastern corner Mr. Bonney entered suddenly, I following, and we passed across the angle and out at another gate, withou any one attempting to hinder us. While we were in the neighborhood of the factories, we were allowed to pursue our way unnoticed, but in the straggling suburbs on the eastern side, we were frequently hailed with the insulting cry of "*Fan-*

kwei!" (Foreign Devil!) One old man, who was at work in his shop, made an exclamation as we passed, which Mr. Bonney translated thus: "I lifted up my eyes, and behold! two devils suddenly appeared before me!" One of these devils however belied the character given him, by carrying with him a bundle of Christian tracts, which he distributed with a liberal hand, every one, old or young, male or female, accepting them with great willingness. They are *too* willing in fact. The carelessness with which they take every thing that is offered them shows a lack of respect for their own faith, an absence of that inherent devotional spirit, which alone can serve as the groundwork of their Christianization.

At a gate near the north-eastern corner, we stopped at a tea-house to take some refreshment. A company of Chinese of the middle class in the white garb of mourning, were waiting there to attend the funeral of some friend. The host brought us steaming cups of tea or rather tea-stew, very strong and invigorating, and a crisp sort of cake seasoned with pork and sugar. Some of the Chinese entered into conversation with Mr. Bonney, in a good-humored friendly way, but one young dandy stretched himself upon the bench beside our table, and indulged in some contemptuous remarks on foreigners. I was well satisfied to be ignorant of the language, for his manner was so insolent, that I could not have replied with the same mildness and prudence as my companion.

The suburbs now ceased, and the open cultivated country reached to the foot of the city wall. To the east extended a fertile plain, dotted with villages, as far as the White Cloud Hills, whose barren summits arose in the distance. We kept on, up a little valley to some springs under a hill on the northern side of the city, which supply the only good water to be had. They gush up, strong and abundant, from the bottom of the dell, which was crowded with water-carriers, going to and from the gates. The hill is crowned with a fort which completely commands the city. It was taken without difficulty by Lord Gough, during the English war, and every preparation was made to open a bombardment, when the ransom of $5,000,000, tendered by the Chinese merchants, was offered and accepted. There is now a small garrison within it, but the sentinel who stood at the entrance, hastily retreated within the walls as we approached, and did not make his appearance again until after we had left.

The view from the fort is very fine, taking in all of Canton, the course of the Pearl River from Whampoa to the mountainous region in the west, the White Cloud Hills, and the rich delta of the river, stretching away to the Bocca Tigris. The mountains which surround this wide landscape are bleak and barren, and contrast strongly with the garden-like beauty of the plain. The broad arms of the river, dotted with boats and junks; the many villages, half-hidden among groves of fruit trees; the lofty pagodas that rise here and there from the banks; and the crowded city itself directly under the eye—the central point which unites the interest of all these scattered objects—combine to form a panorama unique but thoroughly Chinese in its character, and affording as good a type of Chinese scenery as is readily accessible to foreigners. The northern part of Canton rests upon the side of a hill, whose summit is crowned by a great square red temple four stories in height. A slender pagoda, towards the river, is the only other prominent architectural object. About one third of the space with the walls is taken up with gardens. We did not remain long upon the hill, which is in bad repute, on account of the robberies committed in its vicinity. After descending to a little village, and passing several wet fields of lotus and the taro plant, we came again to the filth and crowds of the outer city, and finally reached our starting-point, after an absence of three hours.

The Feast of Lanterns (as it is called, though incorrectly by foreigners) was celebrated during my visit, but with much less splendor than usual, on account of the disturbed state of society. The flower-boats on the river were all ablaze with lamps, and the shops in the principal streets were gaily illuminated. There were also "sing-songs" (theatrical performances), discordant instruments of noise, and other sources of Chinese pleasure, but the whole display was irregular, barbaric, and utterly devoid of grand effect. When I called to mind the fiery mosques of Constantinople, and the cannon thunders of the Night of Predestination, the Feast of Lanterns seemed a farce in comparison.

I was much interested in a visit to Dr. Parker's Chinese Hospital. Some idea of the good accomplished by this institution may be gathered from the fact, that since its establishment more than forty-nine thousand persons have been admitted. Dr. Parker himself is a very accomplished surgeon; his gallery of portraits exhibiting the tumors which he has removed, and the collection of stones which illustrates his skill in lithotomy, would be treasures to the Museum of a Medical College. His operations in lithotomy, especially, have been remarkably successful, as he has lost but *four* out of, I believe, thirty-two patients.

While in Canton I enjoyed the hospitality of Mr. Gideon

Nye, Jr., one of the prominent American merchants, who is well known at home through his taste for Art. My stay was very pleasant and interesting, and I could have agreeably prolonged it; but I was not sorry when my last night on Chinese soil arrived. The reader may have rightly conjectured that I am not partial to China, but this much I must admit: it is the very best country in the world—*to leave.*

CHAPTER XLI.

THE INDIAN ISLES.

Farewell to China—Whampoa—A Musical Good-Bye—The Bogue Forts—The Last Link—The China Sea—Life on the Sea Serpent—The Straits of Mindoro—Picturesque Islands—Calm Sailing—Moonlight in the Tropics—"Summer Isles of Eden"—The Sooloo Sea—The Cagayanes Islands—Straits of Basilan—Mindanao—A Native Proa—The Sea of Celebes—Entering the Straits of Macassar—Crossing the Equator—Off Celebes—Lazy Life—The Java Sea—Passing the Thousand Islands—Approach to the Straits of Sunda.

On the morning of the 9th of September we left Canton in the Macao steamer, which had been chartered to tow the Sea Serpent out to sea. We went swiftly down the crowded stream, passing the Factories, the temple of Ho-nan, and the floating houses of the aquatic Cantonese, and soon reached the long stretch of green paddy-fields extending to Whampoa. The day was shady, but with a soft, cool, clear atmosphere, which mellowed and deepened the rich colors of the landscape. The White Cloud Hills rose high over the undulating region between, which, with its groves, villages and tall pagodas, refreshed the eye, but took not the least hold on the heart. I found myself admiring its beauty with a cold, passionless appreciation, unconnected with the slightest regret at leaving it, or the least wish to behold it again. There may be scenes in China fair to look upon, but they are ennobled by no lofty human interest, lighted by no gleam of poetry or art.

Near the mouth of Lob Creek we passed a tall pagoda, and another within a mile or two of Whampoa, crowning the top of a verdant knoll. The latter was built of dark-red stone, and with the ivy and wild shrubs waving from the horned roofs of its nine stories, was really a picturesque object. The shipping of Whampoa was now visible, and in less than half an hour we lay alongside of the good clipper which was thenceforth to be our ocean home. Whampoa is a long, scattering Chinese town, on the southern bank of the river. The foreign vessels anchored in the reach, for a distance of more than a mile, give the place a lively air, and the low, conical hills which rise from the shore, crowned here and there with Chinese buildings, relieve the tameness of the swampy soil on which the town is built. We were obliged to wait for the flood-tide, which detained us two hours.

The anchor was cheerily lifted at last, and we got under way for New York. In going down the river we had a fair view of all the vessels of war anchored in Blenheim Reach, which was only half a mile distant, on our right. The Mississippi lay nearest to us, and as we drew near the opening of the reach one of her boats appeared, with the band on board, floating side by side with us, while they played our stirring national airs. It was a parting compliment from Capt. Lee to Lieut. Contee. The Sea Serpent's crew gathered on the forecastle, gave three hearty cheers, which the Mississippi's men answered with a will, standing up in the boat. This was our last glimpse of naval life, and a fitting farewell to the service. I looked in vain for the Susquehanna, which was expected from Cumsing moun, but she had not arrived. I would have given much for another sight of her big hull and familiar spars; and, better still, for a hail from some of her jolly men.

The river now became broader and frequently expanded on either side into great arms, some of which extended for many miles into the country. We passed the first bar, which was created by the Chinese sinking junks to prevent the English from reaching Canton. A high hill on the southern shore, near the second bar, which we reached about 5 P. M., is crowned with a pagoda 150 feet high, which is visible at a great distance. Beyond this, the river again expands, to be finally contracted into a narrow pass, at the Bocca Tigris, which we fortunately reached before dusk. It is a fine, bold gateway formed by two mountainous islands, which leave a passage of about half a mile between them. There are several Chinese batteries on either hand, but they are more formidable in appearance than in reality.

By the time we had passed the Bogue, it was dark. The tide was now in our favor, and we stood away towards Lintin. We had a large number of friends, including Messrs. Nye and Tuckerman of Canton, at dinner in the cabin, but about 10 P M. they all bade us good-bye and returned aboard the steamer. We were cast off a little after midnight, and taking a north-east wind ran down past the Ladrones at the rate of ten knots an hour. When I went on deck in the morning, China was no longer visible. The weather was dull and rainy, but we continued to make good progress. On the afternoon of the 12th, by which time we had made 300 miles, a violent squall came on, tearing our maintop-gallant sail and jib into ribbons. Heavy showers of rain succeeded, and during the night the wind gradually settled into the regular south-west monsoon. By noon the following day, we were in Lat. 14° 54′ N.—consequently south of the Paracel Reefs, and beyond the latitude of violent typhoons. As the wind still blew steadily from the south-west, Captain Howland determined to change his course and make for the Straits of Mindoro, Basilan and Macassar, hoping to get the south-east trade wind in the Java Sea, and thus make a better run to Angier than by slowly beating down the China Sea.

I found the Sea Serpent an excellent sea-boat, in every respect. She behaved admirably on a wind, slipping through the water so softly that we would not have suspected the speed she made. Although so sharp in the bows, she was very dry, scarcely a spray flying over the forecastle. In addition to Lieut. Contee and myself, there was but one other passenger, Mr. Parkman of Boston. Capt. Howland was accompanied by his wife and child. The officers were intelligent and obliging, and our party, though small, was large enough to be agreeable. We were all well satisfied with the prospect of a cruise among the Indian Isles, and therefore welcomed the Captain's decision.

At sunset, on the 14th, we made land ahead, at a considerable distance. As the passage required careful navigation, on account of its abundant reefs, we stood off and on until the next morning. Passing the North and North-west Rocks, the mountainous island of Busvagon, or Camelianes, opened to the south and east, its lofty hills, and deep, picturesque valleys clothed in eternal green. The rocky islets which bristled between us and its shores exhibited the most striking peculiarities of form and structure. Some shot upwards like needless or obelisks from the dark-blue sea; others rose in heavy masses, like the turrets or bastions of a fortress, crowned with tufts of shrubbery. The rock of which they were formed was of a dark slate color, in vertical strata, which appeared to have been violently broken off at the top, bearing a strong resemblance to columnar basalt.

Busvagon stretched along, point beyond point, for a distance of forty or fifty miles. The land rose with a long, gentle slope from the beaches of white sand, and in the distance stood the vapory peaks of high mountains. We sailed slowly along the outer edge of the islets, to which the larger island made a warm, rich background. The air was deliciously mild and pure, the sea smooth as glass, and the sky as fair as if it had never been darkened by a storm. Except the occasional gambols of the bonitas, or the sparkle of a flying-fish as he leaped into the sun, there was no sign of life on these beautiful waters.

Towards noon the gentle south-east breeze died away; and we lay with motionless sails upon the gleaming sea. The sun hung over the mast-head and poured down a warm tropical languor, which seemed to melt the very marrow in one's bones. For four hours we lay becalmed, when a light ripple stole along from the horizon, and we saw the footsteps of the welcome breeze long before we felt it. Gradually increasing, it bore us smoothly and noiselessly away from Busvagon and the rocky towers and obelisks, and at sunset we saw the phantomlike hills of the southern point of the island of Mindoro, forty miles distant. The night was filled with the glory of the full moon —a golden tropical radiance, nearly as lustrous, and far more soft and balmy, than the light of day—a mystic, enamored bridal of the sea and sky. The breeze was so gentle as to be felt, and no more; the ship slid as silently through the water as if her keel were muffled in silk; and the sense of repose in motion was so sweet, so grateful to my travel-wearied senses, that I remained on deck until midnight, steeped in a bath of pure indolent happiness.

Our voyage the next day was still more delightful. From dawn until dark we went slowly loitering past the lovely islands that gem those remote seas, until the last of them sank astern in the flush of sunset. Nothing can be more beautiful than their cones of never-fading verdure, draped to the very edge of the waves, except where some retreating cove shows its beach of snow-white sand. On the larger ones are woody valleys, folded between the hills, and opening upon long slopes, overgrown with the cocoa-palm, the mango, and many a strange and beautiful tree of the tropics. The light, lazy clouds, suffused with a crimson flush of heat, that floated slowly through the upper heavens, cast shifting shadows upon the masses of foliage, and deepened, here and there, the dark-purple hue of the sea. Retreating behind one another until they grew dim and soft as clouds on the horizon, and girdled by the most tranquil of oceans, these islands were real embodiments of the joyous fancy of Tennyson, in his dream of the Indies, in "Locksley Hall." Here, although the trader comes, and the flags of the nations of far continents sometimes droop in the motionless air—here are still the heavy-blossomed bowers and the heavy-fruited trees, the summer isles of Eden in their purple spheres of sea. The breeze fell nearly to a calm at noonday, but our vessel still moved noiselessly southward, and island after island faded from green to violet, and from violet to the dim, pale blue that finally blends with the air.

The next day was most taken up with calms. The captain

and mates spent much of their time in shifting the sails so as to get the most of the faint wind-flaws that reached us, watching for distant ripple-lines on the ocean, or whistling over the rail. In the afternoon land was descried ahead—the Cagayanes Islands, a little group in the middle of the Sooloo Sea. We passed between them about four o'clock, and had a fair view on either hand. The shores are smooth walls of perpendicular rock, about a hundred feet in height, and almost completely hidden under a curtain of rich vegetation. Here and there the rock falls away, leaving little beaches of sand, behind which rise thick forests of cocoa or palm. I could distinguish with the glass half a dozen bamboo huts on the shore. A few boats were drawn up on the beach. The islands looked so lovely as we passed them, in the soft lustre of sunset, that I longed for a day of calm, to go ashore where so few Europeans have ever set foot, and have a glance at the primitive barbarism of the natives. The sea still remained as smooth as a mountain lake. We saw great quantities of drift-wood, upon which boobies and cormorants perched in companies of two and three, and watched for fish as they drifted lazily along. In the neighborhood of the islands we frequently saw striped snakes, four or five feet in length.

The lofty coast of Mindanao, one of the largest of the Philippine Islands, was visible at sunrise, on the 19th. Before long Basilan appeared in the south-east, and by noon we were in the mouth of the strait. The observation gave Lat. 7° 3′ N., Long. 121° E. Two vessels were descried ahead, a ship and a brig, both lying close in to Mindanao, and apparently becalmed. In fact, we could easily trace a belt of calm water near the shore, caused by the high hills of the island, which prevented the southern breeze from "blowing home."

Four or five small islands—the commencement of the Sooloo Archipelago—lie to the westward of Basilan. The strait is from six to eight miles wide at its narrowest part, and tolerably free from dangerous points. To the north, the hills of Mindanao, completely mantled with forests, rise grandly to the height of near two thousand feet. The shore presents an almost impenetrable array of cocoa palms. There were two or three cleared spaces on the hills, and as we entered further into the strait, we could see with the glass not only some native huts, but the houses of Spanish residents on the shore. Still further, at the head of a little bight, and protected by a level island of palms, we saw the Spanish settlement of Samboangan. There were several large two-story houses, and a white chapel, before which lay half a dozen small craft at anchor. A native proa put out from the shore, some distance ahead of us, and we at first thought she was making for us with a load of fruit. As she came nearer she hoisted a huge yellow flag, with a red ornamental border, and some large red characters in Chinese. There were six persons on board, and he who appeared to be the leader wore a yellow robe. The boat had an outrigger on each side, and was propelled by paddles and a light canvas sail. She came near us, but to our disappointment dropped astern and passed over to Basilan.

The latter island is remarkably picturesque in its appearance, its long, wavy slopes of foliage shooting into tall conical peaks. In passing through the strait, these piles of eternal vegetation on either hand have an enchanting effect. I took sketches of both islands, which preserved their outlines, but could not give the least idea of their richness and beauty. We had a light westerly wind, with the tide in our favor, and just as the moon arose like a globe of gold, passed the eastern mouth of the strait and entered the Sea of Celebes.

We now experienced a succession of calms and baffling winds for five days, as we stood south by west across the Sea of Celebes, making for the Straits of Macassar. There was an occasional squall of an hour or two, which gave us a "slant" in the right direction. The wind at last shifted, so that we were able to run upon our course close-hauled, and on the afternoon of the 25th we caught a distant and misty view of the Haring Islands. The next morning at sunrise, we saw the lofty headland of Point Kaneoongan, in Borneo, at the western entrance of the straits. Cape Donda, in Celebes, thirty miles distant, appeared for a short time, but was soon hidden by showers. On the 27th, at noon, we were in 0° 5′ S., having crossed the Equator about 11 A. M., and thenceforth, for four days, we slowly loitered along through the Straits of Macassar, with light, variable winds, and seasons of dead, sultry calm. The mercury stood at 88° in the coolest part of the ship. The sea was as smooth as a mirror, and as glossy and oily in its dark-blue gleam, as if the neighboring shores of Macassar had poured upon it libations of their far-famed unguent. Occasionally we saw the shores of Celebes, but so distant and dim that it was rather like a dream of land than land itself. We walked the deck languidly, morning and evening, sat under the the awning by day, alternately dozing and smoking and reading, watched the drift-wood floating by—mangrove logs, with companies of sea-fowl making their fishing excursions—ate for occupation and slept with difficulty: and thus the days passed.

On the 2d of October a light south wind reached us, and we left the dim, far-off headlands of Celebes—the land of sandal-wood groves and birds of Paradise. We made the twin rocks called "The Brothers," off the southern point of Borneo, and about noon passed between the islands of Moresses and Little Pulo Laut. The latter are noble piles of verdure, rising a thousand feet from the water, in long undulating outlines. The Java Sea is a beautiful piece of water, comparatively free from reefs and shoals, and rarely exceeding forty fathoms in depth, so that vessels may anchor in any part of it. Its surface is as smooth as a lake, and even when making eight or nine knots, there was scarcely any perceptible motion in the vessel. The temperature was delicious, and the south wind so bland, sweet and elastic, after the sultry, surcharged atmosphere of Macassar Straits, that the change was perceptible in the temper and spirits of all on board.

We had light but favorable winds, and for four days more stood across the Java Sea, averaging about 100 miles a day. The water was alive with snakes and flying-fish. Passing the Lubeck Islands and Carimon Java, we approached so near the Javanese shores that on the evening of the 6th the delicious land-breeze came off to us, bringing an odor of moist earth and vegetable exhalations. We expected to have a glimpse of Batavia, but made considerable northing, so that we lost sight of the low Java coast before morning. At noon we made the Thousand Islands, and as they have been but very imperfectly explored, we were obliged to go completely to the northward of them, instead of taking one of the numerous channels be tween. They are small and low, but thickly covered with trees, among which the cocoa-palm predominates. I counted thirty-three islands within a sweep of a hundred degrees The wind being dead ahead, we stood on the northern tack until we made the North Watcher, and then fetched a S. by E. course, the current setting us to windward. The same evening, however, the wind changed, and before I turned into my berth, we were thirty miles off Angier Point, the last gateway intervening between us and the Indian Ocean. We had been twenty-eight days in making the voyage from Whampoa—a distance, as we sailed, of 2,613 miles.

CHAPTER XLII.

AROUND THE CAPE.

Entering the Straits of Sunda—Malay Boats—The Mangosteen—Bargaining with the Natives—Scenery of the Straits—Angier—Passing the Straits—Death on Board—The Indian Ocean—A Submarine Earthquake—A Tropical Sunset—A Fatal Escape—The Trade Wind—Mozambique Channel—The Coast of Africa—Doubling the Cape—Southern Constellations—Distant View of Table Mountain—On the Atlantic—The Trades again—Restoration—A Slaver.

I AROSE at sunrise on the morning of the 8th of October, in time to see the Sea Serpent enter the Straits of Sunda. On our left, five or six miles distant, arose the lofty headland of Point St. Nicholas; in front was the rock called "The Cap," and the island of "'Thwart-the-Way," while the mountains of Sumatra were barely visible far to the west. We were scarcely abreast of the headland when two native *prahus*, or boats, were seen coming off to us, the boatmen laboring at their sweeps with a sharp, quick cry, peculiar to semi-barbarous people. One of the boats was soon alongside, with a cargo of yams, plantains and fowls, with such fancy articles as shells, monkeys, parroquets and Java sparrows. The captain and crew were Malays, and nearly all spoke English more or less fluently The former had an account-book, showing his deal ings with ships, and a printed register from the Dutch Govern ment, containing notices of the vessels called upon in the straits. We were gratified to find that we had not been beaten, the shortest passage from Whampoa, previous to our own, being hirty days.

The second boat soon arrived, and between the two Capt. Howland managed to procure about fifteen cwt. of yams, with abundant supplies of potatoes, fowls, and paddy. The fruits they brought off were plantains, cocoa-nuts, ripe and green, and a few *mangosteens*, which were then going out of season. The latter were mostly rotten, but the few fresh ones which we picked out were enough to convince me that its fame as the most exquisite of all fruits had not been overrated. The very look of the snow-white pulp, softly imbedded in its thick, juicy, crimson husk, is refreshing; and its melting coolness and sweetness, relieved by the faintest mixture of a delicious acid flavor, makes it the very nectar and ambrosia of the vegetable world. Certainly no other fruit is comparable to it in flavor and lusciousness.

While the boat went back to Angier for fresh supplies of paddy and other necessaries—an arrangement which deprived us of all chance of landing there—we slowly drifted down the straits with the tide, past Cap Rock and towards 'Thwart-the-Way. I was charmed with the beauty of the Javanese shore. Low hills, completely covered with foliage, rose from the water, with ascending upland slopes beyond, and groups of lofty moun tains in the background. In the almost interminable wealth of tropical vegetation which covered the land, the feathery cocoa-palm and the massive foliage of the banyan could be plainly recognized. Passing the picturesque headlands and leafy wildernesses of "'Thwart-the-Way," we lay to off Angier, waiting for the boat. We were nearly two miles from shore, but the scattered Malay village, the big banyan-tree, the Dutch fort, and the light-house, with its tiled roof, were all distinctly visible. The lofty promontory of Rajah Bassa, on the Sumatra side, loomed in the distance. The wind was blowing fresh from the south, and favorable for us, but we were obliged to lay to nearly an hour for our supplies, surrounded in the mean time with small boats, from which we purchased fish, shells, parroquets and Java sparrows. At last, all the fresh stores were shipped, and we ran off before a spanking breeze. Point St. Nicholas, Button Rock, Angier and 'Thwart-the-Way soon disappeared, and the superb conical peak of the island of Crockatoa rose on our lee bow. We saw Prince's island at dusk, on the weather bow, and entered the Indian Ocean before the twilight had wholly faded—having made the passage through the straits under unusually favorable auspices

At midnight a man who had been shipped by the Consul at Canton, died on board. He was an old sailor, who had fallen ill at Manilla, whence he had been sent to China, and there, by a blind course of drunkenness and harlotry, sealed his own doom. There was no hope of his recovery, for he had himself cut it off. It was a case of deliberate suicide. But he had probably survived all friends, all associations of home, all manly energy and virtue, all pleasure in even mere animal enjoyment, all hope of any thing better in life, and accepted death with a reckless insensibility which disarmed it of fear. He was buried at noon the next day, Capt. Howland reading the funeral service.

The next morning the change from the island seas of the

Indies, to the open ocean, was at once manifest in the dark-blue of the water, the paleness of the sky, the clearness and bracing freshness of the air, the wider stretch of the horizon, and the long, deliberate undulations of the sea, which gave our vessel a motion we had not felt for weeks before. Towards noon the wind abated, leaving us swaying uneasily to and fro, with the sails flapping heavily against the masts.

On Monday evening, the 10th of October, an unusual incident happened to us. The night was clear, and cooler than usual, with a light breeze, not more than three knots at most, and the same heavy swell which we had had for two days previous. I was walking the quarter-deck with Mr. Cornell, the second mate, about a quarter past eleven o'clock, when the ship suddenly stopped, and shook so violently from stem to stern that every timber vibrated. This motion was accompanied by a dull rumbling, or rather humming noise, which seemed to come from under the stern. We were at first completely puzzled and bewildered by this unexpected circumstance, but a moment's reflection convinced us that it proceeded from an earthquake. Capt. Howland and Mr. Contee came on deck just in time to feel a second shock, nearly as violent as the first. Those who were below heard a strong hissing noise at the vessel's side. There did not appear to be any unusual agitation of the water, notwithstanding the vessel was so violently shaken. The length of time which elapsed, from first to last, was about a minute and a half. The breeze fell immediately afterwards, and we had barely steerage way until morning.

The sunset on the following day was one of the most superb I ever saw. The sky was divided into alternate bands of pure blue and brilliant rose-color, streaming upwards and outwards from the sun, without any interfusion or blending of their hues At the horizon the blue became amber-green, and then gold, and the rose-tint a burning crimson. A mountainous line of heavy purple clouds formed a foreground along the horizon, behind which the rayed sky shone with indescribable splendor, doubling its gorgeous hues on the glassy surface of the sea. There was a dead calm all night, and at noon the reckoning showed a progress of twenty-eight miles in twenty-four hours. The swell was worse than ever, and the sails seemed to be slowly beating themselves to pieces against the masts.

On the morning of the 14th I lost a pretty little parroquet which I had bought at Angier. He had become so tame that I took him out of the cage to feed, and while to all appearance contentedly eating rice in my hand, he shot off suddenly, darted through the cabin like a flash, and out of one of the stern-ports. He was gone in an instant, and lost to me for ever—an instance that even freedom may be fatal. The afternoon was cloudy, with frequent squalls, but about midnight the wind came up out of the south and increased at such a rate, that by daylight we were making twelve knots an hour. The swell was still heavy, the sea covered with sparkling foam-caps, and the sky streaked with flying masses of cloud. The air had a bracing, exhilarating freshness and steadiness, which led us to hope that we had at last caught the long-desired "trades."

Our hopes were entirely fulfilled. My log of the voyage showed the consecutive days' runs of 269, 235, 227, 261, and 247 miles, during which time the ship kept on her course, scarce shifting a sail. The weather was gloriously clear and brilliant, with an elastic and bracing air, and a temperature ranging from 70° to 77°. The sunsets were magnificent; and at night the new Southern constellations united themselves to the superb array of Northern stars, reaching from Taurus to Gemini, and formed one sublime and glittering band across the heavens. On the 21st, the wind abated, and we made but 148 miles, but it freshened the next day, and so held until the 29th, when we achieved 268 miles, passed the latitude of Madagascar, and entered the Mozambique Channel. Here we encountered a heavy cross-sea and head current, but were cheered by the sight of the Cape pigeon and albatross, which wheeled and swooped across our wake, in lines as perfectly rhythmical and harmonious as strains of music.

On the 1st of November, the wind shifted to the south-west, obliging us to run close-hauled. In the evening the sea became very rough, rolling in long, heavy swells, which indicated that we had entered the ocean current setting westward around the Cape. The ship plunged so violently that we came down to double-reefed topsails, and logged less than five knots. About four o'clock the next morning, while it was yet perfectly dark, the air was so pervaded with a fresh earthy smell, that the Captain tacked and stood off on a south-east course. Daylight showed us the bold, bleak coast of Africa, about five miles distant. We had made the land about fifty miles south of Port Natal. At nine o'clock, however, we tacked again, the wind having shifted sufficiently to enable us to clear the land, although we ran within eight or ten miles of it during the whole day. The coast rose in long ridges of bleak hills, which, near the sea, were streaked with fields of barren sand, but further inland were green, and covered with thickets. There was not the slightest sign of cultivation, and I should have considered it uninhabited, but for several large fires which were burning on the hills.

The next morning, November 3d, found us becalmed off the Eastern headland of Algoa Bay. It was a warm, cloudless third of May in the lower hemisphere. We sounded, and finding fifty-five fathoms, endeavored to turn the calm to account by fishing for cod; but after sending down the line four times and having two hooks bitten off, a breeze came out of the east and began moving us forward too fast for the sport. The east wind nobly befriended us. At noon on the 4th we reached our Southern Ultima Thule (Lat. 35° 17′ S.), and headed westward for the Atlantic, fifty miles from the African coast. Cape Lagulhas, the southern extremity of the Continent, was 97 miles distant. The sky was cloudless, the sun warm, the air deliciously pure, and just cool enough to make walking on the quarter-deck enjoyable. The sea was smooth, and no sign in air or ocean betokened that we were in the vicinity of the dreaded Cape of Storms.

At night the young moon, Jupiter and Venus, if not exactly in conjunction, were so near it as to shine as with the light of a single planet. But two or three degrees distant from each other, they formed a splendid triangle, the effect of which, on the roseate field of the austral sunset, was indescribably magnificent. The sky was intensely clear, and towards midnight Taurus, Orion, Sirius, Canopus, the Southern Cross and the Magellan Clouds were all visible at once, bewildering the eye with their lustre. The next morning we could plainly distinguish, though at a great distance, the vapors hanging over the Cape and the headlands which bound False, or St. Simon s Bay, on the east. Towards noon they were lifted by the sun, and the far, faint, blue outline of Table Mountain, with that of the four or five broken peaks forming the Cape, was distinctly visible. They were so precisely similar to the pictures I had seen, and to that in my imagination, that I recognized them at once, with a feeling of familiar acquaintance. They slowly passed astern, and at four o'clock faded out of sight behind us. And so farewell, savage old Africa! Shall I ever see your shores again?

Now, at last, I felt that our prow was turned homewards—that our keel ploughed the Atlantic, and the old far-off Asian world lay behind me. We were again sailing for the North Star, for the hemisphere where the strong heart of the world beats, and will beat for ever! We were on our own side of the globe, and I felt—what I had not before felt, since leaving China—that every day was bringing me nearer home. The very sky was changed; the sea was of a deeper blue; the waves danced and sparkled with a merrier life; the clouds gathered into larger masses and grouped themselves together with a sense of power, no longer like the slumberous vapors of the East, smouldering languidly away, in the fires of the sun. There was a prophecy of America in the very air, and I invoked a threefold benediction on the cold south-wind, which filled every inch of our towering piles of canvas, and carried us through the night at twelve knots an hour, dashing the ocean into phosphoric foam.

After making 532 miles in two days, the wind abated, and we dragged along slowly for three days more, through the variable latitudes, before taking the trade-winds again. The albatross and Cape pigeon followed us, past their usual latitudes, until the increase of temperature, in the neighborhood of the

Tropics, warned them to return. The trade-wind, which we took on the 10th of November, was rather sluggish, and even with the addition of sky-sails and royal studding-sails, our pace was languid. The sea was unusually calm, and the swells over which we expected to be "rolling down to St. Helena," according to the sailor's ditty, did not make their appearance. No voyaging could be calmer and more agreeable, and our routine of life had come to be so settled and unvarying, that the day slipped by unawares. I employed this period of quiet and isolation in recalling and rewriting a large package of letters, descriptive of things in India and China, which had gone down in the steamer *Lewiston*, in the China Sea. Floating over that sleepy, deserted sea—for we saw but a single vessel—I was enabled to reproduce the Past so vividly that not a feature was wanting, and, almost word for word, the lost letters were restored.

On the morning of the 11th we passed the meridian of Greenwich, and began to count western longitude. The only other incident was the sight of a rakish-looking brig, which passed several miles astern. Mr. Contee, who had made a cruise in the African Squadron, at once pronounced her to be a slaver. Her movements betrayed an evident anxiety to avoid us.

CHAPTER XLIII.

A DAY AT ST. HELENA.

Proposed Call at St. Helena—First View of the Island—Its Cliffs—Approach to Jamestown—View from the Anchorage—Landing—The Town and Ravine—Ascending the Gorge—Looking Down—"The Briars"—Summit of the Island—Pastoral Landscape—Sea-View—Approach to Longwood—Reception—The Billiard-Room—Scene of Napoleon's Death—His Bedroom—Desecration of Longwood—The New Residence—The Longwood Farm—The "Crown and Rose"—National Peculiarities—The Grave of Napoleon—The Old Woman's Welcome—Condition of the Grave—St. Helena Literature—The Old Woman's Admirable Story—Napoleon's Spring—Return to Jamestown—Departure from the Island.

The three passengers on board the Sea Serpent were greatly delighted to learn from Capt. Howland, on the day when we crossed the Tropic of Capricorn, that the water was getting short, and he had therefore decided to touch at St. Helena for a fresh supply. We had already been more than sixty days on board, and the sea, with all its wonderful fascination, was growing monotonous. Here was an event which, in addition to its positive interest, would give us at least five days of anticipation and a week of active remembrance, virtually shortening our voyage to that extent; for at sea we measure time less by the calendar than by our individual sense of its duration.

I have spent several months on shipboard, when, according to the almanac, barely a fortnight had elapsed.

The trade-wind bore us slowly northward, and when I went on deck at sunrise, on the 14th of November, St. Helena was in sight, about twenty-five miles distant. It was a dark-blue mass, filling about twenty degrees of the horizon, and of nearly uniform elevation above the sea, but gradually resolved itself into sharper and more broken outlines as we approached. Except upon a lofty terrace on the southern side, where there was a tinge of green and some traces of fields, the coast presented a frightfully rocky and inhospitable appearance. Nevertheless it displayed some grand effects of coloring. The walls of naked rock, several hundred feet high, which rose boldly from the sea, in some places overhanging their base, were tinted as by

> " the deep-blue gloom
> Of thunder-shower,"

the hollow chasms between them being filled with gorgeous masses of purple-black shadow, under the sultry clouds which hung over the island. At the south-eastern extremity were two pointed, isolated rocks, probably a hundred feet high. We stood around the opposite extremity of the island, making for the port of Jamestown, which faces the north-west. The coast on this side rises into two bold heads, one of which projects outward like a gigantic capstan, while the other runs slantingly up to a pointed top, which is crowned with a signal station. The rock has a dark, bluish-slate color, with streaks of a warm reddish-brown, and the strata, burst apart in the centre, yet slanting upward toward each other like the sides of a volcano, tell of upheaval by some tremendous subterranean agency. The structure of the island is purely volcanic, and except the rock of Aden, on the coast of Arabia, I never saw a more forbidding spot.

The breeze increased as we drew near the island, but when we ran under the lee of the great cliffs, fell away almost entirely, so that we drifted lazily along within half a mile of them. At length a battery hove in sight, hewn in the face of the precipice, and anchored vessels, one by one, came out behind the point. We stood off a little, urged along by occasional flaws of wind, and in a short time the shallow bight which forms the roadstead of St. Helena lay before us. There was another battery near at hand, at the foot of a deep, barren glen, called Rupert's Valley, from which a road, notched in the rock, leads around the intervening cliffs to the gorge, at the bottom of which Jamestown is built. A sea-wall across the mouth of this gorge, a row of ragged trees, weather-beaten by the gales of the Atlantic, and the spire of a church, were all that appeared of the town. The walls of the fort crowned the lofty cliff above, and high behind them towered the signal station, on the top of a conical peak, the loftiest in the island. The stone ladder which leads from the tower to the fort was marked on the face of the cliff like a white ribbon unrolled from its top. Inland, a summit covered with dark pine-trees, from the midst of which glimmered the white front of a country mansion, rose above the naked heights of the shore. This was the only gleam of fertility which enlivened the terrible sterility of the view.

Further in-shore a few gun-boats and water-boats lay at anchor, and some fishing-skiffs were pulling about. As we forged slowly along to a good anchoring ground, the American consul came off, followed by a boarding-officer, and we at once received permission to go ashore and make the most of our short stay. The consul's boat speedily conveyed us to the landing-place, at the eastern extremity of the town. Every thing had a dreary and deserted air. There were half-a-dozen men and boys, with Portuguese features and uncertain complexions, about the steps, a red-coated soldier at a sentry-box, and two or three lonely-looking individuals under the weather-beaten trees. Passing a row of mean houses, built against the overhanging rock, a drawbridge over a narrow moat admitted us within the walls. A second wall and gate, a short distance further, ushered us into the public square of Jamestown. Even at its outlet, the valley is not more than a hundred and fifty yards wide, and the little town is crowded, or rather jammed, deep in its bottom, between nearly perpendicular cliffs, seven or eight hundred feet in height. At the top of the square is the church, a plain yellowish structure, with a tall, square, pointed spire; and beyond it Market street, the main thoroughfare of the little place, opens up the valley.

A carriage—almost the only one in Jamestown—was procured for Mrs. Howland; my fellow-passenger, Parkman, provided himself with a saddle-horse, and we set out for Longwood. We had a mounted Portuguese postillion, and rattled up the steep and stony main street in a style which drew upon us the eyes of all Jamestown. The road soon left the town, ascending the right side of the ravine by a very long and steep grade. Behind the town are the barracks of the soldiery and their parade-ground—all on a cramped and contracted scale; then some dreary burial-grounds, the graves in which resembled heaps of cinders; then a few private mansions, and green garden-patches, winding upwards for a mile or more. The depth and narrowness of the gorge completely shut out the air; the heat was radiated powerfully from its walls of black volcanic rock, and the bristling cacti and yuccas by the roadside, with full-crowned cocoa-palms below, gave it a fiery, savage, tropical character. The peak of the signal-station loomed high above us from the opposite side, and now the head of the ravine—a precipice several hundred feet high, over which fell a silver thread of water—came into sight. This water supplies the town and shipping, beside fertilizing the gardens in the bed of the ravine. It is clear as crystal, and of the sweetest and freshest quality. Looking backward, we saw the spire of the little church at the bottom projected against the blue plain of ocean, the pigmy hulls of the vessels in the roads, and a great triangular slice of sea, which grew wider and longer as we ascended, until the horizon was full fifty miles distant.

Near the top of the ravine there is a natural terrace about a quarter of a mile in length, lying opposite to the cascade. It contains a few small fields, divided by scrubby hedges, and, near the further end, two pleasant dwelling-houses, surrounded by a garden in which I saw some fine orange-trees. This is "The Briars," memorable for having been Napoleon's first residence on the island. The Balcombe family occupied the larger of the two dwellings, which is flanked by tall Italian cypresses, while the other building, which was then a summer pavilion, but was afterwards enlarged to accommodate the Emperor and his suite, received him on the very night of his landing from the Bellerophon. It stands on a little knoll, overlooking a deep glen, which debouches into the main valley just below. The place is cheerful though solitary; it has a sheltered, sunny aspect, compared with the bleak heights of Longwood, and I do not wonder that the great exile left it with regret. Miss Balcombe's account of Napoleon's sojourn at "The Briars," is among the most striking reminiscences of his life on the island.

Just above the terrace the road turned, and, after a short ascent, gained the crest of the ridge, where the grade became easier, and the cool south-east trade-wind, blowing over the height, refreshed us after the breathless heat of the ravine. The road was bordered with pine-trees, and patches of soft green turf took the place of the volcanic dust and cinders. The flower-stems of the aloe-plants, ten feet in height, had already begun to wither, but the purple buds of the cactus were opening, and thick clusters of a watery, succulent plant were starred with white, pink, and golden blossoms. We had now attained the central upland of the island, which slopes downward in all directions to the summit of the sea-wall of cliffs On emerging again from the wood, a landscape of a very different character met our view. Over a deep valley, the sides of which were alternately green with turf and golden with patches of blossoming broom, we looked upon a ridge of tableland three or four miles long, near the extremity of which, surrounded by a few straggling trees, we saw the houses of Longwood. In order to reach them, it was necessary to pass around the head of the intervening valley. In this direction the landscape was green and fresh, dotted with groves of pine and white country-houses. Flocks of sheep grazed on the turfy hill-sides, and a few cows and horses ruminated among the clumps of broom. Down in the bottom of the valley, I noticed a small enclosure, planted with Italian cypresses, and with a square white object in the centre. It did not need the postillion's words to assure me that I looked upon the Grave of Napoleon

Looking eastward towards the sea, the hills became bare and red, gashed with chasms and falling off in tremendous precipices, the height of which we would only guess from the dim blue of the great sphere of sea, whose far-off horizon was drawn above their summits, so that we seemed to stand in the centre of a vast concavity. In color, form, and magnificent desolation, these hills called to my mind the mountain region surrounding the Dead Sea. Clouds rested upon the high, pine-wooded summits to the west of us, and the broad, sloping valley, on the other side of the ridge of Longwood, was as green as a dell of Switzerland. The view of those fresh pasture slopes, with their flocks of sheep, their groves and cottages, was all the more delightful from its being wholly unexpected. Where the ridge joins the hills, and one can look into both valleys at the same time, there is a small tavern, with the familiar English sign of the "Crown and Rose." Our road now led eastward along the top of the ridge, over a waste tract covered with clumps of broom, for another mile and a half, when we reached the gate of the Longwood Farm. A broad avenue of trees, which all lean inland from the stress of the trade-wind, conducts to the group of buildings, on a bleak spot, overlooking the sea, and exposed to the full force of the wind. Our wheels rolled over a thick, green turf, the freshness of which showed how unfrequent must be the visits of strangers.

On reaching the gate, a small and very dirty boy, with a milk-and-molasses complexion, brought out to us a notice pasted on a board, intimating that those who wished to see the residence of the Emperor Napoleon must pay two shillings a-piece *in advance;* children half-price. A neat little English woman of that uncertain age which made me hesitate to ask her whether she had ever seen the Emperor, was in attendance, to receive the fees and act as cicerone. We alighted at a small green verandah, facing a wooden wing which projects from the eastern front of the building. The first room we entered was whitewashed, and covered all over with the names of visitors, in charcoal, pencil, and red chalk. The greater part of them were French. "This," said the little woman, "was the Emperor's billiard-room, built after he came to live at Longwood. The walls have three or four times been covered with names, and whitewashed over." A door at the further end admitted us into the drawing-room, in which Napoleon died. The ceiling was broken away, and dust and cobwebs covered the bare rafters. The floor was half-decayed, almost invisible through the dirt which covered it, and the plastering, falling off, disclosed in many places the rough stone walls. A winnowing-mill and two or three other farming utensils, stood in the corners. The window looked into a barn-yard filled with mud and dung. Stretched on a sofa, with his head beside this window, the great conqueror, the "modern Sesostris," breathed his last, amid the delirium of fancied battle and the howlings of a storm which shook the island. The corner-stone of the jamb, nearest which his head lay, has been quarried out of the wall, and taken to France.

Beyond this was the dining-room, now a dark, dirty barn floor, filled to the rafters with straw and refuse timbers. We passed out into a cattle-yard, and entered the Emperor's bedroom. A horse and three cows were comfortably stalled there in, and the floor of mud and loose stones was covered with dung and litter. "Here," said the guide, pointing to an unusually filthy stall in one corner, "was the Emperor's bath-room. Mr. Solomon (a Jew in Jamestown) has the marble bathing-tub he used. Yonder was his dressing room"—a big brinded calf was munching some grass in the very spot—"and here" (pointing to an old cow in the nearest corner) "his attendant slept." So miserable, so mournfully wretched was the condition of the place, that I regretted not having been content with an outside view of Longwood. On the other side of the cattle-yard stands the houses which were inhabited by Count Montholon, Las Casas, and Dr. O'Meara; but at present they are shabby, tumble-down sheds, whose stone walls alone have preserved their existence to this day. On the side facing the sea, there are a few pine-trees, under which is a small crescent-shaped fish-pond, dry and nearly filled with earth and weeds. Here the Emperor used to sit and feed his tame fish. The sky, overcast with clouds, and the cold wind which blew steadily from the sea, added to the desolation of the place.

Passing through the garden, which is neglected, like the house, and running to waste, we walked to the new building erected by the Government for Napoleon's use, but which he never inhabited. It is a large quadrangle, one story high, plain but commodious, and with some elegance in its arrangement. It has been once or twice occupied as a residence, but is now decaying from very neglect. Standing under the brow of the hill, it is sheltered from the wind, and much more cheerful in every respect than the old mansion. We were conducted through the empty chambers, intended for billiard, dining, drawing, and bed-rooms. In the bath-room, where yet stands the wooden case which enclosed the marble tub, a flock of geese were luxuriating. The curtains which hung at the windows were dropping to pieces from rot, and in many of the rooms the plastering was cracked and mildewed by the leakage of rains through the roof. Near the building is a neat cottage, in which General Bertrand and his family formerly resided. It is now occupied by the gentleman who leases the farm of Longwood from the Government. The farm is the largest on the island, containing one thousand acres, and is rented at £315 a year. The uplands around the house are devoted to the raising of oats and barley, but grazing is the principal source of profit.

I plucked some branches of geranium and fragrant heliotrope from the garden, and we set out on our return. I prevailed upon Mr. Parkman to take my place in the carriage, and give me his horse as far as the "Crown and Rose," thereby securing an inspiring gallop of nearly two miles. Two Englishmen, of the lower order, had charge of the tavern, and while I was taking a glass of ale, one of them touched his hat very respectfully, and said: "Axin' your pardon, sir, are you from the States?" I answered in the affirmative. "There!" said he, turning to the other and clapping his hands, "I knew it; I've won the bet." "What were your reasons for thinking me an American?" I asked. "Why," said he, "the gentlemen from the States are always *so mild!* I knowed you was one before you got off the horse."

We sent the carriage on by the road, to await us on the other side of the glen, and proceeded on foot to the Grave. The path led down through a garden filled with roses and heliotropes. The peach-trees were in blossom, and the tropical *loquàt*, which

I had seen growing in India and China, hung full of ripe yellow fruit. As we approached tho little enclosure at the bottom of the glen, I, who was in advance, was hailed by a voice crying out, "This way, sir, this way!" and, looking down, saw at the gate a diminutive, wrinkled, old, grizzly-headed, semi-negro semi-Portuguese woman, whom I at once recognized as th *custodienne* of the tomb, from descriptions which the officers of the Mississippi had given me. "Ah! there you are!" said I; "I knew it must be you." "Why, Captain!" she exclaimed "is that you? How you been this long while? I didn't know you was a-comin', or I would ha' put on a better dress, for, you see, I was a-washin' to-day. "Dickey!"—addressing a great, fat, white youth of twenty-two or twenty-three, with a particularly stupid and vacant face—"run up to the garden, and git two or three of the finest *bokys* as ever you can, for the Captain and the ladies!"

At the gate of the enclosure hung a placard, calling upon all visitors to pay, in advance, the sum of one shilling and six-pence each, before approaching the tomb This touching testimony of respect having been complied with, we were allowed to draw near to the empty vault, which, for twenty years, enshrined the corpse of Napoleon. It is merely an oblong shaft of masonry, about twelve feet deep, and with a rude roof thrown over the mouth, to prevent it being filled by the rains. A little railing surrounds it, and the space between is planted with geraniums and scarlet salvias. Two willows—one of which has been so stript by travellers, that nothing but the trunk is left—shade the spot, and half-a-dozen monumental cypresses lift their tall obelisks around. A flight of steps leads to the bottom of the vault, where the bed of masonry which enclosed the coffin still remains. I descended to the lowest step, and there found, hanging against the damp wall, a written tablet stating that the old woman, then waiting for me at the top, told an admirable and excellent story about the burial of Napoleon, which travellers would do well to extract from her and that one shilling was but a fair compensation for the pleasure she would afford them. Appended to the announcement were the following lines, which I transcribed on the spot:

"FIRMLY strike my bounding lyre,
Poet's muse can never tire,
Nosegays gay and flowers so wild,
Climate good and breezes mild,
Humbly ask a shilling, please,
Before the stranger sails the seas.

NAPOLEON was in love with a lady so true,
He gave her a gold ring set with diamonds and pearls,
Which was worthy the honors of many brave earls.
But she died, it is said, in her bloom and her beauty,
So his love broken-hearted
For ever was parted.
He drank of the spring and its water so clear,
Which was reserved for his use, and he held it most dear.
So he died, so he died,
In the bloom of his pride.
In his life he sat under yon lone willow-tree,
And studied the air, the earth, and the sea;
His arms were akimbo, his thoughts far away.
He lived six months at the house on the hill, at his friend's, the brave GENERAL BERTRAND by name, and from thence he would come
To visit the spot,
And stand in deep thought,
Forgotten or not."

If I had been saddened by the neglect of Longwood, I was disgusted by the profanation of the tomb. Is there not enough reverence in St. Helena, to prevent the grave which a great name has hallowed, from being defiled with such abominable doggerel? And there was the old woman, who, having seen me read the notice, immediately commenced her admirable and interesting story in this wise: "Six years he lived upon the island. He came here in 1815, and he died in 1821. Six years he lived upon the island. He was buried with his head to the east. This is the east. His feet was to the west. This is the west. Where you see that brown dirt, there was his head. He wanted to be buried beside his wife Josephine; but, as that couldn't be done, he was put here. They put him here because he used to come down here with a silver mug in his pocket, and take a drink out of that spring. That's the reason he was buried here. There was a guard of a sergeant and six men up there on the hill all the time he was down here a-drinkin' out of the spring with his silver mug. This was the way he walked." Here the old woman folded her arms, tossed back her grizzly head, and strode to and fro with so ludicrous an attempt at dignity, that, in spite of myself, I was forced into laughter. "Did you ever see him?" I asked. "Yes, Captain," said she, "I seed him a many a time, and I always said, 'Good mornin', Sir,' but he never had no conversation with me." A draught of the cool and delicious lymph of Napoleon's Spring completed the farce. I broke a sprig from one of the cypresses, wrote my name in the visitor's book, took the "boky" of gillyflowers and marigolds, which Dickey had collected, and slowly remounted the opposite side of the glen. My thoughts involuntarily turned from the desecrated grave to that fitting sepulchre where he now rests under the banners of a hundred victorious battle-fields, and guarded by the timeworn remnant of his faithful Old Guard. Let Longwood be levelled to the earth, and the empty grave be filled up and turfed over! Better that these memorials of England's treachery should be seen no more!

We hastened back to Jamestown, as it was near sunset. The long shadows already filled the ravine, and the miniature gardens and streets below were more animated than during the still heat of the afternoon. Capt. Howland was waiting for us, as the ship was ready to sail. Before it was quite dark, we had weighed anchor, and were slowly drifting away from the desolate crags of the island. The next morning we saw again the old unbroken ring of the sea.

CHAPTER XLIV.

HOMEWARD.

Trade Weather--Phosphorescence of the Sea—Ocean Nymphs—Butterflies in Mid-Ocean—The North-East Trades—A Gale off the Bermudas—Nautical Alms-Giving—The Gulf Stream—Escape from Cape Hatteras—Fair Wind—Winter Weather—The Last Day of the Voyage—Landing in New York—Retrospect.

For three days after leaving St. Helena we had calm, sluggish weather, but on the 17th took the trade-wind again, and for five days thereafter averaged 200 miles a day. The wind was steady, dead astern, and the sea calm, with very little swell. The sky was overcast, and the atmosphere sultry, with a temperature ranging from 80° to 85°. Flying-fish appeared in greater quantities than I ever noticed before. The phosphorescence of the sea was wonderful. The first half of the night was dark, as the moon was entering her last quarter, and the ship's wake was a dazzling trail of silver fire. The rudder dashed out of the darkness clusters of luminous globes about six inches in diameter, which scattered and spread, growing brighter as they approached the surface. The light rippling of the waves, far and wide, kindled brilliant sparkles, which studded the watery firmament like stars, to which the long, wavy, shining wake of our vessel formed the Milky Way. One who leaned over the stern asked me whether those fiery globes were not the astral lamps with which the Undines lighted their sub-oceanic caverns; but I refused to accept the fancy. The imagination positively forbids any such poetical creatures to inhabit the vast desert spaces of ocean. The Undines are the nymphs of rivers and fountains; the mermaid only haunts the shore. The mid-sea is too vast, too cold in its barren sublimity, to be peopled by human dreams.

At midnight, on the 24th of December, we crossed the Equator in Long. 30° W., having been fifty-nine days in the Southern Hemisphere. We hoped to have taken the north-east trades soon afterwards, but were tantalized for a week with calms, and light, variable winds, during which we did not average more than 125 miles a day. On the 1st of December, in Lat. 12° N. a large butterfly and two dragon-flies came on board. The nearest land, the coast of Guiana, was more than 900 miles distant. I have never seen it stated that these insects are capable of such long flights.

We had been on board the Sea Serpent eighty-one days, and our hopes of spending Christmas at home were rapidly diminishing, when the long-desired trade-wind struck us. On the 2d of December we made 216 miles; on the 3d, 265 miles; and on the 4th, *three hundred* miles, which was our best day's run during the voyage. Our good ship fairly whistled through the water, cutting her way so smoothly that there was scarcely foam enough before her bows to throw a scud over the forecastle, or wake enough behind her stern to tell that she had passed. The beautiful wave-lines of her counter allowed the dead water to close as passively as if the ocean had not been disturbed.

On the morning of December the 11th, in Lat. 32° N. and off the lee of the Bermudas, the wind hauled round to the north-west and blew half a gale for the two following days, during which we ran westward under close-reefed topsails. So it came to pass that on the 14th we were two degrees *west* of New York, and somewhere off Darien, in Georgia. The wind then shifted more to the westward, and by noon on the 16th, we were in the edge of the Gulf Stream, about 75 miles to the south-east of Cape Fear Three or four vessels bound north, were in sight, apparently driven under the lee of Cape Hatteras, like ourselves, by the violence of the northern gale. In the afternoon, an hermaphrodite brig, which had risen on the weather bow, stood down towards us and we saw a boat put off from her. We suspected at first that the brig might be a relief vessel, but were soon undeceived by the boat coming alongside. A raw, rough fellow, in a flannel shirt and red cap, came over the side, and stated that the brig was a Nova Scotian, bound from Magua to Cape Breton, had been out twenty days, and had but four days' provisions on board. He was on a begging errand, and was successful enough to get a barrel each of flour, bread, pork and beef. The brig had encountered strong northerly and north-easterly winds for the previous eight days. The boat's crew were hale, athletic Nova-Scotians and it was refreshing to see such well-knit, sinewy frames, such bold, hearty features, and such ruddiness of warm and healthy blood. As the Bermudas had not suffered us to pass, I hoped that the sailor's couplet would apply both ways, and that Cape Hatteras would let us off easily On Saturday morning, the 17th, a breeze sprang up from the south-east. Gradually increasing, it hauled to the northward and westward, and by noon we were dashing on our course at the rate of ten knots. The sky was too overcast to obtain an observation, but according to the eckoning we were in Lat. 35° 16′ N. and Long. 75° 17′ W. At 2 P. M. we ran across the inner edge of the Gulf Stream, and came at once upon soundings. The line of junction between the dark-blue water of the Gulf, and the pale-green of the shoals was marked with wonderful distinctness. The stern of our vessel was in the former, while the latter reached to her waist. Within the distance of a ship's length, the temperature of the sea changed from 72° to 62°. The water immediately became of a paler green, and we felt an ugly ground swell. At the same instant Mr. Cornell discerned land off the port beam, and a single glance sufficed to show that it was Cape Hatteras, which, according to our reckoning, should have been weathered two hours before. The current of the Gulf Stream had evidently been much retarded by the strong north-eastern gales.

It blew hard during the night, and there was a very heavy sea in the stream, but on soundings the water was smoother. We ran the whole night with no other sail than close-reefed fore and main topsails, and reefed foresail. In the morning the sky was clear and cold, and the air for the first time biting and wintry, rendering our heaviest clothing necessary to support the sudden change from the Tropics. The wind gradually veered to W. N. W., but by noon we were off Cape Henlopen. We ran close-hauled all day, striving to get to windward in order to make Sandy Hook the next morning, but found ourselves at sunrise about 40 miles to the eastward of it. The transition to a winter climate was like a cold-plunge bath. The thermometer sank to 25°, and water froze on deck. At noon a pilot-boat hove in sight, running down towards us. The ship was put about, in order to meet her, but this movement gradually brought a bark, which was to windward of us, between us and the boat, and as the latter hoisted signal, the boat was obliged te give her the only pilot aboard.

We had a tedious night, of alternate calms and snow-squalls, and I slept very little, out of anxiety lest a stiff nor'wester should spring up and blow us out to sea again. But by morning we had a pilot aboard, and taking advantage of a shift of the wind, made a tack which brought us in sight of Sandy Hook and of two steam-tugs. At ten o'clock the *Leviathan* had grappled us; the useless sails were furled, and we sped surely and swiftly, in the clear winter sunshine, up the outer bay, through the Narrows and into the noble harbor of New York. The hills of Staten Island glittered with snow; the trees had long been bare and the grass dead; and for the first time in nearly three years, I looked upon a winter landscape. It was the 20th of December, and 101 days since our departure from Whampoa. We rapidly approached the familiar and beloved city, and at 2 P. M. I landed on one of the East River piers.

I had left New York on the 28th of August, 1851, and had thus been absent two years and four months. During this time I had visited most of the countries of Europe, ascended the Nile to the Negro kingdoms of Central Africa, journeyed in Palestine, Asia Minor, and India, visited China twice, and taken part in the American expedition to Japan. I had travelled altogether about fifty thousand miles, and in all my wanderings, in all my intercourse with men of whatever race or clime, had been received with kindness and attended by uniform good fortune. Let me hope that the reader, who has had the patience to accompany me through the narrative of this long and adventurous journey, will arrive at its close with the same faith in those innate virtues of human nature which no degradation can obscure, and the same dependence on that merciful Providence whose protection extends over all lands and seas.